In the Path of WAR

Children of the American Revolution Tell Their Stories

Edited by
Jeanne Winston Adler

Cobblestone Publishing Company Peterborough, New Hampshire

◈

for Nicholas, David, and Max

Cover photo: Janice Lang
Editorial: Malcolm C. Jensen
Design: C. Porter Designs
Photo research: Winston Adler
Copyediting: Barbara Jatkola

Acknowledgments
The publisher gratefully acknowledges permission to quote from the following material: "The Battle of Lexington," a poem in manuscript by Lemuel Haynes, in the collection of the Houghton Library, Harvard University.

Cobblestone Publishing Company
Simon & Schuster Education Group
30 Grove Street, Suite C
Peterborough, NH 03458

Manufactured in the United States of America
ISBN 0-382443-67-5

Library of Congress Cataloging-in-Publication Data

In the path of war : children of the American revolution tell their stories / edited by Jeanne Winston Adler.
    p. cm.
  Oral accounts of early settlers in northeastern New York collected by Asa Fitch beginning in 1847.
  Includes index.
  Summary: Oral accounts of men and women who were children during the American Revolution, describing local struggles, raids, kidnappings, stolen livestock, and pioneer life in northeastern New York.
  ISBN 0-382-44367-5
  1. New York (State)--History--Revolution, 1775-1783--Personal narratives--Juvenile literature. 2. United States--History--Revolution, 1775-1783--Personal narratives--Juvenile literature. 3. New York (State)--History--Revolution, 1775-1783--Children--Juvenile literature. 4. United States--History--Revolution, 1775-1783--Children--Juvenile literature. 5. Frontier and pioneer life--New York (State)--Juvenile literature. 6. Children--New York (State)--Social life and customs--Juvenile literature. 7. Children--New York (State)--Biography--Juvenile literature. [1. New York (State)--History--Revolution, 1775-1783--Personal narratives. 2. United States--History--Revolution, 1775-1783--Personal narratives. 3. Frontier and pioneer life--New York (State) 4. New York (State)--Social life and customs.] I. Adler, Jeanne Winston, 1946- . II. Fitch, Asa, 1809-1879.
E275.A2I58   1998
973.3'092'2--dc21
[b]
                             98-37074
                                CIP
                                 AC

Contents

Part Two:
Early Pioneer Life

Foreword

In 1847, a country doctor in northeastern New York began to question his elderly patients and friends about the time of their youth — the era of the Revolutionary War. Dr. Asa Fitch was an unusual person. In addition to carrying on his medical practice and helping to run his family's farm, Dr. Fitch also studied insects and made some important discoveries about them. He has been called one of the fathers of American entomology *[the scientific study of insects]*.

Perhaps because he was a scientist and used to making exact observations and taking notes, Dr. Fitch carefully wrote down the words of the people he spoke with. He copied their stories into a series of large notebooks, which his children and grandchildren kept safe. After many years, his descendants gave the notebooks to a New York City library. Today, thanks to the interest and care of Dr. Fitch and his family, Caty Campbell, Robert Blake, Tryphena Angel, Donald McDonald, and others can still speak to us about events they experienced more than two hundred years ago as young people. They are, literally, children of the American Revolution.

A page from one of Dr. Asa Fitch's notebooks.

Dr. Asa Fitch.

Through their eyes, the Revolutionary War looks a lot like a civil war. It was a time when people had to choose sides in a conflict breaking out all around them. Neighbor often turned against neighbor. And yet there were also small, unexpected acts of kindness across the lines that had been drawn between supporters of the American cause and supporters of the king.

The big battles — Bennington and Saratoga — took place just over the horizon from our witnesses. After all, most were too young to fight in the militia or in the regular army. But with these children of the Revolution, we "lie still and quiet in the houses" as British and German troops march past on their way to war. We enter General Burgoyne's camp — a movable city of nearly ten thousand persons — in the weeks before his defeat at Saratoga. We even see Burgoyne shedding tears.

The war for these children was not the American Revolution of the history books. Instead, it was a war of gritty local struggles, rival scouting parties, raids, kidnappings, stolen livestock and food, the ebb and flow of refugees, and an occasional shocking murder.

We can learn much about pioneer life from these children. With them, we visit log homes just cut from the forest and see the work of making farms and towns where none had been before. What few possessions these people had! Yet what an array of skills they possessed! Every settler knew how to turn raw materials — trees, animal skins, flax, wool — into shelter and clothing.

Dr. Fitch had no tape recorder, but he wrote down people's stories exactly as they told them. Sometimes the people he spoke with repeated themselves or went off on tangents. As a result, some of the statements you will read here have been edited. Words, phrases, and sometimes whole sentences have been deleted, but no words have been added to the text. Very occasionally, a word such as "Father" has been substituted for "he" to make the meaning clearer. Even more rarely, the order of sentences within a passage has been altered, again to make the story clearer.

Enjoy your visit with these children of long ago. They have much to tell us about courage, endurance, and hardships overcome.

— *Jeanne Winston Adler*

Part One:
The
Revolutionary
War

The homes of the first settlers in Charlotte County looked like this bark-roofed log cabin in the Adirondack region of New York. The glass windows in this house are "modern." The settlers of the 1700s had only wooden shutters.

CHAPTER ONE

First Settlers

◧ In 1613, the Dutch founded Albany, New York, as a fur-trading post. However, the area along the Hudson northeast of Albany — originally called Charlotte County and later Washington County — was not turned into farms and towns until after the French and Indian War ended in 1763. Like pioneers in many parts of Colonial America, the first settlers brought differences with them. Some were Yankees, which means that they came from the New England colonies to the east. Others were Scotch or Scotch-Irish. (Scotch-Irish were Scots who had lived in Northern Ireland.) Some pioneers were well-to-do. Others had almost nothing at all. Such differences formed cracks, or dividing lines, within communities. Later, as you will see, the Revolution caused some of these cracks to break wide open.

William McCollister of Salem

Father came to Salem when a young man in company with James Turner and Joshua Conkey, who had wives but left them at home. They came from Pelham in Massachusetts and were here two or three years before the town was chartered [*officially started*], coming onto the land as squatters. They first put up a hut on the same spot where the Coffee House now stands in the village of Salem. Flat, level land was the only kind that was much esteemed in those days. We still have Father's old musket which he brought with him at this time and which is marked with his initials and the date 1756 — one of the best guns in the country.

The three men kept bachelor's hall together the first year or two, probably going back to Pelham in the winter. Immediately after erecting their cabin in the woods they commenced clearing up a strip of land each for himself. Each of them put up a small log house on his clearing and by the second year, I think, each was living by himself in his own cabin.

On returning to his house here from Stillwater, he found a large catamount *[mountain lion]* lying dead on the floor. The door was made of soft and perhaps green basswood which he had split into rude boards and pegged or nailed together. The catamount had gnawed a hole through this door and come in and got at some unguentum *[salve]* which was laying on one of the crossbeams overhead — the remedy for itch which in those days was an indispensable article in every dwelling — and had ate and licked the ointment nearly clean from off the beam. This he always supposed had poisoned the animal so that she died on the spot, for he knew not how otherwise to account for her death.

He pulled her out of the door and washed up the floor around where she laid. In the evening, it being a dark night, he was startled at observing at the hole in the door two balls of light like two candles which he well knew were the eyes of another catamount peering in upon him. He grasped his gun but the motion alarmed the animal and the lights disappeared. He now placed his gun at a rest, aiming directly at the hole in the door, and awaited the reappearance of the lights. They soon returned, and cautiously taking a more deliberate aim, he fired. The gun was reloaded with all convenient dispatch, but the lights appeared no more. He now barricaded the hole in the door and laid himself down to sleep. On opening the door next morning, there lay dead a large catamount which was evidently the mate of the one he had found dead in the house.

At the close of the first or second year after Father came here, he returned to Pelham and married his wife and brought her up with him the following season. At Stillwater was the nearest **gristmill,** when Mother first came here, and she used to relate that on one occasion when Father had gone down there — about thirty miles as they then used to go — on horseback, to get a grist ground, a bear came boldly up to the door of the house and grasped and carried off their sow from the midst of her litter of pigs, and she had no means of preventing the depredation.

Susan Lyttle Vance of Salem

I was born at Schuylerville in the **barracks** there in sight of General Schuyler's residence, April 7, 1767, and when four years old was brought to Salem. My father had previously been out to Salem and put up a little cabin. Although it was full of cracks and without a chimney or floor and only a flat stone leaning against one side of the enclosure — against which a fire could be built — on entering

GRISTMILL: A building housing a large piece of machinery, usually powered by running water, in which wheat, corn, and other grains were ground into flour or meal between large stone wheels.

BARRACKS: Large, plain buildings for housing troops or other temporary occupants.

Philip Schuyler owned thousands of acres along the Hudson River north of Albany. The land had been granted to his family in the 1600s by the first Dutch governors of New York. This Dutch aristocrat joined the Patriot cause and fought as a colonel and later a general in the Continental Army.

the cabin Mother with her babe in her arms danced around and around it, so overjoyed was she to set her foot in a house she could call her own.

Tryphena Martin Angel of Salem

I once asked Uncle Adam Martin whether our family was English, Scotch, or Irish in its origin. He said it was neither — that his great-grandfather emigrated from Wales to America. That is all that is known of our origin.

I do not remember particularly what houses were standing here when I was a child. There were a number of them — little huts of no consequence. A Scotch family would come into the town and a day or two after would have a little hut or cabin built of logs and covered with bark — without floor, door or chimney — and would thus become resident citizens in a house of their own the day after their arrival. Mother used to hate these Scotch and Irish families that were coming in so unceremoniously. They were all Tories and never ought to have been allowed to come here.

◨ Many immigrants traveled long distances, not only across the Atlantic Ocean, but also within British North America at a time when much of it was wilderness. Many were veterans of the British army or the sons and daughters of veterans. Some were members of the same Scottish clan [*a large group of relatives having the same last name*]. Almost all had experienced death first-hand, as families were repeatedly broken and re-formed by members' deaths. Immigration was usually, but not always, voluntary. Caty and William Campbell's father was kidnapped by a ship's captain and sold in America as an indentured servant.

Caty Campbell of Greenwich

My father, Duncan Campbell, was born at Craignish or some such-named place in Argyleshire, I think. When he was fourteen years old he went to visit some relations of his in Ireland. With two other boys and three girls, amusing themselves on the seashore, they saw a ship hoisting her sails — as they understood, to make a short cruise around in the harbor — and thinking it would be a pleasant excursion they got on board of her. But she stood directly out to sea, and night coming on they lost sight of their native land forever — crying bitterly but their tears of no avail. The captain brought them to Maryland where he got places for them, binding them out for four years.

William Campbell of Greenwich

Father came to the Highlands [*the West Point region along the Hudson River*] in this state, and when there enlisted as one of the New York troops in the Old French War under Colonel James Clinton and was stationed off on the western frontier as far as Detroit at one time. His company went down Lake Ontario and the St. Lawrence with all the other troops from that direction, forming one of the

A present-day reenactor dressed as a Highland soldier of the 1700s at Fort Ticonderoga. Scotch Highland regiments served in the British army during the French and Indian War (1754–1763). Many veterans of this war settled in northern New York.

three divisions that met at Montreal and forced it to surrender.

Eunice Campbell Reid of Greenwich

My father, William Campbell, was born on the Isle of Skye, Scotland, and at the solicitation of his uncle, Captain Campbell, he enlisted into his company ere he was yet twenty-one years old and came to America. They came to America in time of the Old French War and were at Allegheny, Detroit, Lower Canada, et cetera, in a number of engagements.

My father served nine years in the army and was discharged in Nova Scotia. I think so from the circumstance that he there got acquainted with and married my mother. She was born in Scotland in Argyleshire. Her maiden name was Catherine Kennedy and she had been married to a man named Thompson and was left a widow with eleven children, my half brothers and sisters. I was born in Nova Scotia. My father came thence to New York, and we lived out in New Jersey awhile. Then he came up here and might have settled on land of his own if he had applied for it — soldiers' rights over on the edge of Vermont on Indian River — but he thought it was so entirely out of the world there that he would not go there. So he settled on the corner of Duncan Campbell's lot down the hill this side of Battenville. Stayed there three years.

My mother died there and was buried in the Esquire McNaughton burying ground. *[Esquire was a title of respect given to a man of some property.]* I was my father's only child by her. My half brothers and sisters got scattered about and none of them are now remaining around here. Father then moved to Salem. Here we stayed till the troubles and dangers of the Revolution.

Robert Blake of Jackson

I was born in Scotland on the borders of England on the banks of the Water Liddle. When ten years old, in 1771, I came to this country with my father and my mother, my uncle William Bell and our neighbor George Telford also coming over in company with us.

We came to New York and thence up the Hudson. My mother had been sick all the way and died at Tappan Bay and was buried in a graveyard on the east

shore of the bay. We came on — stopped a few days in Albany, living in the old fort up on the hill — then came up to Saratoga, now called Schuylerville. There was a large barrack on the north side of the mouth of Fish Creek. A Dutchman and his family lived in and kept this barrack. On the flat outside of the ditch were two other barracks — not very large buildings, but very well built with brick chimneys, which were seldom seen so far in the country at that time. These had all been built in the Old French War. General Schuyler's house and sawmills were also there; a man was keeping Schuyler's house, he being away. We emigrant families occupied one of the barracks during our stay there, and there Francis Telford died and was buried.

Thence we came over to this neighborhood, arriving here the last of August, I should think — harvesting was over with.

George Webster of Hebron

My father Alexander Webster was born in Argyleshire in the north of Scotland in 1734. When a young man he went into the south county of Scotland for a time, and thence into England where he lived six years and then embarked for America at Whitehaven in 1772. I was born in England, August 1769. Father had seven children, five of which reached maturity. Two were born in Scotland, two in England and three in this country. One child died on the passage over the ocean. Father landed in New York and came thence direct to Salem where he lived two years on a farm up White Creek, next north the Cleveland farm. Whilst in Salem he was elected onto the **Committee of Safety** for the town. He then moved into Hebron in the McClellan neighborhood where he resided through the war. He was here captain and afterwards major and colonel in the militia in time of the war. In 1777 he was the representative of Charlotte County in the Provincial Congress or Legislature.

Donald McDonald of Hebron

My father, John McDonald, belonged to a regiment of Highland soldiers — the 77th Regiment of Foot — and served in that regiment seven years in America in time of the Old French War. Each soldier discharged from the 77th was entitled to a certain amount of land. A private drew fifty acres, a noncommissioned officer two hundred. Father was with the surveyors as an assistant when they were laying out the soldiers' rights in this country, and selected his land on Indian River. Two-thirds of Father's lot lay in the state of Vermont when the state line came to be settled.

Father returned to Scotland but did not get a deed of his two hundred acres to take home with him. He there married, and December 15th, 1768, I was born in Invernesshire, Parish of Urqhart. When I was five years old Father emigrated to America with Mother, myself, and an uncle of mine, James.

Three months after our arrival in America, Mother died at Normanskill near Albany, giving birth to a daughter, Christine. At Normanskill, so Uncle James used to often say, among the Dutch children I wholly lost my mother tongue, the Gaelic language, in the space of twenty days. The infant Christine was taken care of by some friends in Albany. I also lived two years in Albany with John McDonald who, though of the same name, was no connection of Father's.

Father went to Johnstown with the view of getting a farm of old Sir William Johnson and arrived there as the old baronet was dying of bilious colic *[a painful liver disease or possibly a ruptured appendix]*. He therefore returned to Albany. I suppose he casually fell in with Harry Munro there, as Munro was looking up settlers

COMMITTEE OF SAFETY: Every Whig community had such a committee, which oversaw the local militia and acted as the Revolutionary government at the community level.

Sir William Johnson won the friendship of the Mohawks and other New York tribes and kept them from joining the French. As a reward, Johnson received a title and a 100,000-acre land grant in the Mohawk Valley. The Mohawks and other Iroquois tribes generally remained loyal to the British during the American Revolution.

to move onto his land. *[Munro was a relatively rich settler who owned two thousand acres.]* He then came up here and looked at Munro's land and at his own. Finding his own lot mostly in Vermont, all but sixty-two acres, he gave up the idea of settling on it. Father therefore leased a lot of Munro — one hundred acres. His lot was the northeast one in Munro's Patent *[land grant]*. He took a lease for twenty-one years and paid an annual rent of five pounds per year — one shilling per acre.

Father put up a small log house covering it with black ash bark, without any floor. It was about two miles northeast of the Meadows. Before we moved up, he in the space of two years cleared six or seven acres, and for these two years he had not his axe on a grindstone. His only way of sharpening it was to rub it on a large stone or boulder lying on the ground. The Scotch were not expert with the axe. One Yankee would outchop three Scotchmen.

Before moving us up here, Father married Marjory Cummings, a Highland woman in Albany. She died when I was ten years old, leaving a daughter, Elizabeth. After her death, we grew up — myself, Christine and Elizabeth — in the woods, with no mother and no housekeeper to take care of us or prepare our food and clothes.

◪ Before the American Revolution, both New York and New Hampshire claimed land in what later became the state of Vermont. As a result, settlers were not always sure they legally owned their land. From 1770 to 1775, a war, sometimes called the Hampshire Grants War, took place along the Vermont–New York border in northern New York. Vermonter Ethan Allen and his Green Mountain Boys conducted raids into New York, destroying settlers' homes and burning crops. Many Scotch veterans of the British army held grants of land in the disputed region.

Some of the Scotch and Scotch-Irish were Loyalists, or Tories, favoring British rule, but many did not really care one way or the other. Ethan Allen was a Patriot, or Whig, and favored revolution. Allen was so hated by some Scotch settlers along the border that many of them became Tories — not because they cared about politics, but because Tory was the opposite of what Allen was!

Jacob Bitely of Ticonderoga

I was born in New Jersey, November 9th, 1762. About the year 1765, my father moved from Jersey to Lake Champlain. He settled on the lakeshore, on the south line of the town of Bridport, Vermont. He took a lease for twenty-one years on two hundred acres of land here from Robert Ross of the City of New York. Ross, I think, had served in the French War and received these lands for military service — all the lands along there were soldiers' rights, and the title to them was thus derived directly from the Crown, and was regarded as more secure than any other title. There was a great fuss, I remember, about all the lands there, but we nor our neighbors were never molested — the chief troubles being close up to the foot of the mountains, some ways east and south of us. Our house was seven miles north of Ticonderoga on the lakeshore.

Isabel Duncan McIntyre of Hebron

I was born in Scotland March 15th, 1763. We came to America when I was eight years old, anno Domini 1771. We sailed from Greenoch and after a passage of nine and one-half weeks landed in New York. We came up to Albany and was there some three months. Father there took a lease of some land of Reverend Harry Munro in his patent in Hebron.

Munro was a large, fine-looking man. He promised the folks, as an inducement to settle on his land, that he would preach for them when he had leisure — but I believe I never heard him but once. He was not up to his word in this particular.

From Albany we came in a wagon, passing through Salem and to within five miles of Munro's Meadows. The road was not then opened clear through to the

Meadows — indeed much of the way there was scarcely any road. We got there in August — the weather very hot and flies and mosquitoes very troublesome. We stopped in a house belonging to Munro until we built one of our own, which was done that fall. Father was very handy with a broadaxe and hewed out

Isabel Duncan McIntyre's family probably used a wagon like this on their journey to Munro's Meadows.

puncheons *[slabs of wood]* for making a floor, a door, et cetera. He that fall did not get any land cleared and sowed with wheat, but having plenty of money bought provisions — probably of Munro.

We used to go to Salem, seventeen miles, sometimes to meeting, and Doctor Clark used to come to preach sometimes at the Meadows, baptizing the children. He was a very pious man.

Never saw Ethan Allen — though I heard much of him — that he made a great deal of trouble driving folks from their land and tearing down their houses. They didn't like him very well.

Ethan Allen, accompanied by Jacob Bitely's friend Nathan Beman, surprises De La Place, commander of Fort Ticonderoga. An unknown artist of the early 1800s painted this picture. He included Rosa, the laundress, in her frilly nightcap.

CHAPTER TWO

The Coming of War

1775–1776

2

◘ *Fort Ticonderoga.* On May 10, 1775, Ethan Allen and Benedict Arnold led a group of Green Mountain Boys and Massachusetts soldiers into Fort Ticonderoga and captured it. Fort Ticonderoga is located on the southern end of Lake Champlain, near the entrance to Lake George. Ticonderoga is said to be an Indian word meaning "where the waters meet."

The capture of Fort Ticonderoga is sometimes called the first clear-cut American victory of the Revolutionary War. It occurred about a month after the Battles of Lexington and Concord and a month before the Battle of Bunker Hill. Later, George Washington used the cannon from Ticonderoga to drive the British out of Boston.

As a child, Jacob Bitely lived about seven miles from Fort Ticonderoga. The "Swisher" he refers to is Peter Switzer, carried on both the British payroll list and the American prisoner list as commissary *[one who manages food and equipment]* for the fort.

Jacob Bitely of Ticonderoga

I well remember the taking of Ticonderoga at the breaking out of the war. De La Place, an old fellow no better than an old goose, had charge of the fort which was garrisoned by some thirty or forty old men and cripples that were worn-out in their country's service. Swisher was the commissary's name. He was sixty or seventy years old, and my brother Peter, two years and two months older than me, was

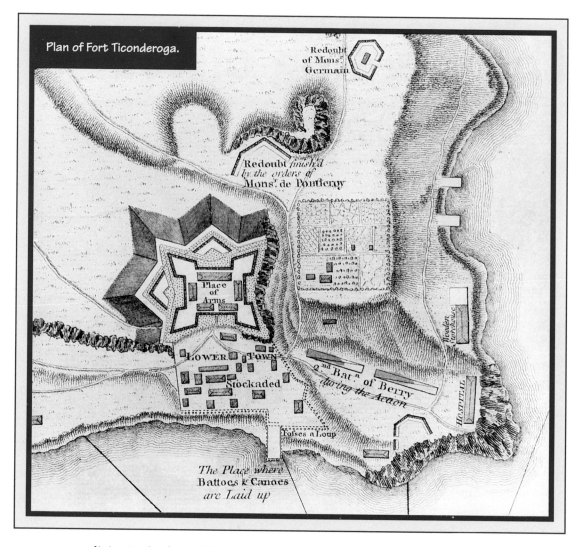

Plan of Fort Ticonderoga.

living in the fort with the commissary at this time. There was a woman whom they called Rosa also living in the fort — she washed for the soldiers and had an equivocal reputation. She was a great favorite with the commissary for a while, till he got mad at her for something and in a rage kicked her outdoors. There might have been one or two other females about the fort.

I used to know Mister Beman very well and his boys Nathan and Samuel were often with us playing ball, et cetera. Boys were so scarce we had to go consid-

The pistols taken from De La Place when he surrendered to Ethan Allen are now on exhibit at Fort Ticonderoga.

erable distances for playmates. When Ethan Allen and his men came, Nathan Beman went with others over to where the **battoes** lay, got them without the slightest alarm, took them over to the Vermont side. Allen and as many men as they could carry embarked and crossed to the fort with muffled oars. Nathan Beman then showed them the way to the little gate. They entered, and the fort was surrendered in the name of the Great Jehovah and the Continental Congress.

Brother Peter was in bed with the commissary at this time; awakened by the noise, he asked what was the matter. Swisher, who had sprung up and was in his shirt flaps looking out the window replied, "The rebels have taken the fort."

"The rebels, who are they?"

"The Yankees," Swisher replied.

The stores of the fort were thrown open and "help yourselves to what you like boys" was the word; the visitors drank freely and had quite a jolly time. What was done with the prisoners or where they were sent I do not know. Brother Peter was well known to several of the captors, and known to be a friend to them and their cause, and was left free to come home.

When Whitehall was taken, [Lord Philip] Skene [see next page] I guess was absent in Montreal. He used to be away from home much of the time, passing to and fro in a little sloop which he owned upon the lake and which was manned by two or three of his blacks. I remember this sloop used to pass our house often and the Negroes landed at our house to get some milk, two of them coming ashore. Skene was not then on board.

BATTOES or BATTEAUX: Flat-bottomed boats of any size, but often about six feet wide and thirty feet long, for use on rivers or lakes. It took three men to navigate a thirty-foot battoe — two to pole or row, one to steer.

⬘ *Attack on Skenesborough.* The local militias enrolled all men between the ages of sixteen and forty-five, or sometimes sixteen and sixty, but not all men were in service at the same time. Small bands of militiamen who made frequent raids or were otherwise active were called scouts or scouting parties. One Salem scouting company was led by John Barnes and included about a dozen local men. Three days after the capture of Ticonderoga, Barnes's scout took part in an attack on the property of Lord Philip Skene.

Skene, who was an officer in the British army, owned a 25,000-acre estate called Skenesborough about ten miles south of Ticonderoga. Skene was looking for tenants to settle on his land and pay him rent. He hoped to become a wealthy landlord, like the aristocrats of England.

The settlers to the south of Skenesborough were mainly small farmers. They owned their lots — usually about one hundred acres per family — and farmed the land themselves. Many small proprietors feared or hated Lord Skene. Indeed, later in the war, a Whig sharpshooter made a special attempt to assassinate Skene but failed.

Barnes's scout believed that Skene had escaped their raid, but actually he was traveling at the time. The following account has much to say about the corpse of Skene's wife. Her coffin was probably being held to send back to England, but the Salem Whigs were ready to think the worst of their enemy.

William McNish of Salem

Barnes' company was ordered out to proceed to Skenesborough and capture Lord Skene. Intending to approach there in the dead of night, they did not start till afternoon. When darkness overtook them they had twelve miles farther to go. A double sentry guarded Skene's house, a fact which they were not aware of. A sentry was placed at the house and another half a mile distant on the road. Before they were suspicious that caution was necessary, a gun was fired towards the residence of Skene. Knowing the alarm was now given they started forwards at their utmost speed. At the same instant, another gun was fired at the house. They rushed on and surrounded the house on all sides.

Reenactors portray Patriot militiamen. They wear leather gaiters [leg protectors] and long shirts or smocks under their jackets. These were the everyday clothes of country men in the 1700s.

Some of their number now searched the house thoroughly — but Skene had escaped. They supposed he had fled into the woods when the alarm was first given. They found the corpse of his wife in a small apartment partitioned off in the cellar. It was laid in a very nice wooden coffin, superior to anything which the carpenters of the country could make. And this was enclosed in a lead coffin which was sealed and soldered up so as to render it quite airtight. His wife had a legacy left her of a

Philip Skene of Skenesborough.

certain sum per day whilst she was above ground, and Skene had placed her there to receive this legacy.

On opening it the corpse was found but little changed. The coffin must have been purchased in Montreal or Quebec. The corpse was taken out and buried. The lead was too much needed for bullets to be buried, and it, together with the choice liquors found in the cellar, was delivered over to the commissaries of the Continental Army. There were about forty Negroes of both sexes upon the premises and these were about the only occupants they found. These Negroes were all full-blooded Africans, save one, a girl six or eight years old named Sylvia who claimed Skene for her father. Captain Barnes brought her home with him on his return. She remained in this town and died but a few years ago.

◻ *Tories and Whigs.* Why did some Colonial Americans become Whigs and others become Tories? This is a question that has many answers, and historians argue about most of them. In northeastern New York, settlers from New England were often, but not always, Whigs. Scotch and Scotch-Irish settlers were often, but not always, Tories or neutrals.

Members of a single community tended to go the same way politically. In some cases, less than ten miles separated communities that were primarily Tory or primarily Whig. Salem, for example, was largely Whig. North of it, the township of Argyle and the portion of Hebron known as Munro's Meadows were either mainly Tory or neutral. As the following accounts show, it was not wise to offend the prevailing community loyalty.

Sarah McCoy McNish of Salem

One John Cloughlin, by trade a cooper *[barrel maker]* at the breaking out of the Revolutionary War, was living, I believe, on Lot Number 3. He was so warm a Loyalist that it was determined to capture him if possible. The party under Barnes proceeded by night to his house. There was an entry-way through which they had to pass to get into the main room of the house. Coming into this entryway awoke him so that as they flung open the inner door, he was discerned escaping out at the window. They fired upon him, but probably without wounding him severely as he made off into the woods.

His wife screamed and cried so violently that she would not hush on their trying to quiet her by words, and they clenched hold of her and shook her to stop her noise. Cloughlin was never seen in the town after this and his wife also disappeared soon after — doubtless joining him and going off together to Canada.

Eunice Campbell Reid of Greenwich

An itinerant minister *[one who traveled from town to town]* came along in the wartime and preached in a barn from the text "I will go and return to my first husband for then it was better with me than now" — Hosea, chapter 2, verse 7. Though he did not apply it to the political condition of the country, some of the Whigs in Salem were so fiery that they denounced him as a Jesuit, a Tory in disguise, et cetera. Where he was from or what his name was, I do not know.

And so of Doctor Clark *[a Salem minister whose congregation was Scotch-Irish]*, who took no active part with either side but advised everyone as he thought was for the good and wished to be regarded by every individual as his friend and well-wisher. He was denounced by the Whigs as a Tory and by the Tories as a rebel so that he often used to say he felt it to be slippery ground on which he was standing.

One Sabbath I remember all the men came to meeting armed with loaded muskets so fearful were they that they would be attacked. The dogs — they too used to be allowed to come to meeting then — probably smelt the powder of the guns, for they kept howling and barking around the church all the time. It was the most doleful meeting I ever attended.

⊡ *1776.* The Declaration of Independence in July 1776 seems not to have been noticed or commented on by the pioneer settlers of the upper Hudson region. For them, there was a war on, and it was already a civil war. Isabel Duncan McIntyre, of Munro's Meadows, Hebron, was a girl of thirteen that year. "All the men were training a great deal of the time," she says. "Some were for the King and some against him."

There were frequent alarms in 1776. Elizabeth Conkey Pratt, who was seven years old in 1776, describes one of many such alarms.

In the fall of 1776, there was an actual invasion via Lake Champlain by British forces under Sir Guy Carleton. A fleet led by Benedict Arnold engaged Carleton at the Battle of Valcour Island on October 11, 1776, and was defeated. Carleton then pressed on to the fort at Crown Point, New York, on October 13, 1776. Because of the lateness of the season, however, Carleton soon withdrew to Canada to spend the winter there. Jacob Bitely, who was not yet fourteen at the time, questions the October dating, but he is mistaken.

Elizabeth Conkey Pratt of Salem

In the Revolutionary War, Father was commissary for the Salem Regiment and Mother did the baking for the troops when they were mustered in Salem. Our oven was outdoors and she had often to bake three ovenfuls of bread per day. Always before putting bread into the oven Father would with his gun take a walk about the surrounding woods to see that there was no enemy lurking about to steal the bread.

We had frequent alarms on the approach of the enemy, when the families would fly from their houses to the woods. Three guns fired in quick succession at the Salem Fort was the signal to all within their hearing that danger was near.

A man, having a gun on his shoulder, was driving a lot of hogs out of a cornfield up Black Creek. Somebody saw him and heard the rustling and saw the moving among the corn and supposed a large number of the enemy were making their way through the cornfield. He ran and gave the alarm. Mother heard the three guns fired in the village. Soon Joseph Slarrow came riding by at full speed exclaiming, "Aunt Dinah, fly from your house — a large body of the enemy are up by Captain McNitt's." Two or three other runners soon passed giving the same intelligence. Mother had a large batch of bread kneaded up which she was loath to leave to spoil. She ran up and met Mistress McCracken coming over the bridge from her house. They concluded if the danger became imminent, their husbands who were at the village would speedily fly home and aid them in getting away. Every family in town forsook their homes during this night except ours and McCracken's. In the evening Father and McCracken came home and told us it was a false alarm.

Jacob Bitely of Ticonderoga

I think there is some mistake in our histories as to the date of the naval battle on Lake Champlain in 1776. My recollection is quite strong that we were haying at the time, and therefore that it must have been in August. The men, having blowed up their boats to prevent their falling into the hands of the British, fled along the shore of the lake, passing and many of them stopping at our house. They were so black with the smoke of the powder that they could scarcely be told from Negroes, and their clothes were all blackened and marked with the burnt powder of the guns.

Carleton following on after the Americans, landed his Indians on Mister Richardson's farm and the regulars opposite to it on Putnam's Creek. He advanced hence to Kirby's Point within three miles of Ticonderoga, but durst *[dared not]* go no nearer. To take the fort by assault could not be done, it was put in such a state of defense. Whole acres around the fort were set with pickets and sharpened stakes or covered with fallen trees — so that he could not approach the walls with any order to scale them.

So he returned to Canada burning the few buildings around Crown Point. The fort there had been previously burnt. All the neighborhood around Crown Point was wholly deserted by both parties through the following winter. I remember of being up there in **pigeon time** that fall hunting, and everybody was gone from around there.

PIGEON TIME: In the fall, the now-extinct passenger pigeon gathered in enormous numbers prior to its annual migration south. The birds were very good to eat and very easy to kill. They were hunted into extinction.

Which on Gen.l Burgoynes. Army advancing, was set Fire to, by the Americans.
Published as the Act directs, 1 Jan.y 1789 by J. Lane Leadenhall Street London.

A sawmill owned by Philip Skene at Fort Ann Creek. Benedict Arnold's troops used planks from this mill to build the fleet (America's first navy) that met the British at Valcour Island in 1776. Carleton's British raiders burned the mill in 1780.

Burgoyne's camp near the southern end of Lake Champlain. The general addresses his Indian allies.

General Burgoyne Arrives

3

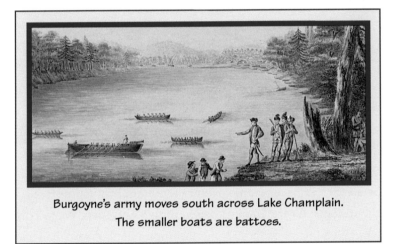

Burgoyne's army moves south across Lake Champlain.
The smaller boats are battoes.

◪ Looked at from far away in time, 1777 was a key year in the Revolutionary War. General John Burgoyne marched into New York and was defeated at the Second Battle of Saratoga. As a result of this great American victory, the French entered the war against Britain. With French aid, America was able to win the Revolutionary War. It is for this reason that the Battle of Saratoga is often described as the turning point of the Revolution.

But, as you will see, the children who lived near Burgoyne's army of seven thousand British regulars, Indians, and German mercenaries were not concerned with grand strategy. They experienced and remembered the small, homely details of their own flights from danger. Depending on political loyalties, some fled *from* Burgoyne, and others fled *to* him. And some, like Jacob Bitely, just stayed put.

Jacob Bitely of Ticonderoga

Burgoyne in 1777 landed on precisely the same spots where Carleton landed the year before — his Indians on Richardson's farm and his regulars at Putnam's Creek on the flats bordering the creek. He laid here some time, I should think two or three weeks. Parties of the Indians were out every day scouting and hunting through the woods. They were always uttering "Curse on the **Bostonians**" in their grum voices whenever we met them; and this was the only English expression they appeared to have learned. They did not molest us or any of the families about there — we being noncombatants and unarmed. My brothers John and Henry had volunteered into the militia and were away from home at this time and indeed through the whole of this year.

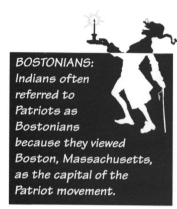

BOSTONIANS: Indians often referred to Patriots as Bostonians because they viewed Boston, Massachusetts, as the capital of the Patriot movement.

Isabel Duncan McIntyre of Hebron

When Burgoyne arrived at Skenesborough all the families from Munro's Meadows went there in a company together to obtain Protection [see page 47] — not from the Indians, for the Indians hadn't joined him then. We hid our beds and other things in thick bushes leaving nothing in the houses when we went away. We found these things all safe and undisturbed when we got back. We started for Skenesborough in the morning; we went on foot driving our cattle with us. Father had one horse, three milch [*milk*] cows and two steers. We followed a path through the woods; got to Skenesborough the same day, the distance being seventeen miles. The settlers there had fled leaving their houses empty; there was but a few houses there at that time. Skene's stone house and barn I remember very well.

We occupied one of the vacant houses. There were not many families that came in there to take Protection, and we were not crowded in our accommodations, and there was no sickness or deaths whilst we were there. We slept upon blankets on the floor, not having any beds with us. The army had their tents pitched, under which they slept, and they were training every day. It was a large army. Our cattle ran at large and the fields of grain were all trampled down and destroyed. We sold the milk to the soldiers every day — they commonly coming

Act, directly or indirectly, endeavour to obstruct the Operation of the King's Troops, or supply or assist those of the Enemy. Every Species of Provision brought to my Camp, will be paid for at an equitable Rate, in solid Coin.----In Consciousness of Christianity, my Royal Master's Clemency, and the Honour of Soldiership, I have dwelt upon this Invitation, and wished for more persuasive Terms to give it Impression ; and let not People be led to disregard it by considering the immediate Situation of my Camp, I have but to give Stretch to the Indian Forces under my Direction, and they amount to Thousands, to overtake the hardened Enemies of Great-Britain ; I consider them the same wherever they may lurk.----If notwithstanding these Endeavours and sincere Inclination to assist them, the Phrenzy of Hostility should remain, I trust I shall stand acquitted in the Eyes of God and Men, in denouncing and executing the Vengeance of the State against the wilful Outcast. The Messengers of Justice and of Wrath await them in the Field, and Devastation, Famine, and every concomitant Horror that a reluctant but indispensible Prosecution of Military Duty must occasion, will bar the Way to their Return.

J. BURGOYNE.

Camp at the River BONGRETT,
June 23d, 1777.
By Order of his Excellency the Lieutenant General,
ROBERT KINGSTON, Sec'ry.

A portion of Burgoyne's proclamation (see page 47). This paper frightened everyone living in the path of the advancing British army and set off the first wave of evacuations. Burgoyne's promise "to give Stretch to the Indian Forces under my Direction...to overtake the hardened Enemies of Great Britain" was particularly ominous.

to us for it, but sometimes we carried it to them.

I remember of seeing the water of the lake there, but do not remember of seeing any relics [remains] of the boats run ashore and burnt. The English army at length struck their tents and marched away from the place. Then a large army of Hessians passed through after them. The troops having thus all gone from the place we returned home; we were there about five weeks. None of the men from the Meadows went to join the army on either side.

Donald McDonald of Hebron

At the time Burgoyne reached Skenesborough the five old Scottish familie which formed the settlement at Munro's Meadows started to go to his camp to take Protection — but my father, John McDonald, stopped upon the way from some cause, I do not know what, and did not go there with our family.

Father was one of the rangers belonging to Captain Barnes' company of Salem, and was out several times upon scouting service — mostly in the last year the war, I suppose. They went to see if Indians had come up the lake from Canad and on similar services — whenever a report of this kind got abroad. The countr was often alarmed by stories of this kind.

John McDonald II of Hebron

Grandfather would gladly have remained neutral in the Revolution, but th was not permitted, and after deliberation he enlisted in Captain Barnes' Ranger This saved him from being harried by the Whigs, and his nationality probably saved him from such of the Tories as were Scotch — as many of that nationality were in and about Hebron, where Grandfather settled.

George Webster of Hebron

When Burgoyne reached Skenesborough the Hebron settlers [who were Whigs] fled down into Salem and stayed with their Salem friends two or three weeks when that town was also evacuated. Our furniture, et cetera, was secreted a by-nook beside Black Creek and covered over with brush. The Tories did not find it. Munro's settlers in the north part of the town came down and took poss sion of our evacuated dwellings — living in them in our absence, fondly hoping to have them for their own when the country was conquered by the King.

We were at Hugh More's near Shushan a few days and thence went south across More's bridge, a rickety structure, tipped and slanting almost as steep as house roof in some places. I do not remember how we travelled, whether on foo

Reenactors dressed as British soldiers. The tall, peaked hat was designed to intimidate the enemy, giving each man an extra foot in height.

or on horseback, but have a faint impression of having rode some of the way in a cart. We came to Albany and thence to Esopus, going all the way by land, Father having to be here to attend the Provincial Legislature at this time. Some other families from Salem accompanied us. McKnight was one of them and continued on from Esopus out into Pennsylvania to some connection of his wife. McCarter from Salem also was with us with his family. We were staying at Esopus when it was burnt by the British — Father being in the Legislature in the village and his family ten miles north. We saw the light of the burning buildings very distinctly, and the Dutch matrons in the neighborhood where we were made a great clamor on seeing the light. Father was pursued by some British soldiers in the street at Esopus but eluded them by turning aside down a by-street.

He returned to Salem in the fall in season to dig his potatoes; he did not move his family back until the latter part of winter. In the spring, I remember, we burnt the meadows over to make them smooth for mowing — the grass not having been cut from them the year before.

Tryphena Martin Angel of Salem

In the war Father was away from home when the families evacuated the town. He was either in the army or away with a scouting party and so was not here to aid us in getting away. We lived then in a log house halfway from the present red house to the kill *[a Dutch word for stream, creek, or river]*.

I remember little about our flight except as I have heard it told by my mother and others. The town was full of exaggerated and alarming reports. Burgoyne was at Whitehall and it was said he had a hundred thousand soldiers with him — British, Hessians, and Indians — and was coming down through this place and would kill every enemy of the King.

Daniel Livingston was living at that time in a house of Father's down near where the old bridge across the kill was. He helped us to get away. Some of our things were buried, others sunk in the well, and the rest were put into the ox-cart in which Aaron and Miriam rode, Livingston driving the oxen. Mother rode on the old mare and I was tied on behind her or had to hold on to her.

I was so young that I remember nothing whatever of this journey except one

incident. It is this. On the road somewhere towards Hoosick was a large slough
hole *[swamp]* or brook across which poles were laid to keep the horses, et cetera,
from miring in it. The foot of the horse we rode got caught between these poles
so that she fell pitching Mother and me off into the mud. We were not hurt but
badly frightened and sadly besmeared with muck and mud. A few days after our
arrival at Brown's my brother Moses was born. We came back before cold weather.

As already stated, part of our things were buried in time of the retreat before
Burgoyne: pots and kettles, a large brass kettle, pewter platters and other dishes,
the iron trammel *[a chain and hook for raising and lowering a kettle]* that hung in
the chimney. When we got back we found all these things had been stolen by the
Tories. We never got any trace as to who it was that had taken them.

A famous American painter, John Vanderlyn, imagined the scene of Jane McCrea's death this way. Vanderlyn painted his *Death of Jane McCrea* some years after the war, in 1804.

CHAPTER FOUR
The Murders

◨ By late July 1777, General Burgoyne's army was in camp near Fort Edward. Burgoyne had issued a proclamation to the inhabitants, calling on them to stay quietly on their farms and put tokens on their hats and their cattle's horns showing they were loyal to the king. (The Loyalist token was a bit of white paper; the Whigs wore sprigs of evergreen.) Burgoyne had also offered "Protection" to all coming into his camp. "Protectioners" swore an oath of allegiance to the king and received a written pass enabling them to go back and forth between the army camp and their homes. Many Tories and neutrals "took Protection" and believed that their lives and property were safe.

On July 26, 1777, some of Burgoyne's Indians murdered a whole family, the George Allens of Argyle. A day later, a young woman, Jane McCrea, was also killed just outside Fort Edward. The Allens and Jane McCrea were Tories, and now no one — Whig, Tory, or neutral — felt safe.

Maria McEachron of Argyle

⬚ Maria was eighteen years old in July of 1777. Two of the murdered women, Catherine Killmore and Mistress Allen, the wife of George Allen, were her sisters.

My father, Yerry Killmore, told my brother Adam to go and help Allen get in his wheat, but Adam felt lazy and wouldn't go, and Father used afterwards to say he could forgive Adam for all his disobedience, he was so glad he disobeyed him at this time. So he sent his Negro Tom, who was a young man grown, in Adam's place, and the wench Sarah, who was about twelve years old, and my sister Catherine also went along. They went on foot early on Saturday morning and were to return home at night.

They wrought together in the harvest field, Mistress Allen binding the sheaves, the black girl carrying them together, Allen and Tom reaping, and Catherine at the house taking care of the babe and getting their dinner — she having gone for this purpose, that Mistress Allen might help in the wheatfield. To make more sure of killing all, it was supposed the Indians lurking in the woods waited till they should be all in the house at dinner, for twas then that the attack was made.

Catherine and the Negroes not coming home at night, on Sunday morning Father sent the boy Abram, Tom's brother, on horseback. Catherine was lame in one foot at this time and he sent the horse for her to ride home on — not knowing but what her foot might have got worse from walking and thus prevented her coming home the night before.

[After coming upon the scene of the massacre] Abram jumped on the horse and rode homewards, three miles to McKallor's — choked and crying, he could scarcely for a time make out to them the tale. He durst not ride any further. They thought at first he was afraid of the Indians in the woods and had lied to them about the family's being murdered as an excuse for his fears, and to get them to send somebody home with him.

Allen was found on the path to the barn and near to the barn. A piece behind him was Catherine; behind her and halfway from the house to the barn was Mistress Allen with her babe in her arms and placed at her breast — where it must have been put by the Indians, for to scalp it they must have had it out of its mother's arms. The two children and the Negro girl had tried to hide themselves in the bed, for they were found there, the bedclothes gashed and bloody from the tomahawks. Blood was tracked all around the floor. Bullet holes were perforated through the door, and there was one bullet through the cupboard door in the northeast corner of the house.

I was living with my husband, Peter McEachron, at the head of the lake [Cossayuna]. On that Saturday he was over at Salem helping them put up pickets around the Presbyterian Church, and came home at night. The next day, Sunday, we heard of the murder and fearing our house would be sought out and we be murdered, we forsook it and in our two boats went onto the island in the lake where we stayed all night, not venturing to kindle a fire lest it should reveal our hiding place to the Indians.

Next day some of our neighbors passing saw our house deserted. Alarmed, they called our names walking along the lakeshore. Hearing and seeing who they were, we answered and came ashore. Cheered up by them, we concluded it was better to stay at home and defend our house if attacked, than forsake it and thus invite its being destroyed.

Daniel Smith of Argyle

◻ Daniel Smith was twelve years old at the time of the murders and was living about four miles from the Allen house.

When John McDougall and James Gillis heard the news they doubted whether it was true and went down to Allen's house to see. Finding it was true, they jumped onto Allen's horses and rode back. Allen's family was not buried that day. It was Sunday. All were too much concerned for their own safety and too poorly furnished with arms and ammunition to venture down there to bury them that day. To add to our terror and alarm, word came from Fort Edward towards night that Mistress McNeil, such was the report we first got, had just been murdered and scalped by the Indians.

All the families around there gathered together on Sunday night at James Gillis' house. It was about a mile north of Yerry Killmore's. A part of the men stood guard around the house through the night. It had been resolved to go down and bury the Allen family the next forenoon. And to be more equipped for this hazardous business, John McDougall kindled a fire out in the yard and was all night casting bullets and buckshot — melting up most of the pewter dishes about the house for this purpose.

The next forenoon, Monday forenoon, the young men rode down to bury the Allen family. They rode down all of them on horseback carrying their guns. Some of the bodies had been torn and mangled by Allen's hogs.

◪ Jane McCrea was twenty-four years old. She and her brother John were the children of a Presbyterian minister and had recently settled in the upper Hudson region. John was a Whig, but Jane was a Tory. She was engaged to an American named David Jones, a Tory serving in Burgoyne's army.

It is possible that Jane McCrea was more or less accidentally killed by an American bullet instead of by the Indians who were taking her into Burgoyne's camp. One eyewitness later claimed that this is what happened. Even so, the Indians scalped her and brought the scalp back with them to camp. General Burgoyne himself always believed that the Indians had committed the murder, and so did many pioneers. Jane McCrea became the subject of stories and songs throughout New York and New England. Although Jane herself was linked with the Tory cause, she became a Patriot heroine. Her death turned many people against Burgoyne and the British cause.

Robert Blake of Jackson

I have often heard Mistress Sarah McNeil tell of her and Miss Jane McCrea's capture and flight towards Burgoyne's camp.

Mistress McNeil was sixty or seventy years old at the time, and had buried three husbands. She was a large fat woman with a good deal of vanity and pride about her. Her maiden name was Fraser, and she claimed to be a cousin of General Fraser of Burgoyne's army. Her house stood, say forty rods [a rod equals five and a half yards] from the fort, up the river a few rods from the river and a few rods from the main road.

Jane McCrea lived with her brother Colonel John McCrea. They lived at that time on the west side of the river, several miles below Fort Edward. Miss McCrea left her brother's house voluntarily and came to Mistress McNeil's hoping for a chance to get from there into the British camp.

Miss McCrea and Mistress McNeil were, as the latter has often told me, sitting outside of the door in the shade on the north side of the house, it being a warm summer's day, engaged in sewing. A party of American soldiers had passed along the road and up the hill a short time before, and their going out had been observed by the ladies, and they had expressed their wishes that them fellows might get a scattering [a volley of musket fire] before they came back. Sitting there and sewing, they were in rather a jocular way conversing when all at once there was a rattling of musket shots among the bushes on the hillside about half a mile distant; and soon emerging from the bushes they descried [saw] the party of Americans pursued hotly by a band of Indians. Alarmed, the ladies ran into the house. As the combatants came on rushing confusedly along the road, to their consternation, some half a dozen Indians separated from the party and made directly for the house. Some of them held of each other's hands, jumping and yelling as they leaped forwards towards the house.

Terror-stricken, they raised a trap door in the floor and jumped into a small cellar hole under it — Miss McCrea, Mistress McNeil, and a younger man about twenty years old named Norman Morrison. A Negress and her children were the only other persons about the house. The wench with her children got partly through the trap door, when Mistress McNeil pushed her back, telling her there was not room for her there, and thereupon pulled down the trap door. The wench hereupon went upstairs with her children, and there found a more secure hiding place than her mistress, for the Indians did not go into the chamber.

Instantly they rushed into the house and probably perceived some motion to the trap door, for they ran directly to it, pulled it up, reached down with their hands, grasped the young man and ladies by their hair and pulled them up through the trap door. Morrison has often told me how they lifted him out of the cellar by the hair on his head. An Indian on each side of Morrison grasped his arms, locked theirs in with his and ran out with him and up the hill. An Indian on each side of Mistress McNeil ran her off in the same way, whilst others placed Miss McCrea in the saddle of the horse and taking hold of the reins ran as fast as they could — for by this time the American party having gained the fort and given the alarm, several companies were drawn up outside the fort and paraded upon the green commenced firing at the Indians. [This was the last Mistress McNeil or Morrison saw of Jane.]

They fired by platoons, as Morrison told me, and instantly as a platoon fired, the Indians would all drop flat upon the ground — that the bullets might pass over them — ordering Morrison to do the same and pulling him down with them as often as they fell. Then jumping up, they would run at their utmost speed till another platoon fired. Thus they scampered up the hill. Morrison being lightest of foot was ahead of the ladies. Mistress McNeil being large and fat could not run to advantage, but the two Indians, one on each side of her holding her arms, pulled her along as fleetly as possible. Mistress McNeil was so exhausted with the race that she was scarcely able to stand when they reached the camp. How far this was, I don't know. Probably two miles or more from her house.

As soon as the Indians were out of sight up the hill, the six hundred American troops at Fort Edward evacuated the fort and retreated down the river to Schuylerville. The British and Tories sneered at this cowardly act — their making no attempt to defend themselves. There were a number of Americans killed by the Indians in the encounter that first alarmed Mistress McNeil. These were gathered up by the British a few days after, and buried just at the foot of the hill near the edge of the bushes. I was passing there to my Uncle Bell's when the British sol-

This woodcut showing Jane McCrea's murder may have been part of General Gates's effort to rouse the local militias to join his army in the fight against Burgoyne. Gates and others believed that two of Burgoyne's Indians quarreled over the right to take McCrea to her fiancé and win a reward. One enraged warrior then killed the prize, McCrea, and scalped her.

diers were gathering up the bodies to bury them or rather to burn them, for they covered them over with logs and wood of pitch pine and set the logs on fire to char and partly consume the bodies, so that they would not taint the air — this was their only object — but for this they would not have touched them I suppose. They were covered up with their clothes on, and when burning, the explosion of their cartridges was repeatedly heard as the fire reached them.

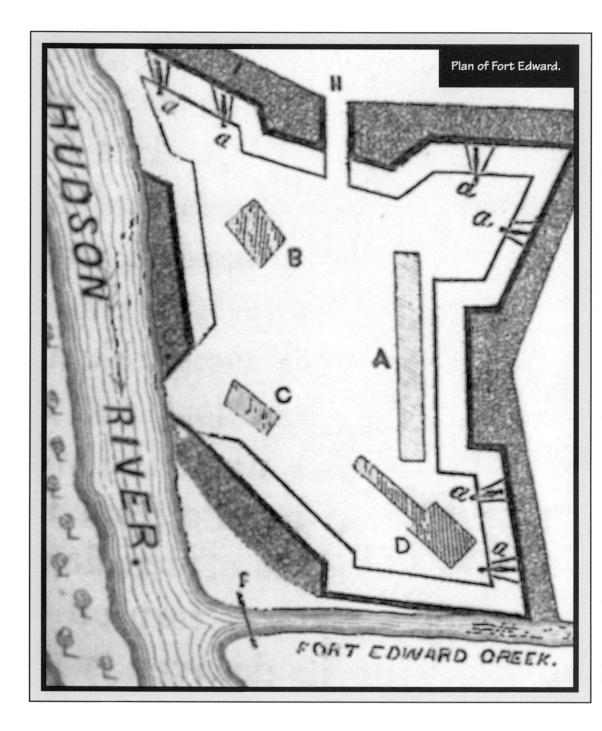

Plan of Fort Edward.

Sutlers, who were often women, traveled with the British army. They sold liquor, soap, candles, fruit, bread, and cheese to the soldiers. This reenactor is preparing a bowl of punch — rum, lemon, sugar, and water.

Jane McCrea was not buried by the Americans, for they had all fled, but by the Tories in the neighborhood. My uncle's folks assisted in her burial and showed me her grave only a few days after it.

I have repeatedly heard Mistress McNeil tell how the Indians held of her arms and made her run, they running like greyhounds and dragging her along and that she was tired all but to death ere she got to the camp. When Burgoyne lay at Fort Edward,

General Simon Fraser, claimed as a relative by Mistress McNeil, was later killed at the Second Battle of Saratoga. This painting shows the mortally wounded Fraser being supported as a German officer, his wife, and several other well-dressed ladies look on.

Archy Livingston, my father, and all the other families around here went over to get Protection from Burgoyne. We were there over a week. I stayed during the time at my Uncle Bell's. Mistress McNeil put up at his house all the time I was there and I knew

her well. She used to go down every day from Uncle's to visit her cousin General Fraser, who with the other officers had their headquarters at Smith's house. This was a large house just below the fort. It was afterwards surrounded by pickets.

Mistress McNeil was talking a great deal at the time about houses that belonged to her in New York City — whether she really had any houses there and was really a cousin to General Fraser, I do not know — and was telling how she was going to give the use of such house to this officer and such house to that for their quarters on their arrival in New York — for that they would reach New York was a fixed fact at that time.

Mary Gillespie Bain of Argyle

◨ **Mary Bain was seven years old at the time of McCrea's murder.**

Mistress McNeil of Fort Edward was an old fat woman, sixty years old or more I should think. She was Scotch and spoke considerably broad *[with a heavy accent]*. I have heard her say she was in bed lying there with nothing on but her chemise *[slip]*. She thence jumped through the trap door into the cellar with Miss McCrea, and I will give you her very expression with regard to her being taken out of the cellar. Said she, "Big and heavy as my arse is, my hair was stout enough to sustain the weight" — meaning she was lifted out of the cellar literally by the hair of her head.

She said the Indians pricked her with their bayonets and pushed her with the butts of their muskets to get her up the hill faster. Arrived at the camp in her chemise, she sent word to her cousin General Fraser of her situation. He stirred around and searched up clothes for her among the women, and thus she was arrayed at last in proper plight to be introduced to him and the other officers and their ladies.

Charlotte Leslie of Salem

> ◙ Charlotte Leslie was a former slave and friend of Dinah McCrea, who had been a slave in the McCrea household. In New York State, most slaves were emancipated, or set free, by law in 1827.

When I first came to live with Judge Edward Savage, Dinah and I became acquainted and were slaves together in his family many years until my marriage and freedom. Then again, after she was emancipated by the state law, she preferred living with us to remaining at Judge Savage's for she felt herself more free and equal at our house than there. So she resided with us until her death some fifteen years ago. I have heard her tell of Jane's murder by the Indians, et cetera, a great many times.

Who John McCrea married for his first wife I do not know. But she was a violent Whig. Jane, his sister, was a violent Tory. Jane and the wife used to quarrel about the war, and Dinah used to say she several times stepped in between them to separate them, so angry would they get with each other.

Jane was up to Fort Edward visiting when she was murdered. Her brother had sent up his wagon for her to ride home but her friends urged her not to go back among the rebels so she stayed. So Dinah used to say. I have no recollection of Dinah's saying that she was with Jane at this time but she used to tell that Jane and Mistress McNeil jumped into the cellar and when the Indians pulled up the trap door Mistress McNeil cried out to them, "Friends! Friends!"

Jane had on a light chintz frock and under this a black callamink [calamanco, a fine woolen cloth] petticoat — so Dinah used to say. When the body was found, the bottom of the chintz gown had been cut off by the Indians — about a third or fourth part of the dress had been cut off. The body was placed on a float in the river for the purpose of bringing it down to her brother's to be buried. But her brother's wife said she did not want it brought there — so they stopped some ways above and buried it on the shore of the river.

African Americans were a significant presence in New York during the Revolutionary era. Like this reenactor, Dinah McCrea would have done much cooking outdoors.

General Stark directs the Patriot forces at the Battle of Bennington.

CHAPTER FIVE

Flight into Danger

The Battle of Bennington

◪ The Allen and McCrea murders horrified everyone because they showed that women and children could also die in the war. In the Whig town of Salem, many members of the militia sent their families south to the towns of Cambridge and Hoosick Falls. From there, some families also continued east into Bennington, Vermont, which was a major supply depot for the Patriot cause.

As Salem was being evacuated, General Burgoyne detached more than eight hundred Hessians and Indians from his army and sent them, commanded by the German colonel Friedrich Baum, to seize the supplies at Bennington. On August 16, 1777, at the Battle of Bennington, some two thousand militiamen inflicted a huge defeat on Baum, killing or capturing his entire force. Burgoyne was thus deprived of badly needed supplies and nearly one-seventh of his army. The actual battle took place in New York, in Walloomsac. It was called the Battle of Bennington because most of the victorious American force came from nearby Bennington, Vermont.

William McCollister of Salem

In 1777, when most of the families from around here fled, Father went with his family to Chesterfield in Massachusetts to his sister's. They left about the first of August and Father had a large field of wheat on the flat which he was obliged to leave unharvested. He had a span of horses. Mother rode one with the eldest boy behind her and the youngest child in her arms. Father rode the other, with the two other children on the horse with him. Judge Ebenezer Russell's wife accompanied them also on horseback with a babe in her arms. Judge Russell, himself, was thus enabled to remain at home. I think Judge Savage's wife also went with them but I am not certain.

Father went and joined the army as soon as his family were safely landed at his sister's. He did not return here to harvest his wheat. He left the premises in charge of one Hunsdale and his wife, who were too old to undertake such a journey and said if they were killed here it would only shorten their lives but a few years.

It must have been late in the fall when the family returned, for Hunsdale had got through with the butchering of the hogs. When mother became childish from old age, she was often talking of Chesterfield and this journey.

Elizabeth Conkey Pratt of Salem

Finally we all forsook our homes for a distant flight to our friends in New England. We had a large quantity of pewter dishes which we could not take and which would be stolen by the Tories unless they were concealed. Father dug a hole near the house and placed them all in it and his handsaw on top of them and covered them up.

The Tories at this time were greatly elated and carried their heads quite high but after Burgoyne's surrender and when we returned, they were greatly humbled and downcast.

I do not know which way our family fled or where we crossed the kill, but we went to Bennington and were there obliged to stay, Father's business as commissary to the militia rendering it impossible for him to go from Bennington for some time. Two of my uncles came up to Bennington from Pelham to take us down there. Eunice was an infant and Mary was sick with the measles, so that Mother had to remain and take care of her. We four older children went with our uncles. I remember nothing of the journey only its close — how we children forgot our fatigue and with light hearts ran up a long hill our uncles having told us "Grandpa's house" was at the top of it. Mother remained in Bennington till after the battle was fought there. After the battle, Father got released long enough to come with her to Pelham.

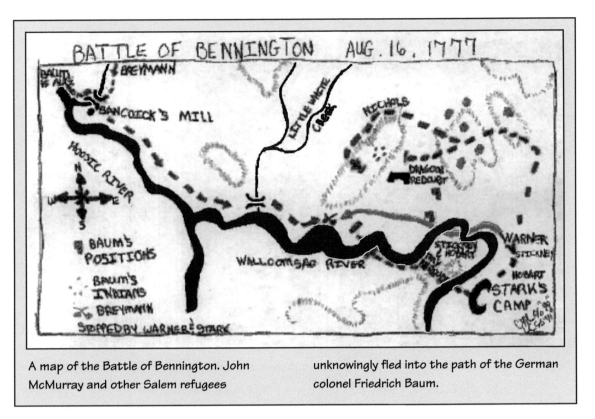

A map of the Battle of Bennington. John McMurray and other Salem refugees unknowingly fled into the path of the German colonel Friedrich Baum.

John McMurray of Salem

When the town was evacuated in 1777, I was an infant and was carried on my mother's back. Our goods were loaded on an ox-sled and the remainder of them buried. Father had many books, some of them that he valued highly. These were all buried and were quite spoiled when they were dug up again. We went south. Somewhere down in Cambridge we made a temporary stop of a day or two. Whilst there, Baum's detachment passed along south of us. It was at the house of a Mistress Miller that we tarried. As the troop of the enemy had passed, it was concluded to be folly to follow in their tracks and that we should be more safe at home. So we returned. Fields of wheat were everywhere standing and the women turned out to reap some in these. The weather was excessively hot and they were constrained to go almost naked. They therefore kept a sharp lookout to see if there was any men anywhere looking at them thus half-clothed, but none ever came in sight of them so entirely had the inhabitants moved off.

Susan Lyttle Vance of Salem

When we moved [in the evacuation] we had but one horse. A fine yoke of oxen was Father's main team at that time, and these oxen had been stolen from them and driven away to Burgoyne's camp by two Salem Tories. They offered Father a receipt for the oxen by which he might get his pay they said, but he would not take their receipt.

We went on foot down into Cambridge and stayed at McCool's. Of the Salem families many stopped around there; others went on to Bennington and down into Massachusetts. On Sabbath, Doctor Clark had the folks all gathered together for divine service. The meeting was on a rise of ground above the Owlkill [River]. I don't remember how long we stayed at McCool's. Father came back first to see about saving his grain, and he was taken sick and sent Mother word — for folks were passing through the country all the time — and so she went back home with me and Jane and Rebecca.

Rebecca and I went out after dinner to **pull flax,** alone, not far from the house. A Hessian soldier with his gun and military clothes came along, enquiring in broken English the way to Bennington. He was deserting from the British at Fort Edward and finding his way through the country to New England. But he told us he was in advance of finding the road to Bennington, and that the whole army was not far behind him. This so alarmed Rebecca that eager to get all the news from him we could we followed him — conversing with him — many rods, till we got to the foot of the hill south of our house. Suddenly we heard a crackling among the bushes. A party of Tories were secreted on the little hill east of the road, at the foot of the big hill. Who they were I do not know. There was more than a dozen of them. They rushed upon the Hessian, took away his gun, pinioned him and said they should take him back to the camp to be shot for deserting. They also said we girls had got to go with them, too, for we were traitors showing a deserter the road for him to escape.

They also captured on the road Judge Hopkins of Rupert, a

PULL FLAX: Flax is the plant from whose seeds comes linseed oil and whose fibers are woven into linen. Flax was harvested by "pulling," or uprooting the whole plant.

A woman in the dress of the 1700s separates flax fibers by combing them with a device called a hatchel.

Spinning flax fibers into thread.

well-known Whig. They marched us along the road past our house, which stood
away from the track we followed, and we got out nearly to where David Russell
now resides when we were met by William McNish who was a frank Tory now
coming from Burgoyne's camp, and knew the party that was taking us away. He
asked what they were doing with us little girls. They told him they were taking us
to Fort Edward for aiding a deserter to escape. He told them they would not do
any such thing — that our mother would go crazy if we were missed and would
think we had been killed by the Indians. On his promising to keep us till after
sundown, they gave us over into his care — their only design probably being to

prevent our going home and telling of their taking off the Hessian till after they could get beyond the reach of a pursuing party which they probably feared would be rallied and sent after them. McNish accompanied us back home and stayed to watch us till dark, when he went on home over the hills.

Simon Nelson of Salem

When the families fled from Salem in 1777, Father had only a span of horses to aid in our flight. Mother and the youngest child rode one of these. Some of our goods and Samuel — who was sick at the time and but a small boy — was taken on the other. I believe there were no wagons in the town at this time. We went down to Sancoick close by the Dutch church. Froman or Vroman wanted Father and John Law to stay there and take charge of his place to allow him to fly to some more secure spot than that was for him, he being a committeeman *[member of a Committee of Safety]* and well-known. So they concluded to tarry there. He had commenced his haying and harvesting. We finished it. Suddenly word was brought us that the British army was coming that way.

About a dozen Salem families were there. Everything was packed up in haste and we were ready to start the next morning, the army being encamped this night at Cambridge. But James More came along and told us all to lay still and quiet in the houses, for then we would not be molested, whereas if we were found moving off all we had would be taken from us. So we concluded to stay. But early next morning all the Salem horses, thirteen in number, were sent a mile down the river, my brother Joseph and others taking them to keep them away from the British. But as ill luck would have it, a man driving away cattle was pursued by a party of Indians and Tories. They followed him south to the Walloomsac River without succeeding in taking him. Then giving over the pursuit they followed up the river and came thus directly upon our horses and seized the whole of them. When the Indians passed back flying from Bennington battle, I saw one of

them riding by on one of our horses and wished with all my heart he would stumble and throw the Indian and escape from him.

I went out in the morning to salt the sheep *[provide salt for the animals — probably table salt, perhaps mixed with grain]*. Running to the top of the knoll and looking towards the house I saw Father entering it and the soldiers and the Indians all about the house and neighborhood like a swarm of bees. I had but one thought — to run and join Father. I first passed through a party of Indians having no fears of them, having been used to the Stockbridge Indians *[a Christianized tribe based in Stockbridge, Massachusetts, that visited the Charlotte County area every fall]* before this. They patted me on the head saying, "Poor little boy — Bostonian boy." I got into the house in safety. The soldiers were plundering it of whatever they could find. One of them told Father to open the oven door, in which was an oven-ful of bread just baked. Father did so, but one of the officers said, "Will you take the bread away from these children?" So they let it remain.

On the day of the battle we were ever and anon receiving reports at Sancoick first that the rebels were beat, then that the Tories were beat, then again that the rebels were getting the worst of it, and so it went first for one then for the other side.

Father and John Law happened to be among a party of Tories when they were all taken prisoner together. They were thus prevented from gathering any of the plunder of the battlefield in which work some of our neighbors were quite success-ful. They were confined three or four days when Doctor John Williams passing by asked, "What are you doing there in that company?" On informing him of their misfortune, they were speedily released. Neighbor Simpson was quite diligent in gathering plunder. He moved his goods from home on an ox-sled, but had three full loads to bring back — knapsacks, carts, wagons, et cetera.

When the discomfited *[defeated]* British were retreating through Sancoick they destroyed all they could not take away. They knocked the hoops from a large quantity of flour in barrels. We durst not gather up any of this flour fearing poison had been scattered amongst it but the hogs fared sumptuously on it.

Immediately after the battle, Father and I came up home to look to our property. Found all safe and unmolested. But that night the hogs broke into our cornfield and we had much trouble in driving them out. Had we not come home

Patriot militiamen wearing long smocks, sometimes called hunting shirts, hurry British and German prisoners from the Bennington battlefield. The Germans are wearing tall fur hats.

as we did our corn crop would have been totally destroyed. A quantity of flour and, I believe, some clothing was sent by Gates' order *[General Horatio Gates commanded the American forces opposing Burgoyne],* I suppose, to Salem to be distributed among those who had fled from their homes and thus lost their crops, which were just ripe as we went away. I know our family drew half a barrel of this flour which we received at Salem Village.

One of Burgoyne's Indian allies, called the Canadian Indians, at a reenactment held at Fort Ticonderoga. The settlers dreaded these powerful warriors.

Back to Burgoyne

6

☑ The McCrea and Allen murders put the Protectioners in a terrible bind. Like the Whigs, they wanted to get away from Burgoyne's army and his murderous Indian allies. But they were unable or unwilling to retreat south.

Most of the wealth of the frontier community was tied up in crops and in farm animals — exactly what an army lives on. Whigs were afraid that their cattle, horses, and sheep would be seized by Tory militias and sold or turned over to Burgoyne's army. Tories were afraid of Whig militias for the same reasons — after all, the American army needed to eat, too. In the end, the Tory families of Greenwich, Argyle, and elsewhere again sought refuge with Burgoyne's army.

Ann McArthur of Argyle

We knew nothing of the murder until the third night after. Uncle Alexander Campbell, who was then with the army as soon as it was ascertained that the scalps brought in by the Indians were those of the Allen family, became alarmed lest we were murdered also. Nobody there had heard anything about us, and he could get nobody to come with him to our house till passing Neal Gillespie's — who was reputedly a cowardly man but showed himself this time more courageous than his neighbors. Neal said he would go with him, for it would be too horrid for Uncle to come here alone and perhaps find us all murdered. So they came together Sunday night when we were all asleep. They found the gate shut

and the cattle all quiet in the yards and hence felt assured we were all safe. They came to the door and aroused us and told us of the murder and the alarm of the country west of us. It was considered that it was no longer safe for us to remain, and we left the house forthwith in the dead of night and went down to my Grandfather Campbell's, taking a direct pathway then running through the woods. I remember I was much gratified with this night's journey through the woods. The moon was very bright at the time. After staying two or three days at Grandfather's we returned home and a company gathered here to go into Burgoyne's camp.

We all felt safe and secure until the Allen murder. Allen was at our house, I believe, the day before the murder, making some arrangement with Father about shooting — that hearing the report of each other's guns they might know it was squirrels or other game they were shooting.

There was a crowd at our house the night we gathered to start for the camp and they were mostly women — scarcely any men among them. Where the men were, I don't know. Uncle Alexander, I know, kept a lookout from a window in the chamber at the end of the house. Two other men stayed in a thicket of woods not far from the house for concealment. Doctor McDonald from Camden *[a Tory section of Salem]*, I remember, was one that came here. He was very sick through the night and on his account the children were stilled as much as possible. A small black girl belonging to Aunt Nancy Campbell was here and sitting on the floor. Her fingers were often stepped on but she was too terrified to cry out.

My grandfather had a considerable flock of sheep to drive over. His was the only wagon then in these parts. Some small children were carried over in it, though they had some difficulty in getting along, the road only being open for passengers on horseback. I walked all the way over. I remember as we passed Allen's house, the cap of the murdered babe, made of calico, was found on a stump beside the house all glued together with the dried blood. We went from here to Fort Edward in a day and stopped at the Campbell house. My sister, six

Reenactors show how some settlers fled on foot through the forests of New York.

years old, was taken sick while we were at Fort Edward and died a few days after we got home.

Caty Campbell of Greenwich

We went to Fort Edward in a company with others from our neighborhood. On our way I went into Allen's house with others of the company. The broken plates, knives and forks and meat from the table were scattered over the floor, which was all tracked with blood — the blood of the poor Negro who it appeared had fought bravely against the Indians. Everyone was screaming and crying when we came out of the house.

I remember when on our way, we came to a party of Indians who had killed a hog and hung it up to dress it. When they saw us they flew for their guns which they snatched up ready to attack us. But on seeing a British officer and his scout of men who were accompanying us for our protection, they fled into the woods and we saw no more of them.

At Fort Edward, I remember seeing Burgoyne talk with Father and shed tears. He was a thickset man, not tall.

Mother died while we were at Fort Edward — of jaundice — the tenth of August. The doctor gave her an emetic *[medicine that causes vomiting]* and she died under the operation of it. "White" Duncan Campbell's wife also died there.

William Campbell of Greenwich

All the families from around here went in company together. My father and his family were the forward one in the train. I think we went from here there in one day, driving our cattle with us. I walked as did all who were able to do so. My mother rode on horseback, being in rather poor health. The children too young to walk were secured on horses. When crossing the Fort Edward flats as we were approaching the house of one Lindsay, the first house on this side of Fort Edward and some two miles from there, an Indian was dressing a hog which he had killed. Seeing us approaching, he caught up his gun and was about shooting at Father, when a British officer came in sight behind him; whereupon he ran into the woods. Soon after this there was a cracking of musket shots out in the woods, perhaps half a mile from

Portrait of General John Burgoyne. Like other educated men of the 1700s, Burgoyne was proud of his ability to shed tears when moved by sad events or stories. A gentleman's willingness to cry proved that he was sensitive and able to feel the proper emotions.

A reenactor in the role of a Mohawk, one of the Iroquois tribes that sided with the British. He is carrying a Brown Bess, the standard British infantry musket.

Lindsay's house, towards Fort Edward. A party of Canadian *[many of Burgoyne's Indians were Ottawas and Caughnawagas from Canada]* and of Stockbridge Indians had encountered each other in the woods, and out of our sight. The firing was

PART ONE: THE REVOLUTIONARY WAR

heard at the post and a party of soldiers was sent out to aid their Indian allies. On their arrival the Stockbridge Indians gave over the fight and fled.

We stayed at Fort Edward a month, I should think, living in the house from which Miss Jane McCrea had been taken. The cows were yarded all together at night. By day they were turned out, but if they got into the woods or out of sight of the fort, they were liable to be killed by the Indians, or at least to be milked dry by the soldiers. So it was my daily employment whilst there, to watch or herd our cattle and keep them in sight of the camp. One day, I remember, a young Indian three or four years older than me came and commenced quarrelling with me, and finally began to cuff me. I hereupon whipped him with my goad so that he halloed out; when a great Indian ran to us, caught me as in a vice, drew his scalping knife, and shook and flourished it about my head. But a British officer now came and took my part, picked up a club and laid it over the back of the Indian, scolding him roundly, and told me to whip every Indian that abused me or attempted to molest me.

Eunice Campbell Reid of Greenwich

The country was greatly alarmed before the Allen murder. This increased it tenfold. It was an awful time — such as the present generation can have no conception of. No families felt safe in remaining in their houses overnight. We forsook the house regularly every night for some time. At first we slept in the hay barrack but not deeming this a secure retreat, we withdrew into the thicket of hemlocks that grew a piece north of the house and there slept night after night.

Scouting parties were continually patrolling the country watching every movement and helping themselves to a meal of victuals whenever they wanted it and continually keeping us in fear. John Barnes led the Salem scout which frequently passed our house. Adams' scout was one of the most active and oftenest heard of. I think this was a British scout but am not certain where it belonged. *[Adams' scout was a Tory militia based in Arlington, Vermont.]* One Sabbath a scouting party came along, caught one of our sheep and butchered it. They came into the house with the mutton and called for whatever they needed for cooking it, dug some potatoes also, then placed their meal upon the table and ate what they wanted, leaving all that remained for our use. Thus they made free with the inhabi-

tants, who had to submit to it passively.

It was in the evening that all the families gathered at Esquire McNaughton's to go into Burgoyne's camp. All the families along [the] Battenkill and its vicinity were in the company. In short, all the families around gathered there with their horses, cattle, and sheep. The sheep were bleating constantly through the whole night.

Much of the stock never returned being sold to the commissaries of Burgoyne's army or killed by the Hessians for beef whenever they could find a cow out of sight of its owner or unguarded.

I do not remember about any alarm that night, but it might have been so, and the youngerly men might have withdrawn. We started early the next morning. The stock was all drove in a herd together. I carried the whole distance a child two or three years old — half sister to Roger Campbell. It was a most fatiguing lug. I think we went entirely through one day. We went past Allen's house and took a resting spell there. The moccasin tracks of the Indians were marked in blood all over the floor; the dishes and knives were scattered about. We also made a pause to rest ourselves at Yerry Killmore's and another at Lindsay's house. At Lindsay's the floor was all torn up by the Indians who had been there searching it for plunder.

At Fort Edward we stayed at Campbell's house. The house was full to overflowing with families that were there for Protection. We were there a week or two — over one Sabbath, I know — for it was said there was preaching in the camp just above us on that day. I also remember a funeral of a lieutenant in the army. The procession came down from the camp to the burying ground and at the close of the burial three volleys were fired over the grave.

The Hessians or Brunswickers as they were called there wore their beards on their upper lips parted each way, and curled around the corners of their mouths.

Both the Duncan Campbells lost their wives there. Old Duncan's wife died

PART ONE: THE REVOLUTIONARY WAR

of dysentery. There was no medical attendance to be had. "Black" Duncan's wife was sick two or three days, speechless all the time. I was going upstairs and found her sitting halfway upstairs looking very unusually. I spoke to her but she made no reply. I ran and told Mistress Livingston that Mistress Campbell would not speak to me. She came and we soon found she could not speak. We got her onto a bed and I watched beside her, brushing off the flies, et cetera, till she died.

A little daughter of Archy Campbell's named Nancy also died there. Archy thought the air was so confined and impure in the crowded house she would do better if she could be in the fresh air. So he made out to get a tent and erected it near the house, and his family and the sick child moved into it — but the child died.

Robert Blake of Jackson

A few days after the murder of the Allen family the families from around here gathered at Alexander McNaughton's house to go into Burgoyne's camp for Protection. Their stock was all turned together into Esquire McNaughton's meadow, and the families were in and about his house overnight to start on our journey early the next morning.

Captain McCracken, with his trained company of Whig soldiers raised from around here, was then garrisoning Salem Fort — as the **picketed** church was called. I don't know how many men he had, but it was a strong company which he had raised some time before. The pickets were then recently placed around the church, the work having been several days in doing, folks turning out from all around to help them.

Sometime in the night, whilst the families were gathered at Esquire McNaughton's, an alarm was given that McCracken's company was on its march to take us prisoners. All was consequently in the utmost terror and confusion, the women weeping and wailing and the men flying from the house, leaving their wives and children, knowing that McCracken's company would not injure them, but that the men would be taken and imprisoned if they were caught. The men withdrew in a body to fly to [Burgoyne's] camp. I was most anxious to accompany the men, but Father forbade me, saying I was so young —

PICKETED: Surrounded by pickets, sharpened stakes or posts stuck into the ground to form a fence of spears.

sixteen years old — that the assailants would do me no harm or wouldn't hurt me. So I had to stay. But in a very short time they sent back for me in haste. They wanted me for their guide, none of them being well enough acquainted with the road to travel it in the night without a risk of losing their way. Glad was I of this.

The next day early, I was sent back to guide and help the families and cattle along. I met them soon after they had started from Killmore's. On our way thence to Fort Edward, I remember well, we met a worthless vagabond, whose name I cannot now recall. He had belonged to Captain McCracken's company and had deserted from it and joined Burgoyne. Six Indians accompanied him. He said they had started out to take the fort at Salem and that we would soon meet a company of six hundred Indians that were on their way for this business. This frightened and appalled the women very much for they expected that their Salem acquaintances would all be murdered. But we met no Indian force and the intelligence was false, but at the moment it scared us excessively.

The fort at Fort Edward was put up in the Old French War, of logs, covered with an embankment of sand. The logs had decayed and the sand slid down when the Revolution commenced, so that only the corner towards the Mistress McNeil house was occupied by the Americans when Miss McCrea was taken. It was some buildings in this corner of the fort from which they came out to fire upon the Indians; all other parts of the fort were dilapidated or nearly worthless. Burgoyne did not occupy the fort at all. His army encamped on the green around it and up near the hill in their tents, and the officers had their headquarters in the Doctor Smith house which was not picketed at that time.

But in the following years of the war pickets were placed around the Doctor Smith house enclosing perhaps an acre of ground and here the garrison was quartered

— the buildings in the corner of the old fort being then occupied only for workshops and baggage rooms.

I remember Colonel Philip Skene [the lord of Skenesborough] well and also his son Major Skene — these were the titles by which they were called in Burgoyne's camp. The Colonel was a large, portly, fine-looking man; his son was smaller and more slender. It was Colonel Skene that administered the oath of allegiance to all the inhabitants who flocked to Burgoyne's army and gave them certificates, under his own signature, of their having taken the oath and being therefore entitled to Protection and permission to pass from the camp to their homes.

[My Uncle Bell's] house was about twenty rods from the main road. It was a log house with but one large room. Two or three rods east of it was a noble, large spring directly from which quite a brook ran. This spring was in great repute at the camp; the washwomen and the men used to come to it, many of them, to wash their clothes.

Duncan Bell and I were employed daily to herd my uncle's and my father's cattle whilst I stayed there. My father drove over but one cow and a yoke of young steers, two or three years old. If they were not watched or got out of sight, there was danger of their being killed by the Indians. The cows all had bells on that rang much louder than the cowbells of a later day. At night they were driven into my uncle's yard, and there were sentries standing there that rendered them safe. A provost master [a military jailer or policeman] was stationed in my uncle's barn, having about twelve American prisoners under his charge in the barn, and a number of Hessians to guard them. The Indians painted the faces of these prisoners in a horrible manner. Some were painted entirely black with a bright red stripe across their necks in front, looking at first glance as though their throats were cut. Others had the black on their faces spotted and marked with red, like the lakes and rivers drawn upon a map. Probably this was intended to represent gashes in the face with the blood streaming from the wounds. They looked awful. A British officer happening in the barn asked why they did not wash the paint off. "I did not know as we had liberty to do so," replied one of the men. Water was immediately thereupon procured and the men gladly washed off the paint. These men were confined there till a day or two before we came home from Fort Edward.

Benedict Arnold, mounted on a
white horse, leads American troops
at the Battle of Freeman's Farm
(First Battle of Saratoga). Brave
and resourceful, Arnold betrayed
the Americans later in the war.

The Battles of Saratoga

◊ The Saratoga campaign called for Burgoyne to march to Albany and there meet up with another British army coming east on the Mohawk River from Lake Erie. Together these armies would control the Hudson River and split off the whole Northeast. But things kept going wrong.

The second British army was stopped at Fort Stanwix. It then turned away and went home. Whenever it left the waterways, Burgoyne's army had great trouble moving through the countryside. It had even greater difficulty getting the food, gunpowder, and other supplies it needed. The Battle of Bennington was fought for supplies, and Burgoyne lost that battle and nearly 15 percent of his army.

After the Battle of Bennington in mid-August, Burgoyne remained in camp at Fort Miller on the east side of the Hudson, about four miles

A reenactment of the American camp at Bemis Heights, looking east.

north of Schuylerville. He waited there for about three weeks collecting supplies, and then, on September 13, he crossed the Hudson and headed south for Albany. Waiting for Burgoyne at Bemis Heights, a fortified plateau, were seven thousand Americans under General Horatio Gates. On September 19, Burgoyne's army and an American detachment under General Benedict Arnold fought a fierce but inconclusive battle at Freeman's Farm, somewhat north of Bemis Heights. This was the First Battle of Saratoga.

PART ONE: THE REVOLUTIONARY WAR

On October 7, Burgoyne attacked the American position at Bemis Heights with fewer than five thousand men. Inspired once again by the daring of Benedict Arnold, the Americans inflicted heavy losses on the British and drove them back toward the Hudson at the Second Battle of Saratoga.

Meanwhile, the American army grew in size from seven thousand to almost twenty thousand and surrounded Burgoyne's force. Faced with the impossibility of retreating or winning against those odds, Burgoyne surrendered on October 17, 1777. It was a stunning victory for the Americans, and it was one of the grand turning points in American history. But as you will see, local farmers mention the battle only in passing.

How did Gates's army grow nearly three times larger in a matter of ten days? It was swelled by farmers from the surrounding countryside. What motivated these farmers? The victories at Bennington and Bemis Heights were key factors, but the murders of Jane McCrea and the Allen family also were important. These murders angered and frightened many, including some who had been neutral in the struggle.

Local Tories suffered from the raids of Whig scouts as well as from the foraging expeditions of Burgoyne's Indians and Hessians in the days immediately before the Saratoga battles. After Saratoga, families who had taken Burgoyne's Protection faced continuing Whig reprisals in northern New York.

Have you ever thought about how great battles get their names?

Long ago, many battles were fought in open, nameless areas where large armies could maneuver. Whoever named the battle — usually, but not always, the winner — looked around for a nearby landmark or a town. Burgoyne's defeat occurred near the village of Saratoga, and so the battle was named the Battle of Saratoga. However, the village of Saratoga later changed its name to Schuylerville, to honor the American general Philip Schuyler. A township that did not exist at that time later took the name Saratoga and even later built a famous resort city called Saratoga Springs, or Saratoga for short. As a result, many people think the Battle of Saratoga took place near Saratoga Springs, but the Battle of Saratoga was really the Battle of Schuylerville.

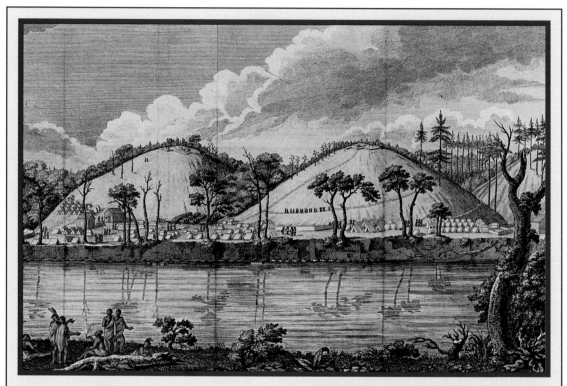

A view of the British camp, drawn from the east side of the Hudson River. The men on the hill to the right represent the funeral procession of the British general Simon Fraser.

Caty Campbell of Greenwich

While we were at Fort Edward, the Whigs tore down our fences and let the cattle into our grain fields, whereby it was nearly destroyed. Father had two horses which he took to Fort Edward and sold, receiving his pay in solid gold. We had four cows. Soon after we got back home, "Mad" [James] More came with some men from Shushan, to drive off our cows. They threw down the fence and went to driving them out of the field, when Father got around them and drove them back. "Mad" More then came up to him, and putting the muzzle of his loaded gun to Father's breast said, "Stand still, you d—d Tory or I'll shoot you through!" And the other men then drove the cattle away, while More kept Father away from them. They took them to Shushan and cast lots for them. One of them fell to Bill

Smith who, the next day, drove her back home to us saying he could not take the milk from motherless children.

More foddered the cows that winter at a stack on the Shushan side of the kill, he living on the opposite side of the stream. At length on the breaking up of winter, high water came running over the top of the ice so that More could not cross it one day to feed the cattle. Towards night the cattle becoming hungry started off upon the path to the house and going on the ice to where the water was running, trying to wade across it, the ice had become so rotten they all fell in and were drowned — the three cows he had stolen from Father, and one of his own, and also a yoke of oxen he had stolen from somebody else.

The oxen that the Whig James More seized from a Tory neighbor
were a very valuable possession.

Mary Gillespie Bain of Argyle

When my father returned home with his family from Burgoyne's camp, he found three fine horses which had been kept in the pasture at home being dead and enormously swollen. They had been killed but a few days before, it was evident. We supposed the Indians had tried to catch them to steal them but not being able to catch them had maliciously shot them.

A day or two after my return, when we were all at dinner, five or six great

Canadian Indians, their faces hideously painted making them look like very demons, came boldly into the door. We all fled from the table, we children affrighted, screaming, "Mama, will they kill us?" — the murder of our neighbor Allen and his children being fresh in our minds. They, without any ceremony, sat down at the table and ate everything that was upon it. A pewter mug holding exactly a quart was on the table filled with milk. An Indian took it up and drank the whole at a draught. Another took the mug, went to the milk pan, dipped it up full and drank it off. Another followed his example, then another and when the last of the milk was poured into the mug, my mother ventured to step up to the Indian and with a look pointed to us children and then to the mug and thus made him understand that we needed the milk more than he did. He thereupon set down the mug.

Having consumed all our eatables, they went out. My father showed them the dead horses and by his motions gave them to understand that Indians had killed them. They looked around and examined the horses very sagely and then shook their heads and made motions to Father to explain to him that it was not Indians' work, but that they had been killed in some other way. But he knew better and insisted upon it to them that it was Indians.

From our house they went south one and one-half miles to old Archy McNeil's. They plundered his house, he and the family not having yet returned from the camp. At length the Indians came back to our house, the same afternoon, each with a great pouch as heavy as he could carry. One of them came up behind Mother and patted her on her left arm, which was bare, with something hard. She supposed it was his tomahawk. She durst not show any resentment but remained perfectly passive. The Indian thereupon struck her arm so hard that she turned her head enough to perceive that it was not his tomahawk but a woman's shoe that was in his hand. He placed the shoe in her hand with a motion from which she knew he intended she should take it as a present from him. She motioned to him that a single shoe was of no value, two being necessary. He put his hand into his bosom and drew out the mate to it and handed it to her.

The next day Mister McNeil and family returned from the camp and stopped at our house to rest on their way. My mother brought the shoes and gave them to Mistress McNeil.

"Where did you find them?" she asked.

"An Indian gave them to me yesterday," my mother replied.

At once Mistress McNeil cried out, "Oh, we are ruined!"

Eunice Campbell Reid of Greenwich

When on our way home from Burgoyne's camp we stopped several days at John McNeil's. Whilst there a large party of the Brunswickers, to the number of thirty or more, came and went into Mister McNeil's potato field and dug a considerable part of the crop. Each of them had three knapsacks or bags which they filled with potatoes and carried off, one knapsack on the back of each and a bag or knapsack under each arm. Two of them had but one knapsack each but they took some pairs of tow cloth *[coarse linen]* trousers that were hanging out to dry, tied up the bottoms of the legs then filled them with potatoes, tied them up, and taking one under each arm went off with the trousers as well as their contents.

Susan Lyttle Vance of Salem

My two brothers Isaac and William were working some land at West Hebron. From this place they were taken prisoners by a party of Tories, and carried to the British camp at Fort Edward where William was attacked by the measles.

It was one of the Gillises of Argyle that came over to Salem to tell us that William was sick with the measles at Fort Edward. Mother was so anxious for him that she determined to go to the British camp to find him and take care of him. She went over on foot to Fort Edward and, finding he was not there, she followed on after the army that was now moving down the river. She overtook the army and was in the camp one night — the night after "The Friday Battle" as it was called *[the First Battle of Saratoga, or Freeman's Farm]*. The scene that she encountered that night beggars description. All was confusion, running to and fro, the blood flowing from the wounded as they were brought into the hospital, and the groans of the dying being everywhere heard. All were too busy and anxious to

After the Second Battle of Saratoga, Lady Harriet Acland traveled by water to the American camp to look for her husband, who had been taken prisoner by the Americans. But Lady Acland's nighttime mission hardly equaled that of Susan Lyttle Vance's mother. Susan's mother walked from Salem to Fort Edward to Schuylerville, then waded across the Hudson River to search for her son in the British camp. Lady Acland's trip by boat with her maid and pet dog looks a lot easier.

notice her or listen to her errand. But she met with a young man who came from the same county in Ireland she came from and who knew some of her relatives and old acquaintances there; and he interested himself in her behalf. She found that William was not there, nor could she gain any intelligence respecting him. Unable to endure another night of such horrors, she next day stole away from the camp with a blanket over her head and wrapped around her, hoping if anyone observed her that they would deem her a squaw wandering about. The river was covered with battoes passing up and down. She reached Schuylerville, and when all was still, late in the night, she waded across the river at Deridder's ferry and next day travelled sixteen miles, reaching Salem, where once more among friends and acquaintances she gladly tarried overnight.

From Fort Edward my brothers were taken down to Ticonderoga where they were confined with many other prisoners. But the Americans attacked and captured the buildings in which they were confined and set them free [September 18, 1777]. The magazines [storehouses] were broken into and boxes of valuables were thrown open and every man told to help himself, to take what he could find by way of remuneration for what they had suffered. A chest was opened and everyone was thrusting in his hands and drawing out for himself. Brother William was too sick to share in this plunder and Isaac went up to the chest and drew out a small neat Bible and a pair of silk stockings, and desisted from taking more. The next man thrust his hand in and drew out a heavy bag, but whether of gold or silver or what it was, they only could judge from the external appearances, for there was no time to pause and examine.

My brothers were released, and contrived to drag themselves over the hills and mountains down to Skenesborough. Thence they sent word home. And Charles Hutchison, our kind neighbor, mounted his horse and rode up to Skenesborough and brought them home, William before and Isaac behind him — William being so feeble he had to support him in his arms the whole distance. A large abscess had formed in his side, so large that Doctor Clark would not venture to open it fearing he might die immediately on the operation. So he could only recommend him to the kind mercy of God. At length the abscess broke and after discharging some time it spontaneously healed.

Isabel Duncan McIntyre of Hebron

All day long we at Munro's Meadows heard the sound of the cannon at the Battle of Saratoga although it was thirty miles away. My mother was confined and my youngest sister was born upon that day.

At the close of the war, Patriot artist John Trumbull painted this view of Burgoyne's surrender to General Gates in 1777. Burgoyne hands his sword to Gates, who introduces his fellow officers, including Colonel Daniel Morgan, leader of a regiment of Virginia riflemen, who is wearing a white hunting shirt. The wounded Benedict Arnold was not present at this ceremony, which took place in Schuylerville, near the banks of the Hudson River. Today this ground is a park with three baseball diamonds.

Caty Campbell of Greenwich

A schoolhouse stood at the top of the hill above the Widow McDougall's, by the side of the road as it ran at that time. The spring after Burgoyne's surrender the house was burnt, set on fire in the night by the Whigs, it was not doubted. The children's books, among which it was said there were over thirty Bibles, burnt in the schoolhouse. This burning the Word of God was much talked about among the Argyle

Tories in the neighborhood and town.

A few nights after the schoolhouse burnt, my father's house was also burnt. It was a log house standing near the Battenkill at the head of the valley, below the Widow McDougall's. Father was at that time making sugar from trees of Archy Campbell's, on the opposite side of the kill a mile or nearly so below our house and wholly out of sight of it. He used to stay at the sugar camp overnight to keep the fires under the kettles, leaving us small children all alone in the house, but coming by day home to see us and get his provisions. That night however, a presentiment *[warning]* came to his mind that he must go home, though he had no particular thought of any danger. He came, crossed the kill in his boat, and got to the house just in time to snatch us children out of our beds and carry us outdoors. Nothing else in the house was saved, though we had no furniture of any great value. That the house had been set on fire was certain, for it was the opposite end of the house from the fireplace that was all on fire when Father first came in sight of it.

Jacob Bitely of Ticonderoga

In 1778 Father left his place in Vermont — it was so risky living there — and we moved to Whitehall where we remained one year. One Burroughs, a Yankee, had evacuated his house there when Burgoyne came down, and was staying down in Salem or somewhere thereabouts. We moved into his house and tilled his land, raising a field of corn. In the fall he came up and wanted half the produce of the farm, and Father gave it to him.

When we were living in Whitehall, there were a few shanties or small buildings, botched up *[built clumsily]* by our men for baking bread for the American army, and only temporarily occupied for this and similar purposes. I well remember, I, with other boys there, used to try to look into the room where Skene had kept his wife unburied. It was in the cellar of his stone house; a small apartment was walled up in one corner. This had a door leading into it and in the door was a single pane of glass. The outer door of the cellar was left open and the door to this vault was closed. We boys used to go in at the outer door, cautiously and silently advance to the door of the vault, raise up on our tiptoes, peek through this pane of glass — all was dark within so that nothing could be distinguished there — then fearing a ghost would appear among us we would scud out of the cellar like scared sheep.

But although the land about Whitehall suited Father well enough, he did not feel that we were safe and secure in making a purchase there. We should be better guarded, he said, to be in the rear of Fort Edward. So he came down here, and bought out a rank Tory on the opposite side of the river, and here we moved in the spring of 1779. The farm was all cleared up and under cultivation. Other Tories about there also sold out and went to Canada about the same time, for they began now to despair of the King's conquering this country; and the Whigs were getting to feel in such high spirits, they could not bear to remain in the neighborhood.

The woods between Glens Falls and Fort George were the most dark, doleful, and dangerous I ever saw. Father and I passed through them in 1779. Having some butter to spare, we took it up there and disposed of it to the garrison, taking salt for pay, which was then difficult to be got and far more valuable than the Continental money. On the way an enemy might anywheres have darted upon us out of the thick woods and murdered us without any chance for our escape.

Reenactors wearing the uniforms of an American Loyalist regiment, the King's Royal Yorkers, advance through the smoke of their own guns. In 1780, the Royal Yorkers took part in attacks on their former communities.

CHAPTER EIGHT

The Great Burning of 1780

8

In the long view of things, not much happened in the northern colonies in 1780. Instead, the British concentrated on the southern colonies. There, they captured the coastal city of Charleston, South Carolina, but lost a big inland battle at Kings Mountain, thus continuing a pattern already set by British generals in the North: success in the port cities and defeat in the countryside.

For the people of northeastern New York, however, 1780 was as eventful as the year of Burgoyne's defeat. In 1780, the British launched a series of devastating raids from Canada that no longer make the history textbooks. In March, they sent a relatively small raiding party against Skenesborough — a small one compared with the great raid of the coming October. In October, Major Carleton sailed south from Canada on Lake Champlain with a fleet of eight large ships and twenty-six flat-bottomed boats carrying about a thousand men — British, Indians, and Tories. One part of the force went east to raid settlements in northern Vermont. The larger part of the expedition, under Carleton himself, struck Forts Ann and George (October 10 and 11), burning them and capturing their garrisons. The raiders also burned the Hudson River settlements as far south as Fort Miller. Among the farmers who suffered in these raids, 1780 was called the "Year of the Great Burning."

Major Guy Carleton, leader of the October 1780 British raids.

Deacon Cook's sister of Granville

When Skenesborough was captured by the Indians, I well remember all the families along Granville River, from its mouth up to Father's on the edge of Pawlet, fled from their dwellings to our house and stayed there a week or two ere they dared venture to return to their homes. Father's was the lowest family on the river that did not forsake their house. McCall, who was murdered by the Indians, kept several cows and sold milk to the garrison. He and his wife were killed, and it was reported the Indians also killed all his cattle — ripping them open and carrying off their unborn calves.

James Rogers of Salem

In 1779, I was in service nine months, stationed most of the time at Whitehall. I went as a substitute for another man who had been drafted. I served his nine months out and received his wages. In 1780 I was captured at Whitehall and kept prisoner in Canada till 1782.

In 1780, Whitehall was the most advanced post occupied by the Americans, Ticonderoga and Crown Point being in ruins. All the settlers along Lake Champlain, too, had evacuated their homes. Whitehall was garrisoned by drafts from the militia of Salem and Cambridge. In March 1780, I was one of sixty men that were drafted to serve for a fortnight.

We were quartered at Skene's house. This house was of stone, some thirty feet by forty in size, two stories high and with windows in the roof. Skene's stone barn stood some distance this side of the house, and there was a third building for a storehouse. These three were all the structures then standing at Whitehall. Skene had ironworks, a gristmill, a sawmill, and probably houses or huts for the workmen, but all these had been destroyed at this time. A path led off east towards Vermont along the south side of the mountain; on this path at a distance of three-quarters of a mile from Skene's house stood a log house in which a man named McCall and his wife lived. She was the washerwoman for the troops. He was an old British soldier who had served in the French War.

Our fortnight expired and the party that was to come to take our places did not arrive. Our provisions were almost all consumed. As the ice on the lake was

A cannon at Fort Ticonderoga points across Lake Champlain. The lake made a smooth, broad highway for Canadian raiders coming south. James Rogers and the other captives taken at Skene's house in March 1780 traveled north with their captors on the frozen lake.

now breaking up, it was thought there was no danger just at this time of any of the enemy coming from Canada to molest us, and it would therefore be safe for most of the men to return home and leave only a guard behind. So a company of twelve men was selected. I was one of this twelve.

On the morning of March 21st our comrades left us — they expecting to reach their homes in Cambridge and Salem before night. As my clothes by this time had become badly soiled and dirty, I set out to take them to the washer-woman, Mistress McCall. On reaching their home, I found them absent — they having started to bring some washed clothes to the soldiers. Returning, when I was onto the main road, I saw McCall and his wife ahead of me. They were near Skene's barn and I some rods behind them, when hearing a rustling in the woods and bushes beside me, I saw two Indians coming out of them towards me. I was unarmed, so I took to my heels, and one of the Indians after me. I saw he was gaining on me — I was then a boy but sixteen years old — when he halloed to me in good English to stop and he wouldn't hurt me. I promptly stopped. He told me that I must go with him to Montreal.

As McCall and his wife were passing Skene's barn, a party of Indians came out of it to take them. McCall had a staff in his hand. I saw him strike at an Indian with this. Immediately thereupon, both he and his wife were stabbed with a sergeant's spontoon, a kind of spear which the Indian had, and fell dead upon the spot. Their bodies were dragged away into the bushes.

At the same time, the men at Skene's house were attacked. The party of the enemy consisted of 130 Canadian Indians, two Canadian Frenchmen for their officers, and a Tory refugee who served as their guide in leading them to the spot. Our men concluded it would be their only chance to escape to rush to the creek and cross it in a battoe moored there. Alas, on reaching the battoe they found it had been drawn onto the land — by some of themselves who had forgotten this circumstance. They took to the water of the flooded and ice-cold stream, but ere they had any of them got across, the Indians reached the shore and ordered them to swim back or they would shoot every man. So they returned and surrendered themselves as prisoners.

We were now started for Canada. When we reached the summit of Whitehall Mountain, all four of the buildings — Skene's house, barn, the rough-boarded storehouse, and the farm dwelling half a mile south — were in flames below us, and not a roof remained where the village of Whitehall stands.

PART ONE: THE REVOLUTIONARY WAR

We went about three or four miles the first day, encamping for the night across East Bay in the present state of Vermont. We, the second day, proceeded by land nearly down to Ticonderoga and there went upon the ice of the lake, which was still firm all the way to Canada. Thus we kept on until, at length, we reached St. John's. From here we were taken by the Indians to their villages, west, at Chateaugee [Chateaugay] and French Mills. My clothes were old and poor and were therefore not meddled with by the Indians. But whoever had a good coat or vest, it was taken from him.

Continental money.

In about a week most of us were taken to Montreal and sold to the British authorities at a joe — eight dollars — apiece. We now went separately before Colonel Campbell for examination. This Colonel Campbell was a son of Duncan Campbell who lived in Argyle. The object of this examination was to tamper with us and induce us to enlist into the British service, and also to gather what information they could, respecting the state of the country.

When I was before him, he inquired all the most minute particulars, the price of provisions, et cetera. Salt was very scarce at this time as the British held New York. None was to be had except what was imported into Boston and brought thence overland to Albany. He inquired the price of liquor. I told him that in the course of the past winter I had known three dollars to be given for a gill of whiskey, and he chuckled at this indication of the straits to which the country was reduced. But when I told him that I had also known a gill of whiskey to be given for a silver sixpence, he readily understood that in the former instance pay had been made in Continental money.

The fort at Chambly.

The company that I was taken with was divided between Montreal and Chambly and two or three of them remained with the Indians at Chateaugee. About thirty prisoners were in the Chambly prison, closely confined and fettered so closely that I could only move my feet the length of my great toe at a step. Our provisions were execrable *[vile]* and our allowance scanty. In the fall of 1781 only seven vessels succeeded in getting into Quebec. The country was therefore in great straits for provisions. Some of the cattle that died of starvation and disease were ate, and horses were slaughtered for the soldiers and prisoners. Horse beef was our main diet for some time. This close confinement and bad fare wore greatly upon my health until I, at length, became so weak that I was taken out and sent to Montreal hospital. After being in the hospital awhile, I was moved to Montreal jail.

Several of our prisoners had enlisted into the British service. Two of these and possibly others were among the guard of Montreal jail. With this influence in the

guard, the prisoners succeeded in inducing the whole guard to join them in an attempt to escape from Canada. John Simpson, also of Salem, was one of the foremost of the prisoners in concerting this scheme.

Arms and provisions were procured for supplying the whole of them well, the prisoners giving the guard their last farthing to buy provisions, et cetera, for their journey. The night was approaching, when John Simpson seeing a stranger among the guard, beckoned to him and communicated the whole plot.

The guards were flogged most severely. I saw their backs just after and it was the worst sight I ever saw — their backs were torn as though a pack of hungry dogs had gnawed and mangled them. The whole were then banished to Cote du Lac Island. John Simpson never returned home after this.

Sometime about September 1781, a merchant of Montreal, being in want of a young man to help him, applied to the general to allow him to take one of the prisoners into his family and I was selected. I now fared very well. The merchant's name was John Gabriel Beak, a Dutchman who before the war had been in business in Boston and there married a Yankee wife. I remained with him until I was exchanged and set at liberty June 10th, 1782. About sixty of us were released at this time. We were brought in the British shipping to Crown Point and thence in battoe to Whitehall, where we bade our British attendants good-bye and came home.

Jacob Bitely of Ticonderoga

In the summer of 1780 a party of men, and one or two women with them, belonging to the garrison at Fort George, took a battoe and went onto one of the islands down the lake to gather huckleberries, fish, et cetera. The huckleberries were very thick on the island and gathering them was their chief errand.

At night they drew the battoe on shore, turned it up sideways and built a fire beside it — the battoe warding off the wind — and lay down to sleep. The light could be, of course, seen a great distance, and attracted thither a party of Indians in their canoes. They found all sound asleep. With their guns, tomahawks, and knives they probably at the same moment of time dispatched the whole company, took off their scalps and made off with themselves, leaving the bodies strewed around the campfire.

Morning comes and one of the group begins to have a return of consciousness. The midsummer sun is pouring down its hot rays upon his naked skull. Unable to stand, he contrives to crawl within reach of some bread. This he soaks in the water of the lake at his side and then covers his aching head with it. The sentries at the fort heard the sound of the firearms, and in the morning a boat was dispatched to ascertain the cause. They approach the island and find the scalpless man sitting erect amid his slain companions.

The surgeon of Warner's regiment, Doctor Washburn, was stationed at Fort Edward and hither the revived man was sent for medical attendance. When he had so far recovered as to be able to walk, he asked permission to go out among the inhabitants where he could obtain milk and better nourishment than the stores of the garrison furnished. Leave was granted, and Father, being at the fort, invited him to come to our house for a few days. He came and was with us three or four days — all the top of his head enveloped in a plaster. He went back to the fort to have it dressed by the surgeon — then he went out for a few days to another family. Thus he passed the time till he recovered. What afterwards became of him I know not.

The year 1780 has always been designated in this quarter as the Year of the Great Burning, to distinguish it from the lesser burnings of separate buildings that occurred in other years. The Tories, as already stated, had mostly sold out their farms around here and moved off to Canada. But such was their feelings of hatred and spite and malevolence towards the Whigs, that it added gall to their feelings to remember that these were living in comfort in their old homes. A large

In the foreground, Loyalist reenactors chase fleeing Whig militiamen.

company of Tory refugees volunteered, it would seem, to come down from Canada in company with Carleton's force and burn our houses.

It was a clear cold night sometime in October that they fell upon us and burnt every house and barn on the west side of the river from Sandy Hill to Fort Miller. This took place the same time that Carleton came down and took Fort Ann and Fort George. Carleton stopped overnight in Kingsbury. The afternoon sun might have been an hour high when we saw the smoke of the houses they were burning in Kingsbury. At the same time, we saw the people rushing down the road on the east side of the river, men, women and children. Some of the folks crossed over to tell us that all Kingsbury was in flames and that all the folks on the east side of the river were flying from their homes. We could scarcely believe the enemy would have the audacity to cross the river and come directly in rear of the fort *[Fort Edward]* and burn our buildings and our neighbors' under the very guns of the fort. Still, we deemed it safest to fly.

My two oldest brothers were not at home at this time. They were enlisted in the American service and were stationed out in the west at Palmerston, where a garrison was kept up to prevent marauding parties from Canada from coming down by the Sacandaga route and falling upon the inhabitants in the neighborhood of Ballston. We had two horses. We tied up our beds and most valuable and necessary clothing and tied them onto the horses' backs. We then went up the river to the fort, three-fourths of a mile above the house, and there crossed to the east side — Father, Mother, my brother and myself. I well remember that I expected we should be fired upon and killed ere we got across the river. We then went down the river, travelling all night, and got to Deridder's opposite Schuylerville, at sunrise the next morning. Father still supposed it was not probable our house was burnt, so he took one of the horses and rode directly back, but on coming in sight he at once perceived all our buildings were in ashes, and all our grain and hay was consumed. They also killed all our cattle and hogs.

George Fowler of Cambridge

In this county, all the men between the ages of sixteen and forty-five were regularly enrolled in companies of militia and frequently assembled for training and drilling. There were few regulars, not more than fifty, stationed at Fort Edward, and to keep the fort garrisoned, men were drafted from the militia companies around to go to Fort Edward and serve there one month.

Thus the garrison was kept up through the season without the service coming very hard on any of us. I was drafted sometime in the summer [he was nineteen years old at this time] and served nine month's time. We had little to do. A file of three men was sent every day up to Fort George to see that all was right up there in the little garrison. I was sent up two or three times during the month I was out.

This was more risky service than any I had to do in Rhode Island, where the land was all cleared and we could espy an enemy at a distance. But from Glens Falls to Fort George, it was all woods and an enemy might at any moment start out from behind the trees along the road and be upon us without a moment's warning.

[In October 1780, when the British raided Forts Ann and George] the Cambridge and the Hoosick companies were forthwith mustered. We reached Fort Edward at the close of the first day, encamping outside of the fort. The commanding officer wanted to take charge of us, at least in some measure, but our officers preferred acting entirely distinct and independent of him.

The next morning we were all paraded, some three hundred in number, and marched up to Glens Falls. A body of the Indians had penetrated down towards Schuylerville and burnt some barracks down that way which were filled with wheat. They had crossed the river about Glens Falls in making this marauding

incursion. We marched on up to Fort George which had been burnt by the enemy who had just gone down the lake. The beams and other timbers of the fort were still smoking and burning when we arrived. The bodies of twelve men were found lying where they fell — scalped and shockingly mangled, bloated and black with partial mortification. It was a most horrid sight, on looking at which I turned faint and sick and had to turn away and lay down in the shade of a tree to recover. I could not aid in burying them. A hole was dug beside them, not very deep, in which they were all placed together and covered up.

We now started on our return and encamped that night part of the way back to Glens Falls. The next day, the third of our being out, we came back to Fort Edward and on halfway or thereabouts to Fort Miller, occupying an old deserted log house around which was a patch of potatoes. We dug some of these, roasted and ate them, for we were most of us quite destitute of provisions. In good season, the next or fourth day, we reached Cambridge and were disbanded.

Austin Wells of Cambridge

◪ Below, Austin Wells mentions finding an African American among the dead at Fort George. African Americans fought in Patriot militias or in regular units of the Continental Army. They also served in the American navy and in American merchant ships. Free blacks faced a special danger. If they were taken prisoner, they were often sold into slavery for profit. The black drummer Wells found may have resisted his Tory captors for this reason.

Lemuel Haynes, an African American from Granville, took the same chance. But that did not stop him from fighting at Lexington, Boston, and Ticonderoga. After the war, Haynes became the minister of a largely white congregation in Granville. "For liberty each Freeman strives," wrote Haynes in a poem about the Battle of Lexington:

REV. LEMUEL HAYNES, A.M.

Sincerely yours
Lemuel Haynes

Lemuel Haynes, an African American soldier and minister.

This motto may adorn their Tombs
(Let tyrants come and view)
"We rather seek these silent Rooms
Than live as Slaves to You."

In April 1776, I enlisted for one year — which was the custom in the early part of the war, short enlistments — and was stationed up the Mohawk at Fort Stanwix. After this I was a sergeant in the Cambridge militia, but we had no regular company enrolled, no regular officers. Men turned out when they pleased, and served under whom they pleased for the time they chose.

Fort Ann was simply a picket fort without ditch or earthy embankment around it. It was square and enclosed about half an acre's space. Within the fort was a single barrack, one story high, some sixteen feet wide and thirty or forty feet long — a framed and clapboarded building. During the summer of 1780, it was garrisoned by drafts and volunteers from the surrounding towns serving a month by turns. In September, I was there a month as sergeant with twelve privates from Cambridge under me. I would not consent to be drafted, but went up as a volunteer with the twelve men. The month expired and we returned, another file of men from Cambridge coming up to supply our places. The number of the garrison was variable, between fifty and one hundred men were always there.

[In October 1780] the alarm was sent and all the militia were ordered out to repel this invasion. We promptly rallied at Fort Edward, Colonel Yates being the commander of the militia there. Some two hundred of us went up to Fort George. We knew the enemy had fled and went up to bury the dead and secure any property that might be left. We found twenty-two slaughtered and mangled men. All

A Frenchman, Jean-Baptiste Antoine De Verger, painted these American foot soldiers from life.

An African American privateer. Privateers were merchant seamen licensed by the government to attack enemy ships.

had their skulls knocked in, their throats cut and their scalps taken. Their clothes were mostly stripped off.

Ruins of the citadel of Fort George.

The officer who came with us recognized Lieutenants Ensign and Eno and cried like a child at beholding them. They laid upon their backs, scalped and with their throats cut. Their stocks *[wide, white, linen neckties]* had been torn from their necks, the silver buckles taken from them, and the stocks laid across their breasts. We buried them both in one grave and buried all the men in graves not very deep in the sand.

One man only had not his throat cut; he was a **mulatto** and was lying on his face — the only one found in this posture. We supposed he was the drummer; and his arms were tied behind him with the cord of his drum, and he had been killed by a spear in his back after he was tied. There were six or eight spear wounds in the middle of his back, on each side of the backbone, and the spear was left in his back. He was scalped. We supposed he had been more obstinate and valiant in withstanding the enemy, and they had therefore bound and tortured him alive. The Negro had his clothes all on; all the other bodies were stripped more or less.

The fort was still burning. A platform was erected in the fort on which a six-pounder *[a cannon shooting a ball that weighed six pounds]* mounted on a carriage was standing. One side of the platform was burnt away, and one of the wheels was so far burnt that the cannon had tipped partly down when we arrived. On the platform, not over three feet from the fire, was also standing a barrel filled with ball cartridges for muskets. These were quickly and eagerly divided among us.

All the enemy's killed were carried away. We buried them all a few rods to the west of where the road then ran.

MULATTO: A Spanish word taken from Arabic, meaning a person of mixed African and European ancestry.

The fighting had been mostly with clubbed muskets *[the soldiers had swung the muskets at each other like clubs]*, and the fragments of these, split and shivered, were laying around with the bodies. The barrel of one I observed had been bent full six inches from a straight line.

Reenactors take the helm of a British gunboat on Lake Champlain. In such vessels, Loyalist raids took place well after the Battle of Yorktown, which ended the war in 1781.

CHAPTER NINE

The War's End and Beyond

9

◘ In 1781, George Washington, leading a combined force of American and French soldiers and assisted by a French squadron of warships, received the surrender of a large British army at Yorktown, Virginia. Two years later, a new British government recognized the independence of the United States. That is the big story.

But for the people who lived on the frontier, near British-controlled lands in Canada and in the West, the war didn't follow the calendar of big events. Instead, much remained unsettled. The rivalry between Whigs and Tories continued, as Mary Bain points out.

Mary Gillespie Bain of Argyle

There was much robbing of stock the last years of the Revolutionary War. The Whigs enlisted men for three months and six months to guard the frontier, and to pay these men, they would take cattle and sheep from the Argyle folks. I know that both cattle and sheep were taken from my father, two or three head at least at different times. The Salem Whigs made themselves rich in this way out of their Argyle neighbors — no restitution being made. But cattle and sheep that were taken down to Saratoga and Stillwater for supplying the army were all paid for afterwards.

The Tories also stole from their Whig neighbors when they were able to do so. Alexander Wright of Salem pilfered sheep from his neighbors' flocks till he collected a large flock. These he drove past my father's house and on to Burgoyne's camp where he sold them and got his pay in silver. But after the surrender, Captain Barnes of Salem commenced a suit against him in court. I remember Wright was over to Father's two or three times to see if he would not be willing to swear to such and such facts — but Father would not swear to all Wright wanted him to.

☑ In the year of Yorktown, Whigs in northern New York kept a sharp eye out for Tory spies. In 1781, as Jacob Bitely relates, a Tory spy, Philip Lovelace, was hanged in Schuylerville. Lovelace was known locally as Lovett.

Jacob Bitely of Ticonderoga

That year *[1781],* I attended the execution of Lovett, the spy, at Schuylerville. He had previously resided about there and was well known to several. Lovett had gone in among the garrison at Schuylerville to spy it out and learn what the plans of the Whigs were. He was taken prisoner. Papers were found on him that showed he was commissioned to enlist men among the Tories in this quarter, to form a company and go to Canada. The papers certified that each man would receive a specified sum in silver on his arrival in Canada, in addition to what was paid down.

I guess it was in September when he was hung. It was the windiest day I ever saw. Of course, a large concourse of people was assembled. He was taken out of the guardhouse; his coffin was placed crosswise on top of the box of a cart drawn by oxen, a rope around his neck, and a mulatto — slave of General Schuyler's, I think — holding the end of the rope, who made him walk close up to the cart. The guards surrounded him, forming a hollow square; thus they marched towards, half a mile, the gallows. The gallows was formed of two long, forked stakes drove into the ground and a pole placed across on the forks. The cart drove under the gallows and stopped. Lovett then got up into the cart, and also the minister who had attended with him after he was tried and sentenced. The minister, I think, was Mister Tanner, a Baptist, who was preaching then up Battenkill. He talked and prayed with him, then shook hands with him and bade him farewell — both standing up in the cart — and then descended.

The Negro then tied the rope to the pole; the cart drove out from under him and he hung till he was dead. Then he was cut down and the guards now marched away. The Negro took off the white frock which he had on over his clothes. He then twitched his silver shirt sleeve buttons and pocketed them; next stripped off his vest; then took hold of the bottoms of his pantaloons and with a violent yank, which drew the body a foot or two forwards, pulled them off and exposed his legs. Some of the spectators could endure the Negro's brutality no longer. They kicked him and forbade his taking off the shirt from the corpse. So the Negro desisted.

For every spy who was hanged, there were many others who simply blended back into the local community. Mary Bain's father was a Tory who was active in the British cause.

Mary Gillespie Bain of Argyle

Lovett was at our house, and stayed in our barn overnight the third day before he was hung on a tree at Schuylerville. Two other men were in company with him at the same time. He was as fine a looking man as I ever saw.

I have no scruples in telling what I know will help you in judging of the state of things here in the Revolutionary War. My father was a Loyalist, as were all the other Argyle settlers. Father used to carry the packet or letters of intelligence from the Canadian officers to the British officers in New York. His part of the route was from here to Albany, commonly. A packet would be brought to him from the north, and he would forthwith start on with it to Albany. These packets were done up in a small compass *[size]* and enveloped in lead — being not more than an inch or two in

You will have heard Dr Sir I doubt not long before this can have reached you that Sir W. Howe is gone from hence. The Rebels imagine that he is gone to the Eastward, by this time however he has filled Chesapeak bay with surprize and terror Washington marched the greatest part of the Rebels to Philadelphia in order to oppose Sir Wm army. I hear he is now returned upon finding none of our troops landed but am not sure of this, great part of his troops are returned for certain I am sure this must be ruin to them. I am left to Command here, half my force may I am sure defend every thing here with as much safety I shall therefore send Sir W. 4 or 5 Batt I have to small a force to invade the New England provinces they are too weak to make any effectual efforts against me and you do not want any diversion in your favor I can therefore very well spare him. 1500 men I shall try some thing certainly towards the close of the year not till then at any rate. It may be of use to inform you that report says all yields to you. I own to you I think the business will quickly be over now. Sir W.s move just at this time has been Capital Washingtons have been the worst he could take in every respect I sincerely give you much joy on your success and am with great Sincerity   your hbl obt st
                                                                          HC

Spy packets like those carried by Mary Gillespie Bain's father often contained coded messages. This letter was read with the aid of a special hourglass-shaped cutout. The words within the hourglass composed the message.

length. He commonly received with them money enough only to pay his expenses. At the close of the war, the money was drawed by Patt Smyth to reward him liberally for his services, as had been promised, but Smyth cleared out and never paid him, preferring to keep the money himself.

I remember on one occasion, it was thought twould be difficult to get the packet through. Mother — who was Dutch — at this time put it into the middle of a biscuit, baking it carefully so as not to burn the paper in the middle. With this and a quantity of similar biscuits for his provisions on the journey, he started off. On his route, he fell in with a scouting party of American soldiers who were without provisions and hungry. They forthwith appropriated Father's biscuits to their own use. Father, now as they were eating the biscuit, regarded himself as a dead man. But to his joy, they returned it to him unbroken with a part of one or two other of the biscuits, having eaten all the rest. Why they passed this and broke all the others, I know not. Mother, in baking it, had been very careful not to heat it enough to burn the paper, and probably they observed it was poorly baked and heavy and therefore preferred all the others to this.

In the spring of the year, when making maple sugar, I and my older sister were one day in the woods keeping up the fire under the kettles, when I heard a whistle — the signal for calling Father. Speaking to my sister to listen, we soon heard it again clear and distinct. We forthwith went to the house to let it be known. Lo, there was a scouting party of the Americans there, and young as we were, we knew it would not do to say anything in their hearing. So, crawling onto Father's lap I contrived to whisper in his ear, "We have heard the whistle." On hearing what I said, he spoke, "Mother, get something for these children to eat. Mary says she is hungry; they have been left at the sugar camp so long. I will go and tend the kettles till they can go back to them." Father accordingly departed, having thus disarmed his guests.

> ◑ About one-third of all the Revolutionary War battles were fought in New York State. According to state historians, the last battle of the Revolution fought in New York was at Johnstown in October 1781, about the time of Yorktown. But the following account by Jacob Bitely shows that even in 1782, the war continued in the form of local raids. The release of numbers of Yankee prisoners from Canadian jails also took place in this year. As you will see, resentment over events of the war years lingered.

Jacob Bitely of Ticonderoga

In the spring of 1782, a party of Tory refugees who had sold out and left this part of the country was dispatched from Canada to come down and capture some of the Whigs in the Fort Edward neighborhood. The party was about twenty in number. Thomas Sherwood was their captain, William Saunders and George Campbell was among them. Saunders afterwards told me their orders from the Canadian officers were not to molest any quiet or neutral inhabitants but to seize and carry off those who were most active in the Whig interest and who had been the most troublesome to the Loyalists in this neighborhood.

The party came up the lake in two boats, and hiding them, came secretly over to their friends here. They stayed out in Argyle and none here knew of their being down. Francis De Long was the main agent in furthering their designs. They did not want to take the men from their houses amid the shrieks and tears of the females and children. So De Long — who lived on the road to Argyle where the Fort Edward and Durkeetown Roads come together — in order to get the men separate from their families, came out here to buy fish. It was then the season for shad fishing. He said he wanted the men to go out that night and catch all the fish they could, and he would come down the next morning and pay for them — he and his neighbors wanting them.

Thus deceived, my two brothers John and Henry Bitely, Silas Bristol, Thomas

Durkee, and Ezra Swain went out together to draw the seine *[a large fishing net]* on Rogers Bar, as it is since called, a mile and a half above here. It was a bright, moonlit night, the 18th of June, 1782. As they threw out their net and were pulling in towards shore in the boat to land and draw the net in, the

party, who had by this time secreted themselves upon the shore, suddenly rose up, presented their guns and ordered them to come ashore and surrender or every one of them was a dead man. Not far off was a vacant house in which Bristol had lived, and adjoining this house he had this season, commenced raising a field of corn. They took the prisoners to this house. Bristol had left the harness with which he had done his plowing. They cut up the harness, and with it securely tied the five captives, and set three or four of their number to guard them.

The remainder of the party now started down the river for Ephraim Crocker's. He and his family were all in bed when the party reached his house. They took him, his brother Levi Crocker, Elijah Dunham, and also a Continental soldier that happened to be there and who was in bed in one of the chambers at the time. They now marched off with their prisoners for Canada, nine in number.

Elijah Dunham was a young man and he begged of them with tears and sobs to let him go. He said he was to be married to Miss Cassel of Kingsbury. The day was set and near at hand for their wedding; but this he did not regard so much as the fact that if he was carried off, the girl would be disgraced. They had been guilty of a misstep; marriage only could save her with reputation. On reaching the lake where their boats lay, having exacted from him the most full and solemn promises never to fight against the King or in any way molest those who were friends to the royal cause, they released him.

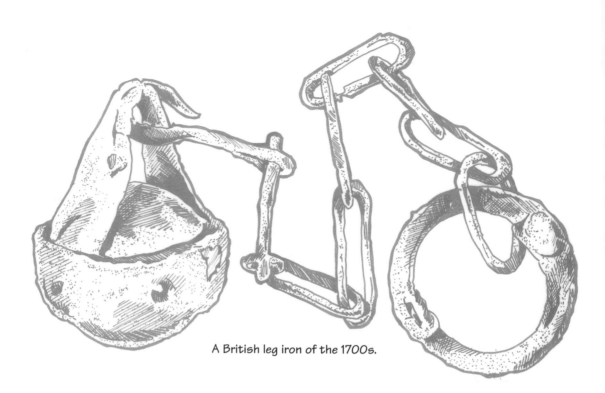

A British leg iron of the 1700s.

The other captives were put in the boats and proceeded down the lake. At Dutchman's Point, which is on the west shore of Lake Champlain, they landed and left the boats; they were within the British lines, as St. Leger with his force was then encamped on an island in the lake opposite this point. From here they marched barefoot from Chambly to Montreal. Durkee was loaded with two packs upon his back and his feet soon became so sore and cut upon the stones that he could be tracked at every step by the blood that ran from them.

They were finally taken to Cote du Lac Island *[an island in the St. Lawrence river near Montreal]*. A large number of American prisoners were there confined and underwent the greatest privations. Not even straw was furnished them to sleep on. I well remember my brother's saying when he got home that his old hat had been his only pillow; his clothes, his sole bed and bedding, all the time he was in prison. They were all alive, moreover, with vermin. And their diet the chief part of the time was sea biscuit and spoiled beef. The biscuit was old and hard enough to almost strike fire like a flint. They could only use it by boiling it a long time with a slice of the beef and thus making it into a kind of soup. So hard was their fare, they looked more like ghosts or skeletons than men. Old Eben Fuller was captured in Kingsbury and carried to Cote du Lac Island. At the surrender of Fort Ann, his son Nathan was taken and sent to the same island; but his father was so changed that the son wholly failed of recognizing him, and could scarcely be persuaded that the person before him was his father.

At length peace was restored, and the prisoners were taken out, as winter was approaching, to be sent home. Some of them were fearful that stress of weather or some other thing would be pled as an excuse for taking them to England, when once on shipboard, and staying with them there till the next season opened. Full of these apprehensions, the two Crockers and Thomas Durkee ran away. The guard soon discovered their absence and pursued after them; but they found a boat and pushed across the river in it, and the guard gave over the pursuit. They came up the west side of the Sorel *[Richelieu River]* nearly to Lake Champlain, and there crossed the river in an old battoe and came down through Vermont. All the settlements in Vermont were broken up, and without shoes and but half clothed, they suffered everything — subsisting upon frogs, birches, sorrel, wintergreens, et cetera, wading through swamps and sleeping in the open air in the frosts of December. Crocker's feet were ever after tormenting him with chilblains *[sores]* caused by this journey, but they finally got home alive.

The vessel on which my brothers embarked was loaded with prisoners. The first days out, the vessel was almost logged with ice by night. Then came on a violent storm, which nearly wrecked them, and drove them into so warm a climate that they were fainting with the heat. At length they reached New York. Here the vessel stopped and discharged all the prisoners that belonged south. An officer, with whom one of my brothers had got well acquainted, was very earnest to have him leave the vessel and go home and live with him in ease and comfort in Carolina, but Brother preferred coming home. The vessel then came up the river, but could only get to Dobbs Ferry, on account of

This painting from the mid-1800s is titled *Veterans of 1776 Returning from the War.* With their wagon, these veterans traveled home in great comfort, compared to the returning prisoners Jacob Bitely tells us about.

the ice. Here the northern prisoners were landed. From the soldiers in the Highlands, they got some old coarse shoes, and came on homewards on foot, so covered with lice they could not ask of the inhabitants a bed to sleep in. They slept in barns or on the floors of houses, but the folks on the way supplied them with enough to eat. They reached home upon the last day of December, the same year they were taken, and the next day was a happy New Year to us, as you may readily suppose.

John Pattison of Fort Miller

Ephraim Crocker was taken prisoner. Mister Wing was the ringleader in capturing him and took him to Montreal and delivered him up to the jailer there. But Crocker broke jail before long and returned, freezing his feet or two of his toes when on his way home.

When Wing delivered Crocker to the Montreal jailer and left him, Crocker said something to this effect to Wing: "My curse upon you, Wing! I shall yet live to see you in as secure a place as this."

After a long series of years had passed away, Wing committed forgery, was convicted and sent to the state's prison at New York City. Now was Crocker's hour of triumph. He rode up to my store one morning for some tobacco, et cetera, which he needed to complete his outfit, put them in his saddlebags, flung them over his saddle, mounted and started away for New York on a brisk trot — the saddlebags going slap-slap-slap against the horse's sides and Crocker's arms flapping up and down with the horse's motion as though he was actually flying. He rode all the way to New York on purpose to see Wing there and remind him of their parting at Montreal jail.

Daniel Carswell of Salem

I was four years old when Father moved to Salem in the year 1779. My brother Abner enlisted for nine months and was stationed at Fort Ann. [My brother] David went up to Fort Ann to take Abner's place and let him come home for a short time. Whilst David was there as Abner's substitute, Fort Ann was taken, and David was carried prisoner to Canada. Caldwell of Cambridge,

Cowan and many others were taken. They were at first confined in Montreal jail. My brother and five others broke jail at one time and made their escape, getting down to Coos *[the northernmost county in New Hampshire]*. They deemed all danger of recapture past and struck up a fire where they encamped at night. This led to their being discovered by a scouting party, by whom they were taken back to Canada. They were now handcuffed and sent to an island *[Cote du Lac]* in the St. Lawrence rapids nine miles above Montreal. Here they were guarded by American Tories who were tenfold more unkind to them than Indians would have been. Although the river was running but a few rods from the prison, they at one time would not give them any water, till some of the men became so dry and thirsty they were attacked with raising of the blood. At length, my brother was exchanged and came home.

A few years after the peace, one Yarnes, a Tory — I think he had been living in Kingsbury — came to Salem when court was sitting, to get compensation for some land that had been unjustly confiscated. My brother was in the courtroom one day and, seeing Yarnes, went to him and asked him if he knew him. Yarnes pretended he did not. "Don't you remember when I was a prisoner in Canada and perishing of thirst, you was one of the guards?" My brother knew he could not be mistaken in the man, and having a whip in his hand, struck him to the floor with the butt of it. A constable was ordered to protect Yarnes out of the court, but he had no sooner got into the hall than he received another blow. Getting into the street he was beset by a crowd who kicked, cuffed, and pounded him without mercy until he was entirely out of the village.

Donald McDonald of Hebron

James Rogers was a noted deer hunter and had a long gun with which he made sure shot at a great distance. He sent word to Simpson's family, when John was reported to be with them on a visit, that Simpson must keep out of reach of his long gun. *[John Simpson had informed on Yankee prisoners trying to escape from the Montreal jail, as James Rogers relates on page 103.]*

◪ The years following the Revolution were not easy ones for many people on the frontier. The Continental money paid to soldiers and others was almost worthless. Almost everyone who spoke to Dr. Fitch about these times mentions money or land troubles of some kind: problems with taxes, bankruptcies, disputed land titles, and so forth. Such discontents erupted in Shays's Rebellion in 1786. This rebellion, led by Daniel Shays of Massachusetts, caused American leaders to write a new Constitution and create a new form of republican government.

Some of the pioneers in northeastern New York sympathized with Shays. Indeed, some of them helped Shays and a handful of his followers hide out in a secret outlaw village in the nearby Vermont mountains. Robert Hanna was sixteen years old in the year of Shays's Rebellion.

Robert Hanna of Salem

I was too young to be called into service in the Revolution, but when I was sixteen years old I was ordered out to quell the rebellion in Granville. Isaac Mitchell was the sergeant of the company who warned me. The captain was old James Stewart or else Armstrong — I ain't certain which. I did not go, but quite a party from Salem did go. The rebellion did not amount to much. It was some men there who would not pay taxes. It was in Shays' time, I remember. Who any of their names were I do not know. But they gave up when they heard the militia were on their way up so it was all settled and over with before the militia got there.

Shays, when he was driven out of Massachusetts, fled through this town. He came here on a stud horse which was so fatigued and jaded out that he was anxious to exchange it for a fresh one, and Sam McCarter traded with him and continued to own this stud horse that he got of Shays a number of years.

Part Two:
Early Pioneer Life

A boy splits a stick of firewood at a reenactment held at Fort Ticonderoga. Donald McDonald would have found this light work.

CHAPTER TEN

Work and Shelter

◨ *Work.* The first settlers in any wooded frontier like northeastern New York faced a lot of hard work. A good deal of this work fell on the shoulders of the young. In poorer families, it was often necessary for boys or girls as young as ten to twelve years old to go to work in more well-to-do households, where they received their meals as compensation.

Donald McDonald of Hebron

One of the first objects of the settlers was to get a small piece of their land into permanent meadow; and for this purpose some low moist tract was cleared and grubbed as clean as possible and sowed with timothy seed *[a type of grass];* the seed being got probably in Albany. The farmers generally calculated on having a small piece thus seeded. Each man aimed to have meadow enough to yield sufficient hay to keep one cow through the winter. The first cow which Father owned he bought of Munro for fifteen dollars paying him in days' work at three shillings per day.

Pasturing cattle in the summer was a thing then unknown. The cows used to be turned daily into the woods and there get their own keep, browsing upon the twigs and leaves. They used to be furnished with bells.

Some would come home regularly at night, others had to be found and drove home. For several years after the first settlement of the country, cattle in the winter were kept on browse mixed with hay. It used to be the prevalent idea that some hay was necessary in order to make the cud for them to chew. Maple and basswood used to be selected for browse for cattle; beech for horses and sheep. Horses could be kept in excellent order on beech browse and grain. Cattle accustomed to browse will eat off basswood twigs as large as a man's finger.

In getting the land under cultivation, the early settlers used to cut down the small trees leaving the largest standing and by throwing the brush around them as much as convenient burn them so as to kill them. Burnt trees would not leaf out the next season; those that were girdled would put forth their leaves two and some of them three years after thus shading the ground. The logs of the cut trees were rolled together in heaps often around the standing large trees when convenient and burnt. This was all done by hand by the first settlers. There was but one span of horses at Munro's Meadows for six years after I came there. By spring half an acre or an acre more would get cleared by each family and this was sowed with oats and grass seed for meadows.

HALF-LAP:
The seed was broadcast — thrown by hand over a wide area. Then a team of horses or oxen dragged a harrow — a large wooden device with spikes to comb the earth — for one length or lap of the field. The harrow was dragged once more over half the strip thus combed — a half-lap. The point was to cover the valuable seed with earth.

Wheat was sowed late for they could not get the ground out and burnt over to sow early. From September 1st to the 20th, they endeavored to sow their wheat but often it was not got in till into October. The seed was sowed on the burnt ground without plowing — sowed broadcast — and harrowed in with a **half-lap.** Some, however, were obliged to hoe in their wheat, teams were so scarce. And it was a good week's work to hoe in an acre. Of course, where a harrow and team could be procured, it made a great savings.

Eunice Campbell Reid of Greenwich

In 1772 there were but two wagons in Argyle township, it was said. They were common lumber two-horse wagons.

Grain and hay was drawn into the barns on wood-shod sleds and on cars having two small wheels and letting most of the load drag on the ground behind them. They would, however, draw a considerable quantity in this way. Boards were carried on horseback. The first boards in this place were brought up from the Point — two miles — in this way: Two bunches were tied together and hung over the backs of the two horses placed one before the other, the forward horse carrying the forward ends by a strap over his back supporting a bunch of boards on each side — the hind horse carrying the hind ends in the same way.

Robert Blake of Jackson

When we came here in the autumn of 1772, Jacobus O'Bail, a Dutchman, had a gristmill on the east and a sawmill on the west side of Black Creek. This was the first gristmill in town or in this section of country. It did but poor work. When William Reid completed his own mill, O'Bail received no more patronage. In 1772, William Reid had got his mill about completed and they were then putting up the dam when we arrived in the neighborhood. There was at the same time a gristmill at Yerry Killmore's in Argyle. Killmore a few years after rebuilt his mill and I remember we turned out from around here to go over and help him raise it — inhabitants were so few they had to gather them from such great distances to accomplish such a job.

Gilbert Robertson a Scotchman, was the first settler in Jackson and put up a house down towards the kill. He was a wheelwright *[a maker of wagon wheels]* by trade, but did all kinds of carpentering and was an enterprising man of some property. He was a good workman and was over to Fort Edward one or two years working for the army there — where I used to see him every two or three weeks and let him know how things were going on at home.

Robertson, in low water, drove stakes in the kill, put sticks across them and slabs from stick to stick thus making a very convenient footbridge — which, of course, went off with the first high water. A few years after this and before the

Revolutionary War was closed, a bridge between here and Gilbert Robertson's was built. McKellips and his neighbors was bitterly opposed to our having a bridge here. A great crib, like a log barn, was built up in the middle of the river and long stringers from this to both shores were put on. But before we got the plank on, there came a great flood in the kill and McKellips having a quantity of logs to be sawed at the mills down the kill now rolled them all together into the stream. They came down, piled up against the crib of our bridge and swept it off. Thus we lost our bridge and McKellips lost his logs too for the kill was up so high and furious they could not stop them at the place intended. The bridge lodged at the bend by Mistress McDougall's whence we drawed back part of it — the folks from away down in Cambridge turning out to help us for they felt indignant at McKellips' conduct. And the next year we got it completed.

Donald McDonald of Hebron

When I first went from home [at age eleven or twelve] in search of some-place to live and support myself, I went to Mister Bell's, a Scotchman. A hurricane had blown down all the trees on a small piece of  Bell's land and I assisted Bell in cutting up the trees. Bell got a new light axe for me and used the old one for himself and I well remember I could easily cut off the tree at its butt, and ere Bell who would take the next cut above me would get his off, I would go on to the third cut and get that off before him. Bell repeatedly telling me, "My child, ye need not work so fast!"

I fared very well at Bell's and it would have been well had I remained there, but Father not knowing I had obtained a place, meeting Armstrong made a bargain with him to have me work for him a year.

The winter of 1779–80 was the hardest ever known in this country. For three months the eaves never dropped from the houses [*the buildup of ice and snow on the roofs never thawed enough to slide off]*, the cold was so severe and steady and the snow was full four feet deep, I presume, all that time. I lived that winter with Captain John Armstrong who resided north of Salem Village — Lot Number 131. It was the hardest winter that a poor boy ever had. He had four horses, four cows, four calves, two or three young cattle and twelve sheep — and about half enough hay to winter them on. It was my work to take care of the stock and provide firewood for the family. He was away from home about all the time frolicking around with his companions. I used daily to tread a path from the barn west over the flat to the hill which was then covered with wood; then cut down a tree; trample the snow down all around the top of it; cut off the limbs and lay them along the path for the cattle, et cetera, to eat; then drive them out to the spot and let them go to feeding; then get up the team, snake the butt of the tree to the house and cut it up for firewood.

The broadaxe was a key tool in pioneer life.

I thus carried all his stock through the winter on browse, cutting over some three or four acres of woods taking all except the largest trees. The wood was all beech, maple and basswood; there were no pines or hemlocks or tamaracks growing along Beaver Brook. Of course for a boy I was constantly employed. But this I should not have minded had I been furnished with suitable fare. Armstrong was a liberal, generous man, but he was little of the time at home and knew not how his wife treated me. My main diet was mush and milk, the milk skimmed — and not only skimmed but profusely watered — ere it was brought onto the table for me. I thus fell away so that I did not appear like the same child in the course of three or four months, and should probably have died had I continued there.

Father becoming aware of how hard I was faring at Armstrong's took me from him, and I next lived with Joseph Welch where my situation was as easy and comfortable as it had previously been hard and laborious.

Samuel Cook of Fort Edward

When Father came here *[Fort Edward]*, our grinding was done at Gillis' Mill five miles from here. But most of the Indian corn for our johnnycakes was ground by hand, in a mortar at the Bell place north of the village. A stump here had been burnt hollow by red-hot cannon balls dropped onto it thus forming a mortar; and the pestle was a long round stone hung to a limb of a tree which bent down with the weight of the stone pestle allowing it to play in the mortar.

Donald McDonald of Hebron

Potatoes were brought here and cultivated when we first came. The early settlers, to economize as much as possible, always sliced the seed. The slices were dropped three or four inches apart around a foot or more and covered with the hoe forming a hill so large around as a bushel basket. No further cultivation was bestowed upon them till they were harvested.

The Spanish potato was the kind first here. It was watery and of an inferior quality but yielded well. Some ten years after, the yellow Rusty-Coats were introduced. These were a round potato with a rough skin and generally cracking open when boiled. Then the Rusty-Coat-Reds. These were small, few of them being larger than a hen's egg — fine for roasting and as white and mealy as flour inside but could not be used for boiling as they would crack all to pieces. I was about nineteen years old *[in 1787, the year of the Constitutional Convention in Philadelphia]* when we took our first load of wheat to Lansingburgh. It required three days to take a load to market and return home. Twenty bushels of wheat were always taken as a load. I was about the first one, I suppose, that showed the folks that more could be taken. Having a good and true team, I was sure I could take more with ease and so put on twenty-five bushels. Going up the Campbell Hill, I told the man ahead of me that I had on twenty-five bushels. It was thought so remarkable a load that he halloed to the man forwards of him, telling him the fact. And thus the announcement was passed forwards from one team to another on the long train upon the road that "there was a fellow behind who had got on twenty-five bushels!"

◻ *Shelter.* In the 1700s, the very first shelters put up by frontier settlers were sometimes lean-tos with only three walls, or rough shacks. The next stage was a cabin made of logs, with the spaces between the logs stuffed, or chinked, with mud and grass. The next step in home construction was to shape the logs with an ax so that they were square and rested upon one another with no open spaces between them. The final step was to build a frame house, with beams and boards.

Asa Fitch made this drawing of the Allen house, following the description given by Maria McEachron.

Until there were sawmills, boards, beams, doors, roof shingles, tables, chairs, and so forth had to be split and shaped with an ax. For this reason, dirt floors were the rule in the first houses. A floor made of planks was a major step up. Wooden pegs took the place of iron nails, which were rare and much prized. Pieces of leather served as hinges for doors and shutters.

Perhaps the hardest fact to grasp for modern Americans is how small pioneer houses were and how little privacy there was. As you will see from the following accounts, even relatively well-off pioneer families cooked, ate, and slept in a space about the size of today's living rooms.

The first settler cabins often had a simple bed in one corner and a trap door leading down to a storage cellar. Here the trap door is actually a number of loose planks.

James Bain of Argyle

☑ On the following page, James Bain describes the Allen house and property. In 1785, he, his mother, and his five brothers moved onto the lot where the Allen family had lived and died.

My father bought Argyle Lot Number 23 in 1785. The west half of this lot had belonged to Allen and has since belonged to and been cultivated by me. My father died just after he bought and before he moved here. My mother with her six boys then moved up.

There was no clearing on the lot when we first came except that made by Allen towards the northwest corner of the lot amounting to some sixteen acres. Allen had cleared in the first place — after clearing his meadow and putting up his house — a field north of his house in which wheat was sowed. The timber originally on the land was mostly oak and chestnut, and west, in the swale *[a low, marshy hollow]* it was all pine — many of the trees of enormous size.

In 1776 this wheat was harvested and a new field on the knoll beyond the meadow south of his house was cleared and sowed with wheat which was ripe when he was murdered. Each of the wheatfields contained about five or six acres and the meadow three or four. Three apple trees were set out by Allen and were mere saplings when we came here. The nearest neighbors to John Allen at the time of the murder were about three miles distant.

The house was of logs and was some eighteen or twenty feet square with the door on its south side and the chimney on the north. Allen had an outdoor oven between the house and the spring. It was about ten rods from the house to the barn.

Samuel Cook of Fort Edward

◪ **Samuel Cook remembers the house of Mistress McNeil because it, too, had been connected with a murder — Jane McCrea's.**

The McNeil house was a small house of round logs some fourteen or sixteen feet broad and somewhat greater in length. It stood some years after I came here — well known as the house from which Jane McCrea was taken. It had an old-fashioned fireplace in one end — the fireplace was without jambs *[sides]*. There was a loft overhead and a ladder or ladder-like stairs leading to this loft — the stairs being on one side of the fireplace.

The door opened on the east side of the house which was the only entrance. There was a cellar hole under the house, not walled up. This was entered by a trap door which was rather south of the middle of the floor. Nearly contiguous to *[next to]* the house, in rear of it, was a little woodshed made of slabs, I think.

This cabin has a ladder leading up to the loft, or chamber, as mentioned in Samuel Cook's description of the McNeil house. Note the chinking between the round logs.

Donald McDonald of Hebron

Donald McDonald remembers the house and property of his father's landlord, Harry Munro. McDonald also talks about how the earliest roofs were made.

Reverend Harry Munro was an Episcopal clergyman. He was chaplain to a Highland regiment, thus ranking as lieutenant.

Munro's house stood near the outlet of the marsh. It was a log house covered with bark and had but a single room some sixteen feet by twenty. No bedroom or pantry. I think it had no floor — the earth trod down firm and hard and could be swept clean.

The first thing Munro did was to ditch the marsh, which covered thirty-five acres. A main ditch was dug along the east side for the brook to run in that comes in at the head of the marsh, and side drains were dug emptying into this. This part of the marsh was so far reclaimed as to produce wild grass. Captain John Armstrong used to come up here and cut hay and draw it home to Salem for several years.

Munro used to assemble his settlers on the Sabbath and preach to them, but it was only occasionally. At such times they gathered by the side of his house and he used to stand with his back to the house and his face towards the meadows; and they used to say that he seemed to be adoring his meadows more than his God.

Most other log houses [were] roofed with black ash bark; though it might have been of oak shingles three or four foot long, like barrel staves, which material was sometimes used. The ash bark was peeled into long strips and flattened by being piled and pressed down with weights upon it till it dried; and then it was placed on the roof the rough side of the bark being uppermost — and held in place by poles running the length of the roof and notched into the end timbers, which were gradually shorter above each other to run the roof up to a ridge.

John Pattison of Fort Miller

☐ Here and there in this land of log cabins and just-cleared farms, there were occasional grand houses built by the powerful men who hoped to rule over the new region. These buildings made a strong impression.

Philip Skene's two-story stone house in Skenesborough was one of these mansions. Philip Schuyler built a large frame house in Schuylerville. Another landowner, William Duer, built a still grander residence at Fort Miller. Like Skene, Duer was a British officer. Unlike Skene, Duer took the American side in the war and was active in Revolutionary councils.

William Duer was born in England and married a daughter of Lord Stirling's. After the war his family lived here, I know. He speculated largely after the war in governme nt securities — so largely that some thought that he meant to own the government — but he was unable to meet his liabilities and thus became a ruined man. When he failed his estate was inventoried and amounted to a hundred and thirty thousand pounds. He was committed to prison in New York and laid there some years. Finally he got released from jail, took cold and died ten days after his enlargement *[release]*.

The Duer mansion had such an air of baronial splendor, I used to delight to go over the river and sit down and look at it. It was so far back from the top of the hill that it could be but partially seen on this side of the river. The main building was fifty-two feet square, two stories high, and a high basement. The roof was four-square and was flattish and surrounded with a balustrade, with a scuttle door to go out onto it. On the east front was a piazza, two stories high, the upper piazza hav-

A substantial house of squared logs built in blockhouse style, with an overhanging second floor. The British general Fraser died here after the Second Battle of Saratoga.

ing a bedroom enclosed off from each end; the lower piazza was open its entire length of fifty-two feet. On each side was a wing twenty-two feet square. The wings stood fourteen feet from the main building, the intervening space being also enclosed. The windows were large and the whole was finished off in a style of elegance such as I had never seen before, I having at that date been no farther south than Albany.

I am surprised that it was pulled down. No one at this day would demolish such a building. But the timber of some of it was wanted for a building or two down here at the falls. And having been unoccupied for a year or two or more, some worthless scamps of the neighborhood had made free to injure it. The window casings were torn off and the leaden weights by which the windows were hung were stolen from every one of the windows. The sheet lead in the gutters of the roofs was also all cut away; in short, whatever any of these fellows had found that they wanted, they had made free to take. The edifice thus becoming so marred and dilapidated, it was taken down.

I measured it all and was for some time occupied in drawing out and straightening the wrought nails from the boards. This work at first I did not fancy at all. But getting used to it, it became a pleasure to me. The iron was so tough, they would be drawn out and straightened so prettily that it was a pastime to me, and I regretted it when it was completed that I had no more such work to do.

Although this reenactor is dressed and decorated as a Mohawk, the war club he is carrying was typical of most Eastern Woodland Indians, including the Stockbridge Indians.

CHAPTER ELEVEN

Indians and Wild Animals

◼ *Indians.* The north-south corridor along Lakes Champlain and George connecting the St. Lawrence and Hudson rivers had been used for centuries by Indians as a trading route and warpath. It also formed a general dividing line between the territories of the Iroquois to the west and the Algonquian tribes to the east. As a result, large parts of the corridor were a sort of neutral zone, which certain Indian tribes visited for the fall hunt or for trading purposes.

Early settlers in this zone had generally good experiences with Indians. Ann McArthur was born in 1770. The "Stockbridge Indians" she talks about below were Mohicans, an Algonquian tribe living in the Stockbridge, Massachusetts, area. Many had been converted to Christianity since the 1730s. Some Stockbridge Indians had fought with the Massachusetts militia in the French and Indian War, and many fought for the American side during the Revolutionary War. Later, the entire tribe moved west.

Ann McArthur of Argyle

The Stockbridge Indians used to come into these parts regularly every autumn to hunt, and remain here some weeks till the weather became cool on the close of the Indian summer. They had their wigwams or camps in the woods. There were several in this vicinity. Each company had its own wigwam to which they regularly came.

One of these stood some sixty rods west of here. I remember it well. It was built of small logs about four inches in diameter, slightly notched together at the end — like a toy house though with wide-open cracks between the logs — and covered over with bark with a hole in the center for the smoke to escape. Their fire was built on the ground in the middle, and three sides were occupied with seats or beds made up by a layer of pine boughs broken from the ends of the limbs, and over this a layer of straw. The Indians, wrapped in their blankets, would then lay on the straw with their heads towards the outer wall and their feet towards the fire

— the fourth side of the wigwam being occupied by the doorway. About a dozen occupied this wigwam coming here every autumn to hunt the deer, bear, raccoon, et cetera. We never used to have any fear of them but were always on friendly terms. An old squaw I used to have some degree of affection for; her name was Rebekah Kack-Kees-Moh.

I well remember on one occasion when I was a little girl our folks had borrowed a knife of the Indians to do some butchering with that day. About dusk the squaw came to our house and wanted to get a bundle of straw. Father told her to go to the barn and get what she wanted. When our folks had got through with the knife they sent me to carry it home. I went to the hut, pushed aside the blanket and went in. Rebekah was not there, and I then felt alarmed at perceiving they were all strangers to me. So I handed them the knife and made my way out and homewards as fast as convenient. On the way, I met Rebekah carrying her bundle of straw and told her I had been to her hut and that I was scared when I found she was not there. She hereupon laughed heartily.

I remember an Indian once came to our house and wanted the loan of a frying pan. He had to motion a long time ere our folks could understand what he wanted — showing that it was long and circular at one end and to be put on the fire and then making a spluttering noise with his mouth exactly resembling the frying of meat. We at once understood him and got him the utensil. He put the meat which he brought with him into the pan and cooked it over the fire and ate it. He then poured some of the grease from the pan onto his hands and rubbed them until they were well and evenly anointed all over. Then stepping to the fire-place, he drew his hands along the chimney-back till the palms were well covered with soot. He next rubbed the palms of his hands together until the soot was mixed with the grease. He now commenced rubbing his face with his hands, step-ping up to the looking-glass to see that he got all parts of his face evenly covered. This being done, with his fingers spread slightly apart he drew the ends of them along his face lengthwise, thus leaving regular stripes of black and flesh color over his whole face. The same motion was next repeated crosswise of his face — thus cutting the stripes up into squares somewhat like a checkerboard. Having thus finished, he turned to us and smiling said, "War! War!" and then left the house.

◘ *Wild Animals.* Some of the wild animals that shared the wilderness with American pioneers — deer, wild turkey, waterfowl — are still to be found in the rural parts of northeastern New York. But pioneers in New York State and else-where soon hunted out dangerous predators such as mountain lions, wolves, and bears, often elimi-nating them locally within a few years of the first settlements.

Samuel Cook of Fort Edward

I well remember the next year after we came here, Moses Harris of Queensbury killed a panther thus. He had two fine hogs fatted. One morning one of them was missing from the pens. It had been carried off by a panther who had partly devoured it and concealed the remainder by covering it with some leaves in the woods. Harris searched and found the carcass. He hereupon fixed his gun with a cord, tied to the carcass and reaching to the trigger of the gun, and left it thus. The following night the panther returned to feast upon the hog; and so skillfully had Harris arranged his apparatus that the gun went off and killed the panther. Harris brought the panther down here to Fort Edward where it was exhibited to all the inhabitants — this being at that date the most considerable place in this vicinity.

Originally wolves thronged the Kingsbury swamp, and this remained their haunt for years after they had been exterminated in all the surrounding country. They were such an annoyance that in 1801 a great wolf hunt was had, all the inhabitants gathering on a specified day and surrounding the swamp. The number killed on this occasion was either nine or eleven, I am not certain which. This broke them up so that after, there was no further trouble from them, though two or three remained in the swamp a few years longer.

John McEachron of Hebron

I know nothing of any panthers having been killed about here. Wolves used

to be plenty and sometimes the sheep, when chased by them, would run directly into the house if the door was left open.

I remember on one occasion when our cattle came home from the woods at night, a two-year-old steer was missing. Father went out to search for it and found it and a large bear that had killed and was eating it. He got word to the Gillis boys; they came over with their dogs and guns. As they approached the bear, he sat himself up on his haunches with his back against a large tree, and the dogs went at him. But with his paws he would knock them hither and thither as fast as they came within his reach. The men had some difficulty in firing at him, the dogs beset him so on every side. They fired as they had chances for doing it without hurting the dogs; and it was not until they had put thirteen bullets through his hide that he was killed. He weighed twelve or thirteen hundred pounds. His head, elevated on the top of a pole, was exhibited a number of years beside the road at my Uncle Peter's.

The Old Burying Ground in Salem. More than one hundred of the American dead from the Second Battle of Saratoga were brought here for burial. Dinah Conkey, the woman who refused to leave her batch of bread during a wartime alarm (see pages 35–36), also is buried here.

CHAPTER TWELVE

Superstitions and Village Life

> ◑ *Superstitions.* In the 1700s and later, farming folk had a number of unusual beliefs, some of them brought from the old country, some of them homegrown.

John Pattison of Fort Miller

When residing at Petersburg *[a town just south of Hoosick]*, I saw a strange instance of popular superstition. The people there were Rhode Islanders and very ignorant. They had among them the belief that when a person died — at least of consumption — and another near relative was taken down with the same disease, there was some part of the deceased person remaining in the grave undecayed, deriving its sustenance from the living person who would consequently pine away and die. The only way to prevent another death in the family was to dig up the dead body, take the part which was thus living and burn it to ashes.

I went with a number of other spectators to see them dig up the body of one who, it was firmly believed, was preying upon a sick person in the same family. The grave was old and grass-grown. They came down to the coffin and raised it from the ground and opened it. There was the bones of the skeleton, the flesh all gone, its remains lying on the bottom of the coffin. In the chest was a lump of a dark color like clay, laying flattened down and decayed. No vestige of anything sound and uncorrupted could be found.

Some of the spectators jeered and laughed at the actors in this affair for their folly and they seemed to be now ashamed. The coffin was now replaced and covered up.

Tryphena Martin Angel of Salem

The mare which Father brought with him from Stillwater was the first horse he ever owned. After some time, he got well enough off to own a second horse. The horse was taken sick. What it was that ailed him nobody knew but from his actions it was concluded to be the blind staggers. He was unable to walk straight, even, at times, to stand. At length, although he was unable to walk on the ground, he was seen to be walking up on the top of a log fence, and actually walked thus a distance of about twenty rods. This was seen by persons whose statement was credited generally. I did not see this feat myself but I saw many strange acts in the horse, and it was concluded on all hands that he was bewitched, for belief in witches was about universal at that time.

Betsey Taylor of Argyle

William Tosh and his wife Jennet were from Scotland or Ireland and lived on the James Cherry Lot, Number 64 Argyle Patent. Mistress Tosh was an active and very inquisitive woman — would work all night and ran about all day to gather the

news. As she knew everything that was going on and would tell folks things which they had said when it was inexplicable how she had got her information, she came to be universally regarded as a witch. She was a great worker and had clothing very nice and good for one in her circumstances.

Mistress Tosh was subject to bleeding at the nose. She and her husband lived alone and

Above: In the 1700s, children wore the same clothes as adults, just in smaller sizes. These girls, who are taking part in a reenactment, are wearing chemises, striped petticoats, and caps. The machine-woven material of their garments would have seemed impossibly fine to Eunice Campbell Reid, Ann McArthur, and the other girls of the Revolutionary era in northern New York. Their clothes were made from wool and linen thread spun and woven into cloth at home. Clothes were few and valuable, as they represented many woman-hours of labor.

Inset: A woman spinning wool.

one night she was taken with bleeding from the nose and mouth so violently that finding they could not stop it by the usual remedies, the husband ran down to Cherry's calling to Mistress Cherry to make haste for Jennie was dying. She was dead before Tosh and Mistress Cherry got to the house.

Upon the same night, Alexander Livingston found a cat in his cellar lapping the cream off from the milk, as the cream had frequently been taken from the milk before. He struck the cat across the nose with a stick or club as it was running past him out of the cellar causing the blood to spurt from its nose and mouth. And it became the current report that Mistress Tosh, the witch, had transformed herself into a cat and come to Livingston's cellar to lick the cream off from his milk and had thus been killed by him.

Mistress Cherry, Mistress Taylor and a Miss Murdock dressed the body for the grave, and had a task of it, she was so large and heavy a woman. The house too was so small that they had not room to move the bed out from the wall. At length, Miss Murdock slipped her shoes off and ventured to get onto the bed behind the corpse to wash it. But she had scarcely got it raised, when the arm slid down and the cold hand of the corpse fell onto her naked foot, which so frighted her — thinking the witch was coming again to life — that at one leap she bounded to the opposite side of the room.

Mistress Cherry, who was my mother-in-law, used to relate that these notions had such an effect on her that for months afterwards when she was at the spinning wheel at night, she durst not step back to draw out the thread any farther than the length of the wheel so powerfully was it wrought into her imagination that the dead Mistress Tosh was standing behind her and would catch her if she went a hair's-breadth beyond the length of the wheel. Night after night has she spun in horror from her thoughts, which she could not dispel, that this witch was behind her in the dark part of the room.

◻ *Village Life.* In the years after the Revolutionary War, many new settlers arrived in northeastern New York, mainly from New England. By 1790, the year of the first national census, some of the rural townships in the area showed substantial populations. The village of Salem, for example, which had begun as a few temporary huts in the 1760s, had become a thriving community by the 1790s. As the following accounts show, village life still had a certain pioneer roughness to it.

Donald McDonald of Hebron

A town meeting or other public gathering never passed, when I was a boy, without a fight. The Armstrongs were noted bullies. They were very athletic men. I remember once seeing Bob Armstrong take the "Salmon Lep" — leap like a salmon as it was called — in a barroom coming from Lansingburgh. This consisted in placing himself on the floor on all fours and then springing up and slapping his hands together three times before striking the floor again. This was a feat that few could accomplish. There was but one man in the county that could whip the Armstrongs. That was Robert Pattison. He was a large man and lived near the **lime kilns** in Hartford and used to burn lime there.

Nathaniel Covill of Greenwich

◩ Covill came to Salem Village in 1792 as a boy of ten. There he learned to be a tanner, one who converts animal skins into leather.

LIME KILNS: Large, dome-shaped ovens of brick or stone in which limestone was burned, turning it into lime, a white, acidic powder used for mortar, plaster, whitewash, and other purposes.

COURT WEEKS: Salem was a county seat. A county judge held court there three times a year — in February, May, and November — for a week at a time. People from the surrounding areas filled Salem Village at these times.

On all public occasions, training days *[when the militia marched and trained]*, **court weeks,** et cetera, there was all sorts of wild rude sports going on in the village — drinking and frolicking, singing songs, and always fighting was going on, wrestling and boxing, et cetera. The town was settled with all kinds of people: Scotch, Irish, Yankee, Dutch and many Negroes. And everyone thought his own nationality the best and greatest and despised all the others, and if any remark derogatory to the Irish, the Dutch or other people was dropped in conversation, someone would instantly say, "That deserves a knockdown," or words of some such purport; and throw-

A tanner at work. Tanning was a long process, which varied according to the type of hide. Cowhides were (1) scraped clean of flesh; (2) soaked in water and lime to loosen the hair; (3) scraped clean again; (4) soaked for days in a mixture of water, manure, and salt to get all the fat out of the hide (so that the leather would not rot later); (5) rinsed; (6) soaked for months in water and ground-up hemlock bark, containing a chemical called tannin, which made the leather flexible; and (7) dried, rubbed, sometimes dyed, and polished.

ing off their coats and rolling up their sleeves, at it they would go.

Bob Pattison was the greatest boxer and most noted bully here in those days. He did not live here [*Salem*] but was always present on public occasions, ready to whip anyone that would box with him. Rowan and he were always having small fights with each other, both claiming to be the best. At length, Doctor Williams got Rowan to fight it out with Pattison and have a final end of it. A time was set for the meeting to take place back of the tan works. Pattison came punctually at the time. It was told to Rowan that Pattison was on the ground. He immediately shut up his bar and came to the spot.

His design was to run and butt his head violently into Pattison's breast or stomach and push him over, but as he came up Pattison knocked him over. At the next round, he managed to knock Pattison down. And then it was first one down and then the other, without any decided

Salem Village in 1795. The line of soldiers on horseback shows that this is a training day for the militia. You can see the courthouse and jail building to the left.

advantage, till they both became so tired out they were no longer able to stand on their feet. Rowan, sitting up on the grass, sent for a bottle of liquor to give him strength to get to his house. It was a drawn game between them, neither one being the victor.

When Ladder Stewart was appointed constable, he did much towards stopping these street fights. I don't know whether his name was Robert Stewart. He was always called Ladder Stewart because at some showman's exhibition he climbed up on a ladder and looked in at a window to see the show without paying for it. He lived off south towards Shushan. Whenever a fight commenced he would command the peace and if they did not stop, he would nab them and clap them under the fish [*put them in Salem's jail, which had a fish-shaped weathervane*]. He was so active in this that it stopped the brawls that had been so common all along till then.

PICTURE CREDITS

Front cover: Janice Lang, Carleton Place, Ottawa (613-253-3435); **back cover:** Courtesy Fort Ticonderoga Museum, Ticonderoga, NY; **inside cover:** Michael Noonan Photography, Saratoga Springs, NY; **page 3:** Janice Lang; **page 6:** Courtesy Rockefeller Library, Colonial Williamsburg Foundation, Williamsburg, VA; **page 8:** Asa Fitch, *Notes for a History of Washington County,* manuscript on microfilm, Washington County Clerk, Hudson Falls, NY; **page 9:** Crisfield Johnson, *History of Washington County, New York, with Illustrations and Biographical Sketches of Some of Its Prominent Men and Pioneers,* Everts & Ensign, Philadelphia, 1878; **page 11:** Janice Lang; **page 12:** Seneca Ray Stoddard, "An Adirondack House," Courtesy Adirondack Museum, Blue Mountain Lake, NY; **page 14:** Courtesy Rockefeller Library, Colonial Williamsburg Foundation; **page 14:** Blanche Cirker, ed., *1800 Woodcuts by Thomas Bewick and His School,* Dover Pictorial Archive Series, Dover Publications, New York, 1962; **page 16:** Engraving after Alonzo Chappel, "Philip Schyler," Miriam and Ira D. Wallach Division of Art, Prints and Photographs, The New York Public Library, New York, NY; **page 17:** *1800 Woodcuts,* Dover Publications; **page 18:** Tonya Condon, Native Sky Photography Studios, Ticonderoga, NY; **page 20:** Benson Lossing, *Pictorial Fieldbook of the American Revolution,* Harper Bros., New York, 1851–52; **page 22:** John Wollaston, "Sir William Johnson," Courtesy Albany Institute of History and Art, Albany, NY; **page 24:** *1800 Woodcuts,* Dover Publications; **page 25:** Courtesy Rockefeller Library, Colonial Williamsburg Foundation; **page 26:** Unknown artist, "Ethan Allen Demanding the Surrender of Fort Ticonderoga," Fort Ticonderoga Museum; **page 28:** Fort Ticonderoga Museum; **page 29:** Fort Ticonderoga Museum; **page 31:** Janice Lang; **page 32:** Courtesy Major William Trotter, CBE DL, The Deanery, Staindrop, Darlington, County Durham; **page 33:** *1800 Woodcuts,* Dover Publications; **page 35:** *1800 Woodcuts,* Dover Publications; **page 37:** Thomas Anburey, *Travels Through the Interior Parts of America,* W. Lane, London, 1789. Courtesy of Fort Ticonderoga Museum; **page 38:** "Burgoyne Addressing His Indians," Courtesy Fort Ticonderoga Museum; **page 39:** James Hunter, "A View of Ticonderoga from a Point on the North Shore of Lake Champlain, 1777," Courtesy of the National Archives of Canada, Ottawa, Ontario; **page 41:** Courtesy Massachusetts Historical Society,

Boston, MA; **page 43:** Tonya Condon; **page 45:** *1800 Woodcuts,* Dover Publications; **page 46:** John Vanderlyn, "The Death of Jane McCrea," Courtesy of the Wadsworth Atheneum, Hartford, CT; **page 47:** Courtesy Rockefeller Library, Colonial Williamsburg Foundation; **page 48:** *1800 Woodcuts,* Dover Publications; **page 53:** "Murder of Jane McCrea," Woodcut, Courtesy of Fort Ticonderoga Museum; **page 54:** Lossing, *Pictorial Fieldbook;* **page 55:** Janice Lang; **page 56:** Samuel Woodforde, "Death of Simon Fraser, 1777," Courtesy of the National Archives of Canada; **page 59:** Courtesy Rockefeller Library, Colonial Williamsburg Foundation; **page 60: Alonzo Chappel, "The Battle of Bennington" (detail), The Bennington Museum, Bennington, VT;** page 63: Courtesy of M. C. Lynne and M. M. Christian, Blue Darter's Guide of the American Revolution; **page 65:** Courtesy Rockefeller Library, Colonial Williamsburg Foundation; **page 66:** Courtesy Rockefeller Library, Colonial Williamsburg Foundation; **page 67:** *1800 Woodcuts,* Dover Publications; **page 69:** Chappel, "The Battle of Bennington" (detail), The Bennington Museum; **page 70:** Todd Condon, Native Sky Photography Studios, Ticonderoga, NY; **page 72:** *1800 Woodcuts,* Dover Publications; **page 73:** Janice Lang; **page 75:** Joshua Reynolds, "General John Burgoyne," Courtesy The Frick Collection, New York, NY; **page 76:** Janice Lang; **page 78:** *1800 Woodcuts,* Dover Publications; **page 80:** *1800 Woodcuts,* Dover Publications; **page 82:** Unknown artist, "Battle of Freeman's Farm" (detail), Fort Ticonderoga Museum; **page 84:** Michael Noonan Photography; **page 86:** Anburey, *Travels Through the Interior Parts of America,* Courtesy of Fort Ticonderoga Museum; **page 87:** Courtesy Rockefeller Library, Colonial Williamsburg Foundation; **page 88:** *1800 Woodcuts,* Dover Publications; **page 90:** Woodcut of Lady Acland, Courtesy of Fort Ticonderoga Museum; **page 92:** John Trumbull, "The Surrender of General Burgoyne at Saratoga, 16 October 1777," Yale University Art Gallery, Trumbull Collection, New Haven, CT; **page 93 top:** Jeanne Winston Adler; **page 93 bottom:** Rusty Riddell, Fine Art Photographer (518-792-4950); **page 94:** Lossing, *Pictorial Fieldbook;* **page 96:** Janice Lang; **page 97:** Unknown artist, "General Sir Guy Carleton," National Archives of Canada; **page 99:** Todd Condon; **page 101:** Lossing, *Pictorial Fieldbook;* **page 102:** Lossing, *Pictorial Fieldbook;* **page 105:** Janice Lang;

page 107: *1800 Woodcuts,* Dover Publications; **page 108:** Frontispiece, Timothy Mather Cooley, *Sketches of the Life and Character of the Reverend Lemuel Haynes, A.M.,* New York, 1837; **page 109:** Jean-Baptiste Antoine De Verger, "American Foot Soldiers, Yorktown Campaign," Anne S. K. Brown Military Collection, Brown University Library, Providence, RI; **page 110:** Unknown artist, "Portrait of a Revolutionary War Privateer," Courtesy of Alexander McBurney, Kingston, RI; **page 111:** *1800 Woodcuts,* Dover Publications; **page 112:** Tonya Condon; **page 114:** *1800 Woodcuts,* Dover Publications; **page 116:** Courtesy Clements Library, University of Michigan, Ann Arbor, MI; **page 117:** *1800 Woodcuts,* Dover Publications; **page 119:** *1800 Woodcuts,* Dover Publications; **page 120:** Drawing by C. Porter; **page 121:** *1800 Woodcuts,* Dover Publications; **page 122:** William Ranney, "Veterans of 1776 Returning from the War," 1848, Dallas Museum of Art, Dallas, TX; **page 128:** Tonya Condon; **page 129:** *1800 Woodcuts,* Dover Publications; **page 131:** *1800 Woodcuts,* Dover Publications; **page 132:** *1800 Woodcuts,* Dover Publications; **page 133:** Courtesy Rockefeller Library, Colonial Williamsburg Foundation; **page 134:** *1800 Woodcuts,* Dover Publications; **page 135:** Fitch, *Notes,* Washington County Clerk; **page 136:** Courtesy Rockefeller Library, Colonial Williamsburg Foundation; **page 138:** Courtesy Rockefeller Library, Colonial Williamsburg Foundation; **page 141:** Lossing, *Pictorial Fieldbook;* **page 142:** Janice Lang; **page 144:** *1800 Woodcuts,* Dover Publications; **page 145:** *1800 Woodcuts,* Dover Publications; **page 146:** *1800 Woodcuts,* Dover Publications; **page 147:** *1800 Woodcuts,* Dover Publications; **page 148:** William D. Cormier, Malta, NY; **page 150:** *1800 Woodcuts,* Dover Publications; **page 151 top:** Tonya Condon; **page 151 inset:** Courtesy Rockefeller Library, Colonial Williamsburg Foundation; **page 154:** *The Book of Trades; or, Library of the Useful Arts,* Tabert & Co., London, 1805; **page 155:** St. John Honeywood, "The Village of Salem in 1795," Photoreproduction in the collection of the Bancroft Library, Salem, NY, whereabouts of the original unknown.

INDEX

Java® Programming
for Android® Developers

2nd edition

by Barry Burd

for
dummies®
A Wiley Brand

Java® Programming for Android® Developers For Dummies®, 2nd Edition

Published by: **John Wiley & Sons, Inc.**, 111 River Street, Hoboken, NJ 07030-5774, www.wiley.com

Copyright © 2017 by John Wiley & Sons, Inc., Hoboken, New Jersey

Published simultaneously in Canada

Contents at a Glance

Table of Contents

Introduction

Android is everywhere. In mid-2016, Android runs on 65 percent of all smartphones in the United States, on 75 percent of all smartphones in EU5 countries, and on 77 percent of all smartphones in China.[1] In a study that spans the Americas, Europe, Asia, and the Middle East, GlobalWebIndex reports that "Android is the most favored OS when it comes to tablets, being used by almost a fifth of internet users and leading iPad by 5 points."[2] More than 2.2 million apps are available for download at the Google Play store.[3] And 9 million developers write code using Java, the language that powers Android devices.[4]

If you read this book in a public place (on a commuter train, at the beach, or on the dance floor at the Coyote Ugly saloon, for example), you can read proudly, with a chip on your shoulder and with your head held high. Android is hot stuff, and you're cool because you're reading about it.

How to Use This Book

You can attack this book in either of two ways: Go from cover to cover or poke around from one chapter to another. You can even do both (start at the beginning, and then jump to a section that particularly interests you). This book was designed so that the basic topics come first, and the more-involved topics follow them. But you may already be comfortable with some basics, or you may have specific goals that don't require you to know about certain topics.

[1] See www.kantarworldpanel.com/global/News/Android-Share-Growth-is-Highest-in-EU5-in-Over-Two-Years. The EU5 countries are France, Germany, Italy, Spain, and the United Kingdom.

[2] See www.globalwebindex.net/hubfs/Reports/GWI_Device_Report_-_Q3_2015_Summary.pdf.

[3] See www.statista.com/statistics/276623/number-of-apps-available-in-leading-app-stores.

[4] See www.java.com/en/about.

In general, my advice is this:

>> If you already know something, don't bother reading about it.

>> If you're curious, don't be afraid to skip ahead. You can always sneak a peek at an earlier chapter, if you need to do so.

Conventions Used in This Book

Almost every technically themed book starts with a little typeface legend, and *Java Programming for Android Developers For Dummies*, 2nd Edition, is no exception. What follows is a brief explanation of the typefaces used in this book:

>> New terms are set in *italics*.

>> If you need to type something that's mixed in with the regular text, the characters you type appear in bold. For example: "Type **MyNewProject** in the text field."

>> You also see this computerese font. I use computerese for Java code, file-names, onscreen messages, and other such things. Also, if something you need to type is really long, it appears in computerese font on its own line (or lines).

>> You may need to change certain things when you type them on your own computer keyboard. For instance, I may ask you to type

```
public void Anyname
```

which means that you type **public void** and then a name that you make up on your own. Words that you need to replace with your own words are set in *italicized computerese*.

What You Don't Have to Read

Pick the first chapter or section that has material you don't already know and start reading there. Of course, you may hate making decisions as much as I do. If so, here are some guidelines you can follow:

>> **If you already know what kind of an animal Java is and you don't care what happens behind the scenes when an Android app runs:** Skip Chapter 1 and go straight to Chapter 2. Believe me — I won't mind.

- » **If you already know how to get an Android app running:** Skip Part 1 and start with Part 2.

- » **If you have experience writing computer programs in languages other than C and C++:** Start with Part 2. You'll probably find Part II to be easy reading. When you get to Part 3, it'll be time to dive in.

- » **If you have experience writing computer programs in C or C++:** Skim Part II and start reading seriously in Part 3. (Java is a bit different from C++ in the way it handles classes and objects.)

- » **If you have experience writing Java programs:** Come to my house and help me write *Java Programming for Android Developers For Dummies,* 3rd Edition.

If you want to skip the sidebars and the paragraphs with Technical Stuff icons, please do. In fact, if you want to skip anything at all, feel free.

Foolish Assumptions

In this book, I make a few assumptions about you, the reader. If one of these assumptions is incorrect, you're probably okay. If all these assumptions are incorrect . . . well, buy the book anyway.

- » **I assume that you have access to a computer.** Access to an Android device is helpful but not absolutely necessary! All the software you need in order to test Android apps on a laptop or desktop computer is freely available. You simply download, install, and get going.

- » **I assume that you can navigate your computer's common menus and dialog boxes.** You don't have to be a Windows, Macintosh, or Linux power user, but you should be able to start a program, find a file, put a file into a certain directory — that sort of thing. Much of the time, when you follow the instructions in this book, you're typing code on the keyboard, not pointing and clicking the mouse.

  On those occasions when you need to drag and drop, cut and paste, or plug and play, I guide you carefully through the steps. But your computer may be configured in any of several billion ways, and my instructions may not quite fit your special situation. When you reach one of these platform-specific tasks, try following the steps in this book. If the steps don't quite fit, consult a book with instructions tailored to your system. If you can't find such a book, send me an email. (My address appears later in the Introduction.)

>> **I assume that you can think logically.** That's all there is to application development — thinking logically. If you can think logically, you've got it made. If you don't believe that you can think logically, read on. You may be pleasantly surprised.

>> **I make very few assumptions about your computer programming experience (or your lack of such experience).** In writing this book, I've tried to do the impossible: make the book interesting for experienced programmers yet accessible to people with little or no programming experience. This means that I don't assume any particular programming background on your part. If you've never created a loop or indexed an array, that's okay.

On the other hand, if you've done these things (maybe in Visual Basic, COBOL, or C++), you'll discover some interesting plot twists in Java. The creators of Java took the best ideas from object-oriented programming, streamlined them, reworked them, and reorganized them into a sleek, powerful way of thinking about problems. You'll find many new, thought-provoking features in Java. As you find out about these features, many of them will seem quite natural to you. One way or another, you'll feel good about using Java.

How This Book Is Organized

This book is divided into subsections, which are grouped into sections, which come together to make chapters, which are lumped, finally, into five parts (like one of those Russian *matryoshka* dolls). The parts of the book are described here.

Part 1: Getting Started with Java Programming for Android Developers

Part 1 covers all the nuts and bolts. It introduces you to the major ideas behind Java and Android software development and walks you through the installation of the necessary software products. You also run a few simple Java and Android programs.

The instructions in these chapters cover both Windows and Macintosh computers. They cover many computer configurations, including some not-so-new operating system versions, 32-bit systems and 64-bit systems, and situations in which you already have some form of Java on your computer. But installing software is always tricky, and you might have a few hurdles to overcome. If you do, check the end of this chapter for ways to reach me (the author) and get some quick advice. (Yes, I answer emails, tweets, Facebook posts, and notes sent by carrier pigeons.)

Part 2: Writing Your Own Java Programs

Chapters 4 through 8 cover Java's basic building blocks. These chapters describe the things you need to know so that you can get your computer humming along.

If you've written programs in Visual Basic, C++, or any other language, some of the material in Part 2 may be familiar to you. If so, you can skip sections or read this stuff quickly. But don't read *too* quickly. Java is a little different from some other programming languages, and Java's differences are worth noting.

Part 3: Working with the Big Picture: Object-Oriented Programming

Part 3 has some of my favorite chapters. This part covers the all-important topic of object-oriented programming. In these chapters, you find out how to map solutions to big problems. (Sure, the examples in these chapters aren't big, but the examples involve big ideas.) You discover, in bite-worthy increments, how to design classes, reuse existing classes, and construct objects.

Have you read any of those books that explain object-oriented programming in vague, general terms? I'm very proud to say that *Java Programming for Android Developers For Dummies,* 2nd Edition, isn't like that. In this book, I illustrate each concept with a simple-yet-concrete program example.

Part 4: Powering Android with Java Code

If you've tasted some Java and want more, you can find what you need in Part 4 of this book. This part's chapters are devoted to details — the things you don't see when you first glance at the material. This part includes some fully functional Android apps. So, after you read the earlier parts and write some programs on your own, you can dive in a little deeper by reading Part 4.

Part 5: The Part of Tens

In The Part of Tens, which is a little Java candy store, you can find lists — lists of tips for avoiding mistakes, tracking down resources, and finding all kinds of interesting goodies.

More on the web!

You've read the *Java Programming for Android Developers* book, seen the *Java Programming for Android Developers* movie, worn the *Java Programming for Android Developers* T-shirt, and eaten the *Java Programming for Android Developers* candy. What more is there to do?

That's easy. Just visit this book's website: www.allmycode.com/Java4Android. There you can find updates, comments, additional information, and answers to commonly asked questions from readers. You can also find a small chat application for sending me quick questions when I'm online. (When I'm not online, you can contact me in other ways. See the end of this chapter for more info.)

Icons Used in This Book

If you could watch me write this book, you'd see me sitting at my computer, talking to myself. I say each sentence in my head. Most of the sentences I mutter several times. When I have an extra thought, a side comment, or something else that doesn't belong in the regular stream, I twist my head a little bit. That way, whoever's listening to me (usually nobody) knows that I'm off on a momentary tangent.

Of course, in print, you can't see me twisting my head. I need some other way to set a side thought in a corner by itself. I do it with icons. When you see a Tip icon or a Remember icon, you know that I'm taking a quick detour.

Here's a list of icons that I use in this book:

TIP

A tip is an extra piece of information — helpful advice that the other books may forget to tell you.

WARNING

Everyone makes mistakes. Heaven knows that I've made a few in my time. Anyway, when I think people are especially prone to make a mistake, I mark the text with a Warning icon.

REMEMBER

Question: What's stronger than a tip but not as strong as a warning?

Answer: A Remember icon.

CROSS-REFERENCE

"If you don't remember what *such-and-such* means, see *blah-blah-blah*," or "For more information, read *blahbity-blah-blah*."

ON THE WEB

This icon calls attention to useful material that you can find online. (You don't have to wait long to see one of these icons. I use one at the end of this introduction!)

TECHNICAL STUFF

Occasionally, I run across a technical tidbit. The tidbit may help you understand what the people behind the scenes (the people who created Java) were thinking. You don't have to read it, but you may find it useful. You may also find the tidbit helpful if you plan to read other (geekier) books about Java and Android.

Beyond the Book

In addition to what you're reading right now, this book comes with a free access-anywhere Cheat Sheet containing code that you can copy and paste into your own Android program. To get this Cheat Sheet, simply go to www.dummies.com and type **"Java Programming for Android Developers For Dummies Cheat Sheet"** in the Search box.

Where to Go from Here

If you've gotten this far, you're ready to start reading about Java and Android application development. Think of me (the author) as your guide, your host, your personal assistant. I do everything I can to keep things interesting and, most importantly, to help you understand.

ON THE WEB

If you like what you read, send me a note. My email address, which I created just for comments and questions about this book, is java4android @allmycode.com. If email and chat aren't your favorites, you can reach me instead on Twitter (@allmycode) and on Facebook (/allmycode). And don't forget — for the latest updates, visit this book's website. The site's address is www.allmycode.com/java4android.

1

Getting Started with Java Programming for Android Developers

Chapter **1**

All about Java and Android

U ntil the mid-2000s, the word *android* represented a mechanical, human-like creature — a rootin'-tootin' officer of the law with built-in machine guns or a hyperlogical space traveler who can do everything except speak using contractions. And then in 2005, Google purchased Android, Inc. — a 22-month-old company creating software for mobile phones. That move changed everything.

In 2007, a group of 34 companies formed the Open Handset Alliance. Its task is "to accelerate innovation in mobile and offer consumers a richer, less expensive, and better mobile experience"; its primary project is *Android,* an open, free operating system based on the Linux operating system kernel.

Though HTC released the first commercially available Android phone near the end of 2008, in the United States the public's awareness of Android and its potential didn't surface until early 2010.

Since then, Android's ecosystem has enjoyed steady growth. Kantar Worldpanel ComTech reports (at `www.kantarworldpanel.com/global/smartphone-os-market-share/article`): "The latest smartphone OS data . . . for the three months ending March 2016 shows Android continuing to grow sales across the EU5, US, and Urban China. There were solid gains in the EU5 (Great Britain, Germany,

France, Italy, and Spain), up 7.1% points to 75.6%. In the US, Android share increased 7.3% points to 65.5%, and in China, it rose nearly 6% points to over 77%."[1]

The Consumer Perspective

A consumer considers the alternatives:

>> **Possibility #1: No mobile phone**

Advantages: Inexpensive; no interruptions from callers.

Disadvantages: No instant contact with friends and family; no calls to services in case of emergencies.

>> **Possibility #2: A feature phone**

This type of mobile phone isn't a smartphone. Though no official rule defines the boundary between feature phone and smartphone, a feature phone generally has an inflexible menu of Home screen options, compared with a smartphone's "desktop" of downloaded apps.

Advantage: Less expensive than a smartphone.

Disadvantages: Less versatile than a smartphone, not nearly as cool as a smartphone, and nowhere near as much fun as a smartphone.

>> **Possibility #3: An iPhone**

Advantages: Great-looking graphics.

Disadvantages: Little or no flexibility with the single-vendor iOS operating system; only a handful of models to choose from.

>> **Possibility #4: A Windows phone or another non-Android, non-Apple smartphone**

Advantage: Having a smartphone without having to belong to a crowd.

Disadvantage: The possibility of owning an orphan product when the smartphone wars come to a climax.

[1]See www.kantarworldpanel.com/global/smartphone-os-market-share/article.

>> **Possibility #5: An Android phone**

   Advantages: Using a popular, open platform with lots of industry support and powerful market momentum; writing your own software and installing it on your own phone (without having to post the software on a company's website); publishing software without having to face a challenging approval process.

   Disadvantages: Security concerns when using an open platform; dismay when iPhone users make fun of your phone.

For me, Android's advantages far outweigh its possible disadvantages. And you're reading a paragraph from *Java Programming for Android Developers For Dummies*, 2nd Edition, so you're likely to agree with me.

The Many Faces of Android

Version numbers can be tricky. My PC's model number is T420s. When I download the users' guide, I download one guide for any laptop in the T400 series. (No guide specifically addresses the T420, let alone the T420s.) But when I have driver problems, knowing that I have a T420s isn't good enough. I need drivers that are specific to my laptop's 7-digit model number. The moral to this story: What constitutes a "version number" depends on who's asking for the number.

With that in mind, you can see a history of Android versions in Figure 1-1.

A few notes on Figure 1-1 are in order:

>> **The platform number is of interest to the consumer and to the company that sells the hardware.**

   If you're buying a phone with Android 5.1, for example, you might want to know whether the vendor will upgrade your phone to Android 6.0.

>> **The API level (also known as the SDK version) is of interest to the Android app developer.**

   For example, the word MATCH_PARENT has a specific meaning in Android API Levels 8 and higher. You might type MATCH_PARENT in code that uses API Level 7. If you do (and if you expect MATCH_PARENT to have that specific meaning), you'll get a nasty-looking error message.

	Platform	API Level	Codename	Features
2008	1.0	1		
2009	1.1	2		
	1.5	3	Cupcake	
	1.6	4	Donut	Maturing app market interface, better voice tools, 800x480
	2.0	5	Eclair	Better user interface, more screen sizes, more camera functionality, Bluetooth 2.1 support, multi-touch support
	2.0.1	6		
	2.1	7		
2010	2.2	8	Froyo	Better performance with just-in-time (JIT) compiler, USB tethering, 720p screen, ability to install apps to the SD card
2011	2.3	9	Gingerbread	System-wide copy/paste, multi-touch soft keyboard, better native code development, concurrent garbage collection
	2.3.3	10		
	3.0	11	Honeycomb	Designed for tablets, new soft keyboard, tabbed browsing, redesigned widgets, "holographic UI", interface fragments
	3.1	12		
	3.2	13		
	4.0	14	Ice Cream Sandwich	Customizable launcher, screenshot capture, face unlock, Chrome browser, near-field communication, Roboto font
	4.0.3	15		
2012	4.1.2	16	Jelly Bean	Expandable notifications, Google Now, smoother drawing, improved voice search
	4.2.2	17		
2013	4.3	18		
	4.4	19	KitKat	Immersive mode for apps, WebViews based on Chromium, text messaging management, UI transitions framework
2011	2.3	9	Gingerbread	System-wide copy/paste, multi-touch soft keyboard, better native code development, concurrent garbage collection
	2.3.3	10		
	3.0	11	Honeycomb	Designed for tablets, new soft keyboard, tabbed browsing, redesigned widgets, "holographic UI", interface fragments
	3.1	12		
	3.2	13		
	4.0	14	Ice Cream Sandwich	Customizable launcher, screenshot capture, face unlock, Chrome browser, near-field communication, Roboto font
	4.0.3	15		
2012	4.1.2	16	Jelly Bean	Expandable notifications, Google Now, smoother drawing, improved voice search
	4.2.2	17		
2013	4.3	18		
	4.4	19	KitKat	Immersive mode for apps, WebViews based on Chromium, text messaging management, UI transitions framework
2014	4.4W	20		API for wrist watches (Android Wear)
	5.0	21	Lollipop	Material Design has shadows and animations
2015	5.1	22		
	6.0	23	Marshmallow	New way of approving permissions, doze mode puts the device on standby to save power
2016	7.0	24	Nougat	Apps can share the screen, virtual reality support

FIGURE 1-1: Versions of Android.

CROSS-REFERENCE

You can read more about the Application Programming Interface (API) in Chapter 2. For more information about the use of Android's API levels (SDK versions) in your code, see Chapter 3. For even more information about Android API levels, visit

```
http://developer.android.com/guide/appendix/api-levels.html-level
```

>> **The code name is of interest to the creators of Android.**

A *code name* refers to the work done by the creators of Android to bring Android to the next official level. Android's code names are desserts, working in alphabetical order starting with Cupcake, Donut, Eclair, and so on. Picture Google's engineers working for months behind closed doors on Project Marshmallow.

In recent years, this naming scheme has become a lot more transparent. For example, Google created an online poll to help decide on an *N* word as the successor to Android Marshmallow. After a month of voting, Android Nougat was announced.

REMEMBER

An Android version may have variations. For example, plain ol' Android 6.0 has an established set of features. To plain ol' Android 6.0 you can add the Google Play Services (the ability to install apps from Google Play) and still be using platform 6.0. You can also add a special set of features tailored for various phone manufacturers.

As a developer, your job is to balance portability with feature-richness. When you create an app, you specify a minimum Android version. (You can read more about this topic in Chapter 3.) The higher the version, the more features your app can have. On the flip side, the higher the version, the fewer devices that can run your app.

The Developer Perspective

Android is a multifaceted beast. When you develop for the Android platform, you use many toolsets. This section gives you a brief rundown.

Java

James Gosling of Sun Microsystems created the Java programming language in the mid-1990s. (Sun Microsystems has since been bought by Oracle.) Java's meteoric rise in use stemmed from the elegance of the language and its well-conceived platform architecture. After a brief blaze of glory with applets and the web, Java settled into being a solid, general-purpose language with a special strength in servers and middleware.

In the meantime, Java was quietly seeping into embedded processors. Sun Microsystems was developing Java Mobile Edition (Java ME) for creating small apps to run on mobile phones. Java became a major technology in Blu-ray disc players. So the decision to make Java the primary development language for Android apps is no big surprise.

An *embedded processor* is a computer chip that is hidden from the user as part of a special-purpose device. The chips in cars are now embedded processors, and the silicon that powers the photocopier at your workplace is an embedded processor. Pretty soon, the flowerpots on your windowsill will probably have embedded processors.

Figure 1-2 describes the development of new Java versions over time. Like Android, each Java version has several names. The *product version* is an official name that's used for the world in general, and the *developer version* is a number that identifies versions so that programmers can keep track of them. (In casual conversation, developers use all kinds of names for the various Java versions.) The *code name* is a more playful name that identifies a version while it's being created.

The asterisks in Figure 1-2 mark changes in the formulation of Java product-version names. Back in 1996, the product versions were *Java Development Kit 1.0* and *Java Development Kit 1.1*. In 1998, someone decided to christen the product *Java 2 Standard Edition 1.2*, which confuses everyone to this day. At the time, anyone using the term *Java Development Kit* was asked to use *Software Development Kit (SDK)* instead.

In 2004 the *1.* business went away from the platform version name, and in 2006, Java platform names lost the *2* and the *.0*. For Java SE 9, the developer versions stopped being numbers like *1.9* and became plain old *9*.

By far the most significant changes for Java developers came about with J2SE 5.0 and Java SE 8. With the release of J2SE 5.0, the overseers of Java made changes to the language by adding many new features — features such as generic types, annotations, varargs, and the enhanced `for` statement. With Java SE 8 came new functional programming features.

To see Java annotations in action, go to Chapter 10. For examples of the use of generic types, varargs, and the enhanced `for` statement, see Chapter 12. To read about functional programming features, see Chapter 11.

Year	Product Version	Developer Version	Codename	Features
1995 (Beta)				
1996	JDK* 1.0	1.0		
1997	JDK 1.1	1.1		Inner classes, Java Beans, reflection
1998	J2SE* 1.2	1.2	Playground	Collections, Swing classes for creation of GUI interfaces
1999				
2000	J2SE 1.3	1.3	Kestrel	Java Naming and Directory Interface (JNDI)
2001				
2002	J2SE 1.4	1.4	Merlin	New I/O, regular expressions, XML parsing
2003				
2004	J2SE 5.0*	1.5	Tiger	Generic types, annotations, enum types, varargs, enhanced for statement, static imports, new concurrency classes
2005				
2006	Java SE* 6	1.6	Mustang	Scripting language support, performance enhancements
2007				
2008				
2009				
2010				
2011	Java SE 7	1.7	Dolphin	Strings in switch statement, catching multiple exceptions try statement with resources , integration with JavaFX
2012				
2013	Java SE 8	1.8		Lambda expressions and other functional programming features
2014				
2015				
2016				
2017	Java SE 9	9*		Division of code into modules and an interactive environment (known as a Read-eval-print loop or a REPL) to test code quickly

FIGURE 1-2:
Versions of Java.

TIP

In addition to all the numbers in Figure 1-2, you'll see codes like *Java SE 8u91*. A code such as *8u91* stands for the 91st update of Java 8. For a novice Java developer, these updates don't make very much difference.

XML

If you find View Source among your web browser's options one day and decide to use it, you'll see a bunch of HyperText Markup Language (HTML) tags. A *tag* is some text, enclosed in angle brackets, that describes something about its neighboring content.

For example, to create boldface type on a web page, a web designer writes

```
<b>Look at this!</b>
```

The b tags in angle brackets turn boldface type on and off.

The *M* in HTML stands for *Markup* — a general term describing any extra text that annotates a document's content. When you annotate a document's content, you embed information about the content into the document itself. For example, in the previous line of code, the content is Look at this! The markup (information about the content) consists of the tags <b> and </b>.

The HTML standard is an outgrowth of Standard Generalized Markup Language (SGML), an all-things-to-all-people technology for marking up documents for use by all kinds of processors running all kinds of software and sold by all kinds of vendors.

In the mid-1990s, a working group of the World Wide Web Consortium (W3C) began developing the eXtensible Markup Language, commonly known as *XML*. The working group's goal was to create a subset of SGML for use in transmitting data over the Internet. It succeeded. XML is now a well-established standard for encoding information of all kinds.

For an overview of XML, see the sidebar "All about XML files" in Chapter 3.

CROSS-REFERENCE

Java is good for describing step-by-step instructions, and XML is good for describing the way things are (or the way they should be). A Java program says, "Do this and then do that." In contrast, an XML document says, "It's this way and it's that way." Android uses XML for two purposes:

>> **To describe an app's data**

An app's XML documents describe the layout of the app's screens, the translations of the app into one or more languages, and other kinds of data.

>> **To describe the app itself**

Every Android app has an AndroidManifest.xml file, an XML document that describes features of the app. A device's operating system uses the

`AndroidManifest.xml` document's contents to manage the running of the app.

For example, an app's `AndroidManifest.xml` file lists the screens that the user sees during a run of the app and tells a device which screen to display when the app is first launched. The same file tells the device which of the app's screens can be borrowed for use by other apps.

CROSS-
REFERENCE

For more information about the `AndroidManifest.xml` file, see Chapter 4.

Concerning XML, I have bad news and good news. The bad news is that XML isn't always easy to compose. At best, writing XML code is boring. At worst, writing XML code is downright confusing. The good news is that automated software tools compose most of the world's XML code. As an Android programmer, I know that the software on your development processor composes much of your app's XML code. You often tweak the XML code, read part of the code for information from its source, make minor changes, and compose brief additions. But you hardly ever create XML documents from scratch.

Linux

An *operating system* is a big program that manages the overall running of a processor or a device. Most operating systems are built in layers. An operating system's outer layers are usually in the user's face. For example, both Windows and Macintosh OS X have standard desktops. From the desktop, the user launches programs, manages windows, and does other important things.

An operating system's inner layers are (for the most part) invisible to the user. While the user plays Solitaire, for example, the operating system juggles processes, manages files, keeps an eye on security, and generally does the kinds of things that the user shouldn't have to micromanage.

At the deepest level of an operating system is the system's kernel. The *kernel* runs directly on the processor's hardware and does the low-level work required to make the processor run. In a truly layered system, higher layers accomplish work by making calls to lower layers. So an app with a specific hardware request sends the request (directly or indirectly) through the kernel.

The best-known, best-loved general purpose operating systems are Windows, Macintosh OS X (which is really Unix), and Linux. Both Windows and Mac OS X are the properties of their respective companies. But Linux is open source. That's one reason why your TiVo runs Linux and why the creators of Android based their platform on the Linux kernel.

As a developer, your most intimate contact with the Android operating system is via the command line, also known as the *Linux shell.* The shell uses commands such as cd to change to a directory, ls to list a directory's files and subdirectories, rm to delete files, and many others.

Google Play has plenty of free terminal apps. A *terminal* app's interface is a plain-text screen on which you type Linux shell commands. And by using one of Android's developer tools, the Android Debug Bridge, you can issue shell commands to an Android device via your development computer. If you like getting your virtual hands dirty, the Linux shell is for you.

From Development to Execution with Java

Before Java became popular, running a computer program involved one translation step. Someone (or something) translated the code that a developer wrote into more cryptic code that a computer could actually execute. But then Java came along and added an extra translation layer, and then Android added another layer. This section describes all those layers.

What is a compiler?

A Java program (such as an Android application program) undergoes several translation steps between the time you write the program and the time a processor runs the program. One of the reasons is simple: Instructions that are convenient for processors to run are not convenient for people to write.

People can write and comprehend the code in Listing 1-1.

LISTING 1-1: Java Source Code

```
public void checkVacancy(View view) {
    if (room.numGuests == 0) {
        label.setText("Available");
    } else {
        label.setText("Taken :-(");
    }
}
```

The Java code in Listing 1-1 checks for a vacancy in a hotel. You can't run the code in this listing without adding several additional lines. But here in Chapter 1, those additional lines aren't important. What's important is that, by staring at the code, squinting a bit, and looking past all its strange punctuation, you can see what the code is trying to do:

```
If the room has no guests in it,
    then set the label's text to "Available".
Otherwise,
    set the label's text to "Taken :-(".
```

The content of Listing 1-1 is *Java source code.*

The processors in computers, phones, and other devices don't normally follow instructions like the instructions in Listing 1-1. That is, processors don't follow Java source code instructions. Instead, processors follow cryptic instructions like the ones in Listing 1-2.

LISTING 1-2: **Java Bytecode**

```
0 aload_0
1 getfield #19 <com/allmycode/samples/MyActivity/room
Lcom/allmycode/samples/Room;>
4 getfield #47 <com/allmycode/samples/Room/numGuests I>
7 ifne 22 (+15)
10 aload_0
11 getfield #41 <com/allmycode/samples/MyActivity/label
Landroid/widget/TextView;>
14 ldc #54 <Available>
16 invokevirtual #56
    <android/widget/TextView/setText
    (Ljava/lang/CharSequence;)V>
19 goto 31 (+12)
22 aload_0
23 getfield #41 <com/allmycode/samples/MyActivity/label
Landroid/widget/TextView;>
26 ldc #60 <Taken :-(>
28 invokevirtual #56
    <android/widget/TextView/setText
    (Ljava/lang/CharSequence;)V>
31 return
```

The instructions in Listing 1-2 aren't Java source code instructions. They're *Java bytecode instructions.* When you write a Java program, you write source code instructions. (Refer to Listing 1-1.) After writing the source code, you run a program (that is, you apply a tool) to the source code. The program is a *compiler:* It translates your source code instructions into Java bytecode instructions. In other words, the compiler translates code that you can write and understand (again, refer to Listing 1-1) into code that a processor can execute. (Refer to Listing 1-2.)

At this point, you might ask, "What will I have to do to get the compiler running?" The answer to your question is "Android Studio." All the translation steps described in this chapter come down to using Android Studio — a piece of software that you download for free using the instructions in Chapter 2. So when you read in this chapter about compiling and other translation steps, don't become intimidated. You don't have to repair an alternator in order to drive a car, and you won't have to understand how compilers work in order to use Android Studio.

REMEMBER

No one (except for a few crazy developers in isolated labs in faraway places) writes Java bytecode. You run software (a compiler) to create Java bytecode. The only reason to look at Listing 1-2 is to understand what a hard worker your computer is.

If compiling is a good thing, compiling twice is even better.

In 2007, Dan Bornstein at Google created *Dalvik bytecode* — another way to represent instructions for processors to follow. (To find out where some of Bornstein's ancestors come from, run your favorite map application and look for Dalvik in Iceland.) Dalvik bytecode is optimized for the limited resources on a phone or a tablet device.

Listing 1-3 contains sample Dalvik instructions.

* To see the code in Listing 1-3, I used the Dedexer program (from `http://dedexer.sourceforge.net`).

LISTING 1-3: | **Dalvik Bytecode**

```
.method public checkVacancy(Landroid/view/View;)V
.limit registers 4
; this: v2 (Lcom/allmycode/samples/MyActivity;)
; parameter[0] : v3 (Landroid/view/View;)
.line 30
    iget-object
    v0,v2,com/allmycode/samples/MyActivity.room
    Lcom/allmycode/samples/Room;
; v0 : Lcom/allmycode/samples/Room; , v2 :
    Lcom/allmycode/samples/MyActivity;
    iget    v0,v0,com/allmycode/samples/Room.numGuests I
; v0 : single-length , v0 : single-length
    if-nez    v0,14b4
```

```
; v0 : single-length
.line 31
    iget-object
    v0,v2,com/allmycode/samples/MyActivity.label
    Landroid/widget/TextView;
; v0 : Landroid/widget/TextView; , v2 :
    Lcom/allmycode/samples/MyActivity;
    const-string    v1,"Available"
; v1 : Ljava/lang/String;
    invoke-virtual
    {v0,v1},android/widget/TextView/setText
    ; setText(Ljava/lang/CharSequence;)V
; v0 : Landroid/widget/TextView; , v1 : Ljava/lang/String;
14b2:
.line 36
    return-void
14b4:
.line 33
    iget-object
    v0,v2,com/allmycode/samples/MyActivity.label
    Landroid/widget/TextView;
; v0 : Landroid/widget/TextView; , v2 :
    Lcom/allmycode/samples/MyActivity;
    const-string    v1,"Taken :-("
; v1 : Ljava/lang/String;
    invoke-virtual
    {v0,v1},android/widget/TextView/setText ;
    setText(Ljava/lang/CharSequence;)V
; v0 : Landroid/widget/TextView; , v1 : Ljava/lang/String;
    goto    14b2
.end method
```

When you create an app, Android Studio performs at least two compilations:

>> **One compilation creates Java bytecode from your Java source files.** The source filenames have the .java extension; the Java bytecode filenames have the .class extension.

>> **Another compilation creates Dalvik bytecode from your Java bytecode files.** Dalvik bytecode filenames have the .dex extension.

But that's not all! In addition to its Java code, an Android app has XML files, image files, and possibly other elements. Before you install an app on a device, Android Studio combines all these elements into a single file — one with the .apk extension. When you publish the app on an app store, you copy that .apk file to the app store's servers. Then, to install your app, a user visits the app store and downloads your .apk file.

To perform the compilation from source code to Java bytecode, Android Studio uses a program named javac, also known as the Java compiler. To perform the compilation from Java bytecode to Dalvik code, Android Studio uses a program named dx (known affectionately as "the dx tool"). To combine all your app's files into one .apk file, Android Studio uses a program named apkbuilder.

What is a virtual machine?

In the section "What is a compiler?" earlier in this chapter, I make a big fuss about phones and other devices following instructions like the ones in Listing 1-3. As fusses go, it's a nice fuss. But if you don't read every fussy word, you may be misguided. The exact wording is ". . . processors follow cryptic instructions *like* the ones in Listing 'blah-blah-blah.'" The instructions in Listing 1-3 are a lot like instructions that a phone or tablet can execute, but computers generally don't execute Java bytecode instructions, and phones don't execute Dalvik bytecode instructions. Instead, each kind of processor has its own set of executable instructions, and each operating system uses the processor's instructions in a slightly different way.

Imagine that you have two different devices: a smartphone and a tablet computer. The devices have two different kinds of processors: The phone has an ARM processor, and the tablet has an Intel Atom processor. (The acronym ARM once stood for Advanced RISC Machine. These days, *ARM* simply stands for ARM Holdings, a company whose employees design processors.) On the ARM processor, the *multiply* instruction is 000000. On an Intel processor, the *multiply* instructions are D8, DC, F6, F7, and others. Many ARM instructions have no counterparts in the Atom architecture, and many Atom instructions have no equivalents on an ARM processor. An ARM processor's instructions make no sense to your tablet's Atom processor, and an Atom processor's instructions would give your phone's ARM processor a virtual headache.

What's a developer to do? Does a developer provide translations of every app into every processor's instruction set?

No. Virtual machines create order from all this chaos. Dalvik bytecode is similar to the code in Listing 1-3, but Dalvik bytecode isn't specific to a single kind of processor or to a single operating system. Instead, a set of Dalvik bytecode instructions runs on any processor. If you write a Java program and compile that Java program into Dalvik bytecode, your Android phone can run the bytecode, your Android tablet can run the bytecode, your Chromebook can run the bytecode, and even your grandmother's supercomputer can run the bytecode. (If your grandmother wants to do this, she should install *Remix OS,* a special port of the Android operating system, on her Intel-based machine. Tell her to visit `www.jide.com/remixos-for-pc`.)

You never have to write or decipher Java bytecode or Dalvik bytecode. Writing bytecode is the compiler's job. Deciphering bytecode is the virtual machine's job.

Both Java bytecode and Dalvik bytecode have virtual machines. Java bytecode's virtual machine is called (big surprise) the *Java virtual machine* (JVM). Dalvik bytecode's virtual machine is called the *Android runtime* (ART).

With the Android runtime, you can take a bytecode file that you created for one Android device, copy the bytecode to another Android device, and then run the bytecode with no trouble. That's one of the many reasons Android has become popular quickly. This outstanding feature, which lets you run code on many different kinds of processors, is called *portability.*

Imagine that you're the Intel representative to the United Nations Security Council, as shown in Figure 1-3. The ARM representative is seated to your right, and the representative from Qualcomm is to your left. (Naturally, you don't get along with either of these people. You're always cordial to one another, but you're never sincere. What do you expect? It's politics!) The distinguished representative from Dalvik is at the podium. The Dalvik representative speaks in Dalvik bytecode, and neither you nor your fellow ambassadors (ARM and Qualcomm) understand a word of Dalvik bytecode.

But each of you has an interpreter. Your interpreter translates from Dalvik bytecode to Intel instructions as the Dalvik representative speaks. Another interpreter translates from bytecode to "ARM-ese." And a third interpreter translates bytecode into "Qualcomm-speak."

Think of your interpreter as a virtual ambassador. The interpreter doesn't really represent your country, but the interpreter performs one important task that a real ambassador performs: It listens to Dalvik bytecode on your behalf. The interpreter does what you would do if your native language were Dalvik bytecode. The interpreter, pretending to be the Intel ambassador, endures the boring bytecode speech, taking in every word and processing each one in some way or another.

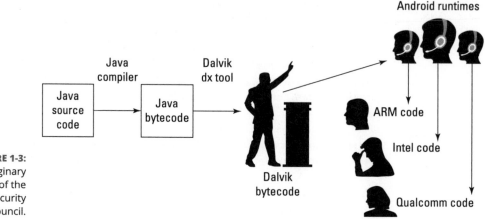

FIGURE 1-3:
An imaginary
meeting of the
U.N. Security
Council.

You have an interpreter — a virtual ambassador. In the same way, an Intel processor runs its own bytecode-interpreting software. That software is the Dalvik virtual machine — a proxy, an errand boy, a go-between. The *Android runtime* serves as an interpreter between Dalvik's run-anywhere bytecode and your device's own system. As it runs, the virtual machine walks your device through the execution of bytecode instructions. It examines your bytecode, bit by bit, and carries out the instructions described in the bytecode. The virtual machine interprets bytecode for your ARM processor, your Intel processor, your Qualcomm chip, or whatever kind of processor you're using. That's a good thing. It's what makes Java code and Dalvik code more portable than code written in any other language.

Java, Android, and Horticulture

"You don't see the forest for the trees," said my Uncle Harvey. To which my Aunt Clara said, "You don't see the trees for the forest." This argument went on until they were both too tired to discuss the matter.

As an author, I like to present both the forest and the trees. The "forest" is the broad overview, which helps you understand why you perform various steps. The "trees" are the steps themselves, getting you from Point A to Point B until you complete a task.

This chapter shows you the forest. The rest of this book shows you the trees.

Chapter **2**

Getting the Tools That You Need

e**rgaliophile** /ɜr gə li ə faɪ əl/ *noun* 1. A lover of tools. 2. A person who visits garage sales for rusty metal implements that might be useful someday but probably won't. 3. A person whose computer runs slowly because of the daily, indiscriminate installation of free software tools.

Several years ago, I found an enormous monkey wrench (more than a yard long and weighing 35 pounds) at a nearby garage sale. I wasn't a good plumber, and to this day any pipe that I fix starts leaking again immediately. But I couldn't resist buying this fine piece of hardware. The only problem was, my wife was sitting in the car about halfway down the street. She's much more sensible than I am about these matters, so I couldn't bring the wrench back to the car. "Put it aside and I'll come back for it later," I told the seller.

When I returned to the car empty-handed, my wife said, "I saw someone carrying the world's largest pipe wrench. I'm glad you weren't the one who bought it." And I agreed with her. "I don't need more junk like that."

So of course I returned later that day to buy the monkey wrench, and to this day the wrench sits in our attic, where no one ever sees it. If my wife ever reads this chapter, she'll be either amused or angry. I hope she's not angry, but I'm taking the risk because I enjoy the little drama. To add excitement to my life, I'm turning this trivial secret into a public announcement.

The Stuff You Need

This book tells you how to write Java programs, and before you can write them, you need some software tools. Here's a list of the tools you need:

>> **The Java Development Kit (JDK)**

This includes a Java virtual machine, the Java code libraries, and some additional software for developing Java code.

>> **An integrated development environment**

You can create Android apps using geeky, keyboard-only tools, but eventually you'll tire of typing and retyping commands. An *integrated development environment* (IDE), on the other hand, is a little like a word processor: A word processor helps you compose documents (memos, poems, and other works of fine literature); in contrast, an IDE helps you compose instructions for processors.

For composing Android apps, you need the Android Studio IDE.

>> **The Android Software Development Kit**

The Android *Software Development Kit (SDK)* includes lots and lots of prewritten, reusable Android code and a bunch of software tools for running and testing Android apps.

The prewritten Android code is the Android *Application Programming Interface (API)*. The API comes in several versions — versions 21 and 22 (both code-named Lollipop), version 23 (Marshmallow), version 24 (Nougat), and so on.

>> **Some sample Android code projects to help you get started**

All examples in this book are available for download from www.allmycode.com/Java4Android.

All these tools run on the *development computer* — the laptop or desktop computer you use to develop Java programs and Android apps. After you create an Android app, you copy the app's code from the development computer to a *target device* — a phone, a tablet, or (someday soon) a refrigerator that runs Android.

Here's good news: You can download from the web all the software you need to run this book's examples for free. The software is separated into three downloads:

» When you visit www.oracle.com/technetwork/java/javase/downloads, you can click a button to install the Java JDK.

» A button at the page http://developer.android.com/studio gives you the Android Studio IDE download and the Android Software Development Kit.

» This book's website (www.allmycode.com/Java4Android) has a link to all code in this book.

WARNING

The Java and Android websites I describe in this chapter are always changing. The software programs you download from these sites change, too. A specific instruction such as "Click the button in the upper-right corner" becomes obsolete (and even misleading) in no time at all. So, in this chapter, I provide explicit steps, but I also describe the ideas behind them. Browse the suggested sites and look for ways to get the software I describe. When a website offers you several options, check the instructions in this chapter for hints on choosing the best option. If your Android Studio window doesn't look quite like the one in this chapter's figures, scan your computer's window for whatever options I describe. If, after all that effort, you can't find the elements you're looking for, check this book's website (www.allmycode.com/Java4Android) or send an email to me at Java4Android@allmycode.com.

If You Don't Like to Read the Instructions . . .

I start this chapter with a brief (but useful) overview of the steps required in order to set up the software you need. If you're an old hand at installing software, and if your computer isn't quirky, these fast-track steps will probably serve you well. If not, you can read the more detailed instructions in the next several sections.

1. **Visit** www.allmycode.com/Java4Android **and download a file containing all the program examples in this book.**

The downloaded file is a .zip archive file. (See the sidebars entitled "Those pesky filename extensions" and "Compressed archive files , later in this chapter.")

2. **Extract the contents of the downloaded file to a place on your computer's hard drive.**

3. **Visit** www.oracle.com/technetwork/java/javase/downloads **and download the Java Standard Edition JDK.**

    Choose a version of the software that matches your operating system (Windows, Macintosh, or whatever) and your operating system's word length (32-bit or 64-bit).

4. **Install the Java Standard Edition JDK.**

    Double-click the .exe file or the .dmg file that you downloaded in Step 3, and proceed with whatever steps you usually take when you install software.

5. **Visit** http://developer.android.com/studio **and download the Android Studio IDE along with the Android Software Development Kit (SDK).**

    The combined download bundle is an .exe file, a .dmg file, or a .zip file (or maybe something else).

6. **Install the software that you downloaded in Step 5.**

    Double-click the downloaded file, accept all kinds of legal disclaimers, drag things, drop things, and so on.

7. **Launch the Android Studio application.**

    The first time you run a fresh, new copy of Android Studio, you see some introductory screens.

8. **Click past the introductory screens until you see a screen with options like Start a New Android Studio Project and Open an Existing Android Studio Project.**

    On your phone, an app is an app and that's all there is to it. But on your development computer, all your work is divided into projects. For professional purposes, you're not absolutely correct if you think of one app as equaling one project. But for the examples in this book, the "one project equals one app" model works just fine.

9. **Select the Open an Existing Android Studio Project option.**

    As a result, the Open dialog box appears.

10. **In the Open dialog box, navigate to the folder containing the stuff that you downloaded from this book's website.**

    That folder contains subfolders with names like 02_01, 03_01, and 03_04.

TIP

You say "directory." I say "folder." Let's call the whole thing off because, in this book, I use these two words interchangeably.

11. **Select the folder named 02_01 (or any of the other such folders) and click OK.**

After a brief pause (or maybe a not-so-brief pause), Android Studio's main window appears. This window displays all the stuff you need in order to work with the Android app that's inside the 02_01 folder.

For details about any of these steps, see the next several sections.

THOSE PESKY FILENAME EXTENSIONS

The filenames displayed in File Explorer or in a Finder window can be misleading. You may browse a directory and see the name MainActivity. The file's real name might be MainActivity.java, MainActivity.class, Mortgage.*somethingElse*, or plain old MainActivity. Filename endings such as .zip, .exe, .dmg, .app, .java, and .class are *filename extensions*.

The ugly truth is that, by default, Windows and the Mac hide many filename extensions. This awful feature tends to confuse people. If you don't want to be confused, change your computer's system-wide settings. Here's how to do it:

- **In Windows 7:** Choose Start ⇨ Control Panel ⇨ Appearance and Personalization ⇨ Folder Options. Then skip to the third bullet.

- **In Windows 8:** On the Charms bar, choose Settings ⇨ Control Panel. In the Control Panel, choose Appearance and Personalization ⇨ Folder Options. Then proceed to the following bullet.

- **In all versions of Windows (7 and newer):** Follow the instructions in one of the preceding bullets. Then, in the Folder Options dialog box, click the View tab. Look for the Hide File Extensions for Known File Types option. Make sure that this check box is *not* selected.

- **In Mac OS X:** On the Finder application's menu, select Preferences. In the resulting dialog box, select the Advanced tab and look for the Show All File Extensions option. Make sure that this check box *is* selected.

Getting This Book's Sample Programs

To get copies of this book's sample programs, visit www.allmycode.com/Java4Android and click the link to download the programs in this book. Save the download file (Java4Android_Projects.zip) to the computer's hard drive.

TIP

In some cases, you can click a download link all you want but the web browser doesn't offer you the option to save a file. If this happens to you, right-click the link (or control-click on a Mac). From the resulting contextual menu, select Save Target As, Save Link As, Download Linked File As, or a similarly labeled menu item.

COMPRESSED ARCHIVE FILES

When you visit www.allmycode.com/Java4Android and you download this book's examples, you download a file named Java4Android_Projects.zip. A *zip* file is a single file that encodes a bunch of smaller files and folders. For example, my Java4Android_Projects.zip file encodes folders named 02_01, 03_04, and so on. The 03_04 folder contains subfolders, which in turn contain files. (The folder named 03_04 contains the code in Listing 3-4 — the fourth listing in Chapter 3. And because Listings 3-1 and 3-4 belong to the same app, the folder named 03_04 also contains the code in Listing 3-1.)

A .zip file is an example of a *compressed archive* file. Other examples of compressed archives include .tar.gz files, .rar files, and .7z files. When you *uncompress* a file, you extract the original files and folders stored inside the larger archive file. (For a .zip file, another word for uncompressing is *unzipping*.) Uncompressing normally re-creates the folder structure encoded in the archive file. So, after uncompressing my Java4Android_Projects.zip file, the hard drive has folders named 02_01, 03_04, with subfolders named gradle, build, and app, which in turn contain files named proguard-rules.pro, build.gradle, and so on.

When you download Java4Android_Projects.zip, the web browser may uncompress the file automatically for you. If not, you can get your computer to uncompress the file. Here's how:

- On a Windows computer, double-click the .zip file's icon. When you do this, Windows File Explorer shows you the files and folders inside the compressed .zip archive. Drag all these files and folders to another place on your computer's hard drive (a place that's not inside the archive file).

- On a Mac, double-click the .zip file's icon. When you do this, the Mac extracts the contents of the archive file and shows you the extracted contents in a Finder window.

Most web browsers save files to the Downloads directory on the computer's hard drive. But your browser may be configured a bit differently. One way or another, make note of the folder containing the downloaded file Java4Android_ Projects.zip.

Setting Up Java

You can get the latest, greatest version of Java by visiting www.oracle.com/ technetwork/java/javase/downloads. Figure 2-1 shows that page circa June 2016. In the figure, I've circled the button that you should click.

The page that you see might not look exactly like the page in Figure 2-1. In particular, you probably won't see *8u91 / 8u92* on your page. Instead, you might see some other numbers, such as *8u105* or *9u13*. If so, that's okay. A version code such as *9u13* stands for the 13th update of Java 9. The version codes on Oracle's download page change all the time.

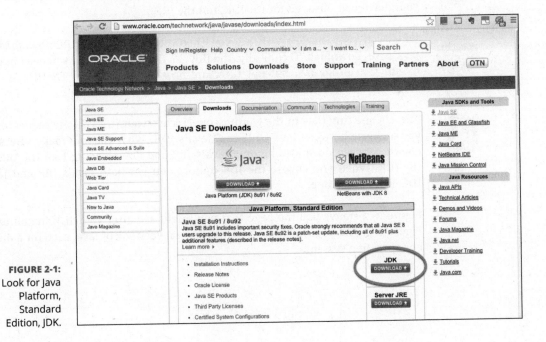

FIGURE 2-1: Look for Java Platform, Standard Edition, JDK.

HOW TO PUT THE CART BEFORE THE HORSE

To run Android's app development software, you need software for creating Java programs. So normally, you install Java and then you install Android's app development software.

Of course, you may already have the required Java software on your laptop or desktop computer. And Google sometimes bundles Java with the Android developer software. You may get lucky and download Java and Android all in one big gulp.

So if you're in a hurry to get started, you can try skipping this "Setting Up Java" section and go straight to the section entitled "Setting up Android Studio and the Android SDK." If you see error messages indicating that Java isn't installed on your computer, come back to this section where you install a fresh, new copy of Java.

REMEMBER

Look for the Standard Edition JDK. Don't bother with the Enterprise Edition or any other such edition. Don't bother to get any other software such as NetBeans with your download. Also, go for the JDK, not the JRE.

TECHNICAL STUFF

When you visit Oracle's website, you choose between Java's JRE download and Java's JDK download. Technically, the JRE has the software that you need in order to run Java programs, but not to create new Java programs. The JDK has the software that you need in order to create new Java programs.

TIP

There's one tiny flaw in the wording on Oracle's website. The site seems to give you a choice between Java's JRE and Java's JDK. What the site really offers is a choice between downloading only Java's JRE and downloading *both* the JRE *and* the JDK. When you choose the JDK option, you get both Java's JRE and Java's JDK. That's just fine.

Figure 2-2 shows you the page that you might see after you click the button in Figure 2-1. The page in Figure 2-2 lists several versions of Java, each for a different operating system.

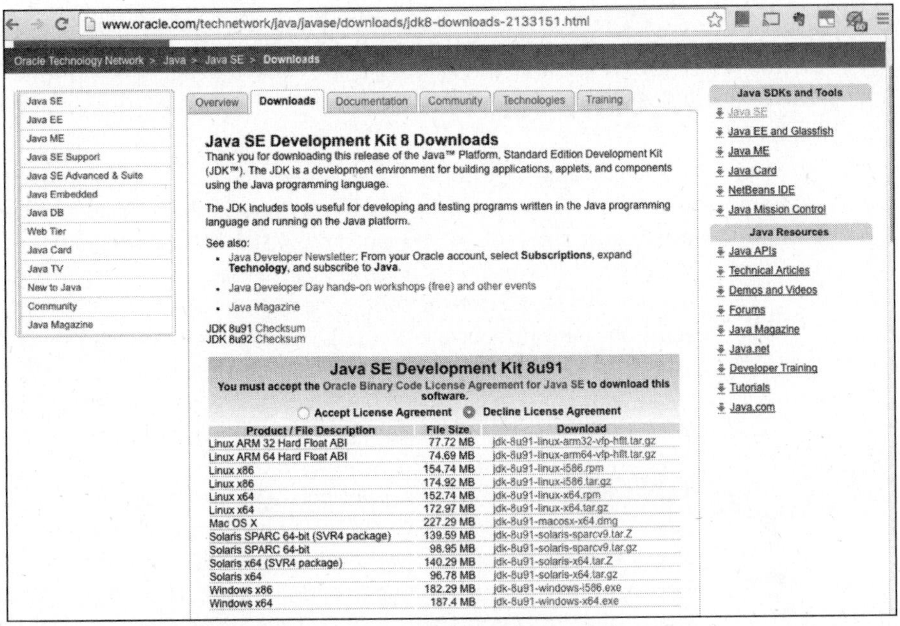

FIGURE 2-2:
Many Java JDK
downloads.

A FISTFUL OF BITS

If you're a Windows user, the www.oracle.com/technetwork/java/javase/downloads page offers you a choice between 32-bit Java and 64-bit Java. The 32-bit alternative might have the digits *586* in its name. More sensibly, the 64-bit alternative probably has the digits *64* in its name. So the question is, which version of Java should you choose?

If you're like most computer users, you want the 64-bit version of Java. Most computers sold in the past several years have 64-bit processors. If you're not sure which version of Java to download, try the 64-bit version.

Some older computers have 32-bit processors, and some newer computers have 64-bit processors with 32-bit operating systems. If your Windows computer falls into one of these categories, an attempt to install 64-bit Java will generate an error message. At best, the message says that this installation file isn't compatible with your version of Windows. At worst, the message says that the thing you're trying to run isn't a valid Windows program. In either case, you want the 32-bit version of Java.

If you want to be safe, you can check to find out how many bits your Windows system has. Search for *Control Panel* in order to launch the Control Panel screen. In the Control Panel's search field, type **About.** When you do, Windows offers System as one of its alternatives. After choosing this System option, you see a panel showing some of your computer's properties. Somewhere in this list of properties, you'll see either *32-bit* or *64-bit*.

THE GREATEST? YES! THE LATEST? MAYBE NOT!

In mid-2016, the page https://developer.android.com/studio/install.html observes ". . . known stability issues in Android Studio on Mac when using JDK 1.8. Until these issues are resolved, you can improve stability by downgrading your JDK to an older version (but no lower than JDK 1.6)." To make things even trickier, I've tried running Android Studio with the soon-to-be-released Java 9 and it's a complete "no go." If you're squeamish about Java versions, you might want to install Java 7 instead of whatever version is foremost on Oracle's download page. Look for the words *Archive* or *Legacy* on the www.oracle.com/technetwork/java/javase/downloads page, and follow the links to download older versions of the Java JDK.

Should you remove existing versions of Java before installing new versions? Not necessarily. Different versions of Java can coexist on a single computer. But sometimes, when you have more than one Java version, Android Studio can't find the most appropriate version. In this case, you can't install Android Studio. Or, if you can install Android Studio, you can't launch Android Studio. Instead, you get a message saying that your computer has no version of the Java JDK or has the wrong version of the Java JDK. If that happens, I recommend uninstalling all versions of Java except the one that you installed most recently. Here's how:

- On Windows, search for *Control Panel* in order to launch the Control Panel screen. In the Control Panel's search field, type **Programs and Features** or type **Add or Remove Programs.** When you've reached the Programs and Features or Add or Remove Programs screen, look for anything with the word *Java* in its name, such as *Java 8 Update 91* or *Java SE Development Kit 8 Update 91*. Try clicking, double-clicking, or right-clicking any item that you want to uninstall.

- On a Mac, look for the Terminal app in the Utilities subfolder of your Applications folder. On the Terminal app's screen, type

      cd /Library/Java/JavaVirtualMachines

  In the computer's response, look for names like jdk-9.jdk, jdk1.8.0_06.jdk, or 1.7.0.jdk. Say, for the sake of argument, that you want to delete jdk1.8.0_06.jdk in order to remove Java 8 from your Mac. Then type the following command in the Terminal window:

      sudo rm -rf jdk1.8.0_06.jdk

  After you do so, the Terminal asks for your password. After typing your password and pressing Enter, you're all set.

Setting Up Android Studio and the Android SDK

WARNING

In the Android world, things change very quickly. The instructions that I write on Tuesday can be out-of-date by Thursday morning. The folks at Google are always creating new features and new tools. The old tools stop working and the old instructions no longer apply. If you see something on your screen that doesn't look like one of my screen shots, don't despair. It might be something very new, or you might have reached a corner of the software that I don't describe in this book. One way or another, send me an email, a tweet, or some other form of communication. (Don't try sending a carrier pigeon. My cat will get to it before I find the note.) My contact info is in this book's introduction.

You download Android's SDK and Android Studio in one big gulp. Here's how:

1. **Visit** http://developer.android.com/studio.

Figure 2-3 shows you what this web page looks like in July of 2016 (commonly known as "the good old days").

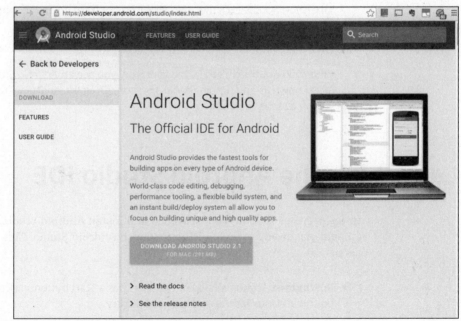

FIGURE 2-3:
Downloading Android Studio.

The page has a big button for downloading Android Studio. The Android Studio download includes the much-needed Android SDK.

By the time you read this book, the web page will probably have changed. But you'll still see an Android Studio download.

2. **Click the Download button on the web page.**

3. **Agree to all the legal mumbo-jumbo.**

4. **Save the download to your local hard drive.**

   If you run Windows, the downloaded file is probably an .exe file. If you have a Mac, the downloaded file is probably a .dmg file. Of course, I make no guarantees. The downloaded file might be a .zip archive or maybe some other exotic kind of archive file.

CROSS-
REFERENCE

For more information on things like .exe and .dmg, refer to the sidebar entitled "Those pesky filename extensions." And, if you need help with .zip files, see the earlier sidebar "Compressed archive files."

What happens next depends on your computer's operating system.

>> **In Windows:** Double-click the .exe file's icon.

When you double-click the .exe file's icon, a wizard guides you through the installation.

>> **On a Mac:** Double-click the .dmg file's icon.

When you double-click the .dmg file's icon, you see an Android Studio icon (also known as an Android Studio.app icon). Drag the Android Studio icon to your Applications folder.

Launching the Android Studio IDE

In the previous section, you download and install Android Studio. Your next task (should you decide to accept it) is to launch Android Studio. This section has the details.

>> **In Windows:** If your version of Windows has a Start button, click the Start button and look for the Android Studio entry.

If you don't have a Start button, press Windows-Q to make a search field appear. In the search field, start typing *Android Studio*. When your computer offers the Android Studio application as one of the options, select that option.

TIP

>> **On a Mac:** Press Command-space to make the Spotlight appear. In the Spotlight's search field, start typing *Android Studio*. When your Mac makes the full name *Android Studio* appear in the Spotlight's search field, press Enter.

If your Mac complains that Android Studio is from an unidentified developer, look for the Android Studio icon in your Applications folder. Control-click the Android Studio icon and select Open. When another "unidentified developer" box appears, click the box's Open button.

When you launch Android Studio for the first time, you might see a dialog box offering to import settings from a previous Android Studio installation. Chances are, you don't have a previous Android Studio installation, so you should firmly but politely decline this offer.

Next, you might see a few dialog boxes with information about installing the development environment (the Android SDK). Accept all the defaults and, if Android Studio offers to download more stuff, let Android Studio do it.

When the dust settles, Android Studio displays a Welcome screen. The Welcome screen has options such as Start a New Android Studio Project, Open an Existing Android Studio Project, and so on. (See Figure 2-4.)

Welcome to Android Studio

Android Studio

Version 2.2 Preview 5 (AI-145.3040006)

✻ Start a new Android Studio project

☐ Open an existing Android Studio project

⬇ Check out project from Version Control ▾

☑ Import project (Eclipse ADT, Gradle, etc.)

☑ Import an Android code sample

✻ Configure ▾   Get Help ▾

FIGURE 2-4:
Android Studio's
Welcome screen.

You'll see this Welcome screen again and again. Stated informally, the Welcome screen says "At the moment, you're not working on any particular project (any particular Android app). So what do you want to do next?"

What you want to do next is to open this book's first project. The next section has all the details.

Opening One of This Book's Sample Programs

When you first launch Android Studio, you see the Welcome screen. It probably looks something like the screen in Figure 2-4. But, because time passes between my writing of this book and your reading the book, the screen might look a bit different. One way or another, the Welcome screen affords you the opportunity to open a full-fledged Android project. Here's what you do:

1. **Follow the steps in this chapter's earlier section "Getting This Book's Sample Programs."**

2. **Make sure that you've uncompressed the file from Step 1.**

For details, refer to that "Getting This Book's Sample Programs" section.

CROSS-REFERENCE

Safari on a Mac generally uncompresses .zip archives automatically, and Windows browsers (Internet Explorer, Firefox, Chrome, and others) do not uncompress .zip archives automatically. For the complete scoop on archive files, see the earlier sidebar "Compressed archive files."

If you look inside the uncompressed download, you notice folders with names such as 02_01, 03_01, 03_04, and so on. With a few exceptions, the names of folders are chapter numbers followed by listing numbers. For example, in the folder named 03_04, the 03 stands for Chapter 3, and the 04 stands for the fourth code listing in that chapter.

3. **Launch Android Studio.**

What you do next depends on what you see when you launch Android Studio.

4. **If you see Android Studio's Welcome screen (refer to Figure 2-4), select Open an Existing Android Project.**

If you see another Android Studio window with a File option on the main menu bar, choose File ⇨ Open in the main menu bar.

Either way, the aptly named Open File or Project dialog box appears.

5. **In the Open File or Project dialog box, navigate to the folder containing the project that you want to open.**

For this experiment, I suggest that you navigate to the 02_01 folder. In the name 02_01, the 02 stands for *Chapter 2*. The 01 stands for this chapter's first (and only) Android project. (There's no code listed anywhere in this chapter. So, in this unusual case, 02_01 doesn't refer to a project whose code is in Listing 2-1.)

TIP

If you're unsure where to find the 02_01 folder, look first in a folder named Downloads. Then look in a subfolder named Java4Android_Projects.

6. Click OK.

WARNING

When you click OK, Android Studio may have to download the default Gradle wrapper from the Internet. If so, downloading this Gradle wrapper might take some time. You may even think that your computer has stalled. Wait for several minutes if that's what it takes.

Eventually, you see Android Studio's main window. In the main window, you find a project containing one of this book's examples. See Figure 2-5.

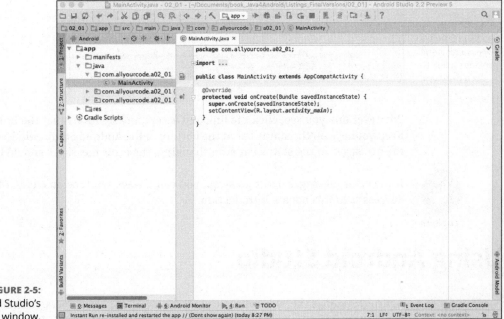

FIGURE 2-5:
Android Studio's
main window.

TIP

If Android Studio's main window looks fairly empty (that is, if you don't see all the stuff in 2-5), look at the status bar on the bottom of Android Studio's main window. If the text in the status bar is changing, Android Studio is taking some time to figure out how the newly opened Android project works. If the status bar is calm and Android Studio's main window still looks mostly empty, look for the word *Project* displayed vertically on the left edge of Android Studio's window. This word *Project* is the label on one of Android Studio's *tool buttons*. Click the Project tool button to reveal some of the stuff that you see earlier, in Figure 2-5.

After opening an example from this book, you may see an error message indicating trouble syncing the Gradle project. If you do, stay calm. The most likely cause is that the tools I used to create the example are older than the tools in your version of Android Studio. You can probably find a link offering to fix the problem in the bottommost pane of the Android Studio window. (See Figure 2-6.) "Fix Gradle wrapper and re-import project Gradle settings," says one such link. "Install missing platform(s) and sync project," says another such link. "Install Build Tools 21.1.2 and sync project," says yet another link.

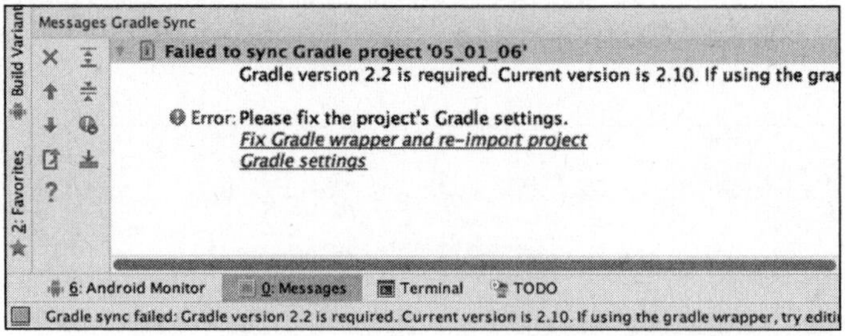

FIGURE 2-6:
Android Studio's
Messages pane
provides a link to
fix a problem.

Whatever link you see, click the link and accept any solutions that the link offers. Keep your eye on the status bar at the bottom of the Android Studio window. When the messages in the status bar stop changing, the error messages should be gone.

REMEMBER

If the error messages don't go away, you can always send me an email. My email address is in this book's introduction.

Using Android Studio

Android Studio is the Swiss army knife for Android app developers. Android Studio is a customized version of IntelliJ IDEA — a general-purpose IDE with tools for Java development, C/C++ development, PHP development, modeling, project management, testing, debugging, and much more.

In this section, you get an overview of Android Studio's main window. I focus on the most useful features that help you build Android apps, but keep in mind that Android Studio has hundreds of features and many ways to access each feature.

Starting up

Each Android app belongs to a project. You can have dozens of projects on your computer's hard drive. When you run Android Studio, each of your projects is either open or closed. An *open* project appears in a window (its own window) on your computer screen. A *closed* project doesn't appear in a window.

Several of your projects can be open at the same time. You can switch between projects by moving from window to window.

TECHNICAL STUFF

I often refer to an open project's window as Android Studio's *main window*. This can be slightly misleading because, with several projects open at a time, you have several main windows open at a time. None of these windows is more "main" than the others.

If Android Studio is running and no projects are open, Android Studio displays its Welcome screen. (Refer to Figure 2-4.) The Welcome screen may display some recently closed projects. If so, you can open a project by clicking its name on the Welcome screen. For an app that's not on the Recent Projects list, you can click the Welcome screen's Open an Existing Android Studio Project option.

If you have any open projects, Android Studio doesn't display the Welcome screen. In that case, you can open another project by choosing File ⇨ Open or File ⇨ Open Recent in an open project's window. To close a project, you can choose File ⇨ Close Project, or you can do whatever you normally do to close one of the windows on your computer. (On a PC, click the X in the window's upper-right corner. On a Mac, click the little red button in the window's upper-left corner.)

TIP

Android Studio remembers which projects were open from one run to the next. If any projects are open when you quit Android Studio, those projects open again (with their main windows showing) the next time you launch Android Studio. You can override this behavior (so that only the Welcome screen appears each time you launch Android Studio). In Android Studio on a Windows computer, start by choosing File ⇨ Settings ⇨ Appearance and Behavior ⇨ System Settings. In Android Studio on a Mac, choose Android Studio ⇨ Preferences ⇨ Appearance and Behavior ⇨ System Settings. In either case, uncheck the Reopen Last Project on Startup check box.

The main window

Android Studio's main window is divided into several areas. Some of these areas can appear and disappear on your command. What comes next is a description of the areas in Figure 2-7, moving from the top of the main window to the bottom.

REMEMBER

The areas that you see on your computer screen may be different from the areas in Figure 2-7. Usually, that's okay. You can make areas come and go by choosing certain menu options, including the View option on Android Studio's main menu bar. You can also click the little tool buttons on the edges of the main window.

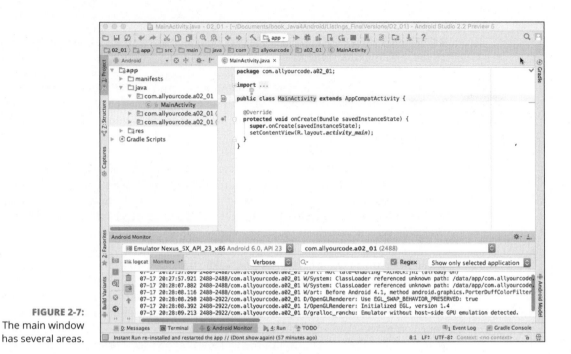

FIGURE 2-7:
The main window
has several areas.

The top of the main window

The topmost area contains the toolbar and the navigation bar.

>> **The *toolbar* contains action buttons such as Open, Save All, Cut, Copy, and Paste.**

Near the middle of the toolbar, you'll find a rightward-pointing green arrow. This arrow is the Run button. You can click that button to run the current Android app.

>> **The navigation bar displays the path to one of the files in your Android project.**

An Android project contains many files and, at any particular moment, you work on one of these files. The navigation bar points to that file.

The Project tool window

Below the main menu and the toolbars you'll see two different areas. The area on the left contains the Project tool window. You use the *Project tool window* to navigate from one file to another within your Android app.

At any given moment, the Project tool window displays one of several possible views. For example, back in Figure 2-7, the Project tool window displays its *Android view*. In Figure 2-8, I click the drop-down list and select the Packages view (instead of the Android view).

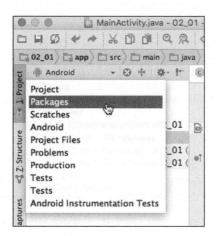

FIGURE 2-8:
Selecting the
Packages view.

The *Packages view* displays many of the same files as the Android view, but in the Packages view, the files are grouped differently. For most of this book's instructions, I assume that the Project tool window is in its default view; namely, the Android view.

REMEMBER

If Android Studio doesn't display the Project tool window, look for the Project tool button — the little button displaying the word *Project* on the left edge of the main window. Click that Project tool button.

TECHNICAL
STUFF

Android Studio has lots of tool buttons on the edge of its main window — buttons with labels such as Project, Structure, Captures, Build Variants, Message, Gradle, and so on. I'm going to be very blunt about the endless number of ways that you can click and unclick these buttons: "For a complete discussion of all the things you can possibly do to customize the Android Studio main window, read someone else's book!" (Editor's note: Barry is tired of writing about tool button-clicking so he's being cantankerous. He also isn't giving himself enough credit. He's actually written more about customizing Android Studio's main window in his *Android Application Development All-in-One For Dummies*, 2nd Edition book. However, you don't need all those main window tweaks in order to follow the examples in this book.)

The Editor area

The area to the right of the Project tool window is the *Editor area*.

What you see in the Editor area depends on the kind of file that you're editing:

>> **When you edit a Java program file, the editor displays the file's text. (Refer to Figure 2-7.)**

You can type, cut, copy, and paste text as you would in other text editors.

The text editor can have several tabs. Each tab contains a file that's open for editing. To open a file for editing, double-click the file's branch in the Project tool window. To close the file, click the little x next to the file's name in the Editor tab.

>> **When you edit a layout file, the Editor area displays the Designer tool.**

A typical Android app contains one or more layout files. A *layout file* describes the buttons, text fields, and other components that appear on a device's screen when a device runs your app. A layout file isn't written in Java.

The Designer tool presents a visual representation of the layout file to help you arrange your app's buttons, text fields, and other components.

For a careful look at Android Studio's Designer tool, see Chapter 3.

CROSS-
REFERENCE Continuing your tour of the areas in Figure 2-7. . . .

The lower area

Below the Project tool window and the editor is another area that contains several tool windows. The tool window that I use most often is the Android Monitor tool window. (Refer to the lower portion of Figure 2-7.)

The Android Monitor tool window displays information about the run of an Android app. This tool window appears automatically when your app starts running on an Android device.

CROSS-
REFERENCE An Android device isn't necessarily a real phone or a real tablet. Your development computer can emulate the behavior of an Android device. For details, see this chapter's later section "Creating an Android virtual device."

The Android Monitor tool window has the Logcat pane, the Monitors pane, and possibly others. (Notice the tabs with these labels earlier, in Figure 2-7.) The pane that I find most useful is the Logcat pane. In the Logcat pane, you see all messages being logged by the Android device that's running your app. If your app isn't running correctly, you can filter the messages that are displayed and focus on the messages that are most helpful for diagnosing the problem.

You can force other tool windows to appear in the lower area by clicking tool buttons near the bottom of the Android Studio window. Here are two other useful tool windows:

» The Terminal tool window displays a PC's MS-DOS command prompt, a Mac's Terminal app, or another text-based command screen that you specify. (See Figure 2-9.)

FIGURE 2-9:
The Terminal tool
window on a Mac.

» The Run tool window displays information about the launching of an Android app. (In Figure 2-10, phrases such as Launching app refer to the movement of an app from your development computer to the Android device.)

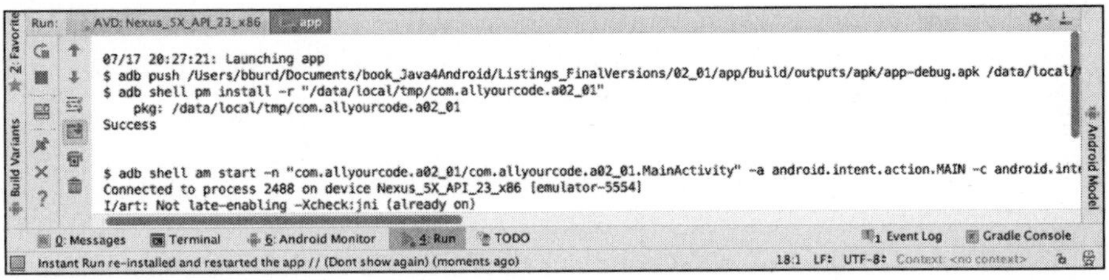

FIGURE 2-10:
The Run tool
window.

A particular tool button might not appear when there's nothing you can do with it. For example, if you're not trying to run an Android app, you might not see the Run tool button.

REMEMBER

Finishing your tour of the areas in Figure 2-7. . . .

The status bar

The status bar is at the very bottom of Android Studio's window.

The status bar tells you what's happening now. For example, if the cursor is on the 37th character of the 11th line in the editor, you see *11:37* somewhere on the status line. When you tell Android Studio to run your app, you see `Gradle: Executing Tasks` on the status line. When Android Studio has finished executing Gradle tasks, you see `Gradle Build Finished` on the status line. Messages like these are helpful because they confirm that Android Studio is doing what you want it to do.

The kitchen sink

In addition to the areas that I mention in this section, other areas might pop up as the need arises. You can dismiss an area by clicking the area's Hide icon. (See Figure 2-11.)

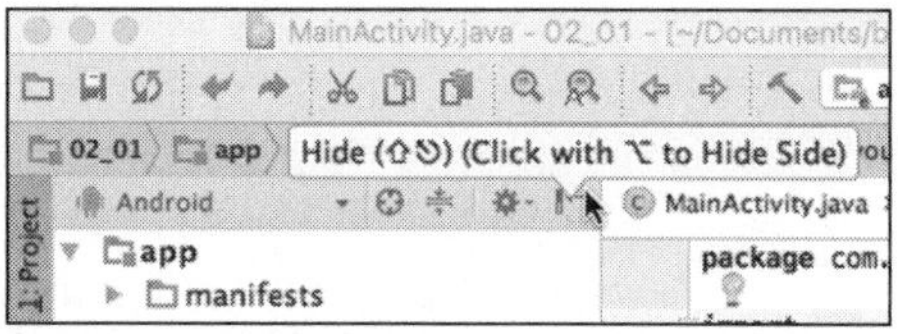

FIGURE 2-11:
Hiding the Project tool window area.

Things You Might Eventually Have to Do

When you download Android Studio, you get the code library (the API) for the current release of Android. You also get several developer tools — tools for compiling, testing, and debugging Android code.

Here's what you don't get:

» **You don't get older Android APIs or older versions of the developer tools.**

Sometimes you have to work with older versions of Android. By the time you read this book, the version of Android that I used to create the book's examples will already be an older version. You'll open one of the examples that you download from this book's web page, and you'll see Android Studio prompting you to install an older Android API. You'll accept the prompt's advice and you'll be well on your way to running the apps that I describe in this book.

» **You don't get future Android APIs or future versions of the developer tools. (You couldn't possibly get those things.)**

Google updates Android frequently, and you might want to follow the latest trends. So, in the near future, you might install a newer release of Android than the release you have now.

You can get older software and newer software by clicking links in Android Studio's notifications, but you can also be proactive and reach out for different versions of Android's tools and APIs. To help you do this, you have two useful "manager" tools — the SDK Manager and the AVD Manager. The next few sections cover these tools in depth.

REMEMBER

When you first install Android Studio, you can probably skip the next two sections. Return to these sections when Google releases updated versions of Android or when you work on a project that requires older versions of Android (versions that you haven't already installed).

Installing new versions (and older versions) of Android

The *Android SDK Manager* lists the versions of Android and helps you download and install the versions that you need on your development computer. Figure 2-12 shows the SDK Manager with the manager's SDK Platforms tab open.

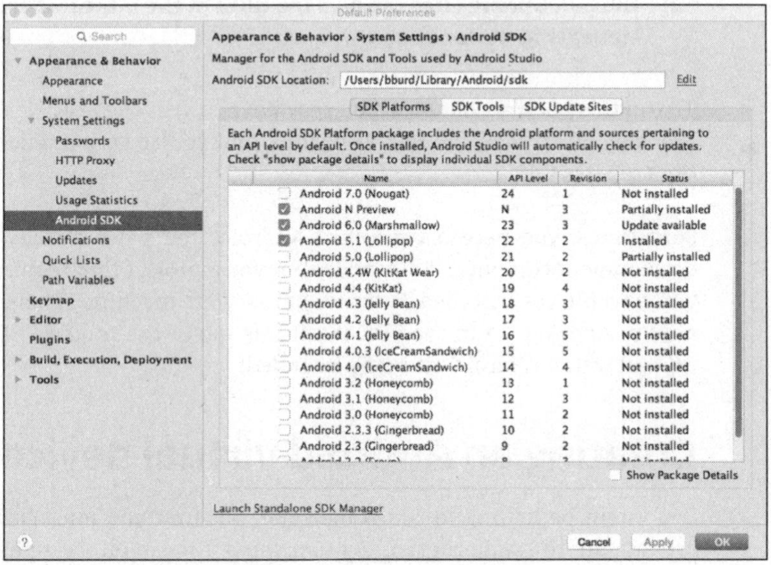

FIGURE 2-12:
The Android SDK Manager.

To open the SDK Manager, go to Android Studio's main menu bar and choose Tools ⇨ Android ⇨ SDK Manager.

TECHNICAL
STUFF

In truth, Android has two SDK managers. The one that I describe in this section is embedded inside Android Studio's Settings dialog box. The other runs on its own, with no help from the Android Studio IDE. The two SDK managers perform roughly the same tasks.

In the Android SDK Manager, you see tabs labeled SDK Platforms, SDK Tools, and SDK Update Sites.

>> **The SDK Platforms tab lists versions of Android.**

In Figure 2-12, the list includes Nougat, a preview release of Nougat when it was called Android N, two versions of Android Lollipop, and many others. The list's rightmost column tells you which Android versions are installed (either fully or partially) on your development computer. The rightmost column may also indicate that an update to an Android version is available for downloading. Adding a check mark next to a version tells the SDK Manager to install that version on your computer.

>> **The SDK Tools tab lists software tools that are already installed, and some that aren't installed but are available for download.**

>> **The SDK Update Sites tab lists the URLs of the places where SDK Manager looks for updates.**

To run this book's examples, you may have to visit the SDK Platforms tab. But you probably won't visit the SDK Tools tab. And you're very unlikely to need the SDK Update Sites tab.

Sometimes, you need a version of Android that's not already installed on your development computer. Somebody sent you a project that requires Android 3.2 and you haven't yet installed Android 3.2 on your machine. Then put a check mark next to Android 3.2 in the SDK Platforms tab of the Android SDK Manager. Click OK and watch Android 3.2 being installed.

Creating an Android virtual device

You might be itching to run some code, but first you must have something that can run an Android program. By *something*, I mean either a physical device or an emulated device.

>> **A *physical device* is a piece of hardware that's meant to run Android. It's a phone, a tablet, an Android-enabled toaster — whatever.**

Another name for a physical device is a *real device*.

>> **An *emulated device* is a picture of a phone or a tablet on your development computer's screen.**

With an emulated device, Android is made to run on your development computer's processor. The emulated device shows you how your code will probably behave when you later run your code on a real phone, a real tablet, or another Android device.

MIMICKING A PHYSICAL DEVICE

An emulated device is really three pieces of software rolled into one:

- **A *system image* is a copy of one version of the Android operating system.**

  For example, a particular system image might be for Android Marshmallow (API Level 23) running on an *Intel x86_64* processor.

- **An *emulator* bridges the gap between the system image and the processor on your development computer.**

  You might have a system image for an Atom_64 processor, but your development computer runs a Core i5 processor. The emulator translates instructions for the Atom_64 processor into instructions that the Core i5 processor can execute.

- **An Android Virtual Device (AVD) is a piece of software that describes a real (physical) device's hardware.**

  An AVD contains a bunch of settings, telling the emulator all the details about the device to be emulated. What's the screen resolution of the device? Does the device have a physical keyboard? Does it have a camera? How much memory does it have? Does it have an SD card? All these choices belong to a particular AVD.

Android Studio's menus and dialog boxes make it easy to confuse these three items. When you download a new AVD, you often download a new system image to go with that AVD. But Android Studio's dialog boxes blur the distinction between the AVD and the system image. You'll also see the word *emulator,* when the correct term is *AVD.* If the subtle differences between system images, emulators, and AVDs don't bother you, don't worry about them.

A seasoned Android developer typically has several system images and several AVDs on the development computer, but only one Android emulator program.

An AVD is a piece of software that tells your development computer all about a particular phone, a particular tablet, or some other kind of device. When you install Android Studio, the installer creates an AVD for you to use. But you can create several additional AVDs and use several different AVDs to run and test your Android apps.

You use the AVD Manager tool to create and customize your Android virtual devices. To open the AVD Manager, go to Android Studio's main menu bar and choose Tools ⇨ Android ⇨ AVD Manager.

Figures 2-13 through 2-16 show the dialog boxes that you might find in the AVD Manager.

I'm reluctant to list instructions for using the AVD Manager, because the look of the AVD Manager tool is constantly in flux. Chances are, what you see on your computer's screen doesn't look much like the mid-2016 screen shots in Figures 2-13 to 2-16.

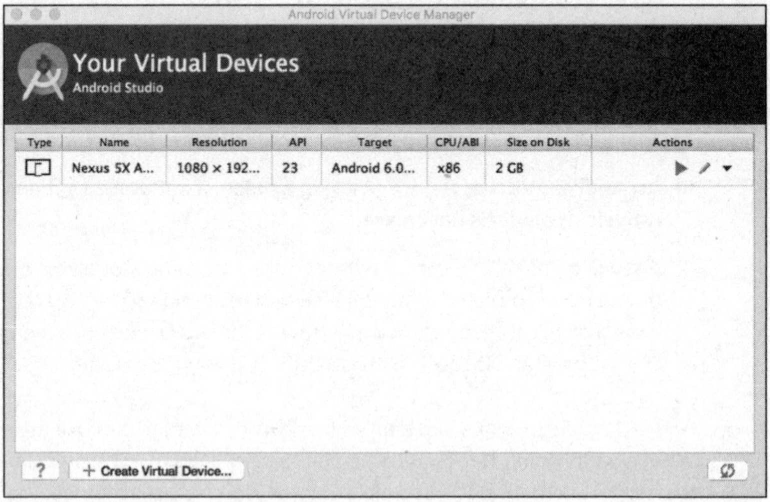

FIGURE 2-13:
The opening page of the AVD Manager.

Instead of giving explicit instructions, my general advice when creating a new AVD is to select the newer phones or tablets and the higher-numbered API levels, and to accept defaults whenever you're tempted to play eeny-meeny-miney-mo. Just keep clicking Next until you can click Finish. If you don't like the AVD that you've created, you can always reopen the AVD Manager and select different options to create another AVD. When you reach the level of proficiency where you're finicky about your AVD's characteristics, you'll probably know your way around many of the AVD Manager's options and you'll be able to choose wisely.

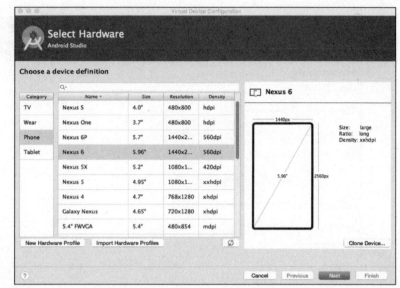

FIGURE 2-14:
The first page
in creating
a new AVD.

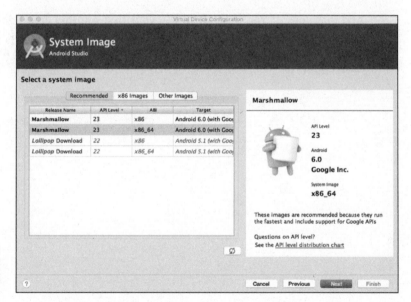

FIGURE 2-15:
The second
page in creating
a new AVD.

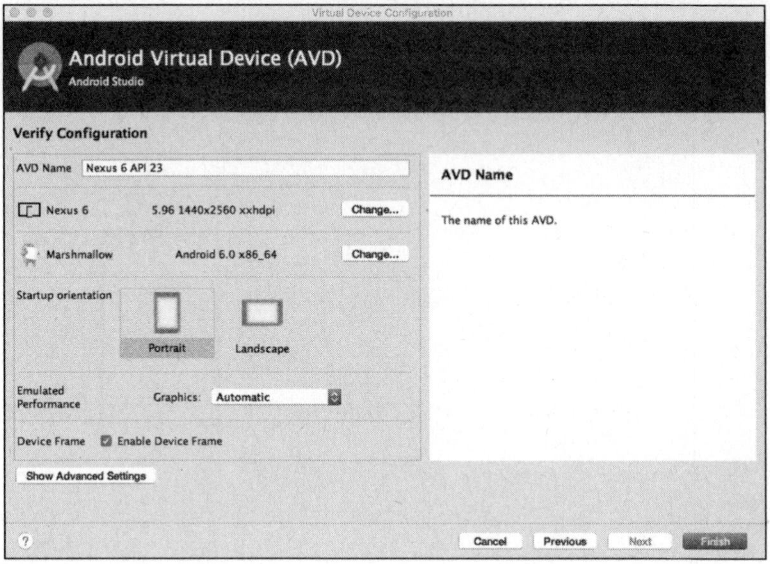

FIGURE 2-16:
The final page
in creating
a new AVD.

And that does it! You're ready to run your first Android app. I don't know about you, but I'm excited. (Sure, I'm not watching you read this book, but I'm excited on your behalf.) Chapter 3 guides you through the running of an Android application. Go for it!

Chapter **3**

Creating and Running an Android App

I n a quiet neighborhood in south Philadelphia, there's a maternity shop named Hello World. I stumbled onto the store on my way to Pat's (to get a delicious Philly cheesesteak, of course), and I couldn't resist taking a picture of the store's sign.

Computer geek that I am, I'd never thought of Hello World as anything but an app. A *Hello World* app is the simplest program that can run in a particular programming language or on a particular platform.* Authors create Hello World apps to show people how to get started writing code for a particular system.

So, in this chapter, you make an Android Hello World app. The app doesn't do much. (In fact, you might argue that the app doesn't do anything!) But the example shows you how to create and run new Android projects.

* For an interesting discussion of the phrase *Hello World*, visit www.mzlabs.com/ JMPubs/HelloWorld.pdf. To see Hello World apps for more than 450 different programming languages, visit www.helloworldcollection.de.)

Creating Your First App

A typical gadget comes with a manual. The manual's first sentence is "Read all 37 safety warnings before attempting to install this product." Don't you love it? You can't get to the good stuff without wading through the preliminaries.

Well, nothing in this chapter can set your house on fire or even break your electronic device. But before you follow this chapter's instructions, you need a bunch of software on your development computer. To make sure that you have this software and that the software is properly configured, return to Chapter 2. (Do not pass Go; do not collect $200.)

When at last you have all the software you need, you're ready to launch Android Studio and create a real, live Android app.

In the Android developer's world, things change quickly. If your screens don't look like the screens that I describe in this chapter, Google may have updated parts of Android Studio. If you have trouble figuring out what to do in any new versions of Android Studio, send me an email. The address is `Java4Android@allmycode.com`.

First things first

To start the IDE and create your first app, you start, naturally, at the beginning:

1. **Launch Android Studio.**

   For details on launching Android Studio, see Chapter 2.

   What you do next depends on what you see on your screen.

2. **If you see a project's main window, go to the window's main menu bar and select File ⇨ New ⇨ New Project.**

   If you see the Welcome screen, select Start a New Android Studio Project.

   As a result, the New Project dialog box appears, as shown in Figure 3-1. The New Project dialog box has fields for the application name, your company domain, and your project location. These fields contain some default values, such as *My Application* for the application name, and *example.com* for the company domain. You can change the values in these fields, as I do in Figure 3-1. But if you accept the defaults, you'll be just fine.

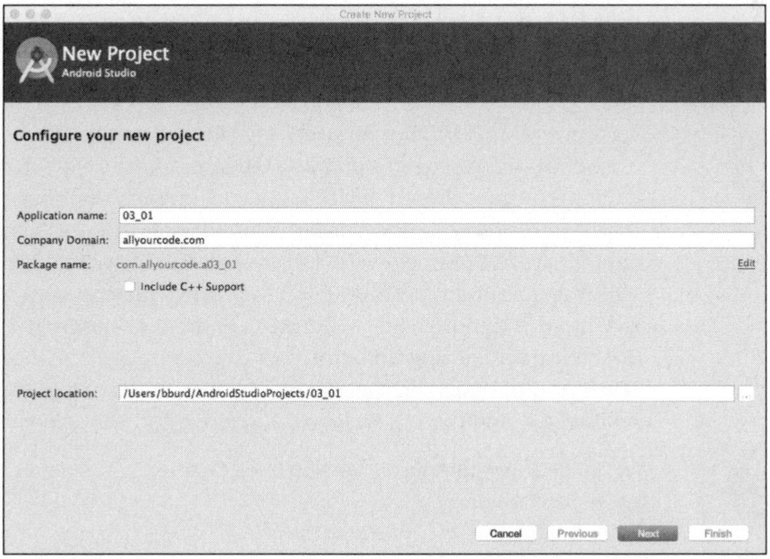

![New Project dialog box screenshot]

Create New Project

New Project
Android Studio

Configure your new project

Application name: 03_01

Company Domain: allyourcode.com

Package name: com.allyourcode.a03_01   Edit

☐ Include C++ Support

Project location: /Users/bburd/AndroidStudioProjects/03_01

Cancel   Previous   **Next**   Finish

FIGURE 3-1:
Configure your
new project.

3. In the New Project window, click Next.

Doing so brings up the Target Android Devices window, as shown in Figure 3-2. This window has check boxes for Phone and Tablet, Wear, TV, Android Auto, and Glass. The window also has a number of Minimum SDK drop-down lists.

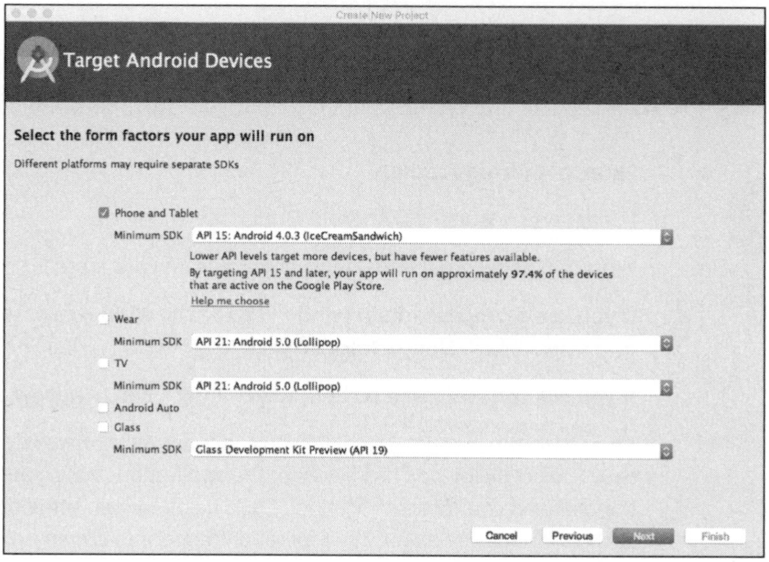

FIGURE 3-2:
Select form factors and minimum SDKs.

In this example, I guide you through the creation of a Phone and Tablet app, so you can accept the minimum SDK value offered in the Phone and Tablet drop-down list. Of course, if you want to try creating a TV, Wear, or Glass app, or if you want to change the choice in the Minimum SDK drop-down list, feel free to do so.

TIP

For a minimum SDK, you can select any API level that's available in the drop-down list. You need a phone, a tablet, or an Android Virtual Device (AVD) that can run your chosen API level, but you probably don't have to worry about that. If you've recently downloaded Android Studio, the installation created an appropriate AVD. For example, if the installation of Android Studio created an AVD that runs Android 6.0, that AVD can handle projects whose minimum SDK is Android 6.0, Android 5.1, Android 5.0, Android 4.4, Android 4.0.3, Android 3.2, and so on. Looking from the other direction, a project whose minimum SDK is Android 4.0.3 can run on a phone or an AVD that has Android 4.0.3, Android 4.4, Android 5.0, Android 5.1, Android 6.0, and so on.

CROSS-REFERENCE

For an overview of Android versions, see Chapter 1. To find out about installing AVDs, see Chapter 2.

4. Click Next.

As a result, the Add an Activity to Mobile window appears. (See Figure 3-3.) On this page, you tell Android Studio to create some Java code for you. The Java code describes an Android activity. The options for the kind of Android activity include Basic Activity, Empty Activity, Fullscreen Activity, and so on.

5. Select the Empty Activity option.

REMEMBER

This is important: In Android developer lingo, an *activity* is one "screenful" of components. Each Android application can contain many activities. For example, an app's initial activity might list the films playing in your neighborhood. When you click a film's title, Android covers the entire list activity with another activity (perhaps an activity displaying a relevant film review).

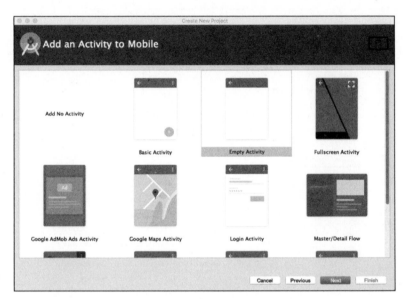

FIGURE 3-3:
Add an activity.

When you select Empty Activity in the Add an Activity to Mobile window, Android Studio writes the Java code for an activity with no bells or whistles. The newly created activity has a text field that displays the words *Hello World!* and not much more. Unlike other choices, Empty Activity has no options menu, no floating action button, no scrollbar, no Google Maps — nothing of the sort. To learn Java, you don't need all that stuff.

6. Click Next again.

You see the Customize the Activity page. (What a surprise!) On this page, you make up the names of things associated with your activity, as shown in Figure 3-4. Again, I recommend the path of least resistance — accepting the defaults.

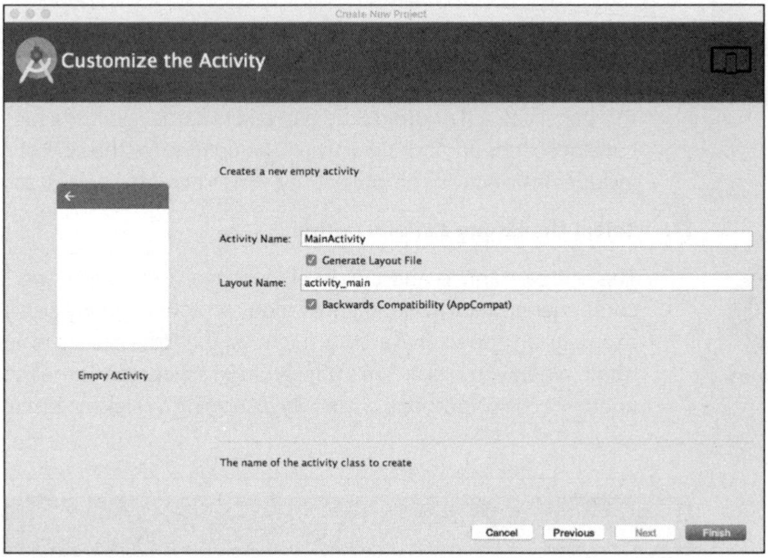

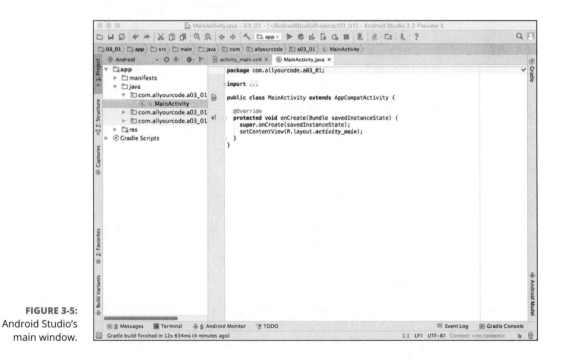

FIGURE 3-4:
Choose options
for your new
activity.

7. Click Finish.

The Customize the Activity page goes away. Android Studio displays its main
window, as shown in Figure 3-5.

FIGURE 3-5:
Android Studio's
main window.

The first time you create a project, you may have to wait a l-o-n-g time for Android Studio to build the Gradle project info (whatever that is). You see a pop-up dialog box indicating that Android Studio is downloading something. Be prepared to wait several minutes for any signs of life on your screen.

Launching your first app

You've started up Android Studio and created your first project. The project doesn't do much except display *Hello World!* on the screen. Even so, you can run the project and see it in action. Here's how you start:

1. **Take a look at Android Studio's main window.**

Refer to Figure 3-5. In Android Studio, your new app consumes the entire main window. If, for some reason, more than one Android Studio window is open, make sure that the window you're looking at is the one containing your newly created Android app.

2. **In Android Studio's main menu, choose Run ⇨ Run 'app'.**

The Select Deployment Target dialog box appears, as shown in Figure 3-6.

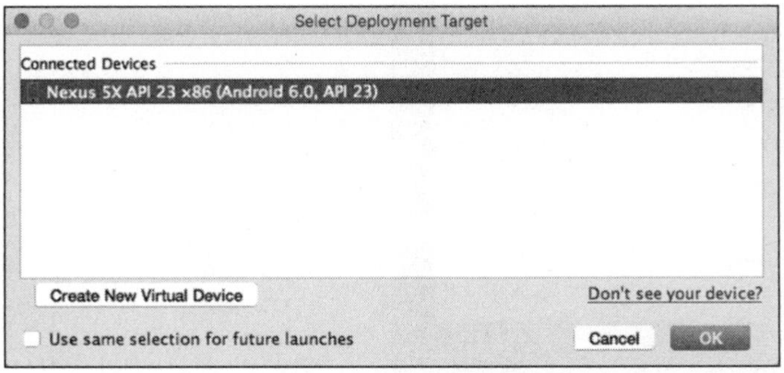

FIGURE 3-6:
The Select Deployment Target dialog box.

In the Select Deployment Target dialog box, you see a list of devices (both physical and emulated) that can run your newly created app. One of them is the AVD that you created when you installed Android Studio. In Figure 3-6, that AVD is named *Nexus 5X API 23 x86*. On your screen, that AVD probably has a different name.

TIP

If the Select Deployment Target dialog box doesn't appear, your computer might be skipping the Select Deployment Target dialog box and going straight to an AVD or a physical device that's the default for this app. If this happens, your app (after a long wait) probably starts running in the emulator window. That's okay, but if you don't like skipping the Select Deployment Target dialog box, visit the section "Testing apps on a physical device," later in this chapter.

3. **Choose an item in the Select Deployment Target dialog box's list.**

If the drop-down list is empty, refer to the section in Chapter 2 on creating an Android Virtual Device.

4. **Click OK.**

When you do, several things happen, though they don't happen all at once. If you wait long enough, you should see your new app running on a device. The device may be a phone that's connected to your development computer. More likely, the device is an emulator window that appears on your development computer's screen. (See Figure 3-7.) The emulator window runs whichever AVD you chose in Step 3.

FIGURE 3-7:
Your Hello World app in action.

WARNING

Android's emulator may take a very long time to get going. For example, my primary development computer has a 3.1GHz processor with 16GB of RAM. On that computer, the emulator takes 75 seconds to start up and run my app. On another computer with a 2.6GHz processor with 8GB of RAM, the emulator takes a few minutes to mimic a fully booted Android device. On yet another computer of mine, one with less than 8GB of RAM, the emulator doesn't even run. If your computer has less than 16GB of RAM, you may need lots of patience when you deal with Android's emulator. If you have trouble getting the emulator to run, consider attaching a real physical device to your development computer, or running a third-party emulator. For more details, refer to this chapter's later section "If the Emulator Doesn't Behave."

Figure 3-7 shows the running of Android's Hello World app. (The screen even has *Hello World!* on it.) Android's development tools create this tiny app when you create a new Android project.

Android's Hello World app has no buttons to click and no fields to fill in. The app doesn't do anything interesting. But the appearance of an app on the Android screen is a very good start. Following the steps in this chapter, you can start creating many exciting apps.

TIP

Don't close an Android emulator unless you know you won't be using it for a while. The emulator is quite reliable after it gets going. While the emulator runs, you can modify your Android code and tell Android Studio to run the code again. When you do, Android Studio implements your changes on the running emulator.

While your app runs, you see the Logcat pane (part of the Android Monitor tool window) along the bottom of Android Studio's main window, as shown in Figure 3-8.

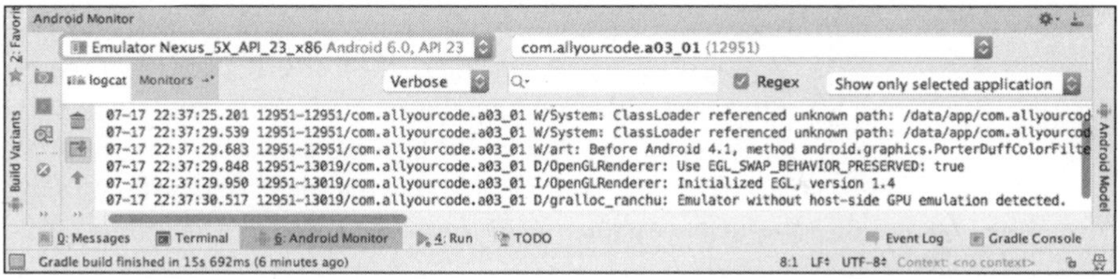

FIGURE 3-8:
The Logcat pane in the Android Monitor tool window.

The *Logcat pane* displays diagnostics about the running of your app.

REMEMBER

You can make parts of Android Studio's window appear and disappear. For example, if you don't see the Logcat pane, look for a tab labeled *logcat* in the lower-left portion of the Android Studio window. (Refer to Figure 3-8.) If you don't see the logcat tab, look for the Android Monitor tool button in the lower-left corner of the Android Studio window. Click that tool button.

If the Emulator Doesn't Behave

The emulator that comes with Android Studio swallows up lots of resources on your development computer. If you're like me and you don't always have the latest, most powerful hardware, you may have trouble running apps in the emulator. This section provides some helpful tips.

If, after five minutes or so, you don't see Android's home screen and you don't see your app running, here are several things you can try:

>> **Lather, rinse, repeat.**

Close the emulator and launch your application again. Sometimes, the second or third time's a charm. On rare occasions, my first three attempts fail, but my fourth attempt succeeds.

>> **If you have access to a computer with more RAM, try running your app on it.**

Horsepower matters.

>> **Try a different AVD.**

The "Creating an Android virtual device" section, back in Chapter 2, tells you how to add a new AVD to your system. An AVD with an *x86* system image is better than an AVD with an *armeabi* image. (Fortunately, when a dialog box lets you choose between *x86* and *armeabi*, you don't have to know what *x86* or *armeabi* means.)

In my experience, AVDs with lower resolution and screen density consume fewer resources on your development computer. So, if the AVD that you're running drags you down, follow the instructions in the "Creating an Android virtual device" section to make yourself a lower-resolution AVD (one that satisfies your app's minimum SDK requirement). Then, when you run an app, Android Studio prompts you with the Select Deployment Target dialog box. Pick the lower-resolution AVD from the dialog box's list, and you'll be on your way.

This section's bulleted list describes a few remedies for problems with Android Studio's emulator. Unfortunately, none of the bullets in this list is a silver bullet. If you've tried these tricks and you're still having trouble, you might try abandoning the emulator that comes with Android Studio. The next two sections have the details.

Running third-party emulators

Android's standard emulator and AVDs (the software that you get when you install Android Studio) don't run flawlessly on every computer. If you don't have at least 16GB of RAM, the emulator's start-up may be very slow. Even after start-up, the emulator's response may be painfully sluggish. If you don't like the standard emulator, you can try one of the third-party emulators.

>> **At** www.genymotion.com, **you can download an alternative to the standard Android emulator.**

This alternative is available for Windows, Macintosh, and some Linux systems. Genymotion's product is free for personal use, but costs $135 per year for commercial use.

>> At www.visualstudio.com/en-us/features/msft-android-emulator-vs.aspx, **you can download Visual Studio Emulator for Android.**

This alternative is free to use, but it runs only on Windows computers.

If you have trouble running the emulator that comes with Android Studio, these third-party emulators are definitely worth considering.

Testing apps on a physical device

You can bypass emulators and test your apps on a real phone, a tablet device, or even an Android-enabled coffee pot. To do so, you have to prepare the device, prepare your development computer, and then hook together the two. This section describes the process.

REMEMBER

Your device's Android version must be at least as high as your project's minimum SDK version.

To test your app on a physical device, follow these steps:

1. **On your Android device, find the USB Debugging option:**

   - If your Android device runs version 3.2 or older, choose Settings ⇨ Applications ⇨ Development.

   - If your Android device runs version 4.0, 4.0.3, or 4.1, choose Settings ⇨ Developer Options.

   - If your Android device runs version 4.2 or higher, choose Settings ⇨ About. In the About list, tap the Build Number item seven times. (Yes, seven times.) Then press the Back button to return to the Settings list. In the Settings list, tap Developer Options.

   Now your Android device displays the Development list (also known as the Developer Options list).

2. **In the Development (or Developer Options) list, turn on USB debugging.**

   Here's what one of my devices displays when I mess with this setting:

   ```
   USB debugging is intended for development purposes.
   Use it to copy data between your computer and your device,
   install apps on your device without notification, and read log data.
   ```

The stewards of Android are warning me that the USB Debugging option can expose my device to malware.

On my device, I keep USB debugging on all the time. But if you're nervous about security, turn off USB debugging whenever you're not using the device to develop apps.

3. **(For Windows users only:) Visit** `https://developer.android.com/studio/run/oem-usb.html` **to download your Android device's Windows USB driver. Install the driver on your Windows development computer.**

4. **When you start running an app, make sure that your development computer displays the Select Deployment Target dialog box.**

   If you don't see the Select Deployment Target dialog box, from Android Studio's main menu choose Run ⇨ Edit Configurations. On the left side of the resulting dialog box, select Android Application ⇨ App. In the main body of the dialog box, under Deployment Target Options, choose the Open Select Deployment Target Dialog option and deselect the Use Same Device for Future Launches check box. Seal the deal by clicking OK.

5. **Make sure that your Android device's screen is illuminated.**

   This particular step might not be necessary, but I've scraped so many knuckles trying to get Android devices to connect with computers that I want every advantage I can possibly get.

   While you follow the next step, keep an eye on your Android device's screen.

6. **With a USB cable, connect the device to the development computer.**

TIP

   Not all USB cables are created equal. Some cables have wires and metal in places where other cables (with compatible fittings) have nothing except plastic. Try to use whatever USB cable came with your Android device. If, like me, you can't find the cable that came with your device or you don't know which cable came with your device, try more than one cable. When you find a cable that works, label that able cable. (If the cable *always* works, label it Stable Able Cable.)

   When you plug in the cable, you see a pop-up dialog box on the Android device's screen. The pop-up asks: Allow USB Debugging?

7. **In response to the Allow USB Debugging? question, click the screen's OK button.**

REMEMBER

   If you're not looking for it, you can miss the Allow USB Debugging? pop-up dialog box. Be sure to look for this pop-up when you plug in your device. If you definitely don't see the pop-up, you might be okay anyway. But if the message appears and you don't respond to it, you definitely won't be okay.

8. **In Android Studio, run your project.**

   Android Studio offers you the Select Deployment Target dialog box. Select your connected device, and (lickety-split) your app starts running on your Android device.

CHECKING THE CONNECTION AND BREAKING THE CONNECTION

To find out whether your physical device is properly connected to your development computer, follow these steps:

1. **Find your computer's ANDROID_HOME directory.**

   What I call your computer's ANDROID_HOME directory is the directory containing the Android SDK. To find your computer's ANDROID_HOME directory, select File ⇨ Project Structure in Android Studio's main menu bar. On the left side of the resulting dialog box, select SDK Location. Then, in the main body of the dialog box, look for a section labeled Android SDK Location. On my Windows computer, the text field in that section points to C:\Users\barry\AppData\Local\Android\Sdk. On my Mac, the text field points to /Users/bburd/Library/Android/sdk.

2. **Select the Terminal tool button at the bottom of Android Studio's main window.**

   When you do, the lower portion of the main window turns into a command window for your computer's operating system. (On Windows, it's like running cmd. On a Mac, it's like running the Terminal app.)

3. **In the command window, use the cd command to navigate to the platform-tools subdirectory of your computer's ANDROID_HOME directory.**

   I'm a rootin'-tootin' two-fisted computer user. On my PC, I type the following, and then press Enter.

   ```
   cd \Users\barry\AppData\Local\Android\Sdk\platform-tools
   ```

   On my Mac, I type the following, and then press Enter.

   ```
   cd /Users/bburd/Library/Android/sdk/platform-tools/
   ```

4. **Type adb devices, and then press Enter. (On a Mac, type ./adb devices, and then press Enter.)**

(continued)

(continued)

If your computer's response includes a very long hexadecimal number (such as 2885046445FF097), that number represents your connected device. For example, with one particular phone connected, my computer's response is

```
emulator-5554 device
emulator-5556 device
2885046445FF097 device
```

If you see the word *unauthorized* next to the long hexadecimal number, you probably didn't answer OK to the Allow USB Debugging? question in Step 7 of the earlier section "Testing apps on a physical device."

If your computer's response doesn't include a long hexadecimal number, you might have missed the boat on one of the other steps in the "Testing apps on a physical device" section.

Eventually, you'll want to disconnect your device from the development computer. If you get the dreaded Not Safe to Remove Device message, then, in the Terminal tool window, type **adb kill-server**. (On a Mac, type **./adb kill-server**.) After that, you get the friendly Safe to Remove Hardware message.

The Project Tool Window

A bare-bones Android project contains over 1,000 files in nearly 500 folders. That's a lot of stuff. If you expand some of the branches in Android Studio's Project tool window, you see the tree shown in Figure 3-9.

To follow this book's examples, you can forget about 99 percent of the stuff in the Project tool window. You can focus on only a few of its branches. I describe them in this section.

The app/manifests branch

The app/manifests branch contains the AndroidManifest.xml file. (Refer to Figure 3-9.) The AndroidManifest.xml file provides information that a device needs in order to run the app. For example, an app may contain several activities. The AndroidManifest.xml file tells Android which of these activities to run when the user launches the app.

CROSS-REFERENCE

You can read more about AndroidManifest.xml files in Chapter 4.

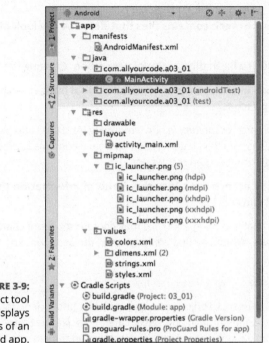

FIGURE 3-9:
The Project tool
window displays
some parts of an
Android app.

The app/java branch

The app/java branch contains your app's Java code. In fact, the branch contains several versions of your app's Java code. Earlier, in Figure 3-9, you see three branches:

>> The com.allyourcode.a03_01 branch contains the code that the user's device will run.

>> The com.allyourcode.a03_01 (androidTest) and com.allyourcode.a03_01 (test) branches contain extra code that you can use to test the app on your development computer.

In this book, you don't bother with the code in the androidTest or test branches.

The app/res branches

The word res stands for *resources*. The res branch contains extra items — items that your app uses other than its own Java code:

>> The app/res/drawable branch contains any regular-size images that your app uses.

>> **The** `app/res/layout` **branch contains files that describe the look of your app's activities.**

You deal with just such a file in this chapter's later section "Creating the 'look.'"

>> **The** `app/res/mipmap` **branch contains some additional images — the images of your app's icons.**

The term *mipmap* stands for *multum in parvo* mapping. And the Latin phrase *multum in parvo* means "much in little." A *mipmap* image contains copies of textures for many different screen resolutions.

>> **The** `app/res/values` **branch contains other kinds of information that an app needs when it runs.**

For example, the branch's `strings.xml` file may contain strings of characters that your app displays. When you first create an app, the `strings.xml` file may contain the line

```
<string name="app_name">My Application</string>
```

If you want Romanian users to enjoy your app, you can right-click or control-click the `strings.xml` file's branch and select Open Translations Editor. In Android Studio's Translations Editor, you can create an additional app/res/values branch (a `strings.xml` (`ro`) branch) containing the following line:

```
<string name="app_name">Aplicatia mea</string>
```

The Gradle scripts branch

Gradle is a software tool. When the tool runs, it takes a whole bunch of files and combines them to form a complete application — a single file that you can post on Google Play. Of course, Gradle can combine files in many different ways, so to get Gradle to do things properly, someone has to provide it with a script of some kind. The heart of that script is in the `build.gradle` (`Module: app`) branch of the Project tool window. That branch describes your app's version number, minimum SDK, and other goodies.

Dragging, Dropping, and Otherwise Tweaking an App

At the start of this chapter, you create a brand-new Android app. The app displays the words *Hello World!* on the device's screen.

Wow! I'll bet you're really impressed!

In this section, I explore new frontiers. I show you how to add components to your app — simple components that copy the user's text. The new app isn't very useful. You wouldn't spend money for this app at Google Play. But with this app, you find out how to get input from the user and how to display text on the user's screen.

Creating the "look"

A general guideline in app development tells you to separate logic from presentation. In less technical terms, the guideline warns against confusing what an app does with how an app looks. The guideline applies to many aspects of life. For example, if you're designing a website, have artists do the layout and have geeks do the coding. If you're writing a report, get the ideas written first. Later, you can worry about fonts and paragraph styles. (I wonder whether this book's copy editor would agree with me about fonts and styles.)

The literature on app development describes specific techniques and frameworks to help you separate form from function. But in this chapter I do the simplest thing — I chop an app's creation into two sets of instructions. The first set is about creating an app's look; the second set is about coding the app's behavior.

To add buttons, boxes, and other goodies to your app, do the following:

1. **Follow the steps earlier in this chapter, in the "First things first" section.**

   When you're finished with these steps, you have a brand-new project with an empty activity. The project appears in Android Studio's main window.

2. **In the new project's `app/res/layout` branch (in the main window's Project tool window), double-click `activity_main.xml`.**

   As a result, Android Studio's Designer tool displays the contents of `activity_main.xml`. The Designer tool has two modes: Design mode for drag-and-drop visual editing and Text mode for XML code editing. So the bottom of the Designer tool has two tabs: a Design tab and a Text tab.

3. **Click the Design tab.**

   In Design mode, you see the palette, the component tree, two preview screens, and the Properties pane. (See Figure 3-10.)

   For details about Android Studio's Design mode, check out the earlier sidebar "Android Studio's Designer tool."

   If you don't see the palette, look for the little Palette button on the left edge of the Designer tool. If you click that button, the palette should appear.

The component tree has a branch labeled *TextView – "Hello World!"* This branch
represents the text *Hello World!* that appears automatically as part of your app.
You don't need this text in your app.

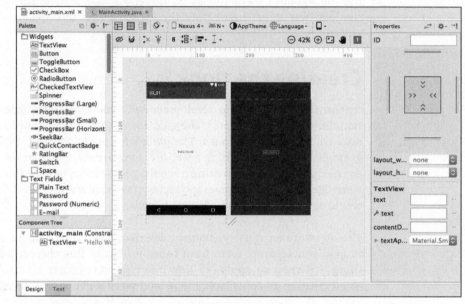

FIGURE 3-10:
The Designer
tool's Design
mode.

4. **Select the** `TextView – "Hello World!"` **branch in the component tree,
    and then press Delete.**

    The `"Hello World!"` branch disappears from the component tree, and the
    words *Hello World!* disappear from the preview screen.

    The next several steps guide you through the creation of the app shown in
    Figure 3-11.

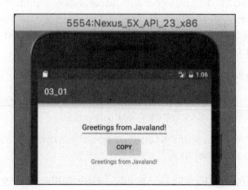

FIGURE 3-11:
Running this
section's app.

The app's layout has three different kinds of components, and each kind of component goes by several different names. Here are the three kinds of components:

- **EditText (also known as Plain Text):** A place where the user can edit a single line of text.

  A common name for this kind of component is a *text field*.

- **Button:** A button is a button is a button.

  Do you want to click the button? Go right ahead and click it.

- **TextView (also known as Plain TextView, Large Text, Medium Text, and so on):** A place where the app displays text.

  Normally, the user doesn't edit the text in a TextView component.

TECHNICAL STUFF

To be painfully precise, Android's EditText, Button, and TextView components aren't really different kinds of components. Every EditText component is a kind of TextView, and every Button is also a kind of TextView. In the language of object-oriented programming, the EditText class *extends* the TextView class. The Button class also extends the TextView class. You can read all about classes extending other classes in Chapter 10 of this book. With or without that chapter, this book's examples don't make use of the relationships between EditText, Button, and TextView. You can forget that you ever read this paragraph, and everything will be okay.

5. **Drag a Plain Text (that is, EditText) item from the palette's Widgets group to either of the preview screens.**

   The Plain Text item may land in an ugly-looking place. That's okay. You're not creating a work of art. You're learning to write Java code.

TIP

My book *Android Application Development All-in-One For Dummies,* 2nd Edition (published by Wiley), has advice on refining the look of your Android layouts.

6. **Repeat Step 5, this time putting a Button item on the preview screen.**

   I suggest putting the Button component below the Plain Text (EditText) component. Later, if you don't like where you put the Button component, you can easily move it by dragging it elsewhere on the preview screen.

7. **Repeat Step 6, this time putting a TextView component on the preview screen.**

   I suggest putting the TextView component below the Button component but, once again, it's up to you.

   In the remaining steps of this section, you change the text that appears in each component.

8. **Select the** Button **component on the preview screen or in the component tree.**

   As a result, the Designer tool's Properties pane displays some of the Button component's properties. (See Figure 3-12.)

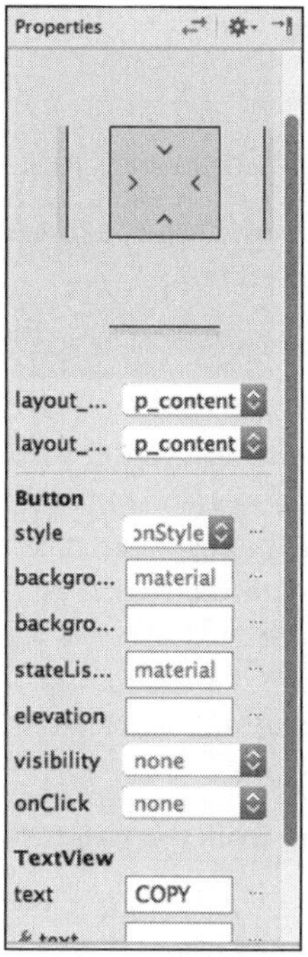

FIGURE 3-12:
Setting the
properties of a
button.

Properties		
layout_...	p_content	
layout_...	p_content	
Button		
style	onStyle	...
backgro...	material	...
backgro...		...
stateLis...	material	...
elevation		...
visibility	none	
onClick	none	
TextView		
text	COPY	...

TIP

After selecting the Button component, you may see the word *TextView* in the Properties pane. Don't confuse this with the TextView component that you dragged from the palette in Step 7. With the button selected, all the fields in the Properties pane refer to that Button component. If the appearance of the word *TextView* in the Properties pane confuses you, refer to the Technical Stuff icon in Step 4. (If the word *TextView* doesn't confuse you, don't bother reading the Technical Stuff icon!)

9. **In the Properties pane, in the field labeled** *text***, type the word** COPY. **(Refer to Figure 3-12.)**

   When you do, the word *COPY* appears on the face of the Button component. You can check this by looking at the wysiwyg preview screen.

In the Properties pane, you may see two fields labeled *text*. If so, one is for testing and the other is for running the app. When in doubt, it doesn't hurt to type the word **COPY** in both of those fields.

10. Repeat Steps 8 and 9 with your activity's `EditText` and `TextView` components, but this time, don't put the word *COPY* into those components. Instead, remove the characters from these components.

When you're finished, the preview screens look similar to the screens in Figure 3-13. If your preview screens don't look exactly like Figure 3-13, don't worry about it. Your components may be scattered in different places on the preview screens, or the creators of Android Studio may have changed the way the preview screens look since the time I wrote this book. As long as you have an `EditText` component, a `Button` component, and a `TextView` component, you're okay.

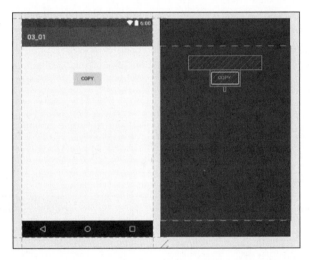

FIGURE 3-13:
Preview screens containing the three components.

11. Choose File ⇨ Save All to save your work so far.

With this section's steps, you edit your app visually. Behind the scenes, Android Studio is editing the text in your app's `activity_main.xml` document. You can see what changes Android Studio has made to your app's `activity_main.xml` document by selecting the Text tab at the bottom of Android Studio's editor. My `activity_main.xml` document is reproduced in Listing 3-1. Your `activity_main.xml` document's contents may be different.

ANDROID STUDIO'S DESIGNER TOOL

A typical Android app has at least one layout file. A layout file describes the look of an Android device's screen. A layout file also describes the positions of text fields, buttons, images, and other items. The layout file can describe other properties of components on the screen. For example, a layout file can indicate the piece of Java code that Android calls when the user clicks a particular button.

Layout files aren't written in Java. They're written in XML. So you don't do anything exciting with layout files in this book. But you can do some simple, fun things with layouts by dragging and dropping components (buttons, text fields, and so on) in Android Studio's Designer tool.

One of the layout files in a typical Android app is named `activity_main.xml`. You may also see a file named `content_main.xml`. When you expand the `app/res/layout` branches in the Project tool window and you double-click the `activity_main.xml` item inside those branches, Android Studio displays its Designer tool. The Designer tool has two modes: Design mode and Text mode. (Refer to Figure 3-10 and the figure in this sidebar.) So the bottom of the Designer tool has two tabs: a Design tab and a Text tab.

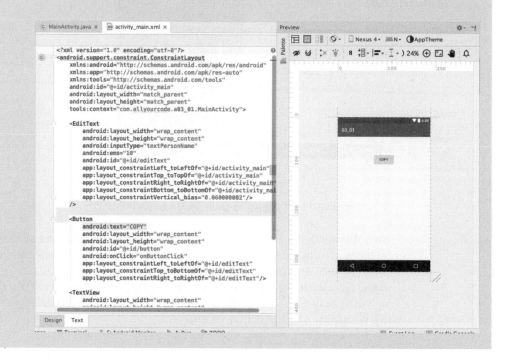

In Design mode, you edit the layout by dragging and dropping components onto one of the Designer tool's preview screens. In Text mode, you edit the same layout by typing text in the XML file.

In Design mode, shown in Figure 3-10, the Designer tool has five parts:

- **The leftmost preview screen is a place to drop new components onto your app's screen.**

  I call this leftmost preview screen the *wysiwyg* ("what you see is what you get") preview screen.

- **To the right of the wysiwyg preview screen is the blueprint preview screen.**

  The *blueprint* screen is good for adjusting the positions of components. However, you can drop new components onto both the wysiwyg and blueprint screens. You can also adjust the positions of components on both the wysiwyg and blueprint screens. Whatever you do to a component on one preview screen automatically changes that same component on the other preview screen.

- **The palette on the left side of the Designer tool is a place to get the components that you drop onto the preview screens.**

  The palette has components such as TextView, Button, CheckBox, and many others.

- **The component tree (immediately below the palette) lists all components on your activity's screen.**

  When you create a project and select Empty Activity, Android Studio places a few of these components on your activity's screen. You may have dropped other components from the palette.

  Some components can live inside other components. That's why the component tree isn't a simple list. Instead, it's a tree with branches within branches.

- **The Properties pane on the right displays facts about the components in your layout. You can change the layout by modifying the values that you find here.**

In Text mode (shown in this sidebar's figure), the Designer tool has two parts:

- **The left half of the Text mode Designer tool is an editor.**

  In the editor, you see the XML file describing the layout of your app.

(continued)

(continued)

- **In the right half of the Text mode Designer tool is yet another preview screen.**

    The Text mode's preview screen is only a viewer. It's not an editor. You can't modify the layout by dragging and dropping items on this preview screen.

    If Android Studio's Designer tool is in Text mode and you don't see the preview, click the Preview tool button. You'll find this button on the rightmost edge of the main window.

When you drag and drop components on Design mode's preview screens, Android Studio automatically updates the XML file. And it works both ways: When you edit the XML file, Android Studio keeps the preview screens up-to-date.

When you go to the Project tool window and double-click a file that's not a layout file, Android Studio dismisses the Designer tool and replaces it with the plain, old editor area.

LISTING 3-1:   **The activity_main.xml Document**

```xml
<?xml version="1.0" encoding="utf-8"?>
<android.support.constraint.ConstraintLayout
    xmlns:android="http://schemas.android.com/apk/res/android"
    xmlns:app="http://schemas.android.com/apk/res-auto"
    xmlns:tools="http://schemas.android.com/tools"
    android:id="@+id/activity_main"
    android:layout_width="match_parent"
    android:layout_height="match_parent"
    tools:context="com.allyourcode.a03_01.MainActivity">

    <EditText
        android:layout_width="wrap_content"
        android:layout_height="wrap_content"
        android:inputType="textPersonName"
        android:ems="10"
        android:id="@+id/editText"
        app:layout_constraintLeft_toLeftOf="@+id/activity_main"
        app:layout_constraintTop_toTopOf="@+id/activity_main"
        app:layout_constraintRight_toRightOf="@+id/activity_main"
        app:layout_constraintBottom_toBottomOf="@+id/activity_main"
        app:layout_constraintVertical_bias="0.06"/>
```

```
<Button
    android:text="COPY"
    android:layout_width="wrap_content"
    android:layout_height="wrap_content"
    android:id="@+id/button"
    app:layout_constraintLeft_toLeftOf="@+id/editText"
    app:layout_constraintTop_toBottomOf="@+id/editText"
    app:layout_constraintRight_toRightOf="@+id/editText"/>

<TextView
    android:layout_width="wrap_content"
    android:layout_height="wrap_content"
    android:id="@+id/textView"
    app:layout_constraintLeft_toLeftOf="@+id/button"
    app:layout_constraintTop_toBottomOf="@+id/button"
    app:layout_constraintRight_toRightOf="@+id/button"/>

</android.support.constraint.ConstraintLayout>
```

REMEMBER

The code in a *something_or_other*.xml file isn't Java code. It's XML (eXtensible Markup Language) code. You don't have to type any XML code in an app's activity_main.xml file. For most of this book's examples, you can create the XML code indirectly by dragging and dropping components, and tweaking properties in Android Studio's Designer tool. That's what this section's instructions are all about. Of course, it's helpful to know something about XML code. That's why I wrote this section's "All about XML files" sidebar.

ALL ABOUT XML FILES

The acronym *XML* stands for eXtensible Markup Language. Every Android app consists of some Java code files, some XML files, and some other files.

Listing 3-1 contains an XML document. You might already be familiar with HTML documents — the bread and butter of the World Wide Web. Like an HTML document, every XML document consists of tags (angle-bracketed descriptions of various pieces of information). But unlike an HTML document, an XML document doesn't necessarily describe a displayable page.

(continued)

(continued)

Here are some facts about XML code:

- **A *tag* consists of text surrounded by angle brackets.**

  For example, the code in Listing 3-1 consists of three tags: The first tag is the `<android.support.constraint.ConstraintLayout ... >` tag. The second tag is the `<EditText ... />` tag. The remaining tags are the `<Button ... />` tag, the `<TextView ... />` tag, and the `</android.support.constraint.ConstraintLayout>` tag.

  With its question marks, the first line in Listing 3-1, `<?xml version="1.0" encoding="utf-8"?>`, doesn't count as a tag.

- **An XML document may have three different kinds of tags: start tags, empty element tags, and end tags.**

  A *start tag* begins with an open angle bracket and a name. A start tag's last character is a closing angle bracket.

  The first tag in Listing 3-1 (the `<android.support.constraint.ConstraintLayout ... >` tag on lines 2 through 9) is a start tag. Its name is `android.support.constraint.ConstraintLayout`.

  An *empty element tag* begins with an open angle bracket followed by a name. An empty element tag's last two characters are a forward slash followed by a closing angle bracket.

  The second tag in Listing 3-1 (the `<EditText ... />` tag on lines 11 through 18 in the listing) is an empty element tag. Its name is `EditText`. The `<Button ... />` and `<TextView ... />` tags are also empty element tags.

  An *end tag* begins with an open angle bracket followed by a forward slash and a name. An end tag's last character is a closing angle bracket.

  The last tag in Listing 3-1 (the `</android.support.constraint.ConstraintLayout>` tag on the last line of the listing) is an end tag. Its name is `android.support.constraint.ConstraintLayout`.

- **An XML *element* has both a start tag and an end tag or it has an empty element tag.**

  In Listing 3-1, the document's `android.support.constraint.ConstraintLayout` element has both a start tag and an end tag. (Both the start and end tags have the same name, `android.support.constraint.ConstraintLayout`, so the name of the entire element is `android.support.constraint.ConstraintLayout`.)

  In Listing 3-1, the document's `EditText` element has only one tag: an empty element tag. The same is true of the `Button` and `TextView` elements.

- **Either elements are nested inside one another or they have no overlap.**

  For example, in the following code, a `TableLayout` element contains two `TableRow` elements:

```
<TableLayout xmlns:android=
        "http://schemas.android.com/apk/res/android"
        android:layout_width="fill_parent"
        android:layout_height="fill_parent" >

  <TableRow>

    <TextView
        android:layout_width="wrap_content"
        android:layout_height="wrap_content"
        android:text="@string/name"/>

  </TableRow>

  <TableRow>

    <TextView
        android:layout_width="wrap_content"
        android:layout_height="wrap_content"
        android:text="@string/address"/>

  </TableRow>


</TableLayout>
```

  The preceding code works because the first `TableRow` ends before the second `TableRow` begins. But the following XML code is illegal:

```
<!-- The following code isn't legal XML code. -->
<TableRow>

    <TextView
        android:layout_width="wrap_content"
        android:layout_height="wrap_content"
        android:text="@string/name"/>
<TableRow>

</TableRow>

    <TextView
        android:layout_width="wrap_content"
        android:layout_height="wrap_content"
        android:text="@string/address"/>
</TableRow>
```

(continued)

(continued)

With two start tags followed by two end tags, this new XML code doesn't pass muster.

- **Each XML document contains a *root element* — one element in which all other elements are nested.**

  In Listing 3-2 (a little later in this chapter), the root element is the `android.support.constraint.ConstraintLayout` element. The listing's other elements (the `EditText`, `Button`, and `TextView` elements) are nested inside that `android.support.constraint.ConstraintLayout` element.

- **Different XML documents use different element names.**

  In every HTML document, the `<br />` element stands for *line break*. But in XML, names such as `android.support.constraint.ConstraintLayout` and `EditText` are particular to Android layout documents. And the names `portfolio` and `trade` are particular to financial product XML (FpML) documents. The names `prompt` and `phoneme` are peculiar to voice XML (VoiceXML). Each kind of document has its own list of element names.

- **The text in an XML document is case-sensitive.**

  For example, if you change `EditText` to `eDITtEXT` in Listing 3-2, the app won't run.

- **Start tags and empty element tags may contain attributes.**

  An *attribute* is a name-value pair. Each attribute has the form *name="value"*. The quotation marks around the *value* are required.

  In Listing 3-1, the start tag (`android.support.constraint.ConstraintLayout`) has seven attributes, and the empty element tag (`EditText`) has seven of its own attributes. For example, in the `EditText` empty element tag, the text `android:layout_width="wrap_content"` is the first attribute. This attribute has the name `android:layout_width` and the value `"wrap_content"`.

- **A non-empty XML element may contain *content*.**

  For example, in the `app/res/values` branch in Android Studio's Project tool window, you can find a file named `strings.xml`. In that `strings.xml` file, you may see

  ```
  <string name="app_name">03_01</string>
  ```

  In the `string` element, the content `03_01` is sandwiched between the start tag (`<string name="app_name">`) and the end tag (`</string>`).

Coding the behavior

Assuming you've followed the instructions in the earlier section "Creating the 'look,'" what's next? Well, what's next depends on how much you want to work. This section describes the easy way. If you read the later section "Going Pro," you'll find out how to do it the not-so-easy way.

Android 1.6 (also known as Donut) introduced an `android:onClick` attribute that streamlines the coding of an app's actions. Here's what you do:

1. **Follow the steps in this chapter's earlier section "Creating the 'look.'"**

2. **If you don't see the Designer tool with its preview screens, double-click the app/res/layout/activity_main.xml branch in the Project tool window. When the Designer tool appears, select the Design tab.**

   For details, refer to Steps 2 and 3 in the "Creating the 'look'" section.

3. **Make note of the labels on the branches in the component tree.**

   The component tree is on the left side of the Designer tool, immediately below the palette. Notice the labels on the branches of the tree. Each element on the screen has an *id* (a name to identify that element). In Figure 3-14, the ids of some of the screen's elements are editText, button, and textView.

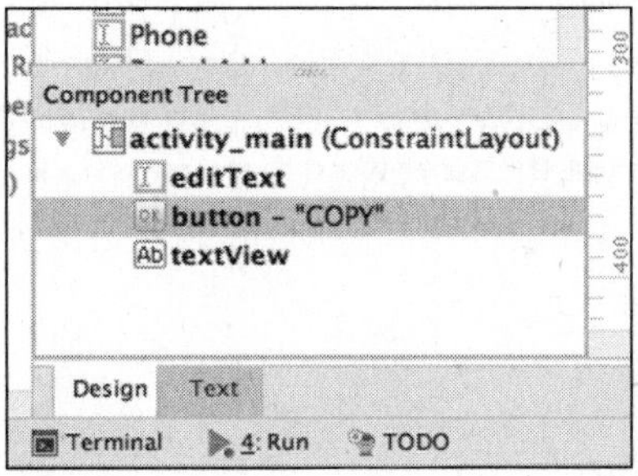

FIGURE 3-14: The component tree.

TIP

You may be wondering why, in place of the word "identification," I use the strange lowercase abbreviation *id* instead of the more conventional English language abbreviation *ID*. To find out what's going on, select the Text tab in Android Studio's designer tool. In the XML code for the activity's layout you'll find lines such as `android:id="@+id/textView"`. In Android's XML files, id is a code word.

When you drop a component onto the preview screen, Android Studio assigns that component an id. You can experiment with this by dropping a second `TextView` component onto the preview screen. If you do, the component tree has an additional branch, and the label on the branch (the id of the new component) is likely to be textView2.

Java is case-sensitive, so you have to pay attention to the way words are capitalized. For example, the word EditText isn't the same as the word editText. In this example, the word EditText stands for a *kind* of component (a kind of text field), and editText stands for a *particular* component (the text field in your app — the text field that you dropped onto the preview screen).

You can change a component's id, if you want. (For example, you can change the name editText to thatTextThingie.) In this example, I recommend accepting whatever you see in the component tree. But before proceeding to the next step, make note of the ids in your app's component tree. (They may not be the same as the ids in Figure 3-14.)

To change a component's id, select that component on the preview screen or in the component tree. Then, in the Properties pane on the right side of the Designer tool, look for an ID field. Change the text that you find in this ID field. (Yes. In the Properties pane, *ID* has capital letters. Don't blame me. It's not my fault.)

4. **On the preview screen or in the component tree, select the COPY button. (Refer to Figure 3-14.)**

   As a result, the Properties pane displays information about your button component.

5. **In the Properties pane, type** onButtonClick **in the** onClick **field. (See Figure 3-15.)**

   Actually, the word you type in the onClick field doesn't have to be **onButtonClick**. But in these instructions, I use the word *onButtonClick*. So please indulge me and use the same word that I use. Thank you!

elevation		...
visibility	none	
onClick	onButtonClick	
TextView		
text	COPY	...
text		...
contentDes...		...
textAppe...	at.Widget.Button	

FIGURE 3-15:
Setting the
button's
onClick value.

6. **Inside the** app/java **branch of the Project tool window, double-click** MainActivity.

   Of course, if you didn't accept the default activity name (MainActivity) when you created the new project, double-click whatever activity name you used.

In the Project tool window, the `MainActivity` branch is located in a branch that's labeled with your app's package name. (The package name is `com.example.myapplication` or `com.allyourcode.a03_01` or something like that.) That package name branch is directly in the `java` branch, which is, in turn, in the `app` branch.

When you're finished with double-clicking, the activity's code appears in Android Studio's editor.

7. **Modify the activity's code, as shown in Listing 3-2.**

   The lines that you type are set in boldface in Listing 3-2.

   For some hints about typing code, see the later sidebar "Make Android Studio do the work."

   In Listing 3-2, I assume that the branches on your app's component tree have the same labels as the tree pictured in Figure 3-14. In other words, I assume that your app's components have the ids `editText`, `button`, and `textView`. If your app's components have different ids, change the code in Listing 3-2 accordingly. For example, if your first `EditText` component has the id `editText2`, change your first `findViewById` call to `findViewById(R.id.editText2)`.

LISTING 3-2: **A Button Responds to a Click**

```
package com.allyourcode.a03_01;

import android.support.v7.app.AppCompatActivity;
import android.os.Bundle;
import android.view.View;
import android.widget.EditText;
import android.widget.TextView;

public class MainActivity extends AppCompatActivity {
  EditText editText;
  TextView textView;

  @Override
  protected void onCreate(Bundle savedInstanceState) {
    super.onCreate(savedInstanceState);
    setContentView(R.layout.activity_main);

    editText = (EditText) findViewById(R.id.editText);
    textView = (TextView) findViewById(R.id.textView);
  }
```

(continued)

LISTING 3-2: *(continued)*

```
public void onButtonClick(View view) {
  textView.setText(editText.getText());
}
}
```

8. **Run the app.**

9. **When the app starts running, type something (anything) in your app's** `EditText` **component. Then click the button.**

   When you click the button, Android copies the text from your `EditText` component to your `TextView` component. The running app is shown in Figure 3-11.

If your app doesn't run, you can ask me for help via email. The address is `Java4 Android@allmycode.com`.

REMEMBER

MAKE ANDROID STUDIO DO THE WORK

When you type code in Android Studio, the editor guesses what you're trying to type and offers to finish typing it for you. In the first sidebar figure, I start to type the word *EditText*. When I type the letters *Ed,* Android Studio displays a drop-down list with entries such as `EditText`, `EdgeEffectCompat`, and `EdgeEffect`. (See the first sidebar figure.) I can select one of these by double-clicking the entry in the pop-up menu. Alternatively, I can select an entry from the pop-up menu and then press Enter or Tab.

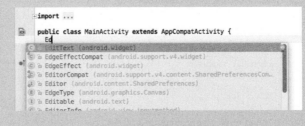

Another cool feature of Android Studio's editor is intention actions. You're minding your own business, typing code, and having a good time — and suddenly you see some commotion in the Editor window. (See the second sidebar figure.) A callout signals the presence of one or more *intention actions* — proposals to make small changes in order to improve your code. In response to the callout's appearance, you press Alt+Enter. Doing so may add an `import` line at the top of your code or make another beneficial change.

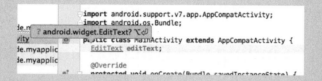

You can tweak Android Studio's settings so that you get the `import` lines at the top of Listing 4-2 without even pressing Alt+Enter. Lines of this kind can appear automatically whenever you type words like `View` or `EditText`. Here's how:

1. **If you have a Windows PC, choose File ⇨ Settings. If you have a Mac, choose Android Studio ⇨ Preferences.**

   A dialog box appears. (The dialog box's title is either Settings or Preferences. Whatever!)

2. **In the panel on the left side of the dialog box, expand the Editor branch.**

3. **In the subbranch labeled General, select Auto Import.**

   Several options appear in the main body of the dialog box. (See the third sidebar figure.)

4. **In the drop-down list labeled Insert Imports on Paste, select All.**

5. **Put a check mark in the Optimize Imports on the Fly check box.**

6. **Put a check mark in the Add Unambiguous Imports on the Fly check box.**

7. **Click OK to commit to these changes.**

Now, when you type a line like `TextView textView`, Android Studio automatically adds the required `import android.widget.TextView` line to your code. That's nice.

What All That Java Code Does

You may be curious about the code in Listing 3-2. If so, a few words of explanation are in order.

Finding the EditText and TextView components

In Listing 3-2, the lines

```
EditText editText;
TextView textView;
```

alert Java to the fact that you use the names `editText` and `textView` in your code. The line

```
EditText editText;
```

says that the name `editText` refers to an `EditText` type of component (a place where the user can type some text). This line might seem redundant, but it's not. You can modify the second word on the line this way:

```
EditText userTypesTextHere;
```

But if you make this change, you have to change the name `editText` in other parts of Listing 3-2.

REMEMBER

In Listing 3-2, you can change the name `editText` to another name, but you can't change `EditText` (starting with an uppercase letter *E*) to another name. In an Android program, the name `EditText` (starting with an uppercase letter *E*) stands for a place where the user can type a single line of text. Similarly, the name `Button` stands for a button, and `TextView` stands for a place where Android displays text.

In Listing 3-2, the line

```
editText = (EditText) findViewById(R.id.editText);
```

finds the `EditText` component that you create in the steps in the earlier section "Creating the 'look.'"

Wait a minute! What does it mean to "find" a component, and how does a line of code in Listing 3-2 accomplish that task? Figure 3-16 illustrates the situation.

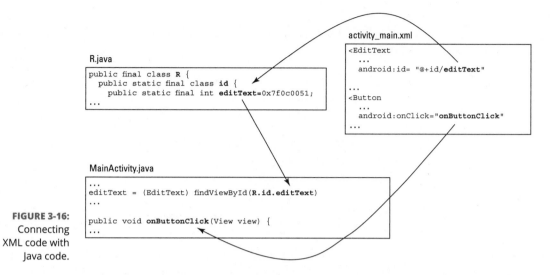

R.java

```
public final class R {
  public static final class id {
    public static final int editText=0x7f0c0051;
...
```

activity_main.xml

```
<EditText
    ...
    android:id= "@+id/editText"
...
<Button
    ...
    android:onClick="onButtonClick"
...
```

MainActivity.java

```
...
editText = (EditText) findViewById(R.id.editText)
...

public void onButtonClick(View view) {
...
```

FIGURE 3-16:
Connecting
XML code with
Java code.

When you follow the directions in the earlier section "Creating the 'look,'" you end up with a file like the one in Listing 3-1. This file contains these lines:

```
<EditText
    android:layout_width="wrap_content"
    android:layout_height="wrap_content"
    ...
    android:id="@+id/editText"
    ... />
```

The EditText component's XML code contains a cryptic @+id/editText attribute. Android Studio sees this @+id/editText attribute and takes it as an instruction to add a line to one of your app's Java files:

```
public final class R {
  public static final class id {
    public static final int editText=0x7f0c0051;
```

TECHNICAL
STUFF

The file that contains this code is named R.java. You don't see the R.java file in Android Studio's Project view unless you select Project or Project Files instead of Android in the drop-down list above the Project tool window. Even if you can see the R.java file, you should never type any of your own changes in the R.java file.

Because of this Java code, the name R.id.editText stands for the number 0x7f0c0051.

So, if you look again at Figure 3-16, you see how a line of Java code says the following:

Look for something that has id number 2131492945. Treat whatever you find as if it's an EditText component, and from here on, in this Java code, refer to that thing by the name editText.

This is how Android connects a component that you create in the Designer tool with a name in your app's Java code.

In Listing 3-2, the line

```
textView = (TextView) findViewById(R.id.textView);
```

serves the same purpose for the TextView component that you add when you follow the instructions in the earlier section "Creating the 'look.'"

TECHNICAL
STUFF

The characters 0x7f0c0051 might not look much like a number but, in a Java program, the characters 0x7f0c0051 form the hexadecimal representation of what we ordinarily call 2131492945. If this number 2131492945 for a little EditText component seems arbitrary, don't worry. It's *supposed* to be arbitrary. Android Studio generates the R.java file automatically from the things that you name in places like Listing 3-1. All the numbers in the R.java file are arbitrary. There's no reason for them not to be arbitrary.

Responding to a button click

The onButtonClick code in Listing 3-2 fulfills the promise that you make in Step 5 of the earlier section "Coding the behavior." Setting the button's onClick property to onButtonClick gets Android Studio to add the additional line android:onClick="onButtonClick" to the code in Listing 3-1. As a result, Android calls the onButtonClick code in Listing 3-2 whenever the user clicks the button.

In Listing 3-2, the lines

```
public void onButtonClick(View view) {
    textView.setText(editText.getText());
}
```

form a *method* whose name is onButtonClick. The first line is the method's *header:*

```
public void onButtonClick(View view)
```

The header has the method's name — onButtonClick. This is the name you typed when you set the button's onClick property in Step 5 of the earlier section "Coding the behavior."

Below the header comes the instruction to be performed whenever the user clicks the button. Figure 3-17 describes what the instruction tells Android to do when the user clicks the button.

```
textView.setText ( editText.getText() );
```

Get the text that's in your activity's editText component, and ...

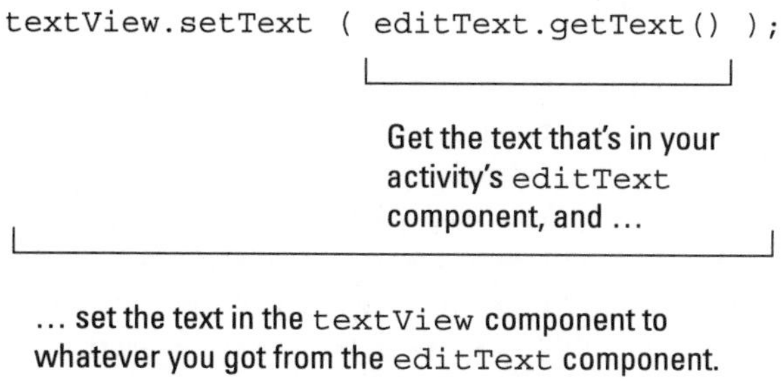

FIGURE 3-17:
An instruction to copy text.

... set the text in the textView component to whatever you got from the editText component.

REMEMBER

You don't have much leeway in the way you create the button click's method header. Instead of public void onButtonClick(View view), you can write something like public void whenClicked(View veryNiceView), but then you must use the words whenClicked and veryNiceView consistently throughout your code.

CROSS-REFERENCE

I confess. I'm getting ahead of myself with this section's talk about a Java method. To read more about Java methods, see Chapters 4 and 7.

The rest of the code

Most of the code in Listing 3-2 is standard stuff. Android Studio composes the code automatically, and you use this code in almost every app that you create. Much of the time, you don't pay attention to this code that Android Studio generates. When you stare at Listing 3-2, you concentrate on the boldface lines and not much else. You take the other lines for granted.

Of course, the boilerplate code in Listing 3-2 isn't magic. In later chapters, I describe lots of Java's features and help you to understand the inner workings of the listing's code. But in this section, I provide only a brief description of that code's purpose. The description is in Listing 3-3.

LISTING 3-3: **A Guide to Listing 3-2**

```
package com.allmycode.a03_03; // The code in this file belongs to
                              // a package named com.allmycode.a03_03.

import android.support.v7.app.AppCompatActivity;
import android.os.Bundle;          // This code uses things that are coded in
import android.view.View;          // other packages -- packages such as
import android.widget.EditText;    // android.widget.EditText, android.os.View,
import android.widget.TextView;    // and others.

public class MainActivity extends AppCompatActivity {
                          // This code defines a class.
                          // The class's name is MainActivity.
                          // This code inherits all the features described in
                          // Android's built-in AppCompatActivity code.
                          // An AppCompatActivity is a kind of Activity.
                          // An Activity is one screenful of stuff that the
                          // user sees. So, this code describes one screenful
                          // for the user.
    EditText editText;
    TextView textView;

    @Override
    protected void onCreate(Bundle savedInstanceState) {
                                          // When an Android device
                                          // creates this screenful
                                          // of stuff...

        super.onCreate(savedInstanceState);  // ... the device recovers
                                             // relevant info from the
                                             // last time this screenful
                                             // appeared, and ...

        setContentView(R.layout.activity_main);  // ... displays the layout
                                                 // that's described in
                                                 // Listing 3-1.
        editText = (EditText) findViewById(R.id.editText);
        textView = (TextView) findViewById(R.id.textView);
    }

    public void onButtonClick(View view) {
        textView.setText(editText.getText());
    }
}
```

If you go to Android Studio's editor and paste the voluminous code of Listing 3-3 in place of Listing 3-2, your app will still run. That's because Listing 3-3 makes use of Java's *comment* feature. When Android runs this code, Android doesn't act on any text that appears on a line after the double slash (//). Text such as // The code in this file belongs to is for humans to read and appreciate.

You can find out more about Java comments in Chapter 4.

CROSS-REFERENCE

Going Pro

This chapter's "Coding the behavior" section describes a way to make your app respond when the user clicks a button. The story isn't complicated: You type a name in the button's onClick field in the Properties pane, and then you use that name in the app's Java code. That's the easy way.

The problem with the easy way is that hard-core Android developers don't do things that way. Using a button's onClick property doesn't work well for more complicated apps. So professional Android developers use a technique that comes from the Java desktop programming world.

In most of this book's examples, I use the easy way to respond to button clicks. But if you want to use the more professional way, read on:

1. **Follow the steps in this chapter's "Creating the 'look'" section.**

2. **Make note of the labels on the branches in the component tree, but don't follow any other instructions in the "Coding the behavior" section.**

In particular, don't bother setting the button's onClick property.

3. **Modify the activity's code, as shown in Listing 3-4.**

The lines that you type are set in boldface in Listing 3-4. Use the labels that you found in Step 2. For example, if your TextView component's id is textView2, modify a line in Listing 3-4 as follows:

```
textView = (TextView) findViewById(R.id.textView2);
```

4. **Run the app.**

LISTING 3-4:   **Event Handling (the Traditional Java Way)**

```java
package com.allyourcode.a03_04;

import android.support.v7.app.AppCompatActivity;
import android.os.Bundle;
import android.view.View;
import android.widget.Button;
import android.widget.EditText;
import android.widget.TextView;

public class MainActivity extends AppCompatActivity
    implements View.OnClickListener {
  EditText editText;
  Button button;
  TextView textView;

  @Override
  protected void onCreate(Bundle savedInstanceState) {
    super.onCreate(savedInstanceState);
    setContentView(R.layout.activity_main);

    editText = (EditText) findViewById(R.id.editText);
    button = (Button) findViewById(R.id.button);
    textView = (TextView) findViewById(R.id.textView);

    button.setOnClickListener(this);
  }

  @Override
  public void onClick(View view) {
    textView.setText(editText.getText());
  }
}
```

Listing 3-4 uses Java's traditional event-handling pattern. The button registers your activity as its click-event listener. In a sense, the setOnClickListener line in Listing 3-4 replaces the button's onClick property in this chapter's "Coding the behavior" section. Your activity declares itself to be an OnClickListener and makes good on this click-listener promise by implementing the onClick method.

The technique that I use in Listing 3-4 involves a callback, and callbacks aren't the easiest things to understand. That's why I wait until Chapter 11 to describe what's going on in Listing 3-4. In the meantime, you can start reading about Java's wonderful features in Chapter 4. Enjoy!

2

Writing Your Own Java Programs

Chapter **4**

An Ode to Code

Hello, hello, hello, . . . hello!
—THE THREE STOOGES IN *DIZZY DETECTIVES* AND OTHER SHORT FILMS

n Chapter 3, you create a Hello World app for Android. You do this with the help of Android Studio and, in the process, Android Studio composes some Java code for you. In Chapter 3, you examine a bit of this Java code.

But in Chapter 3, you only scratch the code's surface. In this chapter, you begin to examine the code in depth. When you understand how the code works, you can forge ahead to create bigger and better Android apps.

Hello, Android!

When you create a new Android app and you select Empty Activity in the Add an Activity dialog box, Android Studio creates the Java code shown in Listing 4-1.

LISTING 4-1: **A Small Android Java Program**

```
package com.allyourcode.a04_01;

import android.os.Bundle;
import android.support.v7.app.AppCompatActivity;

public class MainActivity extends AppCompatActivity {

  @Override
  protected void onCreate(Bundle savedInstanceState) {
    super.onCreate(savedInstanceState);
    setContentView(R.layout.activity_main);
  }
}
```

REMEMBER

In Android developer lingo, an *activity* is one "screenful" of components. Each Android application can contain many activities. For example, an app's initial activity might be a login screen. After the user logs on, Android covers the entire login activity with another, more interesting activity.

When you run the app that Android Studio creates automatically, you see the words *Hello World!*, as shown in Figure 4-1. Now, I admit that writing and running a Java program just to make *Hello World!* appear on a device's screen is a lot of work, but every endeavor has to start somewhere.

FIGURE 4-1:
Running Android
Studio's Blank
Activity app.

Figure 4-2 provides hints about the meaning of the code in Listing 4-1.

The next several sections present, explain, analyze, dissect, and otherwise demystify the Java code shown in Listing 4-1.

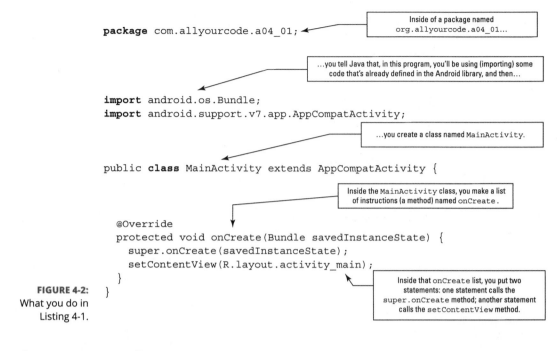

```
package com.allyourcode.a04_01;

import android.os.Bundle;
import android.support.v7.app.AppCompatActivity;

public class MainActivity extends AppCompatActivity {

    @Override
    protected void onCreate(Bundle savedInstanceState) {
        super.onCreate(savedInstanceState);
        setContentView(R.layout.activity_main);
    }
}
```

Inside of a package named org.allyourcode.a04_01...

...you tell Java that, in this program, you'll be using (importing) some code that's already defined in the Android library, and then...

...you create a class named MainActivity.

Inside the MainActivity class, you make a list of instructions (a method) named onCreate.

Inside that onCreate list, you put two statements: one statement calls the super.onCreate method; another statement calls the setContentView method.

FIGURE 4-2:
What you do in Listing 4-1.

The Java Class

Java is an object-oriented programming language. As a Java developer, your primary goal is to describe classes and objects. A *class* is a kind of category, like the category of all customers, the category of all accounts, the category of all geometric shapes, or, less concretely, the category of all MainActivity elements, as shown in Listing 4-1. Just as the listing contains the words class MainActivity, another piece of code to describe accounts might contain the words class Account. The class Account code would describe what it means to be (for example) one of several million bank accounts.

CROSS-REFERENCE The previous paragraph briefly describes what it means to be a *class*. For a more detailed description, see Chapter 9.

The code in Listing 4-1 describes a brand-new Java class. When I create a program like this one, I get to make up a name for my new class. When I created the project, I accepted the default name MainActivity in Android Studio's Customize the Activity dialog box. That's why you have the words class MainActivity in Listing 4-1. (See Figure 4-3.)

TECHNICAL STUFF The code inside the larger box in Figure 4-3 is, to be painfully correct, the *declaration* of a class. (This code is a *class declaration*.) I'm being slightly imprecise when I write in the figure that this code *is* a class. In reality, this code *describes* a class.

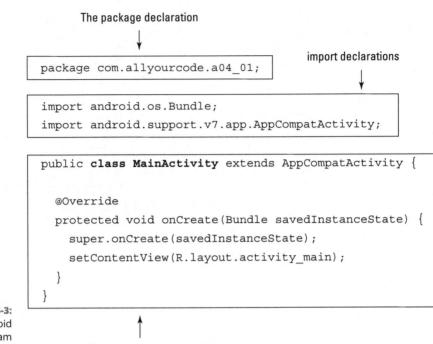

The package declaration

```
package com.allyourcode.a04_01;
```

import declarations

```
import android.os.Bundle;
import android.support.v7.app.AppCompatActivity;
```

```
public class MainActivity extends AppCompatActivity {

    @Override
    protected void onCreate(Bundle savedInstanceState) {
        super.onCreate(savedInstanceState);
        setContentView(R.layout.activity_main);
    }
}
```

The MainActivity class

FIGURE 4-3:
A simple Android
Java program
is a class.

The declaration of a class has two parts: The first part is the *header,* and the rest —
the part surrounded by curly braces, or {} —is the *class body,* as shown in
Figure 4-4.

The word class is a Java *keyword.* No matter who writes a Java program, class is
always used in the same way. On the other hand, MainActivity in Listing 4-1 is
an *identifier* — a name for something (that is, a name that identifies something).
The word MainActivity, which Android Studio made up while I was writing a new
project, is the name of a particular class — the class that I'm creating by writing
this program. When I created the new project, Android Studio gave me the
opportunity to type a new name in place of the name MainActivity. In place of
MainActivity, I could have typed StartHere or EatMoreCheese. It wouldn't have
mattered as long as Android Studio had used the new name consistently throughout the project. (The class's name, whatever it is, appears in several places in the
new Android project's code.)

WARNING

In the previous paragraph, I raise the possibility of giving the class in Listing 4-1
an unusual name. I do this to call attention to the difference between Java keywords (such as the word class), and identifiers (such as the word MainActivity).
I *don't* mean to suggest that creating strange identifiers (such as EatMoreCheese)
is — in any way, shape, or form — a good idea. Strange identifiers confuse other
programmers. Even slightly nonstandard identifiers, such as StartHere in place

of the more commonly used `MainActivity`, make other developers' lives more difficult. So, when you create your own app, use names that other developers will easily recognize. If there's a default name for a particular item in a program, use that default name.

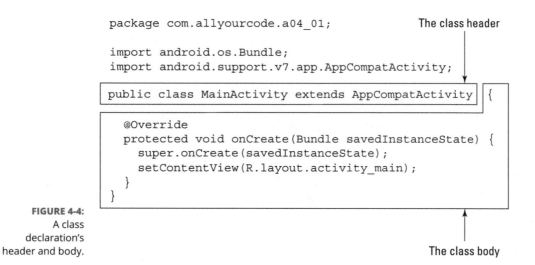

```
package com.allyourcode.a04_01;                    The class header

import android.os.Bundle;
import android.support.v7.app.AppCompatActivity;

public class MainActivity extends AppCompatActivity  {

   @Override
   protected void onCreate(Bundle savedInstanceState) {
      super.onCreate(savedInstanceState);
      setContentView(R.layout.activity_main);
   }
}
                                                    The class body
```

FIGURE 4-4:
A class declaration's header and body.

In Listing 4-1, the words `package`, `import`, `public`, `extends`, `protected`, and `super` are also Java keywords. No matter who writes a Java program, `package` and `class` and the other keywords always have the same meaning. For more jabbering about keywords and identifiers, see the nearby sidebar, "Words, words, words."

CROSS-REFERENCE

To find out what the words `public`, `static`, and `void` mean, see Chapters 7 and 9.

WARNING

tHE jAVA PROGRAMMING LANGUAGE IS cASe-sEnsITiVE. FOR EXAMPLE, iF YOU CHANGE A lowercase LETTER IN A WORD TO UPPERCASE OR CHANGE AN UPPER-CASE WORD TO lowercase, YOU CHANGE THE WORD'S MEANING AND CAN EVEN MAKE THE WORD MEANINGLESS. iN THE FIRST LINE OF lISTING 4-1, FOR EXAMPLE, IF YOU TRIED TO REPLACE `class` WITH `Class`, THE WHOLE PROGRAM WOULD STOP WORKING.

The same holds true, to some extent, for the name of a file containing a particular class. For example, the name of the class in Listing 4-1 is `MainActivity`, with two uppercase letters and ten lowercase letters. So the code in the listing belongs in a file named `MainActivity.java`, with exactly two uppercase letters and ten lowercase letters in front of `.java`.

WORDS, WORDS, WORDS

The Java language uses two kinds of words: keywords and identifiers. You can tell which words are keywords, because Java has only 50 of them. Here's the complete list:

abstract	continue	for	new	switch
assert	default	goto	package	synchronized
boolean	do	if	private	this
break	double	implements	protected	throw
byte	else	import	public	throws
case	enum	instanceof	return	transient
catch	extends	int	short	try
char	final	interface	static	void
class	finally	long	strictfp	volatile
const	float	native	super	while

As a rule, a *keyword* is a word whose meaning never changes (from one Java program to another). For example, in English, you can't change the meaning of the word *if*. It doesn't make sense to say, "I think that I shall never *if* / A poem lovely as a riff." The same concept holds true in a Java program: You can type if (x > 5) to mean "If x is greater than 5," but when you type if (x > if), the computer complains that the code doesn't make sense.

In addition to the keywords, Java has other words that play special roles in the language. You can't make up your own meanings for the words false, null, and true, but, for technical reasons, these words aren't considered keywords. And the words module, requires, exports, dynamic, to, uses, provides, and with are *restricted keywords*. You can make up meanings for them in some parts of your Java code, but not in other parts.

In Listing 4-1, the words class, package, import, public, extends, protected, and super are keywords. Almost every other word in that listing is an *identifier*, which is generally a name for something. The identifiers in the listing include MainActivity, AppCompatActivity, onCreate, and a bunch of other words.

In programming lingo, words such as *Wednesday*, *Barry*, and *university* in the following sentence are identifiers, and the other words (*If*, *it's*, *is*, *at*, and *the*) are keywords:

   If it's Wednesday, Barry is at the university.

As in English and most other spoken languages, the names of items are reusable. For example, a recent web search turns up four people in the United States named Barry Burd (with the same uncommon spelling). You can even reuse well-known names. (A fellow student at Temple University had the name *John Wayne*, and in the 1980s two different textbooks were titled *Pascalgorithms*.) The Android API has a prewritten class named MainActivity, but that doesn't stop you from defining another meaning for the name MainActivity.

Of course, having duplicate names can lead to trouble, so intentionally reusing a well-known name is generally a bad idea. (If you create your own thing named MainActivity, you'll find it difficult to refer to the prewritten MainActivity class in Android. As for my fellow Temple University student, everyone laughed when the teacher called roll.)

The names of classes

I'm known by several different names. My first name, used for informal conversation, is Barry. A longer name, used on this book's cover, is Barry Burd. The legal name that I use on tax forms is Barry A. Burd, and my passport (the most official document I own) sports the name Barry Abram Burd.

In the same way, elements in a Java program have several different names. For example, the class that's created in Listing 4-1 has the name MainActivity. This is the class's *simple name* because, well, it's simple and it's a name.

Listing 4-1 begins with the line package org.allyourcode.a04_01. The first line is a *package declaration*. Because of this declaration, the newly created MainActivity is inside a package named org.allyourcode.a04_01. So org.allyourcode.a04_01. MainActivity is the class's *fully qualified name*.

If you're sitting with me in my living room, you probably call me Barry. But if you've never met me and you're looking for me in a crowd of a thousand people, you probably call out the name Barry Burd. In the same way, the choice between a class's simple name and its fully qualified name depends on the context.

In Listing 4-1, the lines

```
import android.os.Bundle;
import android.support.v7.app.AppCompatActivity;
```

are two import declarations. An *import declaration* uses a class's fully qualified name. In Android's API, the Bundle class is in the android.os package, and the AppCompatActivity class is in the android.support.v7.app package.

Can you do without these import declarations? Yes, you can. Here's how:

```
package com.allyourcode.a04_01_B;

public class MainActivity extends android.support.v7.app.AppCompatActivity {

  @Override
  protected void onCreate(android.os.Bundle savedInstanceState) {
    super.onCreate(savedInstanceState);
    setContentView(R.layout.activity_main);
  }
}
```

This new code is in the com.allyourcode.a04_01_B package, but the Bundle and AppCompatActivity classes aren't in the com.allyourcode.a04_01_B package. In a way, the Bundle and AppCompatActivity classes are foreign to this com.allyourcode.a04_01_B package code. This revised code doesn't start with the import declarations. So, to compensate, the code must use Bundle and AppCompat Activity class's fully qualified names.

If your Java code file doesn't have an import android.support.v7.app.AppCompat Activity declaration, and you refer to the AppCompatActivity class several times in the file, you must use the fully qualified name android.support.v7.app. AppCompatActivity each and every time.

An import declaration, such as

```
import android.support.v7.app.AppCompatActivity;
```

announces that you intend to use the short name AppCompatActivity later in the file's code. The declaration clarifies what you mean by the short name AppCompat Activity. (You mean android.support.v7.app.AppCompatActivity.)

In an import declaration, an asterisk (*) means "all the classes in that package." For example, the android.support.v7.app package contains about 20 different classes. You can import all these classes with a single import declaration. Simply write import android.support.v7.app.*; near the top of your Java file.

TECHNICAL
STUFF

The details of this import business can be nasty, but (fortunately) Android Studio has features to help you write import declarations. Chapter 3 has the details.

TIP

Why Java Methods Are Like Meals at a Restaurant

I'm a fly on the wall at Mom's Restaurant in a small town along Interstate 80. I see everything that goes on at Mom's: Mom toils year after year, fighting against the influx of high-volume, low-quality restaurant chains while the old-timers remain faithful to Mom's menu.

I see you walking into Mom's. Look — you're handing Mom a job application. You're probably a decent cook. If you get the job, you'll get carefully typed copies of every one of the restaurant's recipes. Here's one:

> **Scrambled eggs (serves 2)**
>
> 5 large eggs, beaten
>
> ¼ cup 2% milk
>
> 1 cup shredded mozzarella
>
> Salt and pepper to taste
>
> A pinch of garlic powder
>
> In a medium bowl, combine eggs and milk. Whisk until the mixture is smooth, and pour into preheated frying pan. Cook on medium heat, stirring the mixture frequently with a spatula. Cook for 2 to 3 minutes or until eggs are about halfway cooked. Add salt, pepper, and garlic powder. Add cheese a little at a time, and continue stirring. Cook for another 2 to 3 minutes. Serve.

Before your first day at work, Mom sends you home to study her recipes. But she sternly warns you not to practice cooking. "Save all your energy for your first day," she says.

On your first day, you don an apron. Mom rotates the sign on the front door so that the word *Open* faces the street. You sit quietly by the stove, drumming your fingers. Mom sits by the cash register, trying to look nonchalant. (After 25 years in business, she still worries that the morning regulars won't show up.)

At last! Here comes Joe the barber. Joe orders the breakfast special with two scrambled eggs.

What does Mom's Restaurant have to do with Java?

When you drill down inside the code of a Java class, you find these two important elements:

> » **Method declaration:** The "recipe"
>
> "If anyone ever asks, here's how to make scrambled eggs."

> » **Method call:** The "customer's order"
>
> Joe says, "I'll have the breakfast special with two scrambled eggs." It's time for you to follow the recipe.

TECHNICAL STUFF

Almost every programming language has elements akin to Java's methods. If you've worked with other languages, you may recall terms like *subprogram*, *procedure*, *function*, *subroutine*, *subprocedure*, and PERFORM *statement*. Whatever you call a *method* in your favorite programming language, it's a bunch of instructions, collected in one place and waiting to be executed.

A *method declaration* is a plan describing the steps that Java will take if and when the method is called into action. A *method call* is one of those calls to action. As a Java developer, you write both method declarations and method calls. Figure 4-5 shows you a method declaration and some method calls.

Figure 4-5 doesn't contain a complete Java program, so you can't run the figure's code in Android Studio. But the figure illustrates some facts about method declarations and method calls.

TECHNICAL STUFF

If I'm being lazy, I refer to the code in the upper box in Figure 4-5 as a *method*. If I'm not being lazy, I refer to it as a *method declaration*.

Method declaration

Like one of Mom's recipes, a method declaration is a list of instructions: "Do this, then do that, and then do this other thing." And, like each of Mom's recipes, each method has a name. In Figure 4-5, the method declaration's name is shout. You won't find the shout method in any of Android's API documentation. I made up the shout method especially for this chapter.

REMEMBER

Another term for an instruction in a Java program is a *Java statement*, or simply a *statement*. In Figure 4-5, the shout method's declaration contains two statements. The first statement tells Java to append a message to the text in a particular component (whatever component the name textView refers to). The second statement tells Java to append three asterisks and a blank space to the text in that component.

The shout method's declaration

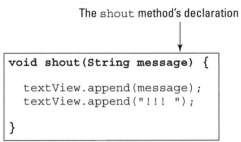

```
void shout(String message) {

    textView.append(message);
    textView.append("!!! ");

}
```

```
shout("Help");
shout("I'm trapped inside a smartphone");
```

Two method calls, each invoking the shout method

FIGURE 4-5:
Declaring and
calling the shout
method.

A method declaration has two parts: the *method header* and the *method body*, as shown in Figure 4-6.

The shout method's header

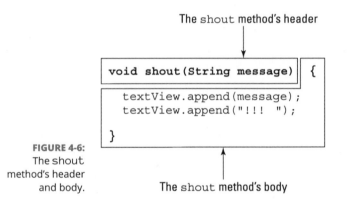

```
void shout(String message)  {

    textView.append(message);
    textView.append("!!! ");

}
```

The shout method's body

FIGURE 4-6:
The shout
method's header
and body.

The method's header has the name of the method and a parameter list. (See Figure 4-7.)

REMEMBER

Package declarations, import declarations, and method declarations are all called *declarations,* but they don't have much in common. A package declaration is typically one line of code — a line at the very beginning of a program, starting with the word package. After one package declaration, a file may contain several import declarations, each consuming one line of code. On the other hand, a typical method declaration is a bunch of lines of code, and those lines don't usually appear at the beginning of a program.

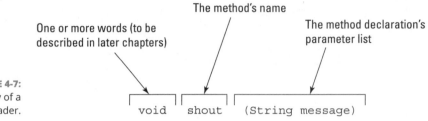

One or more words (to be described in later chapters)

The method's name

The method declaration's parameter list

```
void    shout    (String message)
```

FIGURE 4-7:
Anatomy of a method header.

Method call

A method *call* includes the name of the method being called followed by a parameter list. (See Figure 4-8.)

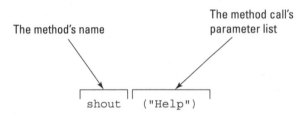

The method's name

The method call's parameter list

```
shout    ("Help")
```

FIGURE 4-8:
Anatomy of a method call.

A method call is like a customer order at Mom's Restaurant. The call in Figure 4-8 says, "It's time to execute whatever instructions are inside the shout method. And in those instructions, use the string "Help"."

Method parameters

A method's declaration has a parameter list, and a method call also has a parameter list. What a coincidence! (Refer to Figures 4-6 and 4-7.)

Of course, it's no coincidence. When Java encounters a method call, Java passes the value in the call's parameter list to the declaration's parameter list. The declaration may use that value in its body's instructions. See Figure 4-9.

A method call parameter conveys specific information — information that may be different from one method call to another. For example, the code shown earlier, in Figure 4-5, contains two method calls. One call conveys the information "Help". The other call conveys different information — namely, "I'm trapped inside a smartphone".

CROSS-
REFERENCE

A method call's parameter list doesn't look exactly like a method declaration's parameter list. You can see this by looking at Figure 4-9. The call's parameter list contains one thing — namely, the string "Help". But the declaration's parameter list contains two things: the word String and the word message. The stuff in the declaration's parameter list says, "When you call this method, send a `String` of characters. I'll refer to that `String` by the name `message`." The word `String` is the name of a Java *type*. To read more about Java types, see Chapter 5.

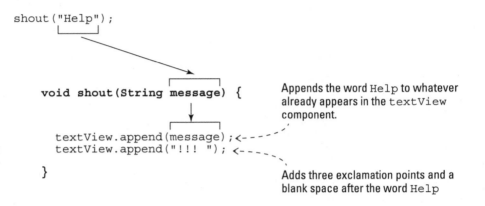

FIGURE 4-9: Passing a value from a call to a declaration.

The chicken or the egg

Which comes first, the method call or the method declaration? Look again at Figure 4-9. The figure contains a call to the `shout` method. The call makes Android execute the statements inside the `shout` method's body.

But the statements inside the `shout` method's body are themselves method calls. They're calls to a method named `append`. In the `shout` method's body, the first `append` call adds the word *Help* to the `textView` component's text. The second `append` call adds three exclamation points and a blank space to the `textView` component's text.

You don't see the `append` method's declaration, because the `append` method is part of Android's built-in API. As an Android developer, you don't deal directly with the method's declaration. All you do is call the method when you need it.

How many parameters?

In Java, double quotation marks denote a string of characters. So the call

```
shout("I'm trapped inside a smartphone")
```

contains one parameter. That single parameter is a string of characters.

Some functions have one parameter. Other functions have more than one parameter. Still other functions have no parameters. Listing 4-2 has an example.

LISTING 4-2: **Overloading a Method**

```
shout("Help");
shout("I'm trapped inside a smartphone");

shout("Put down the phone and start living life", "*");

shout();


void shout(String message) {
  textView.append(message);
  textView.append("!!! ");
}

void shout(String message, String emphasis) {
  textView.append(message);
  textView.append(emphasis);
  textView.append(emphasis);
  textView.append(emphasis);
}

void shout() {
  textView.append("!!!!!!!");
}
```

Like Figure 4-5, the code in Listing 4-2 doesn't contain a complete Java program, so you can't run the figure's code in Android Studio. But Listing 4-2 illustrates the notion of *method overloading*. When you overload a method, you provide several declarations for the method. Each declaration has its own, unique parameter list.

Listing 4-2 contains three shout method declarations — one with a single parameter, another with two parameters, and a third with no parameters.

Listing 4-2 also has four calls to the shout method. For each call, Java decides which declaration to use by matching up the call's parameter list with a declaration's parameter list. Here's what happens when Java executes the shout method calls in Listing 4-2:

» **The first call**, shout("Help"), **has only one parameter, so Java uses the** shout(String message) **declaration.**

Java appends *Help!!!* to the text in the textView component.

» **The second call**, shout("I'm trapped inside a smartphone"), **also has only one parameter. So, again, Java uses the** shout(String message) **declaration.**

Java adds *I'm trapped inside a smartphone!!!* to the textView component.

>> **The third call,** shout("Put down the phone and start living life", "*"), **has two parameters. A comma separates the parameters from one another. Java uses the** shout(String message, String emphasis) **declaration because that declaration also has two parameters.**

Java adds *Put down the phone and start living life**** to the textView component.

>> **The fourth call,** shout(), **has no parameters. The call has a pair of parentheses, but the pair is empty. Java uses the declaration at the end of Listing 4-2, the** shout() **declaration, because that declaration also has no parameters.**

Java adds *!!!!!!!* to the textView component.

CROSS-REFERENCE

In this section's code, you may wonder why the name textView isn't one of the parameters that I pass to the shout method. The short answer is, I want the name textView to refer to the same component anywhere in my MainActivity class's code — not exclusively inside the shout method's declaration. So I declare TextView textView; outside of any method. For more information about this topic, you can read about *fields* in Chapter 9.

Method declarations and method calls in an Android program

The figures and listing in the previous sections contain shout method declarations and shout method calls, but they don't contain a complete Java program. Listing 4-3 contains a complete program using these shout methods. The program's output is shown in Figure 4-10.

LISTING 4-3: **All the Code That's Fit to Print**

```
package com.allyourcode.a04_03;

import android.support.v7.app.AppCompatActivity;
import android.os.Bundle;
import android.widget.TextView;

public class MainActivity extends AppCompatActivity {
  TextView textView;

  @Override
  protected void onCreate(Bundle savedInstanceState) {
    super.onCreate(savedInstanceState);
    setContentView(R.layout.activity_main);
```

(continued)

LISTING 4-3:   *(continued)*

```
        textView = (TextView) findViewById(R.id.textView);
        textView.setText("");

        shout("Help");
        shout("I'm trapped inside a smartphone");

        shout();
    }

    void shout(String message) {
      textView.append(message);
      textView.append("!!! ");
    }

    void shout() {
      textView.append("!!!!!!!");
    }
}
```

ON THE WEB

The code in Listing 4-3 belongs in an Android project — a project containing many other files. You can download the entire project from this book's website: www.allmycode.com/Java4Android.

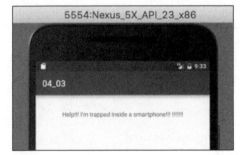

FIGURE 4-10: Running the app in Listing 4-3.

The code in Listing 4-3 describes an activity — one screenful of stuff on the Android device's screen. When an activity first appears, Android calls the activity's onCreate method. That's why Listing 4-3 declares an onCreate method.

REMEMBER

Android's internal code contains a call to an activity's onCreate method. You never write a call to the onCreate method. In fact, you probably never even see a call to the onCreate method.

Here's what happens when Android calls the onCreate method in Listing 4-3:

CROSS-REFERENCE

>> **If a previous run of this activity was interrupted, the call to** super.onCreate(savedInstanceState) **sets the activity back the way it was immediately before the interruption.**

Interruptions can occur when the user takes a phone call, when the user switches to a different activity, or even when the user rotates the phone!

You might wonder why a method named onCreate contains an instruction to execute the instructions inside a method named super.onCreate. The onCreate and super.onCreate methods are related to one another, but they're two different methods. For details about the use of the keyword super, see Chapter 10.

>> **The call to** setContentView **assigns a layout to the activity's screen.**

To read all about layouts and how layouts are created, refer to Chapter 3.

>> **The call to** findViewById **associates the name** textView **with a particular component on the screen.**

To read more about findViewById, see Chapter 3.

>> **The call** textView.setText("") **clears the** textView **component of any text that may already appear in it.**

Two quotation marks with nothing between them is the empty string. This statement puts the empty string in the textView component.

>> **The** shout("Help") **call makes Java execute the instructions in the first of the two** shout **declarations.**

This time, the message that's added to the textView component is *Help*. In addition, the shout method's body adds three exclamation points and a blank space to the stuff in the textView component.

>> **The** shout("I'm trapped inside a smartphone") **call makes Java execute the instructions in the first of the two** shout **declarations again.**

This time, the message that's added to the textView component is *I'm trapped inside a smartphone*.

>> **The** shout() **call makes Java execute the instruction in the second of the two** shout **declarations.**

This time, there's no particular message — only a bunch of exclamation points.

All in all, the code in Listing 4-3 contains ten (count 'em, ten) method calls. The three shout method calls invoke code that's declared right inside Listing 4-3. But the calls to super.onCreate, setContentView, findViewById, setText, and append invoke methods that aren't declared in Listing 4-3. These methods are declared in Android's standard API.

REMEMBER

Listing 4-3 can be deceiving. In Listing 4-3, every statement contains a method call. But in most Java programs, many statements don't contain method calls. The remaining chapters have many such statements.

In a fit of pedagogical zeal, I started making a diagram to illustrate the flow of control from statement to statement in Listing 4-3. When I finished making the diagram, I realized that the diagram may be quite intimidating. Some pictures are worth a thousand words, but this picture may be worth a thousand screams. Anyway, I leave it up to you. If Figure 4-11 helps you understand what happens in Listing 4-3, spend some time staring at the figure. But if Figure 4-11 makes you want to give up Android app development and learn modern dance instead, ignore Figure 4-11. You can understand Listing 4-3 without bothering about that figure.

REMEMBER

Android programs aren't simple. You're in Chapter 4 and, even if you've read every word up to this point, you haven't yet read enough to understand all the code in Listing 4-3. That's okay. The next several chapters fill in the gaps.

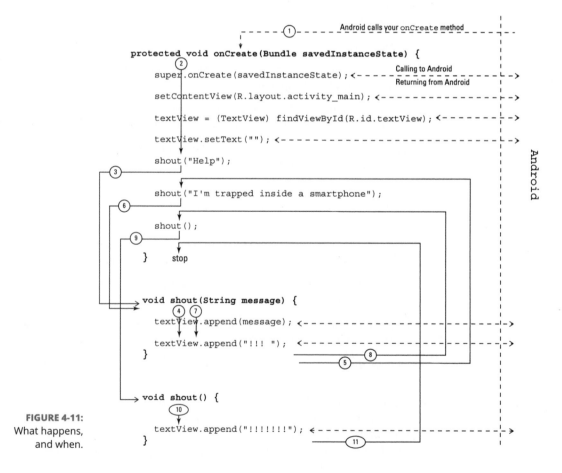

FIGURE 4-11:
What happens, and when.

A CHICKEN IN EVERY DOT

If you look back at Listing 4-3, you see statements such as

```
textView.setText("");
```

and

```
textView.append("!!! ");
```

In these statements, what's the dot all about?

Java is an object-oriented programming language. When you write Java code, you deal with things called *classes* and *objects*. I don't start describing classes and objects in detail until Chapter 9, so at this point I have to blur the terminology. I refer to classes and objects as *object-oriented things*.

> *In Java, every method belongs to an object-oriented thing.*

That's important, so I'll type it again:

> *In Java, every method belongs to an object-oriented thing.*

To call a method, you write

```
the_thing_to_which_the_method_belongs . simple_name_of_the_method
```

For example, in Android, each TextView component has hundreds of methods. One of them is named setText, and another is named append. So, in Listing 4-3, the textView variable has methods named setText and append. That's why you use a dot to call the textView.setText and textView.append methods.

Imagine that your app's screen has two TextView components:

```
textView = (TextView) findViewById(R.id.textView);
textView2 = (TextView) findViewById(R.id.textView2);
```

To put *Boo!* in the first of these components, you write

```
textView.setText("Boo!");
```

To put the words *Buy another copy of this book* in the second of these components, you write

```
textView2.setText("Buy another copy of this book");
```

(continued)

(continued)

The first component, textView, has a setText method, and the second component, textView2, has its own setText method.

What about the shout method in Listing 4-3? Does the shout method belong to anything? It does. The enclosing code (the rest of Listing 4-3) defines an object-oriented thing. Because the shout method's declaration is in Listing 4-3, the shout method belongs to that object-oriented thing.

So now you want to write

```
the_thing_defined_in_all_of_Listing_4-3 . shout
```

But to do that, you have to know the name of the thing defined in all of Listing 4-3. What's the name of the object-oriented thing that's defined in Listing 4-3? You might think that its name is MainActivity, but the story is a bit more complicated than that. In Chapter 9, you settle the issue by reading about classes and objects. But in this chapter, you have to gloss over the whole concept.

Here's the quick-and-dirty (and only partly accurate) story: Inside of Listing 4-3, the thing that Listing 4-3 defines goes by the name this. And when there's no confusion, you can omit the word this.

You can revise these three statements in Listing 4-3:

```
this.shout("Help");
this.shout("I'm trapped inside a smartphone");

this.shout();
```

Alternatively, you can do as I did in Listing 4-3 and omit the word this.

Punctuating Your Code

In English, punctuation is vital. If you don't believe me, ask this book's copy editor, who suffered through my rampant abuse of commas and semicolons in the preparation of this manuscript. My apologies to her — I'll try harder in the next edition.

Anyway, punctuation is also important in a Java program. This list lays out a few of Java's punctuation rules:

>> **Enclose a class body in a pair of curly braces.**

For example, in Listing 4-3, the `MainActivity` class's body is enclosed in curly braces.

```
public class MainActivity extends AppCompatActivity {
  TextView textView;


  ...


  void shout() {
    textView.append("!!!!!!!");
  }
}
```

REMEMBER

The placement of a curly brace (at the end of a line, at the start of a line, or on a line of its own) is unimportant. The only important aspect of placement is consistency. The consistent placement of curly braces throughout the code makes the code easier for you to understand. And when you understand your own code, you *write* far better code. When you compose a program, Android Studio can automatically rearrange the code so that the placement of curly braces (and other program elements) is consistent. To make it happen, click the mouse anywhere inside the editor and choose Code ➪ Reformat Code.

>> **Enclose a method body in a pair of curly braces.**

In Listing 4-3, the `onCreate` method's body is enclosed in curly braces, and the bodies of the two `shout` methods are enclosed in curly braces.

```
public class MainActivity extends AppCompatActivity {
  TextView textView;

  @Override
  protected void onCreate(Bundle savedInstanceState) {
    ...
  }

  void shout(String message) {
    ...
  }

  void shout() {
    ...
  }
}
```

» **A Java statement ends with a semicolon.**

Notice the semicolons in this excerpt from Listing 4-3:

```
super.onCreate(savedInstanceState);
setContentView(R.layout.activity_main);

textView = (TextView) findViewById(R.id.textView);
textView.setText("");
```

» **A package declaration ends with a semicolon. An import declaration also ends with a semicolon.**

In Listing 4-3 each of the first four lines ends with a semicolon.

```
package com.allyourcode.methoddemo;

import android.support.v7.app.AppCompatActivity;
import android.os.Bundle;
import android.widget.TextView;
```

» **In spite of the previous two rules, don't place a semicolon immediately after a closing curly brace (}).**

In Listing 4-3, there's no semicolon after any of the close curly braces.

» **Use parentheses to enclose a method's parameters, and use commas to separate the parameters.**

Listing 4-2 has some examples:

```
shout("Help");
shout("I'm trapped inside a smartphone");

shout("Put down the phone and start living life", "*");

shout();
```

» **Use double quotation marks ("") to denote strings of characters.**

The previous bullet contains four strings — namely, `"Help"`, `"I'm trapped inside a smartphone"`, `"Put down the phone and start living life"`, and, finally, `"*"`.

» **Use dots to separate the parts of a qualified name.**

The fully qualified name of the class in Listing 4-3 is `com.allyourcode.a04_03.MainActivity`.

The `setText` and `append` methods belong to a component named `textView`. So, in Listing 4-3, you write `textView.setText` and `textView.append`.

For details, refer to the earlier section "The names of classes" and the earlier sidebar named "A chicken in every dot."

>> **Use dots within a package name.**

The most blatant consequence of a package name's dots is to determine a file's location on the hard drive. For example, because of its package name, the code in Listing 4-3 must be in a folder named `a04_03`, which must be in a folder named `allyourcode`, which in turn must be in a folder named `com`, as shown in Figure 4-12. Fortunately, Android Studio creates all these folders for you and puts the code in the right place. You don't have to worry about a thing.

FIGURE 4-12:
The folders containing a Java program.

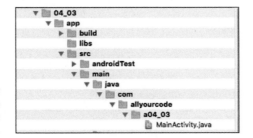

Comments are your friends

Listing 4-4 has an enhanced version of the code in Listing 4-1. In addition to all the keywords, identifiers, and punctuation, Listing 4-4 has text that's meant for human beings (like you and me) to read.

LISTING 4-4: **Three Kinds of Comments**

```
/*
 * Listing 4-4 in
 *    "Java Programming for Android Developers For Dummies, 2nd Edition"
 *
 * Copyright 2016 Wiley Publishing, Inc.
 * All rights reserved.
 */
```

(continued)

LISTING 4-4: **(continued)**

```
package com.allyourcode.a04_04;

import android.support.v7.app.AppCompatActivity;
import android.os.Bundle;

/**
 * MainActivity displays Hello World! on the screen.
 *
 * @author  Barry Burd
 * @version 1.0 07/07/16
 */
public class MainActivity extends AppCompatActivity {

  /**
   * Called when Android creates this activity.
   *
   * @param savedInstanceState
   *
   */
  @Override
  protected void onCreate(Bundle savedInstanceState) {
    super.onCreate(savedInstanceState);        // Restores any previous state
    setContentView(R.layout.activity_main);    // Makes activity_main.xml be
  }                                            //   the layout file
}
```

A *comment* is a special section of text inside a program whose purpose is to help people understand the program. A comment is part of a good program's documentation.

The Java programming language has three kinds of comments:

>> **Block comments:** The first seven lines in Listing 4-4 form one *block* comment. The comment begins with /* and ends with */. Everything between the opening /* and the closing */ is for human eyes only. No information about "Java Programming for Android Developers For Dummies" or Wiley Publishing, Inc. is translated by the compiler.

To read about compilers, see Chapter 1.

CROSS-
REFERENCE

Lines 2 through 6 in Listing 4-4 have extra asterisks (*). I call them *extra* because these asterisks aren't required when you create a comment. They only make the comment look pretty. I include them in the listing because, for some reason that I don't entirely understand, most Java programmers insist on adding these extra asterisks.

» **Line comments:** The text `// Restores any previous state` in Listing 4-4 is a *line* comment — it starts with two slashes and goes to the end of a line of type. Once again, the compiler doesn't translate the text inside a line comment.

  In Listing 4-4, the text `// Makes activity_main.xml be` is a second line comment, and the text `//   the layout file` is a third.

» **Javadoc comments:** A *Javadoc* comment begins with a slash and two asterisks (`/**`). Listing 4-4 has two Javadoc comments — one with the text `MainActivity displays Hello ...` and another with the text `Called when Android creates....`

  A *Javadoc* comment is a special kind of block comment: It's meant to be read by people who never even look at the Java code.

  Wait — that doesn't make sense. How can you see the Javadoc comments in Listing 4-4 if you never look at the listing?

  Well, with a few points and clicks, you can find all the Javadoc comments in Listing 4-4 and turn them into a nice-looking web page, as shown in Figure 4-13.

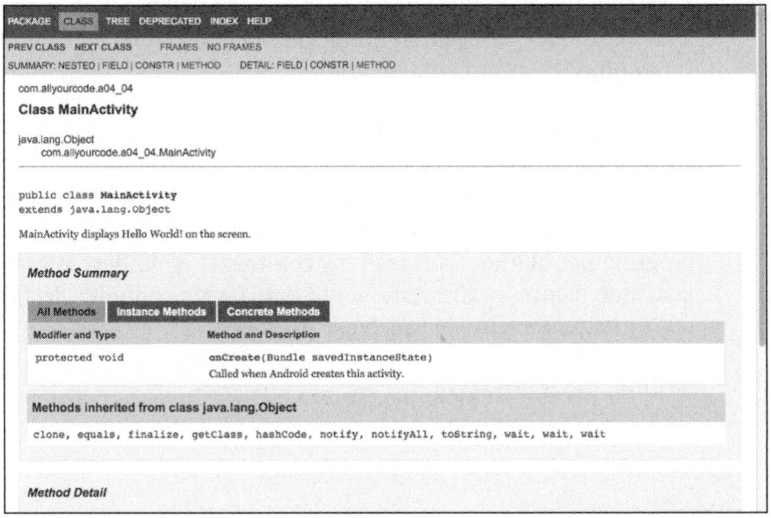

FIGURE 4-13: Javadoc comments, generated from the code in Listing 4-4.

To make documentation pages for your own code, follow these steps:

1. **Put Javadoc comments in your code.**

2. **From the main menu in Android Studio, choose Tools ⇨ Generate JavaDoc.**

   As a result, a dialog box with an awkward title appears. The title is Specify Generate JavaDoc Scope.

3. **In the Specify Generate JavaDoc Scope dialog box, browse to select an Output directory.**

   The computer puts the newly created documentation pages in that directory.

4. **Click OK.**

   As a result, the computer creates the documentation pages.

If you visit the Destination directory and double-click the new `index.html` file's icon, you see your beautiful (and informative) documentation pages.

REMEMBER

You can find the documentation pages for Android's built-in API classes by visiting `https://developer.android.com/reference/packages.html`. Android's API contains thousands of classes, so don't memorize the names of the classes and their methods. Instead, you simply visit these online documentation pages.

What's Barry's excuse?

For years, I've been telling my students to put all kinds of comments in their code, and for years, I've been creating sample code (such as the code in Listing 4-3) containing few comments. Why?

Three little words: "Know your audience." When you write complicated, real-life code, your audience consists of other programmers, information technology managers, and people who need help deciphering what you've done. But when I write simple samples of code for this book, my audience is you — the novice Java programmer. Rather than read my comments, your best strategy is to stare at my Java statements — the statements that Java's compiler deciphers. That's why I put so few comments in this book's listings.

Besides, I'm a little lazy.

All About Android Activities

If you look in the app/manifests branch in Android Studio's Project tool window, you see an AndroidManifest.xml file. The file isn't written in Java; it's written in XML. I don't write much about XML files in this book. Still, I have to write something about an app's manifest file.

Listing 4-5 contains some code from an AndroidManifest.xml file to accompany Listing 4-1. With minor tweaks, this same code could accompany almost any example in this book.

LISTING 4-5:   **The activity Element in an AndroidManifest.xml File**

```
<activity android:name=".MainActivity">
    <intent-filter>
        <action android:name="android.intent.action.MAIN"/>

        <category android:name="android.intent.category.LAUNCHER"/>
    </intent-filter>
</activity>
```

CROSS-
REFERENCE

For a quick introduction to the niceties of XML code, refer to Chapter 3.

Here's what the code in Listing 4-5 "says" to your Android device:

>> **The code's action element indicates that the activity that's set forth in Listing 4-1 (the MainActivity class) is MAIN.**

Being MAIN means that the program in Listing 4-1 is the starting point of an app's execution. When a user launches the app described in Listing 4-1, the Android device reaches inside the Listing 4-1 code and executes the code's onCreate method. In addition, the device executes several other methods that don't appear in Listing 4-1.

>> **The code's category element adds an icon to the device's Application Launcher screen.**

On most Android devices, the user sees the Home screen. Then, by touching one element or another on the Home screen, the user gets to see the Launcher screen, which contains several apps' icons. By scrolling this screen, the user can find an appropriate app's icon. When the user taps the icon, the app starts running.

In Listing 4-5, the category element's LAUNCHER value makes an icon for running the MainActivity class available on the device's Launcher screen.

So there you have it. With the proper secret sauce (namely, the `action` and `category` elements in the `AndroidManifest.xml` file), an Android activity's `onCreate` method becomes an app's starting point of execution.

Extending a class

In Listing 4-1, and in other listings throughout this book, the words `extends` and `@Override` tell an important story — a story that applies to all Java programs, not only to Android apps.

Most of this book's examples contain the lines

```
import android.support.v7.app.AppCompatActivity;


public class MainActivity extends AppCompatActivity {
```

When you *extend* the `android.support.v7.app.AppCompatActivity` class, you create a new kind of Android activity. In Listing 4-1, and in so many other listings, the words `extends AppCompatActivity` tells Java that a `MainActivity` is, in fact, an example of an Android `AppCompatActivity`. That's good because an `AppCompat Activity` is a certain kind of Android activity. The folks at Google have already written thousands of lines of Java code to describe what an Android `AppCompat Activity` can do. Being an example of an `AppCompatActivity` in Android means that you can take advantage of all the `AppCompatActivity` class's prewritten code.

REMEMBER

When you extend an existing Java class (such as the `AppCompatActivity` class), you create a new class with the existing class's functionality. For details of this important concept, see Chapter 10.

Overriding methods

In Listing 4-1, and in many other listings, a `MainActivity` is a kind of Android `AppCompatActivity`. So a `MainActivity` is automatically a screenful of components with lots and lots of handy, prewritten code.

Of course, in some apps, you might not want all that prewritten code. After all, being a Republican or a Democrat doesn't mean believing everything in your party's platform. You can start by borrowing most of the platform's principles but then pick and choose among the remaining principles. In the same way, the code in Listing 4-1 declares itself to be an Android `AppCompatActivity`, but then *overrides* one of the `AppCompatActivity` class's existing methods.

If you bothered to look at the code for Android's built-in `AppCompatActivity` class, you'd see the declaration of an `onCreate` method. In Listing 4-1, the word `@Override` indicates that the listing's `MainActivity` doesn't use the `AppCompat Activity` class's prewritten `onCreate` method. Instead, the `MainActivity` contains a declaration for its own `onCreate` method, as shown in Figure 4-14.

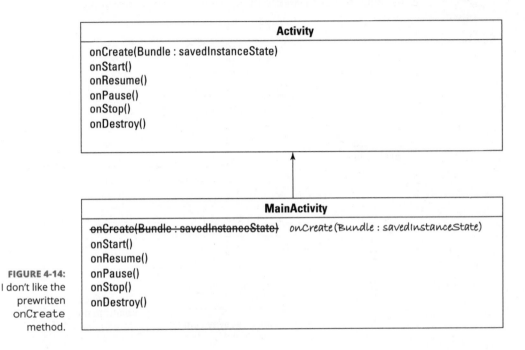

Activity
onCreate(Bundle : savedInstanceState)
onStart()
onResume()
onPause()
onStop()
onDestroy()

MainActivity
~~onCreate(Bundle : savedInstanceState)~~   *onCreate(Bundle : savedInstanceState)*
onStart()
onResume()
onPause()
onStop()
onDestroy()

FIGURE 4-14: I don't like the prewritten `onCreate` method.

In particular, Listing 4-1's `onCreate` method calls `setContentView(R.layout. activity_main)`, which displays the material described in the `res/layout/ activity_main.xml` file. The `AppCompatActivity` class's built-in `onCreate` method doesn't do those things.

For an introduction to the `res/layout/activity_main.xml` file, see Chapter 3.

CROSS-
REFERENCE

An activity's workhorse methods

Every Android activity has a *lifecycle* — a set of stages that the activity undergoes from birth to death to rebirth, and so on. In particular, when your Android device launches an activity, the device calls the activity's `onCreate` method. The device also calls the activity's `onStart` and `onResume` methods. See Figure 4-15.

In most of this book's listings, I choose to declare my own onCreate method, but I don't bother declaring my own onStart and onResume methods. Rather than override the onStart and onResume methods, I silently use the AppCompat Activity class's prewritten onStart and onResume methods.

CROSS-REFERENCE

To find out why you'd choose to override onResume, see Chapter 14.

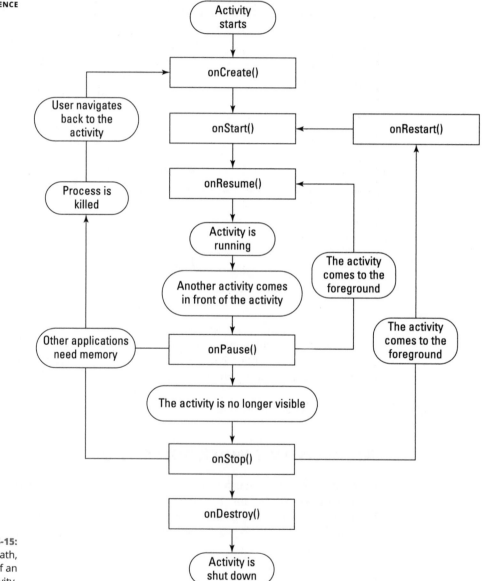

FIGURE 4-15:
The life, death, and rebirth of an Android activity.

When an Android device ends an activity's run, the device calls three additional methods: the activity's onPause, onStop, and onDestroy methods. So, one complete sweep of your activity, from birth to death, involves the run of at least six methods: onCreate, then onStart, and then onResume, and later onPause, and then onStop, and, finally, onDestroy. As it is with all life forms, "ashes to ashes, dust to dust."

Don't despair. For an Android activity, reincarnation is a common phenomenon. For example, if you're running several apps at a time, the device might run low on memory. In this case, Android can kill some running activities. As the device's user, you have no idea that any activities have been destroyed. When you navigate back to a killed activity, Android re-creates the activity for you and you're none the wiser. A call to super.onCreate(savedInstanceState) helps bring things back to the way they were before Android destroyed the activity.

Here's another surprising fact. When you turn a phone from Portrait mode to Landscape mode, the phone destroys the *current* activity (the activity that's in Portrait mode) and re-creates that same activity in Landscape mode. The phone calls all six of the activity's lifecycle methods (onPause, onStop, and so on) in order to turn the activity's display sideways. It's similar to starting on the transporter deck of the *Enterprise* and being a different person after being beamed down to the planet (except that you act like yourself and think like yourself, so no one knows that you're a completely different person).

Indeed, methods like onCreate in this book's examples are the workhorses of Android development.

Chapter **5**

Java's Building Blocks

I've driven cars in many cities, and I'm ready to present my candid reviews:

» Driving in New York City is a one-sided endeavor. A New York City driver avoids hitting another car but doesn't avoid being hit by another car. In the same way, New York pedestrians do nothing to avoid being hit. Racing into the path of an oncoming vehicle is commonplace. Anyone who doesn't behave this way is either a New Jersey driver or a tourist from the Midwest. In New York City, safety depends entirely on the car that's moving toward a potential target.

» A driver in certain parts of California will stop on a dime for a pedestrian who's about to jaywalk. Some drivers stop even before the pedestrian is aware of any intention to jaywalk.

» Boston's streets are curvy and irregular, and accurate street signs are rare. Road maps are outdated because of construction and other contingencies. So driving in Boston is highly problematic. You can't find your way around Boston unless you already know your way around Boston, and you don't know your way around Boston unless you've already driven around Boston. Needless to say, I can't drive in Boston.

» London is quite crowded, but the drivers are polite (to foreigners, at least). Several years ago, I caused three car accidents in one week on the streets of London. And after each accident, the driver of the other car apologized to me!

I was particularly touched when a London cabby expressed regret that an accident (admittedly, my fault) might stain his driving record. Apparently, the rules for London cabbies are quite strict.

This brings me to the subject of the level of training required to drive a taxicab in London. The cabbies start their careers by memorizing the London street map. The map has over 25,000 streets, and the layout has no built-in clues. Rectangular grids aren't the norm, and numbered streets are quite uncommon. Learning all the street names takes several years, and the cabbies must pass a test in order to become certified drivers.

This incredibly circuitous discussion about drivers, streets, and my tendency to cause accidents leads me to the major point of this section: Java's built-in types are easy to learn. In contrast to London's 25,000 streets, and the periodic table's 100-some elements, Java has only eight built-in types. They're Java's *primitive types*, and this chapter describes them all.

Info Is As Info Does

Reality! To Sancho, an inn; to Don Quixote, a castle; to someone else, whatever!

—MIGUEL DE CERVANTES, *AS UPDATED FOR "MAN OF LA MANCHA"*

When you think a computer or some other kind of processor is storing the letter J, the processor is, in reality, storing 01001010. For the letter K, the processor stores 01001011. Everything inside the processor is a sequence of 0s and 1s. As every computer geek knows, a 0 or 1 is a *bit*.

As it turns out, the sequence 01001010, which stands for the letter J, can also stand for the number 74. The same sequence can also stand for $1.0369608636003646 \times 10^{-43}$. In fact, if the bits are interpreted as screen pixels, the same sequence can be used to represent the dots shown in Figure 5-1. The meaning of 01001010 depends on the way the software interprets this sequence of 0s and 1s.

FIGURE 5-1:
An extreme close-up of eight black-and-white screen pixels.

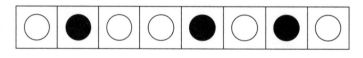

So how do you tell Java what 01001010 stands for? The answer is in the concept of *type*.

The *type* of a variable is the range of values that the variable is permitted to store. Listing 5-1 illustrates this idea.

LISTING 5-1: **Goofing Around with Java Types**

```
package com.allmycode.a05_01;

import android.support.v7.app.AppCompatActivity;
import android.os.Bundle;

public class MainActivity extends AppCompatActivity {

  @Override
  protected void onCreate(Bundle savedInstanceState) {
    super.onCreate(savedInstanceState);
    setContentView(R.layout.activity_main);

    int anInteger = 74;
    char aCharacter = 74;

    System.out.println(anInteger);
    System.out.println(aCharacter);
  }
}
```

CROSS-
REFERENCE

You can download the Android Studio project for Listing 5-1, or you can create it yourself from scratch. To find out how to download the project — as well as how to open the project in Android Studio — see Chapter 2. For info on creating the project from scratch, see Chapter 3.

When you run the code in Listing 5-1, you don't see anything interesting on the emulator screen. But if you scroll around in Android Studio's Logcat pane, you see two interesting lines: one containing the text *I/System.out:* 74 and another containing the text *I/System.out: J*. (Refer to Figure 5-2.)

In Java, `System.out.println` is the name of a method. The `System.out.println` method tells your development computer to display something in Android Studio's Logcat pane. Someone holding an Android device (a phone, a tablet, a watch, or whatever) doesn't see the stuff in Android Studio's Logcat pane, so this output isn't useful in a finished app. But the output can be useful while you're developing a new app to help you see how well the app is running.

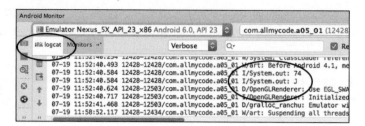

FIGURE 5-2:
Some output
from the code in
Listing 5-1.

TECHNICAL
STUFF

The words `System.out.println` tell Java to display something in a text-only pane. In Android Studio, this text-only pane happens to be the Logcat pane, but in other situations, your text-only pane might be something different. For example, if a Java program is meant to run on a desktop or laptop computer, the text-only pane might be the command prompt in Windows or the Terminal application on a Mac.

CROSS-
REFERENCE

To read about Android Studio's Logcat pane, check out Chapter 2.

WARNING

If you visit `https://source.android.com/source/code-style.html`, you find guidelines describing the kind of code that can and cannot be published on Google Play. The guidelines specifically prohibit the use of `System.out.println` in any code that's distributed on the store. So, for professional Android developers, the code in Listing 5-1 is an anathema. If you show Listing 5-1 on a PowerPoint slide at an Android developers' conference, you'll be booed off the stage. But `System.out.println` is part of Java's API. And apps that can sell on Google Play aren't necessarily the best learning tools. In this chapter, `System.out.println` allows me to describe certain ideas about Java types — ideas that would be hopelessly muddled if I stuck to Google's guidelines. So bear with me and examine the `System.out.println` examples in this chapter. When you finish this chapter, you can rip out the chapter's pages and burn them, if you like. Just remember to read the guidelines mentioned above (yes, available at `https://source.android.com/source/code-style.html`) and never use `System.out.println` in code that you publish on Google Play.

In Figure 5-2, Java interprets 01001010 two different ways. On one line, Java interprets 01001010 as a whole number. And on the next line, Java interprets the same 01001010 bits as the representation of the character J. The difference stems from the two *type declarations* in Listing 5-1:

```
int anInteger = 74;
char aCharacter = 74;
```

Each of these declarations consists of three parts: a variable name, a type name, and an initialization. The next few sections describe these parts.

Variable names

The identifiers `anInteger` and `aCharacter` in Listing 5-1 are variable names, or simply variables. A *variable name* is a nickname for a value (like the value 74).

I made up both variable names for the example in Listing 5-1, and I intentionally made up *informative* variable names. Instead of `anInteger` and `aCharacter` in Listing 5-1, I could have chosen `flower` and `goose`. But I use `anInteger` and `aCharacter` because informative names help other people read and understand my code. (In fact, informative names help me read and understand my own code!)

Like most of the names in a Java program, variable names can't have blank spaces. The only allowable punctuation symbol is the underscore character (_). Finally, you can't start a variable's name with a digit. For example, you can name your variable `close2Call`, but you can't name it `2Close2Call`.

TIP

If you want to look like a seasoned Java programmer, start every variable name with a lowercase letter and use uppercase letters to separate words within the name. For example, `numberOfBunnies` starts with a lowercase letter and separates words by using the uppercase letters O and B. This mixing of upper- and lowercase letters is called *camel case* because of its resemblance to a camel's humps.

CROSS-REFERENCE

Experienced Android programmers begin many variable names with the lowercase letter `m`. For more info on that, refer to Chapter 9.

Type names

In Listing 5-1, the words `int` and `char` are *type names*. The word `int` (in the first type declaration) tells Java to interpret whatever value `anInteger` has as a "whole number" value (a value with no digits to the right of the decimal point). And the word `char` (in the second type declaration) tells Java to interpret whatever value `aCharacter` has as a character value (a letter, a punctuation symbol, or maybe even a single digit). So in Listing 5-1, the line

```
System.out.println(anInteger);
```

tells Android to display the value of `anInteger`, and Android displays the number 74. (Refer to Figure 5-2.) And then the line

```
System.out.println(aCharacter);
```

tells Android to display the value of `aCharacter`, and Android displays the letter J.

In Listing 5-1, the words int and char tell Java what types my variable names have. The names anInteger and aCharacter remind me, the programmer, what kinds of values these variables have, but the names anInteger and aCharacter provide no type information to Java. The declarations int rocky = 74 and char bullwinkle = 74 would be fine, as long as I used the variable names rocky and bullwinkle consistently throughout Listing 5-1.

Assignments and initializations

Both type declarations in Listing 5-1 end with an initialization. As the name suggests, an *initialization* sets a variable to its initial value. In both declarations, I initialize the variable to the value 74.

You can create a type declaration without an initialization. For example, I can turn two of the lines in Listing 5-1 into four lines:

```
int anInteger;
char aCharacter;
anInteger = 74;
aCharacter = 74;
```

A line like

```
int anInteger;
```

is a declaration without an initialization. A line like

```
anInteger = 74;
```

is called an *assignment*. An assignment changes a variable's value. An assignment isn't part of a type declaration. Instead, an assignment is separate from its type declaration (maybe many lines after the type declaration).

You can initialize a variable with one value and then, in an assignment statement, change the variable's value.

```
int year = 2008;
System.out.println(year);
System.out.println("Global financial crisis");
year = 2009;
System.out.println(year);
System.out.println("Obama sworn in as US president");
year = 2010;
System.out.println(year);
System.out.println("Oil spill in the Gulf of Mexico");
```

Sometimes, you need a name for a value that doesn't change during the program's run. In such situations, the keyword `final` signals a variable whose value can't be reassigned.

```
final int NUMBER_OF_PLANETS = 9;
```

A `final` variable is a variable whose value doesn't vary. (As far as I know, no one has ever seriously suggested calling these things *invariables*.)

You can initialize a `final` variable's value, but after the initialization, you can't change the variable's value with an assignment statement. In other words, after you declare `final int NUMBER_OF_PLANETS = 9`, this assignment statement isn't legal:

```
NUMBER_OF_PLANETS = 8;
```

If Pluto is no longer a planet, you can't accommodate the change without changing the 9 in the `final int NUMBER_OF_PLANETS = 9` declaration.

In Java, the word `final` is one of Java's modifiers. A *modifier* is like an adjective in English. A modifier causes a slight change in the meaning of a declaration. For example, in this section, the word `final` modifies the NUMBER_OF_PLANETS declaration, making the value of NUMBER_OF_PLANETS unchangeable.

CROSS-
REFERENCE

For more information about Java's modifiers, see Chapters 9 and 10.

You use `final` variables, as a rule, to give friendly names to values that never (or rarely) change. For example, in a Java program, 6.626068e-34 stands for 6.626068×10^{-34}, which is the same as this:

```
0.00000000000000000000000000000000006626068
```

In a quantum physics application, you probably don't want to retype the number 6.626068e-34 several times in your code. (You can type the number wrong or even make a mistake when you copy-and-paste.) To keep errors from creeping into your code, you declare

```
final double PLANCK_CONSTANT = 6.626068e-34;
```

From that point on, rather than type 6.626068e-34 multiple times in your code, you can type only the name PLANCK_CONSTANT when needed.

TIP

You can use lowercase letters in any variable, including `final` variables. But Java programmers seldom write code this way. To keep from looking like a complete newbie, use only uppercase letters and digits in a `final` variable's name. Use underscores to separate words.

TECHNICAL STUFF

A loophole in the Java language specification allows you, under certain circumstances, to use an assignment statement to give a variable its initial value. For a variable, such as `amount`, declared inside of a method's body, you can write `final int amount;` on one line and then write `amount = 0;` on another line. Want my advice? Ignore this loophole. Don't even read this Technical Stuff icon!

Expressions and literals

In a Java program, an *expression* is a bunch of text that has a value. In Listing 5-1 each occurrence of 74 is an expression, each occurrence of `anInteger` is an expression, and each occurrence of `aCharacter` is an expression. Listing 5-1 is unusual in that all six of these expressions have the same value, namely, the numeric value 74.

If I use the name `anInteger` in ten different places in my Java program, then I have ten expressions, and each expression has a value. If I decide to type `anInteger + 17` somewhere in my program, then `anInteger + 17` is an expression because `anInteger + 17` has a value.

A *literal* is a kind of expression whose value doesn't change from one Java program to another. For example, the expression 74 means "the numeric value 74" in every Java program. Likewise, the expression `'J'` means "the tenth uppercase letter in the Roman alphabet" in every Java program, and the word `true` means "the opposite of `false`" in every Java program. The expressions `true`, 74, and `'J'` are literals. Similarly, the text `"Global financial crisis"` is a literal because, in any Java program, the text `"Global financial crisis"` stands for the same three words.

In Java, single quotation marks stand for a character. You can change the second declaration in Listing 5-1 this way:

```
char aCharacter = 'J';
```

With this change, the program's run doesn't change. The second `I/System.out` line in Figure 5-2 still contains the letter J.

REMEMBER

In Java, a `char` value is a number in disguise. In Listing 5-1, you get the same result if the second type declaration is `char aCharacter = 'J'`. You can even do arithmetic with `char` values. For example, in Listing 5-1, if you change the second declaration to `char aCharacter = 'J' + 2`, you get the letter L.

THE 01000001 01000010 01000011S

What does 01001010 have to do with the number 74 or with the letter J?

The answer for 74 involves the binary number representation. The familiar base-10 (decimal) system has a 1s column, a 10s column, a 100s column, a 1000s column, and so on. But the base-2 (binary) system has a 1s column, a 2s column, a 4s column, an 8s column, and so on. The figure shows how you get 74 from 01001010 using the binary column values.

The connection between 01001010 and the letter J might seem more arbitrary. In the early 1960s, a group of professionals devised the American Standard Code for Information Interchange (ASCII). In the ASCII representation, each character takes up 8 bits. You can see the representations for some of the characters in the sidebar table. For example, our friend 01001010 (which, as a binary number, stands for 74) is also the way Java stores the letter J. The decision to make A be 01000001 and to make J be 01001010 has roots in the 20th century's typographic hardware. (To read all about this, visit `http://citeseerx.ist.psu.edu/viewdoc/summary?doi=10.1.1.96.678`.)

In the late 1980s, as modern communications led to increasing globalization, a group of experts began work on an enhanced code with up to 32 bits for each character. The lower 8 Unicode bits have the same meanings as in the ASCII code, but with so many more bits, the Unicode standard has room for languages other than English. A Java `char` value is a 16-bit Unicode number, which means that, depending on the way you interpret it, a `char` is either a number between 0 and 65535 or a character in one of the many Unicode languages.

In fact, you can use non-English characters for identifiers in a Java program. The sidebar figure shows an Android program with identifiers in Yiddish.

(continued)

(continued)

```
package com.allmycode.yiddish;

import android.support.v7.app.AppCompatActivity;
import android.os.Bundle;

public class MainActivity extends AppCompatActivity {

    @Override
    protected void onCreate(Bundle savedInstanceState) {
        super.onCreate(savedInstanceState);
        setContentView(R.layout.activity_main);

        int אײנס = 1;
        int צװײ = 2;
        int דרײַ = אײנס + צװײ;
        System.out.print("ענטפער : ");
        System.out.println(דרײַ);
    }

}
```

Bits	When Interpreted As an int	When Interpreted As a char	Bits	When Interpreted As an int	When Interpreted As a char
00100000	32	space	00111111	63	?
00100001	33	!	01000000	64	@
00100010	34	"	01000001	65	A
00100011	35	#	01000010	66	B
00100100	36	$	01000011	67	C
00100101	37	%	.	.	.
00100110	38	&	.	.	.
00100111	39	'	etc.	etc.	etc.
00101000	40	(	01011000	88	X
00101001	41	)	01011001	89	Y
00101010	42	*	01011010	90	Z
00101011	43	+	01011011	91	[

Bits	When Interpreted As an int	When Interpreted As a char	Bits	When Interpreted As an int	When Interpreted As a char
00101100	44	,	01011100	92	\
00101101	45	–	01011101	93	]
00101110	46	.	01011110	94	^
00101111	47	/	01011111	95	_
00110000	48	0	01100000	96	`
00110001	49	1	01100001	97	a
00110010	50	2	01100010	98	b
00110011	51	3	01100011	99	c
00110100	52	4	.	.	.
00110101	53	5	.	.	.
00110110	54	6	etc.	etc.	etc.
00110111	55	7	01111000	120	x
00111000	56	8	01111001	121	y
00111001	57	9	01111010	122	z
00111010	58	:	01111011	123	{
00111011	59	;	01111100	124		
00111100	60	<	01111101	125	}
00111101	61	=	01111110	126	~
00111110	62	>	01111111	127	Delete

How to string characters together

In Java, a single character isn't the same as a string of characters. Compare the character 'J' with the string "Bullwinkle J. Moose". A *character* literal has single quotation marks; a *string* literal has double quotation marks.

In Java, a string of characters may contain more than one character, but a string of characters doesn't necessarily contain more than one character. (Surprise!) You can write

```
char aCharacter = 'J';
```

because a character literal has single quotation marks. And because String is one of Java's types, you can also write

```
String myFirstName = "Barry";
```

initializing the String variable myFirstName with the String literal "Barry". Even though "A" contains only one letter, you can write

```
String myMiddleInitial = "A";
```

because "A", with its double quotation marks, is a String literal.

But in Java, a single character isn't the same as a one-character string, so you can't write

```
//Don't do this:
char theLastLetter = "Z";
```

Even though it contains only one character, the expression "Z" is a String value, so you can't initialize a char variable with the expression "Z".

Java's primitive types

Java has two kinds of types: primitive and reference. *Primitive types* are the atoms — the basic building blocks. In contrast, *reference types* are the things you create by combining primitive types (and by combining other reference types).

CROSS-REFERENCE

This chapter covers (mostly) Java's primitive types. Chapter 9 introduces Java's reference types.

TECHNICAL STUFF

Throughout this chapter, I give some attention to Java's String type. The String type in reality belongs in Chapter 9 because Java's String type is a reference type, not a primitive type. But I can't wait until Chapter 9 to use strings of characters in my examples. So consider this chapter's String material to be an informal (but useful) preview of Java's String type.

Table 5-1 describes all eight primitive Java types.

TABLE 5-1   Java's Primitive Types

Type Name	What a Literal Looks Like	Range of Values
Integral types		
byte	(byte)42	–128 to 127
short	(short)42	–32768 to 32767
int	42	–2147483648 to 2147483647
long	42L	–9223372036854775808 to 9223372036854775807
Character type (which is, technically, an Integral type)		
char	'A'	Thousands of characters, glyphs, and symbols
Floating-point types		
float	42.0F	-3.4×10^{38} to 3.4×10^{38}
double	42.0 or 0.314159e1	-1.8×10^{308} to 1.8×10^{308}
Logical type		
boolean	true	true, false

You can divide Java's primitive types into three categories:

» Integral

The *integral* types represent whole numbers — numbers with no digits to the right of the decimal point. For example, the number 42 in a Java program represents the int value 42, as in 42 cents or 42 clowns or 42 eggs. A family can't possibly have 2.5 children, so an int variable is a good place to store the number of kids in a particular family.

The thing that distinguishes one integral type from another is the range of values you can represent with each type. For example, a variable of type int represents a number from –2147483648 to +2147483647.

When you need a number with no digits to the right of the decimal point, you can almost always use the int type. Java's byte, short, and long types are reserved for special range needs (and for finicky programmers).

» Floating-point

The *floating-point* types represent numbers with digits to the right of the decimal point, even if those digits are all zeroes. For example, an old wooden measuring stick might be 1.001 meters long, and a precise measuring stick might be 1.000 meters long.

The double type has a much larger range than the float type and is much more accurate.

In spite of their names, Java programmers almost always use double rather than float, and when you write an ordinary literal (such as 42.0), that literal is a double value. (On the off chance that you want to create a float value, write 42.0F.)

» Logical

A boolean variable has one of two values: true or false. You can assign 74 to an int variable, and you can assign true (for example) to a boolean variable:

```
int numberOfPopsicles;
boolean areLemonFlavored;
numberOfPopsicles = 22;
areLemonFlavored = true;
```

You can do arithmetic with numeric values, and you can do a kind of "arithmetic" with boolean values. For more information, see the next section.

Things You Can Do with Types

You can do arithmetic with Java's *operators*. The most commonly used arithmetic operators are + (addition), − (subtraction), * (multiplication), / (division), and % (remainder upon division).

» When you use an arithmetic operator to combine two int values, the result is another int value.

For example, the value of 4 + 15 is 19. The value of 14 / 5 is 2 (because 5 "goes into" 14 two times, and even though the remainder is bigger than ½, the remainder is omitted). The value of 14 % 5 is 4 (because 14 divided by 5 leaves a remainder of 4).

The same kinds of rules apply to the other integral types. For example, when you add a long value to a long value, you get another long value.

>> **When you use an arithmetic operator to combine two** double **values, the result is another** double **value.**

For example, the value of 4.0 + 15.0 is 19.0. The value of 14.0 / 5.0 is 2.8.

The same kind of rule applies to float values. For example, a float value plus a float value is another float value.

>> **When you use an arithmetic operator to combine an** int **value with a** double **value, the result is another** double **value.**

Java *widens* the int value in order to combine it with the double value. For example, 4 + 15.0 is the same as 4.0 + 15.0, which is 19.0. And 14 / 5.0 is the same as 14.0 / 5.0, which is 2.8.

This widening also happens when you combine two different kinds of integral values or two different kinds of floating-point values. For example, the number 9000000000000000000 is too large to be an int value, so

```
9000000000000000000L + 1
```

is the same as

```
9000000000000000000L + 1L
```

which is

```
9000000000000000001L
```

Two other popular operators are increment ++ and decrement --. The most common use of the increment and decrement operators looks like this:

```
x++;
y--;
```

But you can also place the operators before the variables:

```
++x;
--y;
```

Placing the operator after the variable is called *postincrementing* (or *postdecrementing*). Placing the operator before the variable is called *preincrementing* (or *predecrementing*).

Both forms (before and after the variable) have the same effect on the variable's value; namely, the increment ++ operator always adds 1 to the value, and the decrement -- operator always subtracts 1 from the value. The only difference is what happens if you dare to display (or otherwise examine) the value of something like x++. Figure 5-3 illustrates this unsettling idea.

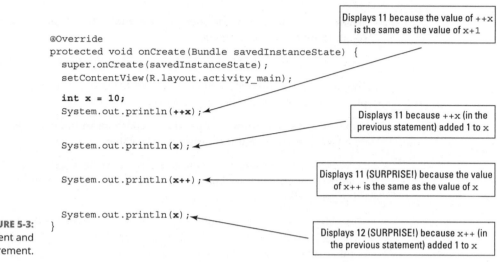

```
@Override
protected void onCreate(Bundle savedInstanceState) {
  super.onCreate(savedInstanceState);
  setContentView(R.layout.activity_main);

  int x = 10;
  System.out.println(++x);

  System.out.println(x);

  System.out.println(x++);

  System.out.println(x);
}
```

Displays 11 because the value of ++x is the same as the value of x+1

Displays 11 because ++x (in the previous statement) added 1 to x

Displays 11 (SURPRISE!) because the value of x++ is the same as the value of x

Displays 12 (SURPRISE!) because x++ (in the previous statement) added 1 to x

FIGURE 5-3:
Preincrement and postincrement.

TIP

In practice, if you remember only that x++ adds 1 to the value of x, you're usually okay.

TECHNICAL
STUFF

The curious behavior shown in Figure 5-3 was inspired by assembly languages of the 1970s. These languages have instructions that perform increment and decrement operations on a processor's internal registers.

Add letters to numbers (Huh?)

You can add String values and char values to other elements and to each other. Listing 5-2 has some examples.

LISTING 5-2: **Java's Versatile Plus Sign**

```
package com.allmycode.a05_02;

import android.support.v7.app.AppCompatActivity;
import android.os.Bundle;

public class MainActivity extends AppCompatActivity {

  @Override
  protected void onCreate(Bundle savedInstanceState) {
    super.onCreate(savedInstanceState);
    setContentView(R.layout.activity_main);
```

```
        int x = 74;
        System.out.println("Hello, " + "world!");
        System.out.println("The value of x is " + x + ".");
        System.out.println("The second letter of the alphabet is " + 'B' + ".");
        System.out.println("The fifth prime number is " + 11 + '.');
        System.out.println
            ("The sum of 18 and 21 is " + 18 + 21 + ". Oops! That's wrong.");
        System.out.println
            ("The sum of 18 and 21 is " + (18 + 21) + ". That's better.");
    }
}
```

REMEMBER

The String type more appropriately belongs in Chapter 9 because Java's String type isn't a primitive type. Even so, I start covering the String type in this chapter.

When you run the code in Listing 5-2, you see the output shown in Figure 5-4.

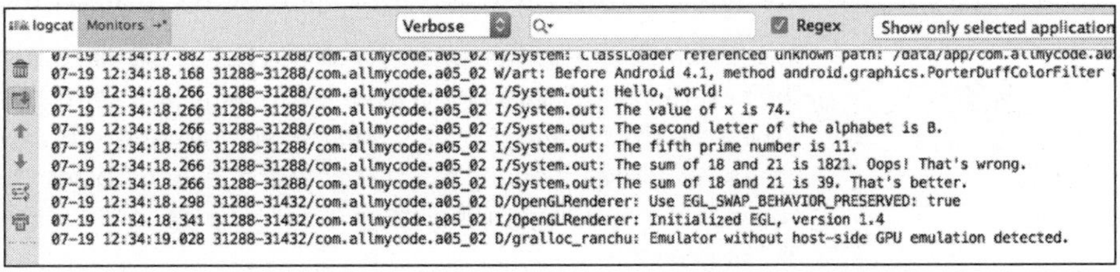

FIGURE 5-4:
A run of the code in Listing 5-2.

Here's what's happening in Figure 5-4:

>> **When you use the plus sign to combine two strings, it stands for string concatenation.**

String concatenation is a fancy name for what happens when you display one string immediately after another. In Listing 5-2, the act of concatenating "Hello, " and "world!" yields the string

```
"Hello, world!"
```

>> **When you add a string to a number, Java turns the number into a string and concatenates the strings.**

In Listing 5-2, the x variable is initialized to 74. The code displays "The value of x is " + x (a string plus an int variable). When adding the string "The value of x is " to the number 74, Java turns the int 74 into the string "74".

So "The value of x is " + x becomes "The value of x is " + "74", which (after string concatenation) becomes "The value of x is 74".

This automatic conversion of a number into a string is handy whenever you want to display a brief explanation along with a numeric value.

TECHNICAL STUFF

Java's internal representation of the number 74 is 0000000000000000000000 001001010 (with 1 in the 64s place, 1 in the 8s place, and 1 in the 2s place). In contrast, Java's internal representation of the string "74" is 000000000011011 10000000000110100. (For some clues to help you understand why these bits represent the "74" string, see the table accompanying this chapter's earlier sidebar, "The 01000001 01000010 01000011s.") The bottom line, as far as Java is concerned, is that the number 74 and the string "74" aren't the same.

>> **When you add a string to any other kind of value, Java turns the other value into a string and concatenates the strings.**

The third System.out.println call in Listing 5-2 adds the char value 'B' to a string. The result, as you can see in Figure 5-4, is a string containing the letter B.

>> **The order in which Java performs operations can affect the outcome.**

The last two System.out.println calls in Listing 5-2 illustrate this point. In the next-to-last call, Java works from left to right. Java starts by combining "The sum of 18 and 21 is " with 18, getting "The sum of 18 and 21 is 18". Then, working its way rightward, Java combines "The sum of 18 and 21 is 18" with 21 getting the screwy string "The sum of 18 and 21 is 1821".

In the last System.out.println call, I fix these problems by grouping 18 and 21 in parentheses. As a result, Java starts by adding 18 and 21 to get 39. Then Java combines "The sum of 18 and 21 is " with 39, getting the more sensible string "The sum of 18 and 21 is 39".

Java's exotic assignment operators

In a Java program, you can add 2 to a variable with a statement like this:

```
numberOfCows = numberOfCows + 2;
```

To a seasoned Java developer, a statement of this kind is horribly *gauche.* You might as well wear white after Labor Day or talk seriously about a "nucular" reactor. Why?

Because Java has a fancy *compound assignment operator* that performs the same task in a more concise way. The statement

```
numberOfCows += 2;
```

adds 2 to `numberOfCows` and lets you easily recognize the programmer's intention. For a silly example, imagine having several similarly named variables in the same program:

```
int numberOfCows;
int numberOfCrows;
int numberOfCries;
int numberOfCrays;
int numberOfGrays;
```

Then the statement

```
numberOfCrows += 2;
```

doesn't force you to check both sides of an assignment. Instead, the `+=` operator makes the statement's intent crystal-clear.

Java's other compound assignment operators include `-=`, `*=`, `/=`, `%=`, and others. For example, to multiply `numberOfCows` by `numberOfDays`, you can write

```
numberOfCows *= numberOfDays;
```

TECHNICAL STUFF

A compound assignment, like `numberOfCrows += 2`, might take a tiny bit less time to execute than the cruder `numberOfCows = numberOfCows + 2`. But the main reason for using a compound assignment statement is to make the program easier for other developers to read and understand. The savings in computing time, if any, is usually minimal.

True bit

A `boolean` value is either `true` or `false`. Those are only two possible values, compared with the thousands of values an `int` variable can have. But these two values are quite powerful. (When someone says "You've won the lottery" or "Your shoe is untied," you probably care whether these statements are true or false. Don't you?)

When you compare things with one another, the result is a `boolean` value. For example, the statement

```
System.out.println(3 > 2);
```

puts the word `true` in Android Studio's Logcat pane. In addition to Java's > (greater than) operator, you can compare values with < (less than), >= (greater than or equal), and <= (less than or equal).

You can also use a double-equal sign (==) to find out whether two values are equal to one another. The statement

```
System.out.println(15 == 9 + 9);
```

puts the word `false` in the Logcat pane. You can also test for inequality. For example, the statement

```
System.out.println(15 != 9 + 9);
```

puts the word `true` in the Logcat pane. (A computer keyboard has no ≠ sign. To help you remember the `!=` operator, think of the exclamation point as a work-around for making a slash through the equal sign.)

An expression whose value is either `true` or `false` is a *condition*. In this section, expressions such as 3 > 2 and 15 != 9 + 9 are examples of conditions.

The symbol to compare for equality isn't the same as the symbol that's used in an assignment or an initialization. Assignment or initialization uses a single equal sign (=), and comparison for equality uses a double equal sign (==). Everybody mistakenly uses the single equal sign to compare for equality several times in their programming careers. The trick is not to avoid making the mistake; the trick is to catch the mistake whenever you make it.

It's nice to display the word `true` or `false` in Android Studio's Logcat pane, but `boolean` values aren't just for pretty displays. To find out how `boolean` values can control the sequence of steps in your program, see Chapter 8.

Java isn't like a game of horseshoes

When you use a double equal sign, you have to be careful. Figure 5-5 shows you what happens in a paper-and-pencil calculation to convert 21 degrees Celsius to Fahrenheit. You get exactly 69.8.

But when you add the following statement to a Java program, you see `false`, not `true`:

```
System.out.println(9.0 / 5.0 * 21 + 32.0 == 69.8);
```

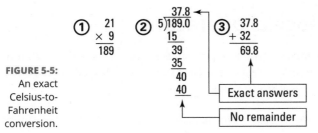

① 21
× 9
189

② 5)189.0
37.8
15
39
35
40
40

③ 37.8
+ 32
69.8

Exact answers

No remainder

FIGURE 5-5:
An exact
Celsius-to-
Fahrenheit
conversion.

Why isn't 9.0 / 5.0 * 21 + 32.0 the same as 69.8? The answer is that Java's arithmetic operators don't use the decimal system — they use the *binary* system. And in binary arithmetic, things don't go as well as they do in Figure 5-5.

Figure 5-6 shows you how Java divides 189.0 by 5. You might not understand (and you might not want to understand) how Java computes the value 100101.110011001100110011 . . ., but when you stop after 64 bits or so, this answer isn't exactly 37.8. It's more like 37.800000000000004, which is slightly inaccurate. In a Java program, when you ask whether 9.0 / 5.0 * 21 + 32.0 is exactly equal to 69.8, Java says "No, that's false."

REMEMBER

Avoid comparing double values or float values for equality (using ==) or for inequality (using !=). Comparing strings for equality (as in the expression "passw0rd" == "passw0rd") is also unadvisable.

CROSS-REFERENCE

For details about comparing strings, see Chapter 8.

```
           100101.110011001100110011 ... etc.
      101)10111101.000000000
           101
             0111
             0101
               1001
               0101
               100 0
               010 1
                 1 10
                 1 01
                   1000
                   0101
                    110
                    101
                      1000
```

FIGURE 5-6:
A division
problem that
never ends.

Use Java's logical operators

Real-life situations might involve complicated chains of conditions. To illustrate that fact, look at the kinds of real-life prose I find myself forced to read late on the evening of April 14 almost every year:

Household income for the purpose of premium tax credit is the sum of [IRC 36B(d)(2); Reg. 1.36B-1(e)]:

1. *The individual's modified adjusted gross income (MAGI) and the aggregate MAGI of all other individuals taken into account for determining family size who are required to file a tax return. Individuals not required to file, but filing to claim a refund are not included in the calculation.*

2. *MAGI for this purpose is the adjusted gross income as reported on Line 37 of Form 1040 increased by the foreign earned income exclusion, tax-exempt income received or accrued and that portion of an individual's social security benefits not included in income.*

The good news is that an app's conditions are not formulated by the same folks who came up with the U.S. tax code — the conditions can be expressed using Java's &&, || and ! operators. The story begins in Listing 5-3. Here, the listing's code computes the price of a movie theater ticket.

LISTING 5-3: **Pay the Regular Ticket Price?**

```
package com.allmycode.a05_03;

import android.support.v7.app.AppCompatActivity;
import android.os.Bundle;

public class MainActivity extends AppCompatActivity {

  @Override
  protected void onCreate(Bundle savedInstanceState) {
    super.onCreate(savedInstanceState);
    setContentView(R.layout.activity_main);

    int age;
    boolean chargeRegularPrice;

    age = 17;
    chargeRegularPrice = 18 <= age && age < 65;
    System.out.println(chargeRegularPrice);
```

```
age = 18;
chargeRegularPrice = 18 <= age && age < 65;
System.out.println(chargeRegularPrice);

age = 75;
chargeRegularPrice = 18 <= age && age < 65;
System.out.println(chargeRegularPrice);
  }
}
```

Figure 5-7 shows part of the Logcat pane when you run the code in Listing 5-3. At first, with the value of age set to 17, the value of chargeRegularPrice is false. So the first I/System.out line says that chargeRegularPrice is false. Then the value of age becomes 18, and chargeRegularPrice becomes true. So the second I/System.out line says that chargeRegularPrice is true. Finally, the code sets the value of age to 75, and once again chargeRegularPrice becomes false.

![logcat pane screenshot]
```
logcat  Monitors →*                          Verbose      Q·              Regex
   07-19 12:46:51.375 4954-4960/? E/art: Failed sending reply to debugger: Broken pipe
   07-19 12:46:51.375 4954-4960/? I/art: Debugger is no longer active
   07-19 12:46:57.940 4954-4954/com.allmycode.a05_03 W/System: ClassLoader referenced unknown path:
   07-19 12:46:58.114 4954-4954/com.allmycode.a05_03 W/art: Before Android 4.1, method android.grap
   07-19 12:46:58.221 4954-4954/com.allmycode.a05_03 I/System.out: false
   07-19 12:46:58.221 4954-4954/com.allmycode.a05_03 I/System.out: true
   07-19 12:46:58.221 4954-4954/com.allmycode.a05_03 I/System.out: false
   07-19 12:46:58.270 4954-5097/com.allmycode.a05_03 D/OpenGLRenderer: Use EGL_SWAP_BEHAVIOR_PRESER
   07-19 12:46:58.337 4954-5097/com.allmycode.a05_03 I/OpenGLRenderer: Initialized EGL, version 1.4
```

FIGURE 5-7:
Three people go to the movies.

CROSS-REFERENCE

This section's example might look peculiar because the code sets the value of age and then tests something about the value of age. Maybe the program's output should be "If you already know the value of age, why are you asking me if it's between 18 and 65?" The answer to that smart-aleck question is that the code for having the user type an age value isn't the world's simplest stuff. I don't want to muddy my discussion of logical operators with lots of user input code. If you want to know how to get input from the user, see Chapter 6.

In Listing 5-3, the value of chargeRegularPrice is true or false depending on the outcome of the 18 <= age && age < 65 condition test. The && operator stands for a logical *and* combination, so 18 <= age && age < 65 is true as long as age is greater than or equal to 18 *and* age is less than 65.

REMEMBER

To create a condition like 18 <= age && age < 65, you have to use the age variable twice. You can't write 18 <= age < 65. Other people might understand what 18 <= age < 65 means, but Java doesn't understand it.

TIP

In the earlier section "Java isn't like a game of horseshoes," I warn against using the == operator to compare two double values with one another. If you absolutely must compare double values with one another, give yourself a little leeway. Rather than write fahrTemp == 69.8, write something like this:

```
(69.7779 < fahrTemp) && (fahrTemp < 69.8001)
```

Listing 5-4 illustrates Java's || operator. (In case you're not sure, you type the || operator by pressing the | key twice.) The || operator stands for a logical *or* combination, so age < 18 || 65 <= age is true as long as age is less than 18 *or* age is greater than or equal to 65.

LISTING 5-4: **Pay the Discounted Ticket Price?**

```
package com.allmycode.a05_04;

import android.support.v7.app.AppCompatActivity;
import android.os.Bundle;

public class MainActivity extends AppCompatActivity {

  @Override
  protected void onCreate(Bundle savedInstanceState) {
    super.onCreate(savedInstanceState);
    setContentView(R.layout.activity_main);

    int age;
    boolean chargeDiscountPrice;

    age = 17;
    chargeDiscountPrice = age < 18 || 65 <= age;
    System.out.println(chargeDiscountPrice);

    age = 18;
    chargeDiscountPrice = age < 18 || 65 <= age;
    System.out.println(chargeDiscountPrice);

    age = 75;
    chargeDiscountPrice = age < 18 || 65 <= age;
    System.out.println(chargeDiscountPrice);

  }
}
```

A run of the code from Listing 5-4 is shown in Figure 5-8. A run of Listing 5-4 looks a lot like a run of Listing 5-3. But where Listing 5-3 outputs true, Listing 5-4 outputs false. And where Listing 5-3 outputs false, Listing 5-4 outputs true.

Listing 5-5 adds Java's ! operator to the logical stew. If you're unfamiliar with languages like Java, you have to stop thinking that the exclamation point means "Yes, definitely." Instead, Java's ! operator means *not*. In Listing 5-5, where isSpecialShowing is true or false, the expression !isSpecialShowing stands for the opposite of isSpecialShowing. That is, when isSpecialShowing is true, !isSpecialShowing is false. And when isSpecialShowing is false, !isSpecialShowing is true.

LISTING 5-5: **What about Special Showings?**

```
package com.allmycode.a05_05;

import android.support.v7.app.AppCompatActivity;
import android.os.Bundle;

public class MainActivity extends AppCompatActivity {

  @Override
  protected void onCreate(Bundle savedInstanceState) {
    super.onCreate(savedInstanceState);
    setContentView(R.layout.activity_main);

    int age;
    boolean isSpecialShowing;
    boolean chargeDiscountPrice;

    age = 13;

    isSpecialShowing = false;
    chargeDiscountPrice = (age < 18 || 65 <= age) && !isSpecialShowing;
    System.out.println(chargeDiscountPrice);
```

(continued)

LISTING 5-5:   *(continued)*

```
isSpecialShowing = true;
chargeDiscountPrice = (age < 18 || 65 <= age) && !isSpecialShowing;
System.out.println(chargeDiscountPrice);
    }
}
```

A run of the code from Listing 5-5 is shown in Figure 5-9.

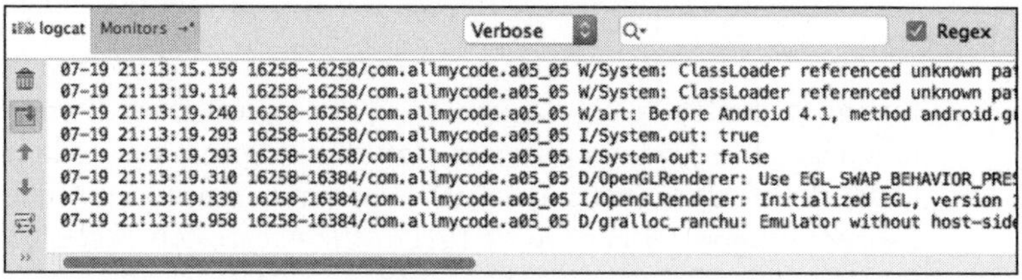

FIGURE 5-9:
Ticket prices for
two movie
showings.

In Listing 5-5, the assignment of a value to `chargeDiscountPrice` grants the discount price to kids and to seniors as long as the current feature isn't a "special showing" — one that the management considers to be a hot item, such as the first week of the run of a highly anticipated movie. When there's a special showing, no one gets the discounted price. Figure 5-10 shows you in detail how `chargeDiscountPrice` gets its values.

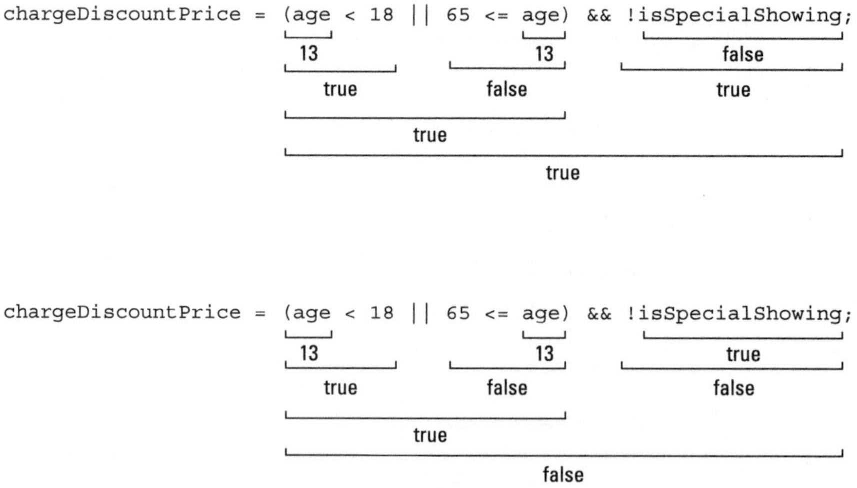

FIGURE 5-10:
Finding the value
of a boolean
expression.

TIP

For any condition you want to express, you always have several ways to express it. For example, rather than test `numberOfCats != 3`, you can be more long-winded and test `!(numberOfCats == 3)`. Rather than test `myAge < yourAge`, you can get the same answer by testing `yourAge > myAge` or `!(myAge >= yourAge)`. Rather than type `a != b && c != d`, you can get the same result with `!(a == b || c == d)`. (A guy named Augustus DeMorgan told me about this last trick.)

Parenthetically speaking . . .

The big condition in Listing 5-5 (the condition `(age < 18 || 65 <= age) && !isSpecialShowing`) illustrates the need for (and the importance of) parentheses (but only when parentheses are needed (or when they help people understand your code)).

When you don't use parentheses, Java's *precedence rules* settle arguments about the meaning of the expression. They tell you whether the line

```
age < 18 || 65 <= age && !isSpecialShowing
```

stands for the expression

```
(age < 18 || 65 <= age) && !isSpecialShowing
```

or for this one:

```
age < 18 || (65 <= age && !isSpecialShowing)
```

According to the precedence rules, in the absence of parentheses, Java evaluates `&&` before evaluating `||`. If you omit the parentheses, Java first checks to find out whether `65 <= age && !isSpecialShowing`. Then Java combines the result with a test of the `age < 18` condition. Imagine a 16-year-old kid buying a movie ticket on the day of a special showing. The condition `65 <= age && !isSpecialShowing` is `false`, but the condition `age < 18` is `true`. Because one of the two conditions on either side of the `||` operator is `true`, the whole nonparenthesized condition is `true` — and, to the theater management's dismay, the 16-year-old kid gets a discount ticket.

Sometimes, you can take advantage of Java's precedence rules and omit the parentheses in an expression. But I have a problem: I don't like memorizing precedence rules, and when I visit Java's online language specifications document (`https://docs.oracle.com/javase/specs/jls/se8/html`), I don't like figuring out how the rules apply to a particular condition.

When I create an expression like the one in Listing 5-5, I almost always use parentheses. In general, I use parentheses if I have any doubt about the way Java behaves without them. I also add parentheses when doing so makes the code easier to read.

Sometimes, if I'm not sure about stuff and I'm in a curious frame of mind, I write a quick Java program to test the precedence rules. For example, I run Listing 5-5 with and without the condition's parentheses. I send a 16-year-old kid to the movie theater when there's a special showing and see whether the kid ever gets a discount ticket. This little experiment shows me that the parentheses aren't optional.

Chapter **6**

Working with Java Types

"**Y**ou can't fit a square peg into a round hole," or so the saying goes. In Java programming, the saying goes one step further: "Like all other developers, you sometimes make a mistake and try to fit a square peg into a round hole. Java's type system alerts you to the mistake and prevents you from running the flawed code."

Working with Strings

Chapter 5 introduces int values, double values, String values, and other kinds of values. Android doesn't let you mix these values willy-nilly. You can't plop an int value into a TextView component and expect things to go smoothly. TextView components want their contents to be String values.

But values don't live in vacuums. Sometimes you want to display a number such as an int value on the user's screen. So what can you do?

You can check some of the ideas in this section. That's what you can do.

Going from primitive types to strings

Chapter 5 gives you one way to get a `String` value from a numeric value: Put a plus sign between the numeric value and some other `String` value. For example, the expression

```
"" + 81
```

doesn't stand for the numeric value 81 (the amount eighty-one). Instead, it stands for the string `"81"` — a string consisting of the two digit characters, `'8'` followed by `'1'`.

Another way to go from a primitive type to a string is with one of Java's `toString` methods. Imagine that, in your code, the variable `amountTextView` refers to a `TextView` component that appears on the user's screen and that the variable `howMany` refers to an `int` value such as 21 or 456. To display the number `howMany` in the `TextView` component, you write

```
amountTextView.setText(Integer.toString(howMany));
```

If `howMany` refers to the number 21, the expression `Integer.toString(howMany)` refers to the Java `String` value `"21"`, and you can set a `TextView` component's text to the `String` value `"21"`.

CROSS-REFERENCE

For an introduction to `TextView` components, see Chapter 3.

The same kind of thing works for other primitive type values. For example, if the `double` variable `howMuch` refers to the value `32.785`, then the expression `Double.toString(howMuch)` refers to the `String` value `"32.785"`. If the `boolean` variable `isGood` refers to the value `true`, then `Boolean.toString(isGood)` refers to the `String` value `"true"`. If the `char` variable `oneLetter` refers to the single letter `'x'`, then the expression `Character.toString(oneLetter)` refers to the `String` value `"x"`.

The words `Integer`, `Double`, `Boolean`, and `Character` are the names of *wrapper types*. These types wrap the primitive types in additional functionality. For more information about wrapper types, see Chapter 12.

REMEMBER

Java's `System.out.println` displays just about any kind of value, including `String` values, `int` values, `double` values, and others. But the display doesn't appear on an Android device's screen. To display a value on a device's screen, you have to put the value into something like a `TextView` component or an `EditText` component. And Android's components can't directly display `int` values or `double` values. Fortunately, Android's components can directly display `String` values.

REMEMBER

To turn an `int` value into a `String`, you don't use `int.toString`. Instead, you use `Integer.toString`. Similarly, you don't use `double.toString`, `boolean.toString`, or `char.toString`. Instead, you use `Double.toString`, `Boolean.toString`, and `Character.toString`.

WARNING

Java's calculations with `double` values isn't always dead-on accurate. When you think your double variable `howMuch` refers to the value 32.785, the expression `Double.toString(howMuch)` might yield a string like `"32.78500001"`.

Going from strings to primitive types

In the previous section, you put an `int` value, a `double` value, or some other primitive type value into a `TextView` component. What about going in the opposite direction? You want to add 10 to some number that the user types in an `EditText` component. How do you get the value from the `EditText` component and turn it into an `int` value? You do it with a `toString` method and with one of Java's `parse` methods.

For example, imagine that the variable `amountEditText` refers to an `EditText` component that appears on the user's screen, and that `howMany` is an `int` variable. As long as the `amountEditText` contains a whole number, you can make `howMany` refer to that number with the following code:

```
howMany = Integer.parseInt(amountEditText.getText().toString());
```

Figure 6-1 shows you what kinds of values you have when you obtain an `int` value from an `EditText` component.

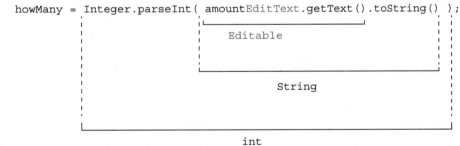

FIGURE 6-1:
Getting an int value from a text field.

If the user types 21 into the `amountEditText`, the expression `amountEditText.getText()` refers to those two digits, 21. Unfortunately, `amountEditText.getText()` isn't quite a Java `String` value. It's an `Editable` value (whatever that means). To get a `String` value from an `Editable` value, you apply `toString`. So the expression `amountEditText.getText().toString()` is the `String` value `"21"`. Then, to get an `int` value from a `String`, you apply `Integer.parseInt`. The expression

```
Integer.parseInt(amountEditText.getText().toString())
```

refers to an `int` value, and if you want, you can add 10 to that `int` value.

The same kind of thing works for other primitive type values. For example, if the user types `105.796` into the `sizeEditText`, the expression

```
Integer.parseDouble(sizeEditText.getText().toString())
```

refers to the `double` value `105.796`.

TIP

If the user types `3.14159` or `cat` into an `EditText` component and you hit that component with the statement in Figure 6-1, your program crashes. Unfortunately, neither 3.14159 nor cat is a whole number, so the `Integer.parseInt` part of the statement simply explodes. Oops! You can prevent this calamity by using the Number and Number (Signed) items from the palette of Android Studio's Designer tool. (See Figure 6-2.) The *Number* item is an `EditText` component that accepts whole numbers with no sign. The *Number (Signed)* item is an `EditText` component that accepts positive, negative, and zero whole numbers. There's also a Number (Decimal) item for `double` values. Of course, it's a good idea for your code to do some extra checking to make sure that the stuff the user types in the `EditText` component is something that `Integer.parseInt` or `Double.parseInt` can handle. For this, you need Java's `if` statements or Java's exception handling features. To find out about `if` statements, see Chapter 8. And for some good reading about exception handling, see Chapter 13.

Getting input from the user

In Chapter 5, I promise that I can make meaningful use of Java's logical operators. With some information from the previous section, I can fulfill that promise. In Listing 6-1, the app gets two pieces of information from the user. The app gets a person's age, and gets a check or no-check, indicating a movie's special showing status.

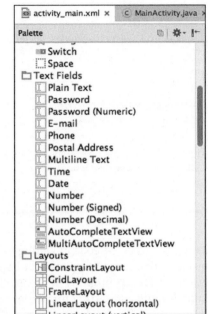

FIGURE 6-2:
Some special text
fields.

LISTING 6-1: **Going Back and Forth Between Strings and Primitives**

```java
package com.allmycode.a06_01;

import android.support.v7.app.AppCompatActivity;
import android.os.Bundle;
import android.view.View;
import android.widget.CheckBox;
import android.widget.EditText;
import android.widget.TextView;

public class MainActivity extends AppCompatActivity {
  EditText ageEditText;
  CheckBox specialShowingCheckBox;
  TextView outputTextView;

  @Override
  protected void onCreate(Bundle savedInstanceState) {
    super.onCreate(savedInstanceState);
    setContentView(R.layout.activity_main);

    ageEditText = (EditText) findViewById(R.id.ageEditText);
    specialShowingCheckBox =
                    (CheckBox) findViewById(R.id.specialShowingCheckBox);
```

(continued)

LISTING 6-1: *(continued)*

```
    outputTextView = (TextView) findViewById(R.id.outputTextView);
  }

  public void onButtonClick(View view) {
    int age = Integer.parseInt(ageEditText.getText().toString());
    boolean isSpecialShowing = specialShowingCheckBox.isChecked();

    boolean chargeDiscountPrice = (age < 18 || 65 <= age) && !isSpecialShowing;
    outputTextView.setText(Boolean.toString(chargeDiscountPrice));
  }
}
```

**CROSS-
REFERENCE**

There's more to the app in Listing 6-1 than the code in Listing 6-1. To create this app, you have to design the layout with its text fields, its check box, and its button. You also have to set the button's `onClick` property to `"onButtonClick"`. I've described the steps for designing layouts and setting properties in Chapter 3.

Figures 6-3 and 6-4 show runs of the code in Listing 6-1.

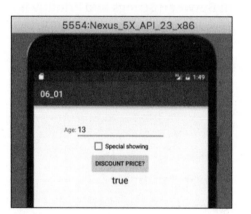

FIGURE 6-3:
Getting a
discounted movie
ticket.

In Listing 6-1, the `age` variable gets its value using the tricks that I describe earlier in this chapter, in the "Going from strings to primitive types" section. And the `String` value for the `outputTextView` comes from the techniques earlier in this chapter, in the "Going from primitive types to strings" section.

Every check box has an `isChecked` method, and, in Listing 6-1, the `isSpecialShowing` variable gets its value from a call to the `isChecked` method. In Figure 6-3, the user hasn't selected the check box. So, when Android executes the code in Listing 6-1, the expression `specialShowingCheckBox.isChecked()` has the value `false`. But, in Figure 6-4, the user has selected the check box. So for

Figure 6-4, when Android executes the code in Listing 6-1, the expression `specialShowingCheckBox.isChecked()` has the value `true`.

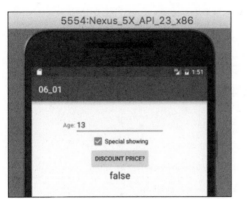

FIGURE 6-4:
Paying the full
price for a movie
ticket.

**CROSS-
REFERENCE**

To make the code in Listing 6-1 work, you have to associate the variable names `ageEditText`, `specialShowingCheckBox`, and `outputTextView` with the correct thingamajigs on the device's screen. The `findViewById` statements in Listing 6-1 help you do that. For details, refer to Chapter 3.

Practice Safe Typing

In the previous section, you convert primitive values to `String` values and `String` values to primitive values. It's very useful, but the story about converting values doesn't end there. Java is *fussy* about the types of its values. In Java, you can't even move seamlessly among the different kinds of primitive values. Here's an example:

By one measure, the average number of children per family in the United States in 2010 was 1.16. But by 2010, the Duggar family (featured on a well-known cable television show in the United States) had 19 children. Measuring the average family size in a population of 300 million people is tricky. But, no matter how you measure it, the average number of children has digits to the right of the decimal point. In my Java program, the average number of children is a `double` value. In contrast, the number of children in a particular family is an `int` value.

In Figure 6-5, I try to calculate the Duggar family's divergence from the national average. I don't even show you a run of this program, because the program doesn't work. It's defective. It's damaged goods. As cousin Jeb would say, "This program is a dance party on a leaky raft in a muddy river."

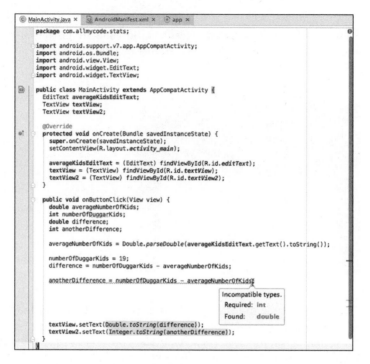

```
 © MainActivity.java ×    AndroidManifest.xml ×    © app ×

    package com.allmycode.stats;

   import android.support.v7.app.AppCompatActivity;
   import android.os.Bundle;
   import android.view.View;
   import android.widget.EditText;
   import android.widget.TextView;

   public class MainActivity extends AppCompatActivity {
       EditText averageKidsEditText;
       TextView textView;
       TextView textView2;

       @Override
       protected void onCreate(Bundle savedInstanceState) {
           super.onCreate(savedInstanceState);
           setContentView(R.layout.activity_main);

           averageKidsEditText = (EditText) findViewById(R.id.editText);
           textView = (TextView) findViewById(R.id.textView);
           textView2 = (TextView) findViewById(R.id.textView2);
       }

       public void onButtonClick(View view) {
           double averageNumberOfKids;
           int numberOfDuggarKids;
           double difference;
           int anotherDifference;

           averageNumberOfKids = Double.parseDouble(averageKidsEditText.getText().toString());

           numberOfDuggarKids = 19;
           difference = numberOfDuggarKids - averageNumberOfKids;

           anotherDifference = numberOfDuggarKids - averageNumberOfKids

                                                    ┌──────────────────────┐
                                                    │ Incompatible types.  │
                                                    │ Required: int        │
                                                    │ Found:    double     │
                                                    └──────────────────────┘

           textView.setText(Double.toString(difference));
           textView2.setText(Integer.toString(anotherDifference));
       }
   }
```

FIGURE 6-5:
Trying to fit a
square peg into a
round hole.

The code in Figure 6-5 deals with double values (such as the averageNumberOfKids variable) and int values (such as the numberOfDuggarKids variable). You might plan to type 1 in the app's averageKidsEditText. But, because of the declaration

```
double averageNumberOfKids;
```

the value stored in the averageNumberOfKids variable is of type double. The user's typing 1 instead of 1.0 doesn't scare Java into storing anything but a double in the averageNumberOfKids variable.

The expression numberOfDuggarKids - averageNumberOfKids is an int minus a double, so (according to my sage advice in Chapter 5) the value of numberOf DuggarKids - averageNumberOfKids is of type double. Sure, if you type 1 in the averageKidsEditText, then numberOfDuggarKids - averageNumberOfKids is 18.0, and 18.0 is sort of the same as the int value 18. But Java doesn't like things to be "sort of the same."

Java's *strong typing* rules say that you can't assign a double value (like 18.0) to an int variable (like anotherDifference). You don't lose any accuracy when you chop the *.o* off *18.o*. But with digits to the right of the decimal point (even with *o* to the right of the decimal point), Java doesn't trust you to stuff a double value into an `int` variable. After all, rather than type `1.0` in the `averageKidsEditText`, you can type `0.9`. Then you'd definitely lose accuracy, from stuffing *18.1* into an `int` variable.

You can try to assure Java that things are okay by using a plain, old assignment statement, like this:

```
double averageNumberOfKids;
averageNumberOfKids = 1;
```

When you do, `numberOfDuggarKids - averageNumberOfKids` is always 18.0. Even so, Java doesn't like assigning 18.0 to the `int` variable `anotherDifference`. This statement is still illegal:

```
anotherDifference = numberOfDuggarKids&#x00A0;- averageNumberOfKids;
```

WARNING

When you put numbers in your Java code (such as `1` in the previous paragraph or the number `19` in Figure 6-5), you *hardcode* the values. In this book, my liberal use of hardcoding keeps the examples simple and (more importantly) concrete. But in real applications, hardcoding is generally a bad idea. When you hardcode a value, you make it difficult to change. In fact, the only way to change a hardcoded value is to tinker with the Java code, and all code (written in Java or not) can be brittle. It's much safer to input values in a dialog box than to change a value in a piece of code. If getting a value from a dialog box doesn't suit your needs, you can create a name for the value using Java's `final` keyword. (See Chapter 5.) You can even read the value from the device's SD card.

Remember to do as I say and not as I do. Avoid hardcoding values in your programs.

Widening is good; narrowing is bad

Java prevents you from making any assignment that potentially *narrows* a value, as shown in Figure 6-6. For example, with the declarations

```
int numberOfDuggarKids = 19;
long lotsAndLotsOfKids;
```

the following attempt to narrow from a `long` value to an `int` value is illegal:

```
numberOfDuggarKids = lotsAndLotsOfKids; //Don't do this!
```

An attempt to *widen* from an `int` value to a `long` value, however, is fine:

```
lotsAndLotsOfKids = numberOfDuggarKids;
```

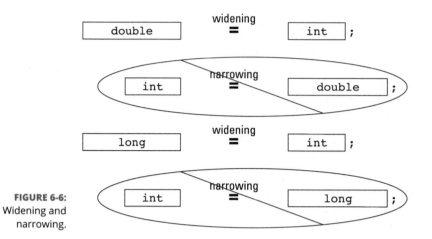

FIGURE 6-6:
Widening and
narrowing.

Earlier, in fact, in Figure 6-5, I subtract a double value from an int value with no trouble at all:

```
double averageNumberOfKids;
int numberOfDuggarKids;
double difference;

difference = numberOfDuggarKids - averageNumberOfKids;
```

Combining a double value with an int value is legal because Java automatically widens the int value.

Incompatible types

Aside from the technical terms *narrowing* and *widening*, there's another possibility — plain, old incompatibility — trying to fit one element into another when the two have nothing in common and have no hope of ever being mistaken for one another. You can't assign an int value to a boolean value or assign a boolean value to an int value:

```
int numberOfDuggarKids;
boolean isLarge;
numberOfDuggarKids = isLarge; //Don't do this!
isLarge = numberOfDuggarKids; //Don't do this!
```

You can't do either assignment, because boolean values aren't numeric. In other words, neither of these assignments makes sense.

REMEMBER

Java is a *strongly typed* programming language. It doesn't let you make assignments that might result in a loss of accuracy or in outright nonsense.

Using a hammer to bang a peg into a hole

In some cases, you can circumvent Java's prohibition against narrowing by *casting* a value. For example, you can create the long variable lotsAndLotsOfKids and make the assignment numberOfDuggarKids = (int) lotsAndLotsOfKids, as shown in Listing 6-2.

LISTING 6-2: **Casting to the Rescue**

```
package com.allmycode.a06_02;

import android.support.v7.app.AppCompatActivity;
import android.os.Bundle;
import android.view.View;
import android.widget.TextView;

public class MainActivity extends AppCompatActivity {
  TextView numberTextView;

  @Override
  protected void onCreate(Bundle savedInstanceState) {
    super.onCreate(savedInstanceState);
    setContentView(R.layout.activity_main);
    numberTextView = (TextView) findViewById(R.id.numberTextView);
  }

  public void onButtonClick(View view) {
    long lotsAndLotsOfKids = 2147483647;
    int numberOfDuggarKids;

    numberOfDuggarKids = (int) lotsAndLotsOfKids;

    numberTextView.setText(Integer.toString(numberOfDuggarKids));
  }
}
```

In Listing 6-2, the type name (int) in parentheses is a *cast operator*. It tells Java that you're aware of the potential pitfalls of stuffing a long value into an int variable and that you're willing to take your chances.

When you run the code in Listing 6-2, the value of lotsAndLotsOfKids might be between −2147483648 and 2147483647. If so, the assignment numberOfDuggar Kids = (int) lotsAndLotsOfKids is just fine. (*Remember:* An int value can be between −2147483648 and 2147483647. Refer to Table 5-1 in Chapter 5.)

But if the value of lotsAndLotsOfKids isn't between −2147483648 and 2147483647, the assignment statement in Listing 6-2 goes awry. When I run the code in Listing 6-2 with the different initialization

```
long lotsAndLotsOfKids = 2098797070970970956L;
```

the value of numberOfDuggarKids. becomes −287644852 (a negative number!).

When you use a casting operator, you're telling Java, "I'm aware that I'm doing something risky but (trust me) I know what I'm doing." And if you don't know what you're doing, you get a wrong answer. That's life!

IN THIS CHAPTER

» Matching Java types

» Calling methods effectively

» Understanding method parameters

Chapter **7**

Though These Be Methods, Yet There Is Madness in't

I n Chapter 4, I compare a method declaration to a recipe for scrambled eggs. In this chapter, I compute the tax and tip for a meal in a restaurant. And in Chapter 9 (spoiler alert!), I compare a Java class to the inventory in a cheese emporium. These comparisons aren't far-fetched. A method's declaration is a lot like a recipe, and a Java class bears some resemblance to a blank inventory sheet. But instead of thinking about methods, recipes, and Java classes, you might be reading between the lines. You might be wondering why I use so many food metaphors.

The truth is, my preoccupation with food is a recent development. Like most men my age, I've been told that I should shed my bad habits, lose a few pounds, exercise regularly, and find ways to reduce the stress in my life. (I've argued to my Wiley editors that submission deadlines are a source of stress, but so far the editors aren't buying a word of it. I guess I don't blame them.)

Above all, I've been told to adopt a healthy diet: Skip the chocolate, the cheeseburgers, the pizza, the fatty foods, the fried foods, the sugary snacks, and everything else that I normally eat. Instead, eat small portions of vegetables, carbs, and protein, and eat these things only at regularly scheduled meals. Sounds sensible, doesn't it?

I'm making a sincere effort. I've been eating right for about two weeks. My feelings of health and well-being are steadily improving. I'm only slightly hungry. (Actually, by "slightly hungry," I mean "extremely hungry." Yesterday I suffered a brief hallucination, believing that my computer keyboard was a giant Hershey's bar. And this morning I felt like gnawing on my office furniture. If I start trying to peel my mouse, I'll stop writing and go out for a snack.)

One way or another, the gustatory arena provides many fine metaphors for Java programming. A method's declaration is like a recipe. A declaration sits quietly, doing nothing, waiting to be executed. If you create a declaration but no one ever calls your declaration, then — like a recipe for worm stew — your declaration goes unexecuted.

On the other hand, a method call is a call to action — a command to follow the declaration's recipe. When you call a method, the method's declaration wakes up and follows the instructions inside the body of the declaration.

In addition, a method call may contain parameters. You call

```
textEdit.setText("Don't vote for that narcissist!");
```

with the parameter `"Don't vote for that narcissist!"`. The parameter, `"Don't vote for that narcissist!"` tells Android exactly what to display in the `textEdit` component on the user's screen. In the world of food, you might call `meatLoaf(6)`, which means, "Follow the meatloaf recipe, and make enough to serve six people."

Minding Your Types When You Call a Method

In Chapter 4, I introduce method parameters. And in Chapters 5 and 6, I make a big fuss about Java types. In this section, I pull those two ideas together.

A method call involves values going both ways — from the call to the running method and from the running method back to the call. Consider the code in Listing 7-1.

LISTING 7-1: **Parameter Types and Return Types**

```
package com.allmycode.a07_01;

import android.os.Bundle;
import android.support.v7.app.AppCompatActivity;
import android.view.View;
import android.widget.TextView;

import java.text.NumberFormat;

public class MainActivity extends AppCompatActivity {
  TextView paymentView;

  @Override
  protected void onCreate(Bundle savedInstanceState) {
    super.onCreate(savedInstanceState);
    setContentView(R.layout.activity_main);

    paymentView = (TextView) findViewById(R.id.paymentView);
  }

  public void onButtonClick(View view) {
    double principal = 100000.00, ratePercent = 5.25;
    double payment;
    int years = 30;
    String paymentString;

    payment = monthlyPayment(principal, ratePercent, years);

    NumberFormat currency = NumberFormat.getCurrencyInstance();
    paymentString = currency.format(payment);
    paymentView.setText(paymentString);
  }

  double monthlyPayment(double dPrincipal, double dRatePercent, int dYears) {
    double rate, effectiveAnnualRate;
    int paymentsPerYear = 12, numberOfPayments;

    rate = dRatePercent / 100.00;
    numberOfPayments = paymentsPerYear * dYears;
    effectiveAnnualRate = rate / paymentsPerYear;
```

(continued)

LISTING 7-1: *(continued)*

```
    return dPrincipal * (effectiveAnnualRate /
        (1 - Math.pow(1 + effectiveAnnualRate, -numberOfPayments)));
  }

}
```

Figure 7-1 shows a run of the code in Listing 7-1.

FIGURE 7-1:
Pay it and weep.

In Listing 7-1, I choose the parameter names `principal` and `dPrincipal`, `ratePercent` and `dRatePercent`, and `years` and `dYears`. I use the letter `d` to distinguish a declaration's parameter from a call's parameter. I do this to drive home the point that the names in the call aren't automatically the same as the names in the declaration. In fact, there are many variations on this call/declaration naming theme, and they're all correct. For example, you can use the same names in the call as in the declaration:

```
//In the call:
payment = monthlyPayment(principal, ratePercent, years);

//In the declaration:
double monthlyPayment(double principal, double ratePercent, int years) {
```

You can use expressions in the call that aren't single variable names:

```
//In the call:
payment = monthlyPayment(amount + fees, rate * 100, 30);

//In the declaration:
double monthlyPayment(double dPrincipal, double dRatePercent, int dYears) {
```

When you call a method from Java's API, you don't even know the names of parameters used in the method's declaration. And you don't care. The only things that matter are the positions of parameters in the list and the compatibility of the parameters. The value of the call's leftmost parameter becomes the value of the declaration's leftmost parameter, no matter what name the declaration's leftmost parameter has. The value of the call's second parameter becomes the value of the declaration's second parameter, no matter what name the declaration's second parameter has. And so on.

REMEMBER

In this section's example, I hardcode the values of the variables `principal`, `ratePercent`, and `years`, making Listing 7-1 useless for anything except one particular calculation. The only people who hardcode values are book authors and bad programmers. In a real app, you'd probably get values for these variables from `EditText` components on the user's screen. If you didn't have `EditText` components, you'd manage to get the values for `principal`, `ratePercent`, and `years` some other way.

Method parameters and Java types

Listing 7-1 contains both the declaration and a call for the `monthlyPayment` method. Figure 7-2 illustrates the type matches between these two parts of the program.

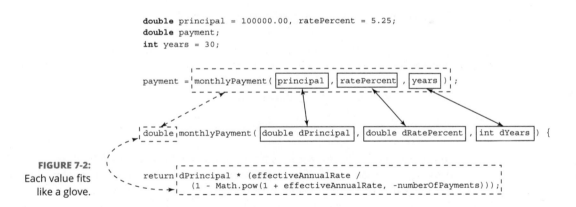

FIGURE 7-2:
Each value fits
like a glove.

In Figure 7-2, the `monthlyPayment` method call has three parameters, and the `monthlyPayment` declaration's header has three parameters. The call's three parameters have the types `double` and then `double` and then `int`:

```
double principal = 100000.00, ratePercent = 5.25;
...
int years = 30;

payment = monthlyPayment(principal, ratePercent, years);
```

And sure enough, the declaration's three parameters have the types `double` and then `double` and then `int`:

```
double monthlyPayment(double dPrincipal, double dRatePercent, int dYears) {
```

The expressions in the call must have types that are compatible with the corresponding parameters in the method's declaration. But "compatible" doesn't necessarily mean "exactly the same." You can take advantage of widening, which I describe in Chapter 6. For example, in Listing 7-1, the following call would be okay:

```
payment = monthlyPayment(100000, 5, years);
```

You can pass an `int` value (like `100000`) to the `dPrincipal` parameter, because the `dPrincipal` parameter is of type `double`. Java widens the values `100000` and `5` to the values `100000.0` and `5.0`. But, once again, Java doesn't narrow your values. The following call causes a squiggly red underline in Android Studio's editor:

```
payment = monthlyPayment(principal, ratePercent, 30.0);
```

You can't stuff a `double` value (like `30.0`) into the `dYears` parameter, because the `dYears` parameter is of type `int`.

If at first you don't succeed . . .

If you don't like the types of the parameters in a method declaration, you can take matters into your own hands. You can create another method declaration with the same name but with different parameter types. For example, in Listing 7-1, you can add a method with the following header:

```
double monthlyPayment(String lenderName, String borrowerName, double amount) {
```

In other words, you can overload a method name. Java figures out which method declaration to use by looking for a match with the types of parameters in the method call. For more information about overloading, refer to Chapter 4.

Return types

A method declaration's header normally looks like this:

```
maybeSomeWords returnType methodName(parameters) {
```

For example, Listing 7-1 contains a method declaration with the following header:

```
double monthlyPayment(double dPrincipal, double dRatePercent, int dYears) {
```

In this header, the *returnType* is double, the *methodName* is monthlyPayment, and the *parameters* are double dPrincipal, double dRatePercent, int dYears.

An entire method call can have a value, and the declaration's returnType tells Java what type that value has. In Listing 7-1, the returnType is double, so the call

```
monthlyPayment(principal, ratePercent, years)
```

has a value of type double. (Refer to Figure 7-2.)

I hardcoded the values of principal, ratePercent, and years in Listing 7-1. So when you run Listing 7-1, the value of the monthlyPayment method call is always 552.20. The call's value is whatever comes after the word return when the method is executed. And in Listing 7-1, the expression

```
return dPrincipal * (effectiveAnnualRate /
       (1 - Math.pow(1 + effectiveAnnualRate, -numberOfPayments)));
```

always comes out to be 552.20. Also, in keeping with the theme of type safety, the expression after the word return is of type double.

In summary, a call to the monthlyPayment method has the *return value* 552.20 and has the *return type* double.

The great void

A method to compute a monthly mortgage payment naturally returns a value. But some methods have no reason to return a value. Consider, for example, the onButtonClick method in Listing 7-1. This method's purpose is to make text appear in the paymentView. That's not what you'd call a calculation, and it's not the kind of work that ends up with an answer of some kind. So, in Listing 7-1, the onButtonClick method doesn't return a value of any kind.

In Listing 7-1, the onButtonClick method doesn't return a value, so the method's body has no return statement. And, in place of a return type, the header in the method's declaration contains the word void.

TECHNICAL
STUFF

To be painfully precise, you can put a `return` statement in a method that doesn't return a value. When you do, the `return` statement has no expression. It's just one word, `return`, followed by a semicolon. When Java executes this `return` statement, Java ends the run of the method and returns to the code that called the method. This form of the `return` statement works well in a situation in which you want to end the execution of a method before you reach the last statement in the method's declaration.

Displaying numbers

Here are a few lines that are scattered about in Listing 7-1:

```
import java.text.NumberFormat;


NumberFormat currency = NumberFormat.getCurrencyInstance();
paymentString = currency.format(payment);
```

Taken together, these statements format numbers into local currency amounts. On my phone, when I call `getCurrencyInstance()` with no parameters, I get a number (like $552.20) formatted for United States currency. (Refer to Figure 7-1.) But if your phone is set to run in Germany, you see the payment amount shown in Figure 7-3.

FIGURE 7-3:
Displaying the
euro symbol and
a comma for the
decimal
separator.

552,20 €

A country, its native language, or a variant of the native language is a *locale*. And by adding a parameter to the `getCurrencyInstance` call, you can format for locales other than your own. For example, by calling

```
NumberFormat.getCurrencyInstance(Locale.GERMANY)
```

anyone in any country can get the message box shown in Figure 7-3.

You can even cobble together a locale from a bunch of pieces. For example, one variant of the Thai language uses its own, special digit symbols. (See Figure 7-4.) To form a number with Thai digits, you write

```
NumberFormat.getCurrencyInstance(new Locale("th", "TH", "TH"))
```

In the list ("th", "TH", "TH"), the lowercase "th" stands for the Thai language. The first uppercase "TH" stands for the country Thailand. The last uppercase "TH" indicates the language variant that uses its own digit symbols.

FIGURE 7-4:
Thai digit
symbols.

THB๔๔๖.๒๐

Primitive Types and Pass-by Value

Java has two kinds of types: primitive and reference. The eight primitive types are the atoms — the basic building blocks. In contrast, the reference types are the things you create by combining primitive types (and by combining other reference types).

CROSS-
REFERENCE

I cover Java's primitive types in Chapter 5, and my coverage of Java's reference types begins in Chapter 9.

Here are two concepts you should remember when you think about primitive types and method parameters:

>> **When you assign a value to a variable with a primitive type, you're identifying that variable name with the value.**

The same is true when you initialize a primitive type variable to a particular value.

>> **When you call a method, you're *making copies* of each of the call's parameter values and initializing the declaration's parameters with those copied values.**

This scheme, in which you make copies of the call's values, is named *pass by value*. Listing 7-2 shows you why you should care about any of this.

LISTING 7-2: **Rack Up Those Points!**

```
package com.allmycode.a07_02;

import android.support.v7.app.AppCompatActivity;
import android.os.Bundle;
import android.widget.TextView;
```

(continued)

LISTING 7-2:   *(continued)*

```java
public class MainActivity extends AppCompatActivity {
  TextView textView;

  @Override
  protected void onCreate(Bundle savedInstanceState) {
    super.onCreate(savedInstanceState);
    setContentView(R.layout.activity_main);
    textView = (TextView) findViewById(R.id.textView);

    int score = 50000;
    int points = 1000;
    addPoints(score, points);
    textView.setText(Integer.toString(score));
  }

  void addPoints(int score, int points) {
    score += points;
  }

}
```

In Listing 7-2, the addPoints method uses Java's compound assignment operator to add 1000 (the value of points) to the existing score (which is 50000). To make things as cozy as possible, I've used the same parameter names in the method call and the method declaration. (In both, I use the names score and points.)

So what happens when I run the code in Listing 7-2? I get the result shown in Figure 7-5.

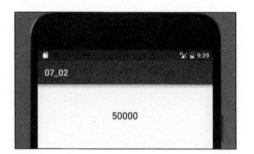

FIGURE 7-5: Getting 1000 more points?

But wait! When you add 1000 to 50000, you don't normally get 50000. What's wrong?

With Java's pass-by value feature, you *make a copy* of each parameter value in a call. You initialize the declaration's parameters with the copied values. So, immediately after making the call, you have two pairs of variables: the original `score` and `points` variables in the `onCreate` method and the new `score` and `points` variables in the `addPoints` method. The new `score` and `points` variables have copies of values from the `onCreate` method. (See Figure 7-6.)

PERILS AND PITFALLS OF PARAMETER PASSING

How would you like to change the value of 2 + 2? What would you like 2 + 2 to be? Six? Ten? Three hundred? In certain older versions of the FORTRAN programming language, you could make 2 + 2 be almost anything you wanted. For example, the following chunk of code (translated to look like Java code) would display 6 for the value of 2 + 2:

```
void increment(int score) {
  score++;
}
...
increment(2);
print(2 + 2);
```

When computer languages were first being developed, their creators didn't realize how complicated parameter passing can be. They weren't as careful about specifying the rules for copying parameters' values or for doing whatever else they wanted to do with parameters. As a result, some versions of FORTRAN indiscriminately passed memory addresses rather than values. Though address-passing alone isn't a terrible idea, things become ugly if the language designer isn't careful.

In some early FORTRAN implementations, the computer automatically (and without warning) turned the literal 2 into a variable named two. (In fact, the newly created variable probably wasn't named two. But in this story, the actual name of the variable doesn't matter.) FORTRAN would substitute the variable name two in any place where the programmer typed the literal value 2. But then, while running this sidebar's code, the computer would send the address of the two variable to the `increment` method. The method would happily add 1 to whatever was stored in the two variable and then continue its work. Now the two variable stored the number 3. By the time you reached the `print` call, the computer would add to itself whatever was in two, getting 3 + 3, which is 6.

If you think parameter passing is a no-brainer, think again. Different languages use all different kinds of parameter passing. And in many situations, the minute details of the way parameters are passed makes a big difference.

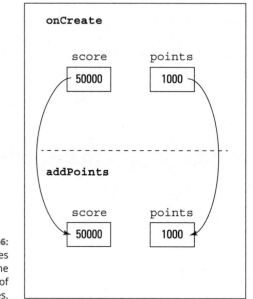

FIGURE 7-6:
Java makes
copies of the
values of
variables.

The statement in the body of the addPoints method adds 1000 to the value stored in its score variable. After adding 1000 points, the program's variables look like the stuff shown in Figure 7-7.

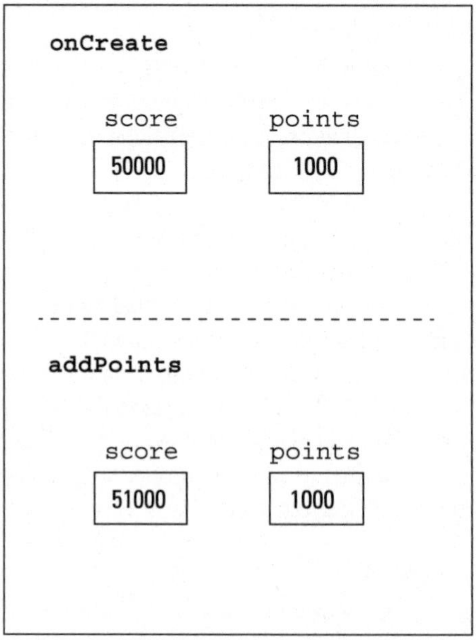

FIGURE 7-7:
Java adds 1000 to
only one of the
two score
variables.

Notice how the value of the onCreate method's score variable remains unchanged. After returning from the call to addPoints, the addPoints method's variables disappear. All that remains is the original onCreate method and its variables. (See Figure 7-8.)

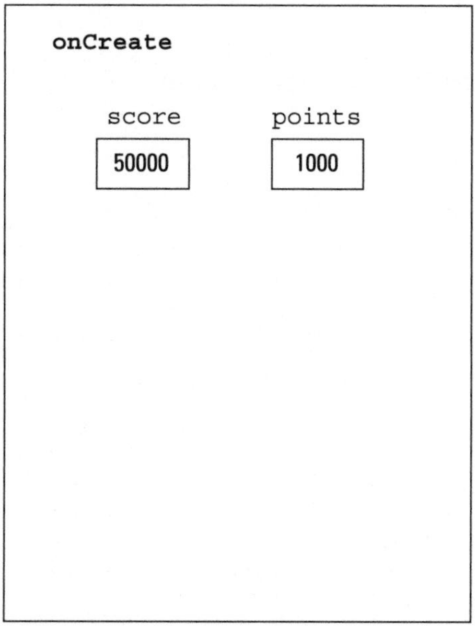

```
onCreate

        score           points
        ┌─────────┐     ┌────────┐
        │  50000  │     │  1000  │
        └─────────┘     └────────┘
```

FIGURE 7-8:
The variable with
value 51000 no
longer exists.

Finally, in Listing 7-2, Java calls textView.setText to display the value of the onCreate method's score variable. And (sadly, for the game player) the value of score is still 50000.

What's a developer to do?

The program in Listing 7-2 has a big, fat bug. The program doesn't add 1000 to a player's score. That's bad.

You can squash the bug in Listing 7-2 in several different ways. For example, you can avoid calling the addPoints method by inserting score += points along with the other code in the onCreate method.

```
int score = 50000;
int points = 1000;
score += points;
textView.setText(Integer.toString(score));
```

But that's not a satisfactory solution. Methods such as addPoints are useful for dividing work into neat, understandable chunks. And avoiding problems by skirting around them is no fun at all.

A better way to get rid of the bug is to make the addPoints method return a value. Listing 7-3 has the code.

LISTING 7-3: **A New-and-Improved Scorekeeper Program**

```java
package com.allmycode.a07_03;

import android.support.v7.app.AppCompatActivity;
import android.os.Bundle;
import android.widget.TextView;

public class MainActivity extends AppCompatActivity {
  TextView textView;

  @Override
  protected void onCreate(Bundle savedInstanceState) {
    super.onCreate(savedInstanceState);
    setContentView(R.layout.activity_main);
    textView = (TextView) findViewById(R.id.textView);

    int score = 50000;
    int points = 1000;
    score = addPoints(score, points);
    textView.setText(Integer.toString(score));
  }

  int addPoints(int score, int points) {
    return score + points;
  }

}
```

In Listing 7-3, the new-and-improved addPoints method returns an int value — namely, the value of score + points. So the value of the addPoints(score, points) call is 51000. Finally, I change the value of score by assigning the method call's value, 51000, to the score variable.

TECHNICAL STUFF

Java's nitpicky rules ensure that the juggling of the score variable's values is reliable and predictable. In the statement score = addPoints(score, points), there's no conflict between the old value of score (50000 in the addPoints parameter list) and the new value of score (51000 on the left side of the assignment statement).

A run of the code in Listing 7-3 is shown in Figure 7-9. You probably already know what the run looks like. (After all, 50000 + 1000 is 51000.) But I can't bear to finish this example without showing the correct answer.

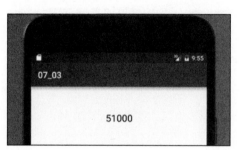

FIGURE 7-9:
At last, a higher
score!

CROSS-
REFERENCE

Making addPoints return a value isn't the only way to correct the problem in Listing 7-2. At least two other ways (using member variables and passing objects) are among the subjects of discussion in Chapter 9.

A final word

The program in Listing 7-4 displays the total cost of a $100 meal.

LISTING 7-4: **Yet Another Food Example**

```
package com.allmycode.a07_04;

import android.support.v7.app.AppCompatActivity;
import android.os.Bundle;
import android.view.View;
import android.widget.TextView;

import java.text.NumberFormat;

public class MainActivity extends AppCompatActivity {
    TextView totalView;
```

(continued)

LISTING 7-4: *(continued)*

```java
@Override
protected void onCreate(Bundle savedInstanceState) {
  super.onCreate(savedInstanceState);
  setContentView(R.layout.activity_main);
  totalView = (TextView) findViewById(R.id.totalView);
}

public void onButtonClick(View view) {
  NumberFormat currency = NumberFormat.getCurrencyInstance();
  totalView.setText(currency.format(addAll(100.00, 0.05, 0.20)));
}

double addAll(double bill, double taxRate, double tipRate) {
  bill *= 1 + taxRate;
  bill *= 1 + tipRate;
  return bill;
}

}
```

A run of the program in Listing 7-4 is shown in Figure 7-10.

FIGURE 7-10:
Support your
local eating
establishment.

Listing 7-4 is nice, but this code computes the tip after the tax has been added to the original bill. Some of my less generous friends believe that the tip should be based on only the amount of the original bill. (Guys, you know who you are!) They believe that the code should compute the tax but that it should remember and reuse the original $100.00 amount when calculating the tip. Here's my friends' version of the addAll method:

```
double addAll(double bill, double taxRate, double tipRate) {
  double originalBill = bill;
  bill *= 1 + taxRate;
  bill += originalBill * tipRate;
  return bill;
}
```

The new (stingier) total is shown in Figure 7-11.

FIGURE 7-11:
A dollar saved is a
dollar earned.

The revised addAll method is overly complicated. (In fact, in creating this example, I got this little method wrong two or three times before getting it right.) Wouldn't it be simpler to insist that the bill parameter's value never changes? Rather than mess with the bill amount, you make up new variables named tax and tip and total everything in the return statement:

```
double addAll(double bill, double taxRate, double tipRate) {
  double tax = bill * taxRate;
  double tip = bill * tipRate;
  return bill + tax + tip;
}
```

When you have these new tax and tip variables, the bill parameter always stores its original value — the value of the untaxed, untipped meal.

After developing this improved code, you make a mental note that the bill variable's value shouldn't change. Months later, when your users are paying big bucks for your app and demanding many more features, you might turn the program into a complicated, all-purpose meal calculator with localized currencies and tipping etiquette from around the world. Whatever you do, you always want easy access to that original bill value.

After your app has gone viral, you're distracted by the need to count your earnings, pay your servants, and maintain the fresh smell of your private jet's leather seats. With all these pressing issues, you accidentally forget your old promise not to change the `bill` variable. You change the variable's value somewhere in the middle of your 1000-line program. Now you've messed everything up.

But wait! You can have Java remind you that the `bill` parameter's value doesn't change. To do this, you add the keyword `final` (one of Java's modifiers) to the method declaration's parameter list. And while you're at it, you can add `final` to the other parameters (`taxRate` and `tipRate`) in the `addAll` method's parameter list:

```
double addAll (final double bill, final double taxRate, final double tipRate) {
  double tax = bill * taxRate;
  double tip = bill * tipRate;
  return bill + tax + tip;
}
```

With this use of the word `final`, you're telling Java not to let you change a parameter's value. If you plug the newest version of `addAll` into the code in Listing 7-4, `bill` becomes 100.00 and `bill` stays 100.00 throughout the execution of the `addAll` method. If you accidentally add the statement

```
bill += valetParkingFee;
```

to your code, Android Studio flags that line as an error because a `final` parameter's value cannot be changed. Isn't it nice to know that, with servants to manage and your private jet to maintain, you can still rely on Java to help you write a good Android app?

Chapter **8**

What Java Does (and When)

uman thought centers around nouns and verbs. Nouns are the "stuff," and verbs are the stuff's actions. Nouns are the pieces, and verbs are the glue. Nouns are, and verbs do. When you use nouns, you say "book," "room," or "stuff." When you use verbs, you say "do this," "do that," "tote that barge," or "lift that bale."

Java also has nouns and verbs. Java's nouns include `int` and `String`, along with Android-specific terms such as `AppCompatActivity`, `EditText`, and `TextView`. Java's verbs involve assigning values, choosing among alternatives, repeating actions, and taking other courses of action.

This chapter covers some of Java's verbs. (In the next chapter, I bring in the nouns.)

Making Decisions

When you're writing Java programs, you're continually hitting forks in roads. Did the user type the correct password? If the answer is yes, let the user work; if it's no, kick the bum out. The Java programming language needs a way to make a program branch in one of two directions. Fortunately, the language has a way: It's the `if` statement. The use of the `if` statement is illustrated in Listing 8-1.

LISTING 8-1: **Using an if Statement**

```
package com.allmycode.a08_01;

import android.support.v7.app.AppCompatActivity;
import android.os.Bundle;
import android.view.View;
import android.widget.CheckBox;
import android.widget.EditText;
import android.widget.TextView;

import java.text.NumberFormat;

public class MainActivity extends AppCompatActivity {
  EditText ageEditText;
  CheckBox specialShowingCheckBox;
  TextView outputView;

  @Override
  protected void onCreate(Bundle savedInstanceState) {
    super.onCreate(savedInstanceState);
    setContentView(R.layout.activity_main);

    ageEditText = (EditText) findViewById(R.id.ageEditText);
    specialShowingCheckBox =
        (CheckBox) findViewById(R.id.specialShowingCheckBox);
    outputView = (TextView) findViewById(R.id.outputView);
  }

  public void onButtonClick(View view) {
    int age = Integer.parseInt(ageEditText.getText().toString());
    boolean isSpecialShowing = specialShowingCheckBox.isChecked();
    double price;
    NumberFormat currency = NumberFormat.getCurrencyInstance();

    if ((age < 18 || 65 <= age) && !isSpecialShowing) {
      price = 7.00;
    } else {
      price = 10.00;
    }

    outputView.setText(currency.format(price));
  }
}
```

Listing 8-1 revives a question that I pose in Chapters 5 and 6: How much should a person pay for a movie ticket? Most people pay $10. But when the movie has no special showings, youngsters (under 18) and seniors (65 and older) pay only $7.

In Listing 8-1, a Java if statement determines a person's eligibility for the discounted ticket. If this condition is true:

```
(age < 18 || 65 <= age) && !isSpecialShowing
```

the price becomes 7.00; otherwise, the price becomes 10.00. In either case, the code displays the price in a TextView component. (See Figure 8-1.)

FIGURE 8-1:
Checking the
ticket price.

Java if statements

An if statement has this form:

```
if (condition) {
    statements to be executed when the condition is true
} else {
    statements to be executed when the condition is false
}
```

In Listing 8-1, the condition being tested is

```
(age < 18 || 65 <= age) && !isSpecialShowing
```

The condition is either true or false — true for youngsters and seniors when there's no special showing and false otherwise.

Conditions in if statements

The condition in an if statement must be enclosed in parentheses. The condition must be a boolean expression — an expression whose value is either true or false. For example, the following condition is okay:

```
if (numberOfTries < 17) {
```

But the strange kind of condition that you can use in other (non-Java) languages — languages such as C++ — is not okay:

```
if (17) { //This is incorrect.
```

CROSS-REFERENCE See Chapter 5 for information about Java's primitive types, including the boolean type.

Omitting braces

You can omit an if statement's curly braces when only one statement appears between the condition and the word else. You can also omit braces when only one statement appears after the word else. For example, the following chunk of code is right and proper:

```
if ((age < 18 || 65 <= age) && !isSpecialShowing)
   price = 7.00;
else
   price = 10.00;
```

The code is correct because only one statement (price = 7.00) appears between the condition and the else, and only one statement (price = 10.00) appears after the word else.

An if statement can also enjoy a full and happy life without an else part. The following code snippet contains an assignment statement followed by a complete if statement:

```
price = 10.00;
if ((age < 18 || 65 <= age) && !isSpecialShowing)
   price = 7.00;
```

Compound statements

An if statement is one of Java's *compound* statements because an if statement normally contains other Java statements. For example, the if statement in Listing 8-1 contains the two assignment statements price = 7.00 and price = 10.00.

A compound statement might even contain other compound statements. In this example:

```
price = 10.00;
if (age < 18 || 65 <= age) {
  if (!isSpecialShowing) {
    price = 7.00;
  }
}
```

one if statement (with the condition age < 18 || 65 <= age) contains another if statement (with the condition !isSpecialShowing).

Choosing among many alternatives

A Java if statement creates a fork in the road: Java chooses between two alternatives. But some problems lend themselves to forks with many prongs. What's the best way to decide among five or six alternative actions?

For me, multipronged forks are scary. In my daily life, I hate making decisions. (If a problem crops up, I would rather have it be someone else's fault.) So, writing the previous sections (on making decisions with Java's if statement) knocked the stuffing right out of me. That's why my mind boggles as I begin this section on choosing among many alternatives.

This section's example is a tiny calculator. The user types in two numbers and then presses one of four buttons. I label the buttons with the symbols of the four common arithmetic operations. See Figure 8-2.

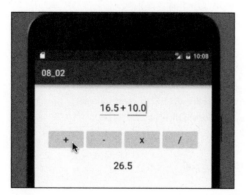

FIGURE 8-2: Running a tiny calculator app.

When I create the four buttons, I give each button an id value. How about the names buttonAdd, buttonSubtract, buttonMultiply, and buttonDivide for the buttons' id values? That sounds good.

CROSS-REFERENCE

For a reminder about id values, refer to Chapter 3.

I also give each button an onClick attribute. In fact, I set each button's onClick attribute to the name onButtonClick. So if the user clicks one of the buttons, Android calls my activity's onButtonClick method.

But wait! Any of the four buttons sends Android to my activity's onButtonClick method. How does my code know which of the buttons the user clicked? Listing 8-2 has the answer.

LISTING 8-2: **Switching from One Button to Another**

```java
package com.allmycode.a08_02;

import android.support.v7.app.AppCompatActivity;
import android.os.Bundle;
import android.view.View;
import android.widget.EditText;
import android.widget.TextView;

public class MainActivity extends AppCompatActivity {
  EditText numberLeftEditText, numberRightEditText;
  TextView operatorView, resultView;

  @Override
  protected void onCreate(Bundle savedInstanceState) {
    super.onCreate(savedInstanceState);
    setContentView(R.layout.activity_main);

    numberLeftEditText = (EditText) findViewById(R.id.numberLeftEditText);
    numberRightEditText = (EditText) findViewById(R.id.numberRightEditText);
    operatorView = (TextView) findViewById(R.id.operatorView);
    resultView = (TextView) findViewById(R.id.resultView);
  }

  public void onButtonClick(View view) {
    double numberLeft =
        Double.parseDouble(numberLeftEditText.getText().toString());
    double numberRight =
        Double.parseDouble(numberRightEditText.getText().toString());
```

```
String operatorSymbol = "";
double result;

switch (view.getId()) {
  case R.id.buttonAdd:
    operatorSymbol = "+";
    result = numberLeft + numberRight;
    break;
  case R.id.buttonSubtract:
    operatorSymbol = "-";
    result = numberLeft - numberRight;
    break;
  case R.id.buttonMultiply:
    operatorSymbol = "x";
    result = numberLeft * numberRight;
    break;
  case R.id.buttonDivide:
    operatorSymbol = "/";
    result = numberLeft / numberRight;
    break;
  default:
    operatorSymbol = "?";
    result = 0;
    break;
}

operatorView.setText(operatorSymbol);
resultView.setText(Double.toString(result));
  }
}
```

In Figure 8-2, the user enters the numbers 16.5 and 10.0 in the two EditText components. Then the user clicks the button that has a plus sign on its face. As a result, Android calls the onButtonClick method in Listing 8-2. What happens next?

The program enters the switch statement in Listing 8-2. The switch statement starts with the line

```
switch (view.getId()) {
```

That line contains the expression view.getId(). The name view (a parameter of the onButtonClick method) refers to whatever component the user clicked. That component's getId method returns the component's id. For example, if the user clicks the plus-sign button, the value of view.getId() is the same as the value of `R.id.buttonAdd`. If the user clicks the times-sign button, the value of `view.getId()` is the same as the value of `R.id.buttonMultiply`. And so on.

A `switch` statement contains `case` clauses, followed (optionally) by a `default` clause. In Listing 8-2, Java compares the value of `view.getId()` with `R.id.buttonAdd` (the value in the first of the `case` clauses). If the user clicked the plus-sign button, the value of `view.getId()` is the same as the value of `R.id.buttonAdd`, and the program executes the statements after the words `case R.id.buttonAdd`.

In Listing 8-2, the statements immediately after `case R.id.buttonAdd` are

```
operatorSymbol = "+";
result = numberLeft + numberRight;
break;
```

The first two statements set the values of `operatorSymbol` and `result` in preparation for displaying these values on the user's screen. The third statement (the `break` statement) jumps out of the entire `switch` statement, skipping past all the other `case` clauses and past the `default` clause to get to the last part of the program.

After the `switch` statement, the statements

```
operatorView.setText(operatorSymbol);
resultView.setText(Double.toString(result));
```

display the `operatorSymbol` and `result` values in `TextView` components on the user's screen. (Refer to Figure 8-2.)

Take a break

This news might surprise you: The end of a `case` clause (the beginning of another `case` clause) doesn't automatically make the program jump out of the `switch` statement. If you forget to add a `break` statement at the end of a `case` clause, the program finishes the statements in the `case` clause *and then continues executing the statements in the next* `case` *clause*. Imagine that I write the following code (and omit the `R.id.buttonAdd` `case`'s `break` statement):

```
case R.id.buttonAdd:
    operatorSymbol = "+";
    result = numberLeft + numberRight;
case R.id.buttonSubtract:
    operatorSymbol = "-";
    result = numberLeft - numberRight;
    break;
... etc.
```

With this modified code (and with `view.getId()` equal to `R.id.buttonAdd`), the program sets `operatorSymbol` to "+", sets `result` to `numberLeft + numberRight`, sets `operatorSymbol` to "−", sets `result` to `numberLeft − numberRight`, and, finally, breaks out of the `switch` statement (skipping past all other `case` clauses and the `default` clause). The upshot of the whole thing is that `operatorSymbol` has the value "−" (not "+") and that `result` is `numberLeft − numberRight` (not `numberLeft + numberRight`).

This phenomenon of jumping from one `case` clause to another (in the absence of a `break` statement) is called *fall-through,* and, sometimes, it's useful. Imagine a dice game in which 7 and 11 are instant wins; 2, 3, and 12 are instant losses; and any other number (from 4 to 10) tells you to continue playing. The code for such a game might look like this:

```
switch (roll) {
  case 7:
  case 11:
    message = "win";
    break;
  case 2:
  case 3:
  case 12:
    message = "lose";
    break;
  case 4:
  case 5:
  case 6:
  case 8:
  case 9:
  case 10:
    message = "continue";
    break;
  default:
    message = "not a valid dice roll";
    break;
}
```

If you roll a 7, you execute all statements immediately after `case 7` (of which there are none), and then you fall-through to `case 11`, executing the statement that assigns "win" to the variable `message`.

Every beginning Java programmer forgets to put a `break` statement at the end of a `case` clause. When you make this mistake, don't beat yourself up about it. Just remember what's causing your program's unexpected behavior, add `break` statements to your code, and move on. As you gain experience in writing Java programs, you'll make this mistake less and less frequently. (You'll still make the mistake occasionally, but not as often.)

In this section, I harp on the use of the break statement as if it's the only way to avoid fall-through. But in truth, there are other ways. You can see another way in this chapter's later section "Take a break from using the break statement." With or without these other ways, reminding yourself about fall-through by thinking "break, break, break!" is a good idea.

Java selects a case clause

When you run the code in Listing 8-2, you can click any of the four buttons. If you click the times-sign button, Java looks for a match between the times-sign button's id and the values in the case expressions. Java skips past the statements in the case R.id.buttonAdd clause and then skips past the statements in the R.id.buttonSubtract clause. The program hits pay dirt when it reaches the case R.id.buttonMultiply clause and executes that clause's statements, making operatorSymbol be "x" and making result be numberLeft * numberRight. Then the case R.id.buttonMultiply clause's break statement makes the program skip the rest of the stuff in the switch statement.

The default clause

A switch statement's optional default clause is a catchall for values that don't match any of the case clauses' values. You might enhance the calculator app by adding a square root button to the activity's screen but then forget to create a case clause for the new button. Then, if you run the app and click the square root button, Java doesn't fix on any of the case clauses. Java skips past all the case clauses and executes the code in the default clause, making operatorSymbol be "?" and making result be 0.

When you create a switch statement, your switch statement doesn't have to have a default clause. But if it doesn't, you probably haven't planned for all possible contingencies. You should always plan for contingencies. Good planning makes a good, sturdy app, and a good, sturdy app gets high ratings on Google Play.

The last break statement in Listing 8-2 tells Java to jump to the end of the switch statement, skipping any statements after the default clause. But look again. Nothing comes after the default clause in the switch statement! Which statements are being skipped? The answer is none. I put a break at the end of the default clause for good measure. This extra break statement doesn't do anything, but it doesn't do any harm, either.

Oops!

Figures 8-3 and 8-4 show you what happens when the app in Listing 8-2 divides a number by zero.

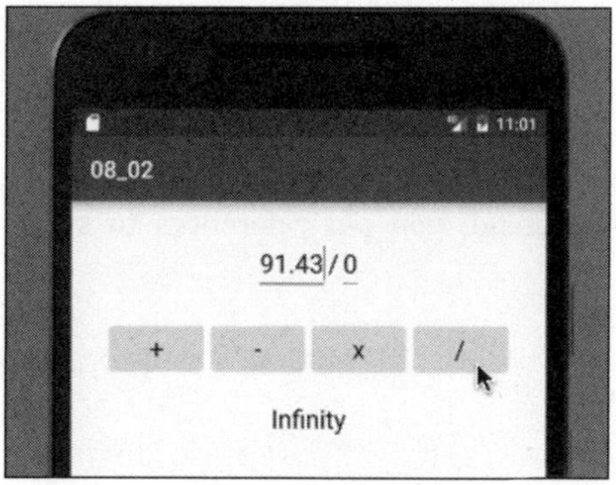

FIGURE 8-3: Dividing almost any number by zero.

FIGURE 8-4: Dividing zero by zero.

Dividing a number by zero might give you *Infinity* — an inspiring value. But dividing zero by zero gives you *NaN*, which stands for *Not a Number*. In general, you probably don't want the user to divide by zero, so you can add code that makes dividing by zero a "no-no." Here's the code:

```java
if (Double.isInfinite(result) || Double.isNaN(result)) {
    resultView.setText("Bad value!");
} else {
    resultView.setText(Double.toString(result));
}
```

The `Double.isInfinite` and `Double.isNaN` methods do what their names advertise. If the user becomes frisky and tries to crash your app with a zero divisor, your app tells the user to behave.

TIP

In this book, I create examples with the novice developer in mind. In some cases, I break with recommended Android coding guidelines to keep the code simple and readable. For example, in an industrial-strength Android program, you should avoid statements such as

```
resultView.setText("Bad value!");
```

This statement displays the English language phrase *Bad value!* on every device, even if the device's language setting is for German or Chinese. To create an app that adapts to non-English languages, you don't put `String` values in the app's `setText` method calls. Instead, you put references to string resources in the `setText` method calls.

At this point, you may ask "What's a reference to string resource?" To that question I reply "See Chapter 11."

Some formalities concerning Java switch statements

A `switch` statement has the following form:

```
switch (expression) {
case constant1:
    statements to be executed when the
    expression has value constant1
case constant2:
    statements to be executed when the
    expression has value constant2
case ...

default:
    statements to be executed when the
    expression has a value different from
    any of the constants
}
```

You can't put any old expression in a `switch` statement. The expression that's tested at the start of a `switch` statement must have

>> One of these primitive types: `char`, `byte`, `short`, or `int`

or

>> One of these wrapper types: `Character`, `Byte`, `Short`, or `Integer`

or

>> The String type

or

>> An enum type

CROSS-
REFERENCE
For some words of wisdom concerning Java's wrapper types, see Chapter 12.

An enum type is a type whose values are limited to the few that you declare. For example, the line

```
enum TrafficSignal {GREEN, YELLOW, RED};
```

defines a type whose only values are GREEN, YELLOW, and RED. Elsewhere in your code, you can write

```
TrafficSignal signal;
signal = TrafficSignal.GREEN;
```

to make use of the TrafficSignal type.

Repeating Instructions Over and Over Again

In 1966, the company that brings you Head & Shoulders shampoo made history. On the back of the bottle, the directions for using the shampoo read, "Lather, rinse, repeat." Never before had a complete set of directions (for doing anything, let alone shampooing hair) been summarized so succinctly. People in the direction-writing business hailed it as a monumental achievement. Directions like these stood in stark contrast to others of the time. (For instance, the first sentence on a can of bug spray read, "Turn this can so that it points away from your face." Duh!)

Aside from their brevity, the characteristic that made the Head & Shoulders directions so cool was that, with three simple words, they managed to capture a notion that's at the heart of all step-by-step instruction-giving, namely, the notion of repetition. That last word, *repeat,* turned an otherwise bland instructional drone into a sophisticated recipe for action.

When you follow directions, you usually don't just follow one instruction after another. Instead, you make turns in the road. You make decisions ("If HAIR IS DRY, then USE CONDITIONER,") and you repeat steps ("LATHER-RINSE, and then LATHER-RINSE again."). In application development, you use decision-making and repetition all the time.

Check, and then repeat

In this chapter's earlier "Take a break" section, I describe a simplified version of the dice game called Craps. Keep rolling the dice until you roll 2, 3, 7, 11, or 12. If you finish with 7 or 11, you win. But if you finish with 2, 3, or 12, you lose.

The program in Listing 8-3 uses Java's Random class to simulate a round of play.

LISTING 8-3: **Look Before You Leap**

```
package com.allmycode.a08_03;

import android.os.Bundle;
import android.support.v7.app.AppCompatActivity;
import android.view.View;
import android.widget.TextView;

import java.util.Random;

public class MainActivity extends AppCompatActivity {
  TextView textView;

  @Override
  protected void onCreate(Bundle savedInstanceState) {
    super.onCreate(savedInstanceState);
    setContentView(R.layout.activity_main);

    textView = (TextView) findViewById(R.id.textView);
  }

  public void onButtonClick(View view) {
    Random random = new Random();
    String message = "continue";

    textView.setText("");

    while (message.equals("continue")) {
      int numberA = random.nextInt(6) + 1;
      int numberB = random.nextInt(6) + 1;
      int total = numberA + numberB;
      message = getMessage(total);
```

```
      textView.append(numberA + " + " + numberB + " = " + total +
                                        " " + message + "\n");
  }
}

String getMessage(int total) {
  switch (total) {
    case 7:
    case 11:
      return "win";
    case 2:
    case 3:
    case 12:
      return "lose";
    case 4:
    case 5:
    case 6:
    case 8:
    case 9:
    case 10:
      return "continue";
    default:
      return "not a valid dice roll";
  }
}
}
```

A run of the code in Listing 8-3 is shown in Figure 8-5.

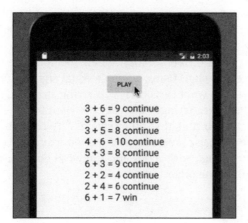

FIGURE 8-5:
Try, try, try again.

Take your chances

In Listing 8-3, I spread the statements

```
import java.util.Random;

Random random = new Random();

int numberA = random.nextInt(6) + 1;
int numberB = random.nextInt(6) + 1;
```

across the code to produce two randomly chosen int values. A single call to random.nextInt(6) returns a randomly chosen int value from 0 to 5 inclusive. (Yes, you read it correctly. The number 6 means "return 0, 1, 2, 3, 4, or 5.") By adding 1 to the value returned by random.nextInt(6), you get a randomly chosen int value from 1 to 6 — exactly the kind of value you get when you roll a single die. Calling random.nextInt(6) +1 twice is like rolling two dice.

TECHNICAL STUFF

Java's Random class generates sequences of numbers that, by the most stringent technical standards, are "almost random." To use the correct terminology, the Random class creates *pseudo-random* sequences of numbers. You wouldn't use Java's Random class for a multimillion-dollar, government-sponsored lottery game. But you can use the Random class to help demonstrate loops in an introductory programming book.

Testing String values for equality

Java has several ways to test for equality: "Is this value the same as that value?" None of these ways is the first one you'd consider. In particular, to find out whether someone's age is 35, you *don't* write if (age = 35). Instead, you use a double equal sign (==): if (age == 35). In Java, the single equal sign (=) is reserved for *assignment.* So age = 35 means "Let age stand for the value 35", and age == 35 means "True or false: Does age stand for the value 35"?

Comparing two strings is a different story. When you compare two strings, you don't use the double equal sign. Using a double equal sign would ask a question that's usually not what you want to ask: "Is this string stored in exactly the same place in memory as that other string?" Instead, you want to ask, "Does this string have the same characters in it as that other string?" To ask the second question (the more appropriate one), use Java's equals method. To call this equals method, follow one of the two strings with a dot and the word equals, and then with a parameter list containing the other string:

```
while (message.equals("continue")) {
```

The equals method compares two strings to see whether they have the same characters in them. In Listing 8-3, the variable message refers to a string, and the text "continue" refers to a string. The condition message.equals("continue") is true if message refers to a string whose characters are the letters in the "continue" string.

Repeat, repeat, repeat

A while statement tells Java to do things repeatedly. In plain language, the while statement in Listing 8-3 says:

```
while ( message is "continue" ) {

    roll the dice and add new information to the textView

}
```

The while statement is one of Java's compound statements. It's also one of Java's *looping* statements because, when executing a while statement, Java can go into a loop, spinning around and around, executing a certain chunk of code over and over again.

In a looping statement, each go-around is an *iteration*.

TIP

In Listing 8-3, notice how the string that I append to the textView component's text ends with "\n". The \n says "go to a new line before adding more text after this." That's why, in Figure 8-5, each simulated dice roll appears on its own, separate line. The \n business is an example of an *escape sequence*. Other escape sequences include \t for tab, \b for backspace, \" for a double quotation mark, and \\ for the backslash itself.

Some formalities concerning Java while statements

A while statement has this form:

```
while (condition) {
    statements inside the loop
}
```

Java repeats the *statements inside the loop* over and over again as long as the condition in parentheses is true:

```
Check to make sure that the condition is true;
Execute the statements inside the loop.

Check again to make sure that the condition is true;
Execute the statements inside the loop.

Check again to make sure that the condition is true;
Execute the statements inside the loop.

And so on.
```

For Listing 8-3, the repetition looks like this:

```
Check to make sure that the message is "continue";
Roll the dice, get a message, and display stuff on the screen.

Check again to make sure that the message is "continue";
Roll the dice, get a message, and display stuff on the screen.

Check again to make sure that the message is "continue";
Roll the dice, get a message, and display stuff on the screen.

And so on.
```

At some point, the while statement's condition becomes false. (Generally, this happens because one of the statements in the loop changes one of the program's values.) When the condition becomes false, Java stops repeating the statements in the loop. (That is, Java stops *iterating*.) Instead, Java executes whatever statements appear immediately after the end of the while statement:

```
Check again to make sure that the condition is true;
Execute the statements inside the loop.

Check again to make sure that the condition is true;
Execute the statements inside the loop.

Check again to make sure that the condition is true;
Oops! The condition is no longer true!
Execute any code that comes immediately after the while statement.
```

For Listing 8-3, the repetition looks like this:

```
Check to make sure that the message is "continue";
Roll the dice, get a message, and display stuff on the screen.

Check again to make sure that the message is "continue";
Roll the dice, get a message, and display stuff on the screen.

Check again to make sure that the message is "continue";
Oops! The message is no longer "continue"!
Execute any code that comes immediately after the while statement.
```

In Listing 8-3, the onButtonClick method has no code after the while statement. So, when the message.equals("continue") condition is no longer true, the code in Listing 8-3 doesn't do anything. The code sits and waits for the user to click another button, for the user to back away from the activity, or for some other interesting event to happen.

Take a break from using the break statement

In this chapter's earlier section "Take a break," I promise to show you an alternative way of avoiding unwanted fall-through. The switch statement in Listing 8-3 avoids fall-through by jumping clear out of getMessage method.

For example, if the value of total is 7, the switch statement matches total with the first case 7 clause. The case 7 clause has no statements to execute. But because of fall-through, Java marches onward into the case 11 clause. Inside that case 11 clause, Java encounters the return "win" statement. With this return "win" statement, Java ends execution of anything inside the getMessage method and returns to the statements in while loop. It all works very nicely!

Variations on a theme

A while statement's condition might become false in the middle of an iteration, before all the iteration's statements have been executed. When this happens, Java doesn't stop the iteration dead in its tracks. Instead, Java executes the rest of the loop's statements. After executing the rest of the loop's statements, Java checks the condition (finding the condition to be false) and marches on to whatever code comes immediately after the while statement.

TECHNICAL
STUFF

The previous paragraph should come with some fine print. To be painfully accurate, I should point out a few ways for you to stop abruptly in the middle of a loop iteration. You can execute a break statement to jump out of a while statement immediately. (It's the same break statement that you use in a switch statement.) Alternatively, you can execute a continue statement (the word continue, followed by a semicolon) to jump abruptly out of an iteration. When you jump out with a `continue` statement, Java ends the current iteration immediately and then checks the `while` statement's condition. A `true` condition tells Java to begin the next loop iteration. A `false` condition tells Java to go to whatever code comes after the `while` statement.

Many of the `if` statement's tricks apply to `while` statements as well. A `while` statement is a compound statement, so it might contain other compound statements. Also, when a `while` statement contains only one statement, you can omit curly braces. Here's an example:

```
int newNumber = 1;

while (newNumber < 4)
  newNumber = random.nextInt(6) + 1;
```

This code repeatedly fetches randomly generated values for `newNumber` as long as `newNumber` is less than 4.

Priming the pump

Java's `while` statement uses the policy "Look before you leap." Java always checks a condition before executing the statements inside the loop. Among other things, this forces you to prime the loop. When you prime a loop, you create statements that affect the loop's condition before the beginning of the loop. (Think of an old-fashioned water pump and how you have to prime the pump before water comes out.) In Listing 8-3, the initialization in

```
String message = "continue";
```

primes the loop. This initialization — the = part — gives `message` its first value so that when you check the condition `message.equals("continue")` for the first time, the variable `message` refers to a value that's worth checking.

Here's something you should consider when you create a `while` statement: Java can execute a `while` statement without ever executing the statements inside the loop. For example, in Listing 8-3, change the `message` variable's initialization to

```
String message = "win";
```

The code checks the condition `message.equals("continue")` before performing any loop iterations. But before performing any loop iterations, the condition `message.equals("continue")` is `false`. Java skips past the statements inside the loop and goes immediately to a place after `while` statement. In this situation, Java never rolls the dice and never displays any info about a roll.

Repeat, and then check

The while statement (which I describe in the previous section) is the workhorse of repetition in Java. Using while statements, you can do any kind of looping that you need to do. But sometimes it's convenient to have other kinds of looping statements. For example, occasionally you want to structure the repetition so that the first iteration takes place without checking a condition. In that situation, you use Java's do statement. Listing 8-4 is almost the same as Listing 8-3. But in Listing 8-4, I replace a while statement with a do statement.

LISTING 8-4: **Leap before You Look**

```
package com.allmycode.a08_04;

import android.os.Bundle;
import android.support.v7.app.AppCompatActivity;
import android.view.View;
import android.widget.TextView;

import java.util.Random;

public class MainActivity extends AppCompatActivity {
  TextView textView;

  @Override
  protected void onCreate(Bundle savedInstanceState) {
    super.onCreate(savedInstanceState);
    setContentView(R.layout.activity_main);

    textView = (TextView) findViewById(R.id.textView);
  }

  public void onButtonClick(View view) {
    Random random = new Random();
    String message;

    textView.setText("");

    do {
      int numberA = random.nextInt(6) + 1;
      int numberB = random.nextInt(6) + 1;
      int total = numberA + numberB;
      message = getMessage(total);
```

(continued)

LISTING 8-4: *(continued)*

```
        textView.append(numberA + " + " + numberB + " = " + total +
                                          " " + message + "\n");

    } while (message.equals("continue"));

}

String getMessage(int total) {
  switch (total) {
    case 7:
    case 11:
      return "win";
    case 2:
    case 3:
    case 12:
      return "lose";
    case 4:
    case 5:
    case 6:
    case 8:
    case 9:
    case 10:
      return "continue";
    default:
      return "not a valid dice roll";
    }
  }
}
```

With a do statement, Java jumps right in, takes action, and then checks a condition. If the condition is true, Java goes back to the top of the loop for another go-round. If the condition is false, execution of the loop is done.

REMEMBER

A do statement contains the while keyword, but a while statement never contains the do keyword. If it helps, think of Java's do statement as a do...while statement.

Walls built with braces

Unlike a while statement, a do statement generally doesn't need to be primed. In Listing 8-4, I don't even bother to give message an initial value.

Because message isn't checked until the last line of the do statement, you might be tempted to declare message inside the do statement.

```
// Don't "do" this... (ha ha!)
do {
    int numberA = random.nextInt(6) + 1;
    int numberB = random.nextInt(6) + 1;
    int total = numberA + numberB;

    String message;
    message = getMessage(total);

    textView.append(numberA + " + " + numberB + " = " + total +
        " " + message + "\n");

} while (message.equals("continue"));
```

Unfortunately, declaring message inside of the do statement doesn't work. In Figure 8-6, the shaded area marks the code where the declaration of message is in play.

```
public void onButtonClick(View view) {
    Random random = new Random();

    textView.setText("");

    do {
        int numberA = random.nextInt(6) + 1;
        int numberB = random.nextInt(6) + 1;
        int total = numberA + numberB;
        String message = getMessage(total);

        textView.append(numberA + " + " + numberB + " = " + total +
            " " + message + "\n");

    } while (message.equals("continue"));

}
```

FIGURE 8-6:
A declaration inside of a do statement's block.

In this incorrect code snippet, you can use the variable message only between the do statement's open curly brace and the do statement's close curly brace. But the words while (message.equals("continue")) aren't between the two curly braces. With this snippet, Android Studio displays an error message and refuses to run your code. Too bad!

The stuff between an open curly brace and its corresponding close curly brace is called a *block*. Here's the story:

>> **Every block, whether it's part of a method declaration, a do statement, an if statement, a while statement, or any other Java construct, traps any of its variable declarations for use only inside the block.**

If you declare a variable inside a block, you can't use that variable outside the block.

But if you go from outside a block to the inside of a block, the opposite is true. . . .

>> **If a variable's declaration is in force immediately before the start of a block, you can use that variable inside the block, and you can use that variable in the code that comes after the block.**

In Figure 8-7, I declare message before the do statement's block. The shaded area marks the code where this declaration of message is in play.

This second bullet explains why it's okay to declare message before the start of the do statement in Listing 8-4. For the same reason, in Listing 8-4, I'm able to declare textView before any of the method declarations, and then use the textView variable in two of those method declarations.

```
public void onButtonClick(View view) {
    Random random = new Random();
    String message;

    textView.setText("");

    do {
        int numberA = random.nextInt(6) + 1;
        int numberB = random.nextInt(6) + 1;
        int total = numberA + numberB;
        message = getMessage (total);

        textView.append(numberA + " + " + numberB + " = " + total +
            " " + message + "\n");

    } while (message.equals("continue"));
}
```

FIGURE 8-7:
A declaration outside of a do statement's block.

TECHNICAL
STUFF

If you want, you can use a name such as message in two different declarations. You can put one declaration outside the do statement's block, and a second declaration inside the do statement's block. But if you try this, you've declared two different variables, both with the same name message. It's like having two people named "Barry Burd" living in the same town. They have the same name, but they're not the same person. The two message variables don't share any values. Except for coincidentally having the same spelling, the two variable names bear no relation to one another.

Some formalities concerning Java do statements

A do statement has the following form:

```
do {
    statements inside the loop
} while (condition)
```

Java executes the *statements inside the loop* and then checks to see whether the condition in parentheses is true. If the condition in parentheses is true, Java executes the *statements inside the loop* again. And so on.

Java's do statement uses the policy "Leap before you look." The statement checks a condition immediately *after* each iteration of the statements inside the loop.

A do statement is good for situations in which you know for sure that you should perform the loop's statements at least once. But in practice, you see many more while statements than do statements. In the lion's share of your processing scenarios, you check a condition before you start repeating things.

Count, count, count

Java's while and do statements check conditions to decide whether to keep repeating things. That's great but, sometimes, the condition is mundane. You don't check for a special showing or a "continue" message. You simply want to repeat something a certain number of times. To do that, you should use Java's for statement.

Suppose that you want to estimate how many times a player wins or loses in this chapter's simplified dice game. You can use mathematics to calculate probabilities, but you can also experiment by rolling the dice 100 times. To do that, you put the dice-rolling statements inside a Java for statement. Listing 8-5 shows you what to do.

LISTING 8-5: **A Loop That Counts**

```
package com.allmycode.a08_05;

import android.os.Bundle;
import android.support.v7.app.AppCompatActivity;
```

(continued)

LISTING 8-5: *(continued)*

```java
import android.view.View;
import android.widget.TextView;

import java.util.Random;

public class MainActivity extends AppCompatActivity {
  TextView textView;

  @Override
  protected void onCreate(Bundle savedInstanceState) {
    super.onCreate(savedInstanceState);
    setContentView(R.layout.activity_main);

    textView = (TextView) findViewById(R.id.textView);
  }

  public void onButtonClick(View view) {
    Random random = new Random();
    String message;
    int winCount = 0, loseCount = 0;

    for (int i = 1; i <= 100; i++) {
      int numberA = random.nextInt(6) + 1;
      int numberB = random.nextInt(6) + 1;
      int total = numberA + numberB;
      message = getMessage(total);

      if (message.equals("win")) {
        winCount++;
      } else if (message.equals("lose")) {
        loseCount++;
      }
    }

    textView.setText("Wins: " + winCount + "\nLosses: " + loseCount);
  }

  String getMessage(int total) {
    switch (total) {
      case 7:
      case 11:
        return "win";
      case 2:
      case 3:
```

```
      case 12:
        return "lose";
      case 4:
      case 5:
      case 6:
      case 8:
      case 9:
      case 10:
        return "continue";
      default:
        return "not a valid dice roll";
    }
  }
}
```

Listing 8-5 declares an int variable named i. This declaration is inside the first line of the for statement. The starting value of i is 1. As long as the condition i <= 100 is true, Java repeatedly executes the statements inside the loop. After each iteration of the statements inside the loop, Java executes i++ (adding 1 to the value of i).

After 100 iterations, the value of i gets to be 101, in which case the condition i <= 100 is no longer true. At that point, Java stops repeating the statements inside the loop and moves on to execute any statements that come after the for statement.

In Listing 8-5, the statements inside the for loop simulate a roll of the dice, and keep tallies of the number of winning and losing rolls. The only statement that comes after the for loop is a statement that displays the tallies in the textView component. A run of the code is shown in Figure 8-8.

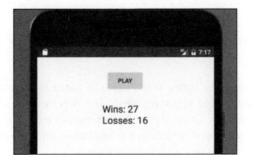

FIGURE 8-8: One run of the code in Listing 8-5.

Notice the combination of if statements in Listing 8-5. Some programming languages have their own special elseif keywords, but Java doesn't have such a thing. Instead, you can put an if statement inside the else clause of another if statement. In Listing 8-5, Java checks to find out if the message is "win". When the message is "win", it's the end of the if statement story. But when the message isn't "win", Java goes on to check whether the message is "lose". When the message is neither "win" nor "lose", the execution of these if statements doesn't change either of the tallies' values.

Some formalities concerning Java for statements

A for statement has the following form:

```
for (initialization ; condition ; update) {
    statements inside the loop
}
```

» An *initialization* (such as int i = 1 in Listing 8-5) defines the action to be taken before the first loop iteration.

» A *condition* (such as i <= 100 in Listing 8-5) defines the value to be checked before an iteration. If the condition is true, Java executes the iteration. If the condition is false, Java doesn't execute the iteration, and it moves on to execute whatever code comes after the for statement.

» An *update* (such as i++ in Listing 8-5) defines an action to be taken at the end of each loop iteration.

You can omit the curly braces when only one statement is inside the loop.

What's Next?

This chapter describes several ways to jump from one place in your code to another.

Java provides other ways to move from place to place in a program, including enhanced for statements and try statements. But descriptions of these elements don't belong in this chapter. To understand the power of enhanced for statements and try statements, you need a firm grasp of classes and objects, so Chapter 9 dives fearlessly into the classes-and-objects waters.

I'm your swimming instructor. Everyone into the pool!

3

Working with the Big Picture: Object-Oriented Programming

IN THIS PART . . .

Understanding object-oriented programming (at last!)

Writing code that other developers can use

Reusing other developers' code

Chapter **9**

Why Object-Oriented Programming Is Like Selling Cheese

Andy's Cheese and Java Emporium carries fine cheeses and freshly brewed java from around the world (especially from Java in Indonesia). The Emporium is in Cheesetown, Pennsylvania, a neighborhood along the Edenville–Cheesetown Road in Franklin County.

The emporium sells cheese by the bag, each containing a certain variety, such as Cheddar, Swiss, Munster, or Limburger. Bags are labeled by weight and by the number of days the cheese was aged (admittedly, an approximation). Bags also carry the label *Domestic* or *Imported,* depending on the cheese's country of origin.

Before starting up the emporium, Andy had lots of possessions — material and otherwise. He had a family, a cat, a house, an abandoned restaurant property, a bunch of restaurant equipment, a checkered past, and a mountain of debt. But for the purpose of this narrative, Andy had only one thing: a form. Yes, Andy had developed a form for keeping track of his emporium's inventory. The form is shown in Figure 9-1.

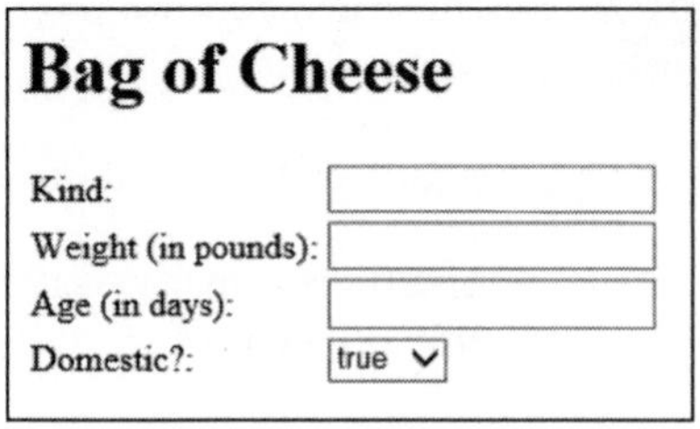

FIGURE 9-1:
An online form.

Exactly one week before the emporium's grand opening, Andy's supplier delivered one bag of cheese. Andy entered the bag's information into the inventory form. The result is shown in Figure 9-2.

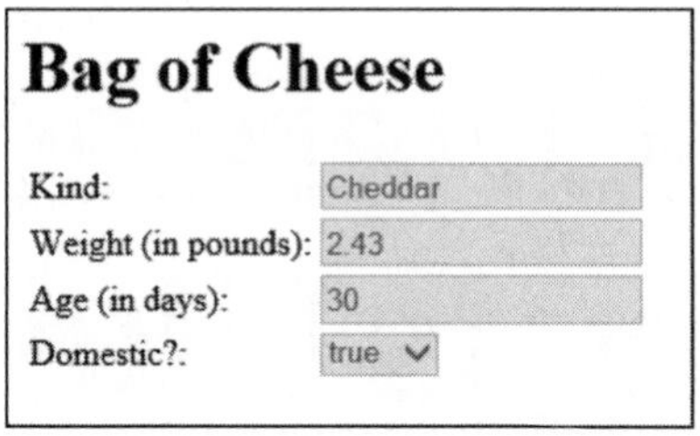

FIGURE 9-2:
A virtual bag
of cheese.

Andy had only a form and a bag of cheese (which isn't much to show for all his hard work), but the next day the supplier delivered five more bags of cheese. Andy's second entry looked like the one shown in Figure 9-3, and the next several entries looked similar.

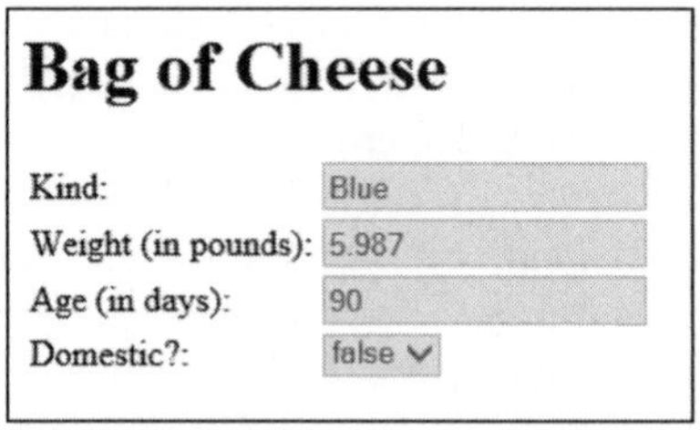

FIGURE 9-3:
Another virtual
bag of cheese.

At the end of the week, Andy was giddy: He had exactly one inventory form and six bags of cheese.

The story doesn't end here. As the grand opening approached, Andy's supplier brought many more bags so that, eventually, Andy had his inventory form and several hundred bags of cheese. The business even became an icon on Interstate Highway 81 in Cheesetown, Pennsylvania. But as far as you're concerned, the business had, has, and always will have only one form and any number of cheese bags.

That's the essence of object-oriented programming!

Classes and Objects

Java is an object-oriented programming language. A program that you create in Java consists of at least one class.

A class is like Andy's blank form, described in this chapter's introduction. That is, a class is a general description of some kind of thing. In the introduction to this chapter, the class (the form) describes the characteristics that any bag of cheese possesses. But imagine other classes. For example, Figure 9-4 illustrates a bank account class:

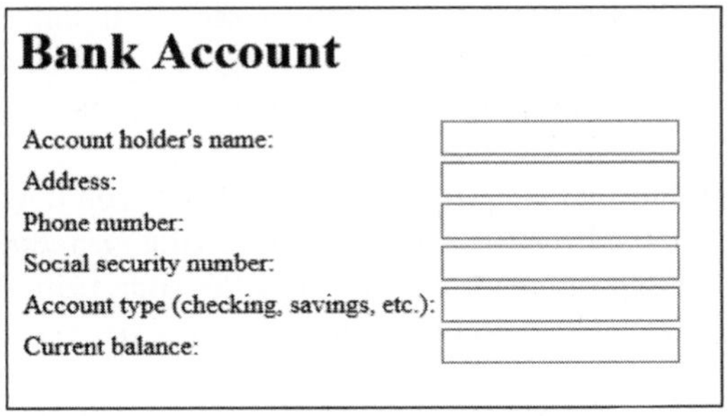
Bank Account

Account holder's name:
Address:
Phone number:
Social security number:
Account type (checking, savings, etc.):
Current balance:

FIGURE 9-4: A bank account class.

Figure 9-5 illustrates a sprite class, which is a class for a character in a computer game:

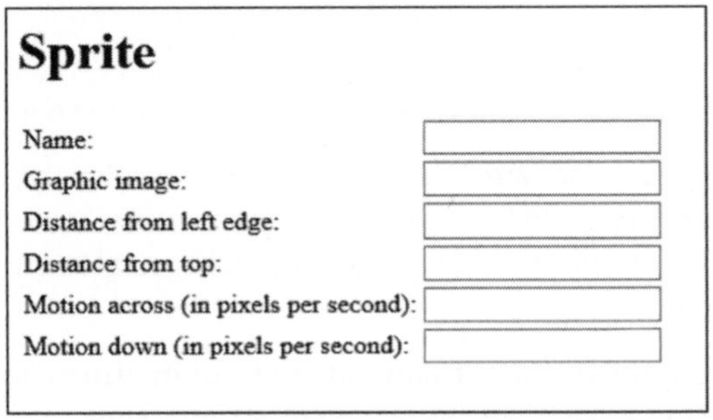
Sprite

Name:
Graphic image:
Distance from left edge:
Distance from top:
Motion across (in pixels per second):
Motion down (in pixels per second):

FIGURE 9-5: A sprite class.

What is a class, really?

In practice, a class doesn't look like any of the forms in Figures 9-1 through 9-5. In fact, a class doesn't look like anything. Instead, a Java class is a bunch of text describing the kinds of things that I refer to as "blanks to be filled in." Listing 9-1 contains a real Java class — the kind of class you write when you program in Java.

LISTING 9-1: A Class in the Java Programming Language

```
package com.allmycode.a09_01;

public class BagOfCheese {
  public String kind;
  public double weight;
  public int daysAged;
  public boolean isDomestic;
}
```

REMEMBER As a developer, your primary job is to create classes. You don't develop attractive online forms like the form shown earlier, in Figure 9-1. Instead, you write Java language code — code containing descriptions, like the one in Listing 9-1.

WARNING You won't find a folder named *09_01* in the stuff that you downloaded from this book's website. That's because the code in Listing 9-1 doesn't constitute a complete, runnable app. Instead, you can find the code from Listing 9-1 in this chapter's other projects — projects named *09_02*, *09_03*, and so on.

Compare Figure 9-1 with Listing 9-1. In what ways are they the same, and in what ways are they different? What does one have that the other doesn't have?

> » **The form in Figure 9-1 appears on a user's screen. The code in Listing 9-1 does not.**
>
> A Java class isn't necessarily tied to a particular display. Yes, you can display a bank account on a user's screen. But the bank account isn't a bunch of items on a computer screen — it's a bunch of information in the bank's computers.
>
> In fact, some Java classes are difficult to visualize. Android's SQLiteOpenHelper class assists developers in the creation of databases. An SQLiteOpenHelper doesn't look like anything in particular, and certainly not like an online form or a bag of cheese.
>
> » **Online forms appear in some contexts but not in others. In contrast, classes affect every part of every Java program's code.**

Forms show up on web pages, in dialog boxes, and in other situations. But when you use a word processing program to type a document, you deal primarily with free-form input. I didn't write this paragraph by filling in some blanks. (Heaven knows! I wish I could!)

The paragraphs I've written started out as part of a document in a word processing application. In the document, every paragraph has its own alignment, borders, indents, line spacing, styles, and many other characteristics. As a Java class, a list of paragraph characteristics might look something like this:

```
class Paragraph {
    int alignment;
    int borders;
    double leftIndent;
    double lineSpacing;
    int style;
}
```

When I create a paragraph, I don't fill in a form. Instead, I type words, and the underlying word processing app deals silently with its Paragraph class.

>> **The form shown in Figure 9-1 contains several fields, and so does the code in Listing 9-1.**

In an online form, a field is a blank space — a place that's eventually filled with specific information. In Java, a *field* is any characteristic that you (the developer) attribute to a class. The BagOfCheese class in Listing 9-1 has four fields, and each of the four fields has a name: kind, weight, daysAged, or isDomestic.

Like an online form, a Java class describes items by listing the characteristics that each of the items has. Both the form in Figure 9-1 and the code in Listing 9-1 say essentially the same thing: Each bag of cheese has a certain kind of cheese, a certain weight, a number of days that the cheese was aged, and a domestic-or-imported characteristic.

>> **The code in Listing 9-1 describes exactly the kind of information that belongs in each blank space. The form in Figure 9-1 is much more permissive.**

Nothing in Figure 9-1 indicates what kinds of input are permitted in the Weight field. The weight in pounds can be a whole number (0, 1, 2, and so on) or a decimal number (such as 3.14159, the weight of a big piece of "pie"). What happens if the user types the words *three pounds* into the form in Figure 9-1? Does the form accept this input, or does the computer freeze up? A developer can add extra code to test for valid input in a form, but, on its own, a form cares little about the kind of input that the user enters.

In contrast, the code in Listing 9-1 contains this line:

```
double weight;
```

This line tells Java that every bag of cheese has a characteristic named weight and that a bag's weight must be of type double. Similarly, each bag's daysAged value is an int, each bag's isDomestic value is boolean, and each bag's kind value has the type String.

REMEMBER

The unfortunate pun in the previous paragraph makes life more difficult for me, the author! A Java String has nothing to do with the kind of cheese that peels into strips. A Java String is a sequence of characters, like the sequence "Cheddar" or the sequence "qwoiehasljsal" or the sequence "Go2theMoon!". So the String kind line in Listing 9-1 indicates that a bag of cheese might contain "Cheddar", but it might also contain "qwoiehasljsal" cheese or "Go2theMoon!" cheese. Well, that's what happens when Andy starts a business from scratch.

If you look at Listing 9-1, you may notice my liberal use of the word public. In declaring the BagOfCheese class, I've decided that everything should be public. The class itself is public, kind field is public, the weight field is public, and so on.

When you declare a class, you don't have to make things public. But in this chapter's examples, the keyword public helps a lot. To find out why, see the later section "Java's Modifiers."

REMEMBER

In an online form, fields are places where the user types text. And in a Java class such as the class in Listing 9-1, variables such as kind, weight, daysAged, and isDomestic are fields. In this section, I emphasize the similarity between a form's fields and a Java class's fields. But don't mistake form fields for Java class fields. Form fields and Java class fields are two different kinds of things. A form's field may or may not be associated with a Java class's variable. And a Java class's field may or may not make an appearance on any device's screen.

What is an object?

At the start of this chapter's detailed Cheese Emporium exposé, Andy had nothing to his name except an online form — the form in Figure 9-1. Life was simple for Andy and his dog Fido. But eventually the suppliers delivered bags of cheese. Suddenly, Andy had more than just an online form — he had things whose characteristics matched the fields in the form. One bag had the characteristics shown in Figure 9-2; another bag had the characteristics shown in Figure 9-3.

In the terminology of object-oriented programming, each bag of cheese is an *object*, and each bag of cheese is an *instance* of the class in Listing 9-1.

You can also think of classes and objects as part of a hierarchy. The BagOfCheese class is at the top of the hierarchy, and each instance of the class is attached to the class itself. See Figures 9-6 and 9-7.

TECHNICAL STUFF

The diagrams in Figures 9-6 and 9-7 are part of the standardized Unified Modeling Language (UML). For more info about UML, visit www.omg.org/spec/UML.

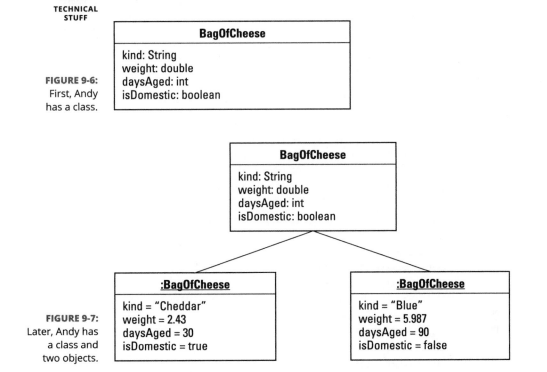

FIGURE 9-6:
First, Andy has a class.

FIGURE 9-7:
Later, Andy has a class and two objects.

REMEMBER

An object is a particular thing. (For Andy, an object is a particular bag of cheese.) A class is a description with blanks to be filled in. (For Andy, a class is a form with four blank fields: a field for the kind of cheese, another field for the cheese's weight, a third field for the number of days aged, and a fourth field for the Domestic-or-Imported designation.)

And don't forget: Your primary job is to create classes. You don't develop attractive online forms like the form in Figure 9-1. Instead, you write Java language code — code containing descriptions, like the one in Listing 9-1.

Creating objects

Listing 9-2 contains real-life Java code to create two objects: two instances of the class in Listing 9-1.

LISTING 9-2: **Creating Two Objects**

```
package com.allmycode.a09_02;

import android.support.v7.app.AppCompatActivity;
import android.os.Bundle;
import android.widget.TextView;

import com.allmycode.a09_01.BagOfCheese;

public class MainActivity extends AppCompatActivity {
  TextView textView;

  @Override
  protected void onCreate(Bundle savedInstanceState) {
    super.onCreate(savedInstanceState);
    setContentView(R.layout.activity_main);

    textView = (TextView) findViewById(R.id.textView);

    BagOfCheese bag1 = new BagOfCheese();
    bag1.kind = "Cheddar";
    bag1.weight = 2.43;
    bag1.daysAged = 30;
    bag1.isDomestic = true;

    BagOfCheese bag2 = new BagOfCheese();
    bag2.kind = "Blue";
    bag2.weight = 5.987;
    bag2.daysAged = 90;
    bag2.isDomestic = false;

    textView.setText("");

    textView.append(bag1.kind + ", " + bag1.weight + ", " +
        bag1.daysAged + ", " + bag1.isDomestic + "\n");

    textView.append(bag2.kind + ", " + bag2.weight + ", " +
        bag2.daysAged + ", " + bag2.isDomestic + "\n");
  }
}
```

A run of the code in Listing 9-2 is shown in Figure 9-8.

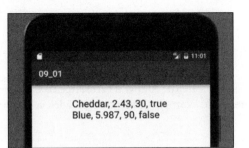

FIGURE 9-8:
Running the code
from Listing 9-2.

TECHNICAL STUFF

To vary the terminology, I might say that the code in Listing 9-2 creates "two BagOfCheese objects" or "two BagOfCheese instances," or I might say that the new BagOfCheese() statements in Listing 9-2 *instantiate* the BagOfCheese class. One way or another, Listing 9-1 declares the existence of one class, and Listing 9-2 declares another class — a class that declares the existence of two objects.

CROSS-REFERENCE

In Listing 9-2, each use of the words new BagOfCheese() is a *constructor call*. For details, see the "Calling a constructor" section, later in this chapter.

In Listing 9-2, I use ten statements to create two bags of cheese. The first statement (BagOfCheese bag1 = new BagOfCheese()) does three things:

» With the words

```
BagOfCheese bag1
```

the first statement declares that the variable bag1 refers to a bag of cheese.

» With the words

```
new BagOfCheese()
```

the first statement creates a bag with no particular cheese in it. (If it helps, you can think of it as an empty bag reserved for eventually storing cheese.)

» Finally, with the equal sign, the first statement makes the bag1 variable refer to the newly created bag.

The next four statements in Listing 9-2 assign values to the fields of bag1:

```
bag1.kind = "Cheddar";
bag1.weight = 2.43;
bag1.daysAged = 30;
bag1.isDomestic = true;
```

REMEMBER

To refer to one of an object's fields, follow a reference to the object with a dot and then the field's name. (For example, follow bag1 with a dot and then the field name kind.)

The next five statements in Listing 9-2 do the same for a second variable, bag2, and a second bag of cheese.

ONE APP; TWO JAVA FILES

To run the code in Listing 9-2, I put two Java files (BagOfCheese.java from Listing 9-1 and MainActivity.java from Listing 9-2) in the same Android Studio project. To up the ante a bit more, I put the two Java files into two different packages. As you can see at the top of each listing, my BagOfCheese class is in the com.allmycode.a09_01 package, and my MainActivity class is in the com.allmycode.a09_02 package. I didn't have to create different classes for these two packages. But I was following my convention of naming the packages after listing numbers. Then I realized that, with two different package names, I can show you how to deal with new packages in Android Studio. So here goes:

When you create a new project, Android Studio creates a package containing the project's main activity. To add an additional package to the project, follow these steps:

1. Select the app/java branch in the Project tool window.

2. In the main menu bar, choose File ➪ New ➪ Package.

   A Choose Destination Directory dialog box appears. If this dialog box is the same as the one that I see in mid-2016, the dialog box lists three directories — androidTest/java, main/java, and test/java.

3. Select the main/java directory.

4. Click OK.

   The New Package dialog box appears.

5. In the New Package dialog box, type the name of your new package.

   When I started this section's project, I already had a package named
   `com.allmycode.a09_02`. So, in the New Package dialog box, I typed
   com.allmycode.a09_01, the name of the package for Listing 9-1.

6. Click OK.

Voilà! Your project has a new package.

To add an additional class (such as BagOfCheese in Listing 9-1) to your project, follow
these steps:

1. In the Project tool window, select the branch of the package that will contain your
   new class.

   For example, if you're adding the BagOfCheese class in Listing 9-1, select the
   `app/java/com.allmycode/a09_01` branch.

2. In the main menu bar, choose File ⇨ New ⇨ Java Class.

   A Create New Class dialog box appears.

3. In the Name field of the Create New Class dialog box, type the name of your new
   class.

   To create the class in Listing 9-1, I typed **BagOfCheese**.

4. Make sure that the new class's package name appears in the dialog box's
   Package field.

5. Click OK.

And there you have it — a brand-new Java class in your Android app's project.

Reusing names

In Listing 9-2, I declare two variables — bag1 and bag2 — to refer to two different
BagOfCheese objects. That's fine. But sometimes, having only one variable and
reusing it for the second object works just as well, as shown in Listing 9-3.

LISTING 9-3: **Reusing the bag Variable**

```
package com.allmycode.a09_03;

import android.support.v7.app.AppCompatActivity;
import android.os.Bundle;
import android.widget.TextView;

import com.allmycode.a09_01.BagOfCheese;

public class MainActivity extends AppCompatActivity {
  TextView textView;

  @Override
  protected void onCreate(Bundle savedInstanceState) {
    super.onCreate(savedInstanceState);
    setContentView(R.layout.activity_main);

    textView = (TextView) findViewById(R.id.textView);

    BagOfCheese bag = new BagOfCheese();
    bag.kind = "Cheddar";
    bag.weight = 2.43;
    bag.daysAged = 30;
    bag.isDomestic = true;

    textView.setText("");

    textView.append(bag.kind + ", " + bag.weight + ", " +
        bag.daysAged + ", " + bag.isDomestic + "\n");

    bag = new BagOfCheese();
    bag.kind = "Blue";
    bag.weight = 5.987;
    bag.daysAged = 90;
    bag.isDomestic = false;

    textView.append(bag.kind + ", " + bag.weight + ", " +
        bag.daysAged + ", " + bag.isDomestic + "\n");
  }
}
```

In Listing 9-3, when Java executes the second bag = new BagOfCheese( ) statement, the old object (the bag containing cheddar) has disappeared. Without bag (or any other variable) referring to that cheddar object, there's no way your code can do anything with the cheddar object. Fortunately, by the time you reach the second bag = new BagOfCheese( ) statement, you're finished doing everything you want to do with the original cheddar bag. In this case, reusing the bag variable is acceptable.

When you reuse a variable (like the one and only bag variable in Listing 9-3), you do so by using an assignment statement, not an initialization. In other words, you don't write BagOfCheese bag a second time in your code. If you do, you see error messages in the Android Studio editor.

To be painfully precise, you can, in fact, write BagOfCheese bag more than once in the same piece of code. For an example, see the use of shadowing later in this chapter, in the "Constructors with parameters" section.

In Listing 9-1, none of the BagOfCheese class's fields is final. In other words, the class's code lets you reassign values to the fields inside a BagOfCheese object. With this information in mind, you can shorten the code in Listing 9-3 by one more line, as shown in Listing 9-4.

LISTING 9-4: **Reusing a bag Object's Fields**

```
package com.allmycode.a09_04;

import android.support.v7.app.AppCompatActivity;
import android.os.Bundle;
import android.widget.TextView;

import com.allmycode.a09_01.BagOfCheese;

public class MainActivity extends AppCompatActivity {
  TextView textView;

  @Override
  protected void onCreate(Bundle savedInstanceState) {
    super.onCreate(savedInstanceState);
    setContentView(R.layout.activity_main);

    textView = (TextView) findViewById(R.id.textView);

    BagOfCheese bag = new BagOfCheese();
    bag.kind = "Cheddar";
```

(continued)

LISTING 9-4: *(continued)*

```
    bag.weight = 2.43;
    bag.daysAged = 30;
    bag.isDomestic = true;

    textView.setText("");

    textView.append(bag.kind + ", " +  bag.weight + ", " +
        bag.daysAged + ", " + bag.isDomestic + "\n");

    // bag = new BagOfCheese();
    bag.kind = "Blue";
    bag.weight = 5.987;
    bag.daysAged = 90;
    bag.isDomestic = false;

    textView.append(bag.kind + ", " +  bag.weight + ", " +
        bag.daysAged + ", " + bag.isDomestic + "\n");
  }
}
```

With the second constructor call in Listing 9-4 commented out, you don't make the bag variable refer to a new object. Instead, you economize by assigning new values to the existing object's fields.

In some situations, reusing an object's fields can be more efficient (quicker to execute) than creating a new object. But whenever I have a choice, I prefer to write code that mirrors real data. If an actual bag's content doesn't change from cheddar cheese to blue cheese, I prefer not to change a BagOfCheese object's kind field from "Cheddar" to "Blue".

Calling a constructor

In Listing 9-2, the words new BagOfCheese( ) look like method calls, but they aren't — they're constructor calls. A *constructor call* creates a new object from an existing class. You can spot a constructor call by noticing that

>> **A constructor call starts with Java's** new **keyword:**

```
new BagOfCheese( )
```

and

>> **A constructor call's name is the name of a Java class:**

```
new BagOfCheese()
```

When Java encounters a method call, Java executes the statements inside a method's declaration. Similarly, when Java encounters a constructor call, Java executes the statements inside the constructor's declaration. When you create a new class (as I did in Listing 9-1), Java can create a constructor declaration automatically. If you want, you can type the declaration's code manually. Listing 9-5 shows you what the declaration's code would look like:

LISTING 9-5: **The Parameterless Constructor**

```
package com.allmycode.a09_05;

public class BagOfCheese {
  public String kind;
  public double weight;
  public int daysAged;
  public boolean isDomestic;

  public BagOfCheese() {
  }
}
```

In Listing 9-5, the boldface code

```
public BagOfCheese() {
}
```

is a very simple constructor declaration. This declaration (unlike most constructor declarations) has no statements inside its body. This declaration is simply a *header* (BagOfCheese()) and an empty body ({}).

CROSS-
REFERENCE

You can type Listing 9-5 exactly as it is. Alternatively, you can omit the code in boldface type, and Java creates that constructor for you automatically. (You don't see the constructor declaration in the Android Studio editor, but Java behaves as if the constructor declaration exists.) To find out when Java creates a constructor declaration automatically and when it doesn't, see the "Constructors with parameters" section, later in this chapter.

A constructor's declaration looks much like a method declaration. But a constructor's declaration differs from a method declaration in two ways:

>> **A constructor's name is the same as the name of the class whose objects the constructor constructs.**

In Listing 9-5, the class name is BagOfCheese, and the constructor's header starts with the name BagOfCheese.

>> **Before the constructor's name, the constructor's header has no type.**

Unlike a method header, the constructor's header doesn't say int BagOfCheese() or even void BagOfCheese(). The header simply says BagOfCheese().

The constructor declaration in Listing 9-5 contains no statements. That isn't typical of a constructor, but it's what you get in the constructor that Java creates automatically. With or without statements, calling the constructor in Listing 9-5 creates a brand-new BagOfCheese object.

More About Classes and Objects (Adding Methods to the Mix)

In Chapters 4 and 7, I introduce parameter passing. In those chapters, I unobtrusively avoid details about passing objects to methods. (At least, I hope it's unobtrusive.) In this chapter, I shed my coy demeanor and face the topic (passing objects to methods) head-on.

I start with an improvement on an earlier example. The code in Listing 9-2 contains two nasty-looking textView.append calls. This code has two nearly identical occurrences of a complicated expression:

```
textView.append(bag1.kind + ", " + bag1.weight + ", " +
    bag1.daysAged + ", " + bag1.isDomestic + "\n");

textView.append(bag2.kind + ", " + bag2.weight + ", " +
    bag2.daysAged + ", " + bag2.isDomestic + "\n");
```

You can streamline the code by moving this complicated expression to a method. Here's how:

1. **View the code from Listing 9-2 in the Android Studio editor.**

This `MainActivity.java` file is in the 09_02 project, which is in the `Java4Android_Projects.zip` file that you download in Chapter 2.

2. **Use the mouse to select the entire expression inside the parameter list of the first call to `textView.append`.**

Be sure to highlight everything in the expression, starting with `bag1.kind` and ending with `"\n"`.

3. **On the Android Studio main menu, choose Refactor ⇨ Extract ⇨ Method.**

The Extract Method dialog box in Android Studio appears, as shown in Figure 9-9.

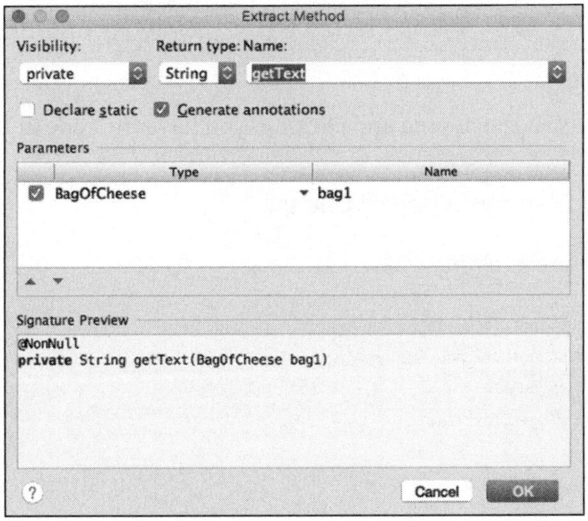

FIGURE 9-9:
The Extract
Method
dialog box.

In the next two steps, you make the names in your code the same as the names in this book's examples.

4. **(Optional) In the Name field in the Extract Method dialog box, type** toString.

5. **(Optional) In the Name column of the Parameters list, change** bag1 **to** bag.

6. **Click OK.**

Android Studio dismisses the Extract Method dialog box.

Android Studio creates a method named toString and replaces the string in the first textView.append call with a call to the new toString method.

Android Studio also displays a dialog box like the one in Figure 9-10.

7. **In the dialog box, click Yes.**

Clicking Yes tells Android Studio to replace the string in the second textView.append call with a call to the new toString method.

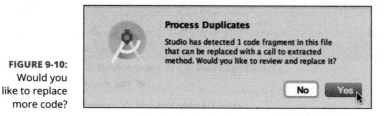

FIGURE 9-10:
Would you
like to replace
more code?

As a result of all this typing and clicking, you have the code in Listing 9-6.

LISTING 9-6: **A Method Displays a Bag of Cheese**

```
package com.allmycode.a09_06;

import android.support.annotation.NonNull;
import android.support.v7.app.AppCompatActivity;
import android.os.Bundle;
import android.widget.TextView;

import com.allmycode.a09_05.BagOfCheese;

public class MainActivity extends AppCompatActivity {
  TextView textView;

  @Override
  protected void onCreate(Bundle savedInstanceState) {
    super.onCreate(savedInstanceState);
    setContentView(R.layout.activity_main);

    textView = (TextView) findViewById(R.id.textView);
```

```
        BagOfCheese bag1 = new BagOfCheese();
        bag1.kind = "Cheddar";
        bag1.weight = 2.43;
        bag1.daysAged = 30;
        bag1.isDomestic = true;

        BagOfCheese bag2 = new BagOfCheese();
        bag2.kind = "Blue";
        bag2.weight = 5.987;
        bag2.daysAged = 90;
        bag2.isDomestic = false;

        textView.setText("");

        textView.append(toString(bag1));

        textView.append(toString(bag2));
    }

    @NonNull
    private String toString(BagOfCheese bag) {
        return bag.kind + ", " + bag.weight + ", " +
            bag.daysAged + ", " + bag.isDomestic + "\n";
    }
}
```

According to the toString declaration (refer to Listing 9-6), the toString method takes one parameter. That parameter must be a BagOfCheese instance. Inside the body of the method declaration, you refer to that instance with the parameter name bag. (You refer to bag.kind, bag.weight, bag.daysAged, and bag.isDomestic.)

In the onCreate method, you create two BagOfCheese instances: bag1 and bag2. You call toString once with the first instance (toString(bag1)), and call it a second time with the second instance (toString(bag2)).

CROSS-
REFERENCE

The @NonNull business in Listing 9-6 is an *annotation*. For the story on Java annotations, see Chapter 10.

Constructors with parameters

Listing 9-7 contains a variation on the theme from Listing 9-2.

LISTING 9-7: **Another Way to Create Two Objects**

```
package com.allmycode.a09_07;

import android.support.v7.app.AppCompatActivity;
import android.os.Bundle;
import android.widget.TextView;

import com.allmycode.a09_08.BagOfCheese;

public class MainActivity extends AppCompatActivity {
  TextView textView;

  @Override
  protected void onCreate(Bundle savedInstanceState) {
    super.onCreate(savedInstanceState);
    setContentView(R.layout.activity_main);

    textView = (TextView) findViewById(R.id.textView);

    BagOfCheese bag1 = new BagOfCheese("Cheddar", 2.43, 30, true);
    BagOfCheese bag2 = new BagOfCheese("Blue", 5.987, 90, false);

    textView.setText("");

    textView.append(toString(bag1));
    textView.append(toString(bag2));
  }

  private String toString(BagOfCheese bag) {
    return bag.kind + ", " + bag.weight + ", " +
        bag.daysAged + ", " + bag.isDomestic + "\n";
  }
}
```

Listing 9-7 calls a BagOfCheese constructor with four parameters, so the code has to have a four-parameter constructor. In Listing 9-8, I show you how to declare that constructor.

LISTING 9-8: **A Constructor with Parameters**

```
package com.allmycode.a09_08;

public class BagOfCheese {
  public String kind;
  public double weight;
  public int daysAged;
  public boolean isDomestic;

  public BagOfCheese() {
  }

  public BagOfCheese(String dKind, double dWeight,
                     int dDaysAged, boolean dIsDomestic) {
    kind = dKind;
    weight = dWeight;
    daysAged = dDaysAged;
    isDomestic = dIsDomestic;
  }
}
```

Listing 9-8 borrows some tricks from Chapters 4 and 7. In those chapters, I introduce the concept of *overloading* — reusing a name by providing different parameter lists. Listing 9-8 has two different BagOfCheese constructors — one with no
parameters and another with four parameters. When you call a BagOfCheese constructor (as in Listing 9-7), Java knows which declaration to execute by matching
the parameters in the constructor call. The call in Listing 9-7 has parameters of
type String, double, int, and boolean, and the second constructor in Listing 9-8
has the same types of parameters in the same order, so Java calls the second constructor in Listing 9-8.

You might also notice another trick from Chapter 7. In Listing 9-8, in the second
constructor declaration, I use different names for the parameters and the class's
fields. For example, I use the parameter name dKind and the field name kind.
What happens if you use the same names for the parameters and the fields, as in
this example:

```
// DON'T DO THIS
public class BagOfCheese {
  public String kind;
  public double weight;
```

```
public int daysAged;
public boolean isDomestic;


public BagOfCheese() {
}


public BagOfCheese(String kind, double weight,
                   int daysAged, boolean isDomestic) {
  kind = kind;
  weight = weight;
  daysAged = daysAged;
  isDomestic = isDomestic;

  }
}
```

Figure 9-11 shows you exactly what happens. (Spoiler alert! Nothing good happens!)

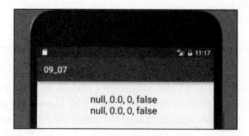

FIGURE 9-11:
Some unpleasant
results.

The code with duplicate parameter and field names gives you the useless results from Figure 9-11. The code has two kind variables — one inside the constructor and another outside of the constructor, as shown in Figure 9-12.

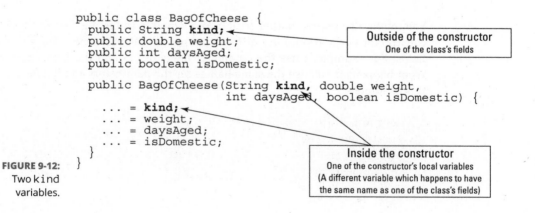

```
public class BagOfCheese {
  public String kind;          Outside of the constructor
  public double weight;        One of the class's fields
  public int daysAged;
  public boolean isDomestic;

  public BagOfCheese(String kind, double weight,
                     int daysAged, boolean isDomestic) {
    ... = kind;
    ... = weight;
    ... = daysAged;
    ... = isDomestic;
  }
}
```

Inside the constructor
One of the constructor's local variables
(A different variable which happens to have
the same name as one of the class's fields)

FIGURE 9-12:
Two kind
variables.

Inside a constructor or method, a parameter *shadows* any identically named field. So, outside the constructor declaration, the word `kind` refers to the field name. Inside the constructor declaration, however, the word `kind` refers only to the parameter name. In the horrible code with duplicate names, the statement

```
kind = kind;
```

does nothing to the `kind` field. Instead, this statement tells Java to make the `kind` parameter refer to the same string that the `kind` parameter already refers to.

If this explanation sounds like nonsense to you, it is.

The `kind` variable in the constructor declaration's parameter list is *local* to the constructor. Any use of the word `kind` outside the constructor cannot refer to the constructor's local `kind` variable.

Fields are different. You can refer to a field anywhere in the class's code. For example, in Listing 9-8, the second constructor declaration has no local `kind` variable of its own. Inside that constructor's body, the word `kind` refers to the class's field.

One way or another, the second constructor in Listing 9-8 is cumbersome. Do you always have to make up peculiar names like `dKind` for a constructor's parameters? No, you don't. To find out why, see the "This is it!" section, later in this chapter.

The default constructor

I don't see any constructors in Listing 9-1. So why can I make a constructor call (the call `new BagOfCheese()`) in Listing 9-2? I can call `new BagOfCheese()` because, without explicitly adding text to the code in Listing 9-1, Java silently creates a parameterless constructor for me.

But Listing 9-8 is different. In Listing 9-8, if I didn't explicitly type the parameterless constructor in my code, Java wouldn't have created a parameterless constructor for me. A call to `new BagOfCheese()` with no parameters would have been illegal. If I added a `new BagOfCheese()` call, Android Studio's editor would tell me that *The BagOfCheese() in BagOfCheese cannot be applied*. Sounds bad. Doesn't it?

Here's how it works: When you declare a class, Java creates a parameterless constructor (known formally as a *default constructor*) if, and only if, you haven't explicitly declared any constructors in your class's code. When Java encounters Listing 9-1, Java automatically adds a parameterless constructor to your `BagOfCheese` class. But when Java encounters Listing 9-8, with its 4-parameter constructor already declared, you don't get a parameterless constructor unless you explicitly type the lines

```
public BagOfCheese() {
}
```

into your code. Without a parameterless constructor, calls to new BagOfCheese() (with no parameters) will be illegal.

This is it!

The naming problem that crops up earlier in this chapter, in the "Constructors with parameters" section, has an elegant solution. Listing 9-9 illustrates the idea.

LISTING 9-9: **Using Java's this Keyword**

```
package com.allmycode.a09_09;

public class BagOfCheese {
  public String kind;
  public double weight;
  public int daysAged;
  public boolean isDomestic;

  public BagOfCheese() {
  }

  public BagOfCheese(String kind, double weight,
                     int daysAged, boolean isDomestic) {
    this.kind = kind;
    this.weight = weight;
    this.daysAged = daysAged;
    this.isDomestic = isDomestic;
  }
}
```

To use the class in Listing 9-9, you can run the MainActivity code in Listing 9-7. When you do, you see the run shown earlier, in Figure 9-8.

You can persuade Android Studio to create the big constructor that you see in Listing 9-9. Here's how:

1. **Start with the code from Listing 9-1 (or Listing 9-5) in the Android Studio editor.**

2. **Click the mouse cursor anywhere inside the editor.**

3. **On the Android Studio main menu, select Code ⇨ Generate ⇨ Constructor.**

   The Choose Fields to Initialize by Constructor dialog box appears, as shown in Figure 9-13.

4. **In the Choose Fields to Initialize by Constructor dialog box, make sure that all four of the** BagOfCheese **fields are selected.**

   To do so, start by selecting the topmost field (the kind field). Then, with your computer's Shift key pressed, select the bottommost field (the isDomestic field).

   This ensures that the new constructor will have a parameter for each of the class's fields.

5. **Click OK.**

   That does it! Android Studio dismisses the dialog box and adds a freshly brewed constructor to the editor's code.

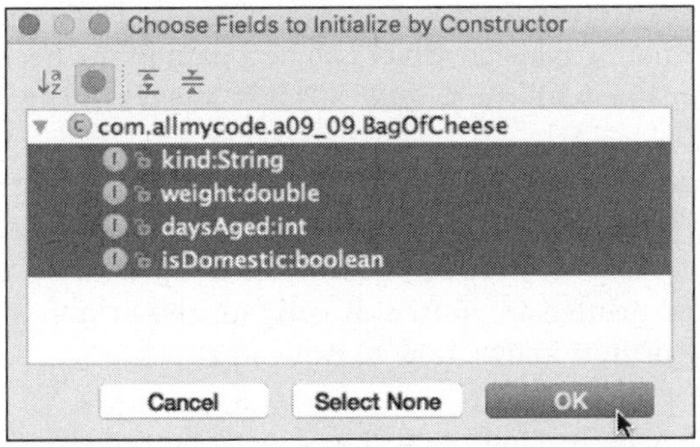

FIGURE 9-13:
Choose Fields to
Initialize by
Constructor.

Java's this keyword refers to "the object that contains the current line of code." So in Listing 9-9, the word this refers to an instance of BagOfCheese (that is, to the object that's being constructed). That object has a kind field, so this.kind refers to the first of the object's four fields (and not to the constructor's kind parameter). That object also has weight, daysAged, and isDomestic fields, so this.weight, this.daysAged, and this.isDomestic refer to that object's fields, as shown in Figure 9-14. And the assignment statements inside the constructor give values to the new object's fields.

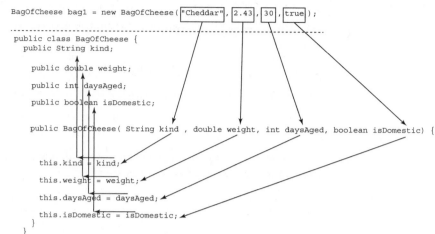

FIGURE 9-14:
Assigning values to an object's fields.

Giving an object more responsibility

You have a printer and you try to install it on your computer. It's a capable printer, but it didn't come with your computer, so your computer needs a program to *drive* the printer: a printer *driver*. Without a driver, your new printer is nothing but a giant paperweight.

But, sometimes, finding a device driver can be a pain in the neck. Maybe you can't find the disk that came with the printer. (That's always my problem.)

I have one off-brand printer whose driver is built into its permanent memory. When I plug the printer into a USB port, the computer displays a new storage location. (The location looks, to ordinary users, like another of the computer's disks.) The drivers for the printer are stored directly on the printer's internal memory. It's as though the printer knows how to drive itself!

Now consider the code in Listings 9-7 and 9-8. You're the MainActivity class (refer to Listing 9-7), and you have a new gadget to play with — the BagOfCheese class in Listing 9-8. You want to display the properties of a particular bag, and you don't like dealing with a bag's nitty-gritty details. In particular, you don't like worrying about commas, blank spaces, and field names when you display a bag:

```
bag.kind + ", " + bag.weight + ", " +
      bag.daysAged + ", " + bag.isDomestic + "\n"
```

You'd rather have the BagOfCheese class figure out how to display one of its own objects.

Here's the plan: Move the big string with the bag's fields, the commas and the spaces from the `MainActivity` class to the `BagOfCheese` class. That is, make each `BagOfCheese` object be responsible for describing itself in `String` form. With the Andy's Cheese Emporium metaphor that starts this chapter, each bag's form has its own Display button, as shown in Figure 9-15.

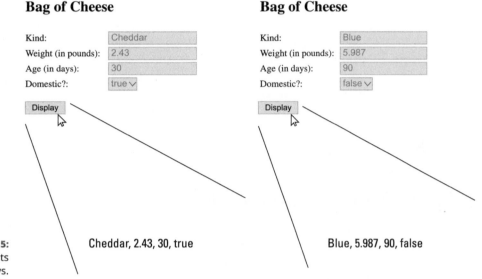

FIGURE 9-15:
Two bag objects and two displays.

The interesting characteristic of a Display button is that when you press it, the text you see depends on the bag of cheese you're examining. More precisely, the text you see depends on the values in that particular form's fields.

The same thing happens in Listing 9-11 when you call `bag1.toString()`. Java runs the `toString` method shown in Listing 9-10. The values used in that method call — `kind`, `weight`, `daysAged`, and `isDomestic` — are the values in the `bag1` object's fields. Similarly, the values used when you call `bag2.toString()` are the values in the `bag2` object's fields.

LISTING 9-10: **A Self-Displaying Class**

```
package com.allmycode.a09_10;

public class BagOfCheese {
    public String kind;
    public double weight;
    public int daysAged;
    public boolean isDomestic;
```

(continued)

LISTING 9-10: *(continued)*

```
public BagOfCheese() {
}

public BagOfCheese(String kind, double weight,
                   int daysAged, boolean isDomestic) {
  this.kind = kind;
  this.weight = weight;
  this.daysAged = daysAged;
  this.isDomestic = isDomestic;
}

public String toString() {
  return kind + ", " + weight + ", " + daysAged + ", " + isDomestic + "\n";
}
}
```

LISTING 9-11: Having a Bag Display Itself

```
package com.allmycode.a09_11;

import android.support.v7.app.AppCompatActivity;
import android.os.Bundle;
import android.widget.TextView;

import com.allmycode.a09_10.BagOfCheese;

public class MainActivity extends AppCompatActivity {
  TextView textView;

  @Override
  protected void onCreate(Bundle savedInstanceState) {
    super.onCreate(savedInstanceState);
    setContentView(R.layout.activity_main);

    textView = (TextView) findViewById(R.id.textView);

    BagOfCheese bag1 = new BagOfCheese("Cheddar", 2.43, 30, true);
    BagOfCheese bag2 = new BagOfCheese("Blue", 5.987, 90, false);

    textView.setText("");
```

```
    textView.append(bag1.toString());
    textView.append(bag2.toString());
  }
}
```

In Listing 9-10, the BagOfCheese object has its own, parameterless toString method. And in Listing 9-11, the following two lines make two calls to the toString method — one call for bag1 and another call for bag2:

```
textView.append(bag1.toString());
textView.append(bag2.toString());
```

A call to toString behaves differently depending on the particular bag that's being displayed. When you call bag1.toString(), you see the field values for bag1, and when you call bag2.toString(), you see the field values for bag2.

REMEMBER

To call one of an object's methods, follow a reference to the object with a dot and then the method's name.

Members of a class

Notice the similarity between fields and methods:

>> As I say earlier in this chapter, in the "Creating objects" section:

To refer to one of an object's fields, follow a reference to the object with a dot and then the field's name.

>> As I say earlier in this chapter, in the "Giving an object more responsibility" section:

To call one of an object's methods, follow a reference to the object with a dot and then the method's name.

The similarity between fields and methods stretches far and wide in object-oriented programming. The similarity is so strong that special terminology is necessary to describe it. In addition to each BagOfCheese object having its own values for the four fields, you can think of each object as having its own copy of the toString method. So the BagOfCheese class in Listing 9-10 has five *members*. Four of the members are the fields kind, weight, daysAged, and isDomestic, and the remaining member is the toString method.

Reference types

Here's a near-quotation from the earlier section "Creating objects:"

> In Listing 9-2, the initialization of bag1 makes the bag1 variable refer to the newly created bag.

In the quotation, I choose my words carefully. "The initialization makes the bag1 variable *refer to* the newly created bag." Notice how I italicize the words *refer to*. A variable of type `int` *stores* an int value, but the bag1 variable in Listing 9-2 *refers to* an object.

What's the difference? The difference is similar to holding an object in your hand versus pointing to it in the room. Figure 9-16 shows you what I mean.

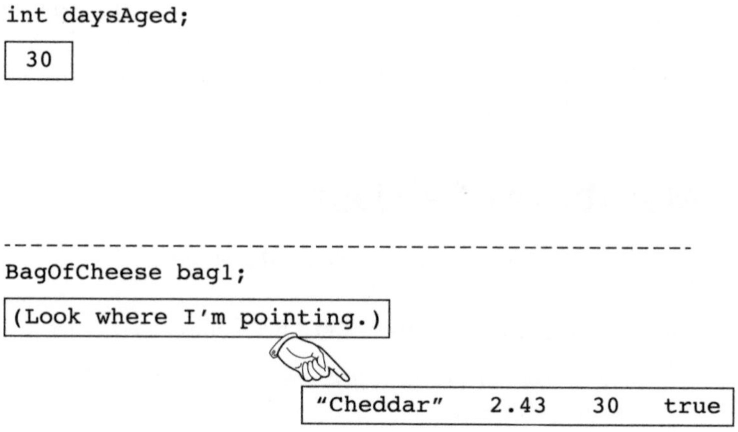

```
int daysAged;
```
```
30
```

```
BagOfCheese bag1;
```
```
(Look where I'm pointing.)
```

```
"Cheddar"    2.43    30    true
```

FIGURE 9-16: Primitive types versus reference types.

Java has two kinds of types: primitive types and reference types.

>> I cover primitive types in Chapter 5. Java's eight primitive types are `int`, `double`, `boolean`, `char`, `byte`, `short`, `long`, and `float`.

>> A *reference type* is the name of a class or (as you see in Chapter 10) an interface.

In Figure 9-16, the variable daysAged contains the value 30 (indicating that the cheese in a particular bag has been aged for 30 days). I imagine the value 30 being right inside the daysAged box because the daysAged variable has type `int` — a primitive type.

But the variable bag1 has type BagOfCheese, and BagOfCheese isn't a primitive type. (I know of no computer programming language in which a bag of cheese is a built-in, primitive type!) So the bag1 variable doesn't contain "Cheddar" 2.43 30 true. Instead, the variable bag1 contains the information required to locate the "Cheddar" 2.43 30 true object. The variable bag1 stores information that *refers to* the "Cheddar" 2.43 30 true object.

REMEMBER

The types int, double, boolean, char, byte, short, long, and float are primitive types. A primitive type variable (int daysAged, double weight, and boolean isDomestic, for example) stores a value. In contrast, a class is a reference type, such as String, which is defined in Java's API, and BagOfCheese, which you or I declare ourselves. A reference type variable (BagOfCheese bag and String kind, for example) *refers* to an object.

TECHNICAL STUFF

The String type is a reference type, so Figure 9-16 would be slightly more accurate if the bottommost box had another hand pointing to the letters 'C', 'h', 'e', 'd', 'd', 'a', and 'r'. (See Figure 9-17.) To keep my diagrams uncluttered, I don't put that other hand in Figure 9-16 and I don't put the other hand in similar diagrams in this chapter.

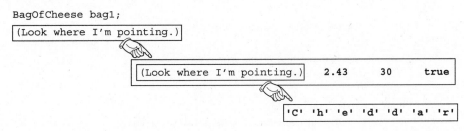

FIGURE 9-17: The String type is also a reference type.

TECHNICAL STUFF

In this section, I say that the bag1 variable *refers to* the "Cheddar" 2.43 30 true object. It's also common to say that the bag1 variable *points to* the "Cheddar" 2.43 30 true object. Alternatively, you can say that the bag1 variable stores the number of the memory address where the "Cheddar" 2.43 30 true object's values begin. Neither the pointing language nor the memory language expresses the truth of the matter, but if the rough terminology helps you understand what's going on, there's no harm in using it.

Pass by reference

In the previous section, I emphasize that classes are reference types. A variable whose type is a class contains something that refers to blah, blah, blah. You might ask, "Why should I care?"

Look at Listing 7-2, over in Chapter 7, and notice the result of passing a primitive type to a method:

> When the method's body changes the parameter's value, the change has no effect on the value of the variable in the method call.

This principle holds true for reference types as well. But in the case of a reference type, the value that's passed is the information about where to find an object, not the object itself. When you pass a reference type in a method's parameter list, you can change values in the object's fields.

See, for example, the code in Listing 9-12.

LISTING 9-12: **Another Day Goes By**

```
package com.allmycode.a09_12;

import android.support.v7.app.AppCompatActivity;
import android.os.Bundle;
import android.widget.TextView;

import com.allmycode.a09_10.BagOfCheese;

public class MainActivity extends AppCompatActivity {
  TextView textView;

  @Override
  protected void onCreate(Bundle savedInstanceState) {
    super.onCreate(savedInstanceState);
    setContentView(R.layout.activity_main);

    textView = (TextView) findViewById(R.id.textView);

    BagOfCheese bag1 = new BagOfCheese("Cheddar", 2.43, 30, true);

    addOneDay(bag1);

    textView.setText("");
    textView.append(bag1.toString());
  }
```

```
void addOneDay(BagOfCheese bag) {
    bag.daysAged++;
}

}
```

A run of the code in Listing 9-12 is shown in Figure 9-18. In that run, the constructor creates a bag that is aged 30 days, but the addOneDay method successfully adds a day. In the end, the display in Figure 9-18 shows 31 days aged.

Unlike the story with int values, you can change a bag of cheese's daysAged value by passing the bag as a method parameter. Why does it work this way?

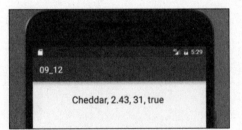

When you call a method, you make a copy of each parameter's value in the call. You initialize the declaration's parameters with the copied values. Immediately after making the addOneDay call in Listing 9-12, you have two variables: the original bag1 variable in the onCreate method and the new bag variable in the addOneDay method. The new bag variable has a copy of the value from the onCreate method, as shown in Figure 9-19. That "value" from the onCreate method is a reference to a BagOfCheese object. In other words, the bag1 and bag variables refer to the same object.

The statement in the body of the addOneDay method adds 1 to the value stored in the object's daysAged field. After one day is added, the program's variables look like the information in Figure 9-20.

Notice how both the bag1 and bag variables refer to an object whose daysAged value is 31. After returning from the call to addOneDay, the bag variable goes away. All that remains is the original onCreate method and its bag1 variable, as shown in Figure 9-21. But bag1 still refers to an object whose daysAged value has been changed to 31.

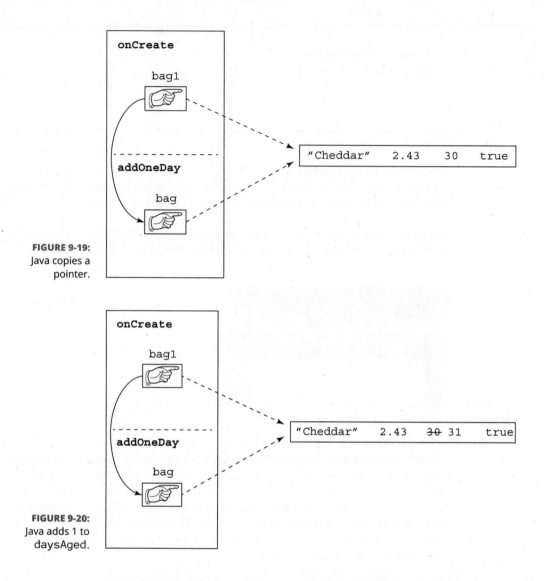

FIGURE 9-19:
Java copies a pointer.

FIGURE 9-20:
Java adds 1 to daysAged.

In Chapter 7, I show you how to pass primitive values to method parameters. Passing a primitive value to a method parameter is called *pass-by value*. In this section, I show you how to pass both primitive values and objects to method parameters. Passing an object (such as bag1) to a method parameter is called *pass-by reference*.

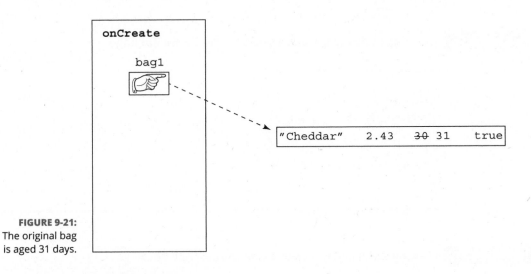

FIGURE 9-21:
The original bag
is aged 31 days.

Java's Modifiers

Throughout this book, you see words like `public` and `protected` peppered throughout the code listings. You might wonder what these words mean. (Actually, if you're reading from front to back, you might have grown accustomed to seeing them and started thinking of them as background noise.) In the next few sections, I tackle some of these *modifier* keywords.

Public classes and default-access classes

Most of the classes in this chapter's listings begin with the word `public`. When a class is public, any program in any package can use the code (or at least some of the code) inside that class. If a class isn't public, then for a program to use the code inside that class, the program must be inside the same package as the class. Listings 9-13, 9-14, and 9-15 illustrate these ideas.

LISTING 9-13: **What Is a Paragraph?**

```
package com.allyourcode.wordprocessor;

class Paragraph {
  int alignment;
  int borders;
  double leftIndent;
  double lineSpacing;
  int style;
}
```

LISTING 9-14: **Making a Paragraph with Code in the Same Package**

```
package com.allyourcode.wordprocessor;

class MakeAParagraph {
  Paragraph paragraph = new Paragraph();

  {
    paragraph.leftIndent = 1.5;
  }
}
```

LISTING 9-15: **Making a Paragraph with Code in Another Package**

```
// THIS IS BAD CODE:

package com.allyourcode.editor;

import com.allyourcode.wordprocessor.Paragraph;

public class MakeAnotherParagraph {
  Paragraph paragraph = new Paragraph();

  {
    paragraph.leftIndent = 1.5;
  }
}
```

The Paragraph class in Listing 9-13 has *default access* — that is, the Paragraph class isn't public. The code in Listing 9-14 is in the same package as the Paragraph class (the com.allyourcode.wordprocessor package). So in Listing 9-14, you can declare an object to be of type Paragraph, and you can refer to that object's leftIndent field.

The code in Listing 9-15 isn't in the same com.allyourcode.wordprocessor package. For that reason, the use of names like Paragraph and leftIndent (from Listing 9-13) aren't legal in Listing 9-15, even if Listings 9-13 and 9-15 are in the same Android Studio project. When you type Listings 9-13, 9-14, and 9-15 into the Android Studio editor, you see a red, blotchy mess for Listing 9-15, as shown in Figure 9-22.

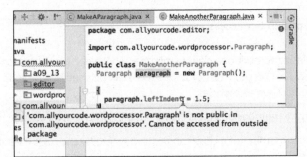

FIGURE 9-22:
Errors in
Listing 9-15.

TECHNICAL
STUFF

Have you ever seen an assignment statement that's not inside of a method? Think about it. When you work with the textView variable in Listing 9-12, you declare TextView textView outside of any method, and then you assign textView = (TextView) findViewById... inside the onCreate method. Outside of a method, you can't assign values to things unless you create an initializer block. Like any other kind of block, an *initializer block* has open and close curly braces. Between the braces, the initializer block has statements that assign values to things. In Listing 9-14, an initializer block assigns the value 1.5 to a paragraph's leftIndent field. In Listing 9-15, an initializer block tries to assign a value, but the assignment doesn't work because the Paragraph class isn't public.

The .java file containing a public class must have the same name as the public class. For example, the file containing the code in Listing 9-1 must be named BagOfCheese.java.

Even the capitalization of the filename must be the same as the public class's name. You see an error message if you put the code in Listing 9-1 inside a file named bagofcheese.java. In the file's name, you have to capitalize the letters B, O, and C.

Because of the file-naming rule, you can't declare more than one public class in a .java file. If you put the public classes from Listings 9-1 and 9-2 into the same file, would you name the file BagOfCheese.java or CreateBags.java? Neither name would satisfy the file-naming rule. For that matter, *no* name would satisfy it.

Access for fields and methods

A class can have either public access or nonpublic (default) access. But a member of a class has four possibilities: public, private, default, and protected.

REMEMBER

A class's fields and methods are the class's *members*. For example, the class in Listing 9-10 has five members: the fields kind, weight, daysAged, and isDomestic and the method toString.

Here's how member access works:

>> A default member of a class (a member whose declaration doesn't contain the words public, private, or protected) can be used by any code inside the same package as that class.

>> A private member of a class cannot be used in any code outside the class.

>> A public member of a class can be used wherever the class itself can be used; that is:

- Any program in any package can refer to a public member of a public class.

- For a program to reference a public member of a default access class, the program must be inside the same package as the class.

To see these rules in action, check out the public class in Listing 9-16.

LISTING 9-16: **A Class with Public Access**

```
package com.allyourcode.bank;

public class Account {
  public String customerName;
  private int internalIdNumber;
  String address;
  String phone;
  public int socialSecurityNumber;
  int accountType;
  double balance;

  public static int findById(int internalIdNumber) {
    Account foundAccount = new Account();
    // Code to find the account goes here.
    return foundAccount.internalIdNumber;
  }
}
```

The code in Figures 9-23 and 9-24 uses the Account class and its fields.

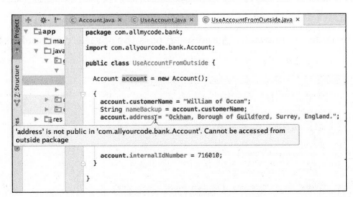

```
 C Account.java ×    © UseAccount.java ×    C UseAccountFromOutside.java ×

    package com.allyourcode.bank;

    public class UseAccount {

        Account account = new Account();

        {
            account.customerName = "William of Occam";
            String nameBackup = account.customerName;
            account.address = "Ockham, Borough of Guildford, Surrey, England.";
            account.internalIdNumber = 716010;
        }
    'internalIdNumber' has private access in 'com.allyourcode.bank.Account'

        }
    }
```

FIGURE 9-23:
Referring to a
public class in the
same package.

The error messages in Figures 9-23 and 9-24 point to some troubles with the code. Here's a list of facts about these two pieces of code:

>> The UseAccount class is in the same package as the Account class.

>> The UseAccount class can create a variable of type Account.

>> The UseAccount class's code can refer to the public customerName field of the Account class and to the default address field of the Account class.

>> The UseAccount class cannot refer to the private internalIdNumber field of the Account class, even though UseAccount and Account are in the same package. (Refer to Figure 9-23.)

>> The UseAccountFromOutside class is not in the same package as the Account class. (In Figure 9-24, notice allyourcode versus allmycode.)

```
 ✦  ✿ ↑    C Account.java ×    © UseAccount.java ×    © UseAccountFromOutside.java ×

 app               package com.allmycode.bank;
   ▶  mar
   ▼  java          import com.allyourcode.bank.Account;
     ▼
       ▼            public class UseAccountFromOutside {

       ▶                Account account = new Account();
       ▶
     ▶  res            {
 res                       account.customerName = "William of Occam";
                           String nameBackup = account.customerName;
                           account.address = "Ockham, Borough of Guildford, Surrey, England.";
    'address' is not public in 'com.allyourcode.bank.Account'. Cannot be accessed from
    outside package

                           account.internalIdNumber = 716010;
                       }
                   }
```

FIGURE 9-24:
Referring to a
public class in a
different package.

>> The UseAccountFromOutside class can create a variable of type Account. (An import declaration keeps me from having to repeat the fully qualified com.allyourcode.bank.Account name everywhere in the code.)

>> The UseAccountFromOutside class's code can refer to the public customerName field of the Account class.

>> The UseAccountFromOutside class's code cannot refer to the default address field of the Account class or to the private internalIdNumber field of the Account class. (Figure 9-24 shows the address field's error message.)

Now examine the nonpublic class in Listing 9-17.

LISTING 9-17: **A Class with Default Access**

```
package com.allyourcode.game;

class Sprite {
  public String name;
  String image;
  double distanceFromLeftEdge, distanceFromTop;
  double motionAcross, motionDown;
  private int renderingValue;

  void render() {
    if (renderingValue == 2) {
      // Do stuff here
    }
  }
}
```

The code in Figures 9-25 and 9-26 uses the Sprite class and its fields.

FIGURE 9-25:
Referring to a
default access
class in the same
package.

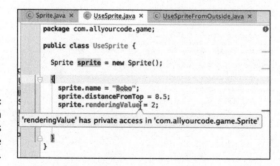

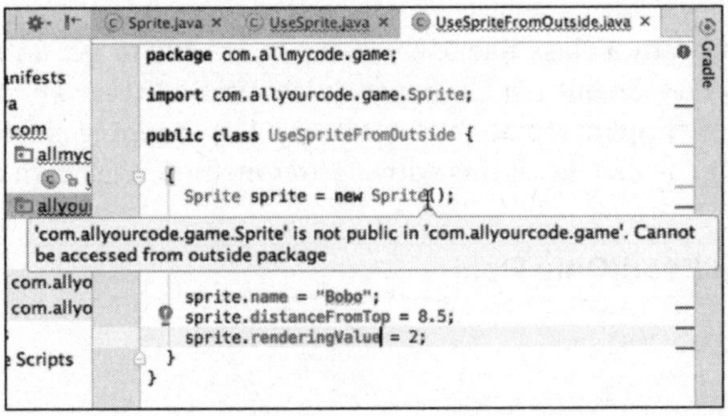

FIGURE 9-26:
Referring to a default access class in a different package.

The error messages in Figures 9-25 and 9-26 point to some troubles with the code. Here's a list of facts about these two pieces of code:

>> The UseSprite class is in the same package as the Sprite class.

>> The UseSprite class can create a variable of type Sprite.

>> The UseSprite class's code can refer to the public name field of the Sprite class and to the default distanceFromTop field of the Sprite class.

>> The UseSprite class cannot refer to the private renderingValue field of the Sprite class, even though UseSprite and Sprite are in the same package. (Refer to Figure 9-25.)

>> The UseSpriteFromOutside class isn't in the same package as the Sprite class. (In Figure 9-26, notice allyourcode versus allmycode.)

>> The UseSpriteFromOutside class cannot create a variable of type Sprite. (Not even an import declaration can save you from an error message here.)

>> Inside the UseAccountFromOutside class, references to sprite.name, sprite.distanceFromTop, and sprite.renderingValue are all meaningless because the sprite variable doesn't have a type.

Using getters and setters

In Figures 9-23 and 9-24, the UseAccount and UseAccountFromOutside classes can set an account's customerName and get the account's existing customerName:

```
account.customerName = "Occam";
String nameBackup = account.customerName;
```

But neither the UseAccount class nor the UseAccountFromOutside class can tinker with an account's internalIdNumber field.

What if you want a class like UseAccount to be able to get an existing account's internalIdNumber but not to change an account's internalIdNumber? (In many situations, getting information is necessary, but changing existing information is dangerous.) You can do all this with a *getter* method, as shown in Listing 9-18.

LISTING 9-18: **Creating a Read-Only Field**

```
package com.allyourcode.bank;

public class Account {
  public String customerName;
  private int internalIdNumber;
  String address;
  String phone;
  public int socialSecurityNumber;
  int accountType;
  double balance;

  public static int findById(int internalIdNumber) {
    Account foundAccount = new Account();
    // Code to find the account goes here.
    return foundAccount.internalIdNumber;
  }

  public int getInternalIdNumber() {
    return internalIdNumber;
  }
}
```

With the Account class in Listing 9-18, another class's code can call

```
int backupIdNumber = account.getInternalIdNumber();
```

The Account class's internalIdNumber field is still private, so another class's code has no way to assign a value to an account's internalIdNumber field. If you want to enable other classes to change an account's private internalIdNumber value, you can add a setter method to the code in Listing 9-18, like this:

```
public void setInternalIdNumber(int internalIdNumber) {
  this.internalIdNumber = internalIdNumber;
}
```

Getter and setter methods aren't built-in features in Java — they're simply ordinary Java methods. But this pattern (having a method whose purpose is to access an otherwise inaccessible field's value) is used so often that programmers use the terms *getter* and *setter* to describe it.

REMEMBER

Getter and setter methods are *accessor* methods. Java programmers almost always follow the convention of starting an accessor method name with `get` or `set` and then capitalizing the name of the field being accessed. For example, the field `internalIdNumber` has accessors named `getInternalIdNumber` and `setInternalIdNumber`. The field `renderingValue` has accessors named `getRenderingValue` and `setRenderingValue`.

You can have Android Studio create getters and setters for you. Here's how:

1. **Start with the code from Listing 9-16 in the Android Studio editor.**

2. **Click the mouse cursor anywhere inside the editor.**

3. **On the Android Studio main menu, select Code ⇨ Generate ⇨ Getter and Setter.**

The Select Fields to Generate Getters and Setters dialog box appears, as shown in Figure 9-27.

Alternatively, you can generate only getters by selecting Code ⇨ Generate ⇨ Getter. And you can generate only setters by selecting Code ⇨ Generate ⇨ Setter.

A dialog box lists the fields in the class that appears in Android Studio's editor.

4. **Select one or more fields in the dialog box's list of fields.**

To create the code in Listing 9-18, I selected only the `internalIdNumber` field.

Alternatively, you can generate only getters by selecting Code

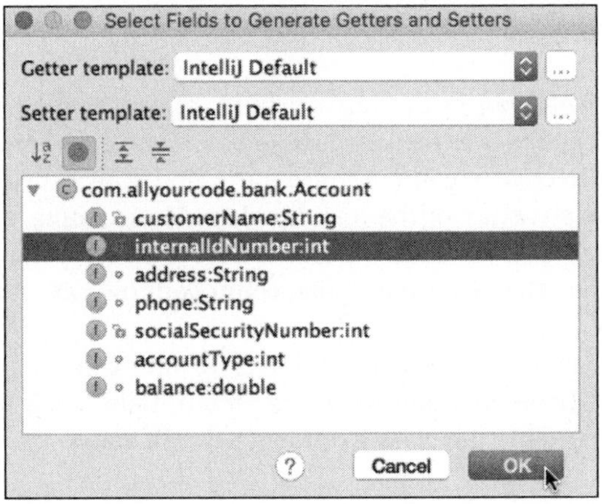

FIGURE 9-27: Select Fields to Generate Getters and Setters.

5. **Click OK.**

Android Studio dismisses the dialog box and adds freshly brewed getter and setter methods to the editor's code.

CROSS-REFERENCE

I cover protected access in Chapter 10.

What does static mean?

This chapter begins with a discussion of cheese and its effects on Andy's business practices. Andy has a blank form that represents a class. He also has a bunch of filled-in forms, each of which represents an individual bag-of-cheese object.

One day, Andy decides to take inventory of his cheese by counting all the bags of cheese. (See Figure 9-28.)

Bag of Cheese

Kind:	
Weight (in pounds):	
Age (in days):	
Domestic?:	☑
Bag count:	377

FIGURE 9-28:
Counting bags of cheese.

Compare the various fields shown in Figure 9-28. From the object-oriented point of view, how is the daysAged field so different from the count field?

The answer is that a single bag can keep track of how many days it has been aged, but it shouldn't count *all* the bags. As far back as Listing 9-1, a BagOfCheese object has its own daysAged field. That makes sense. (Well, it makes sense to an object-oriented programmer.)

But giving a particular object the responsibility of counting all objects in its class doesn't seem fair. To have each BagOfCheese object speak on behalf of all the others violates a prime directive of computer programming: The structure of the program should imitate the structure of the real-life data. For example, I can post a picture of myself on Facebook, but I can't promise to count everyone else's pictures on Facebook. ("All you other Facebook users, count your own @#!% pictures!")

A field to count all bags of cheese belongs in one central place. That's why, in Figure 9-29, I have one, and only one, count field. Each object has its own daysAged value, but only the class itself has a count value.

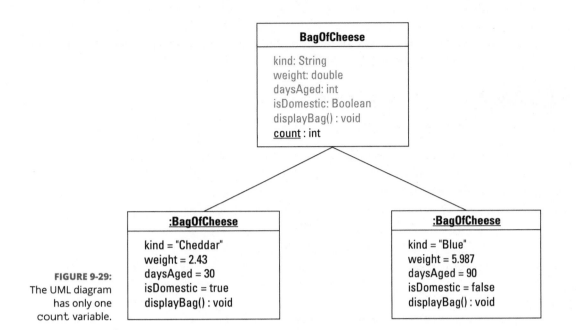

FIGURE 9-29:
The UML diagram
has only one
count variable.

A field or method that belongs to an entire class rather than to each individual object is a *static* member of the class. To declare a static member of a class, you use Java's `static` keyword (what a surprise!), as shown in Listing 9-19.

LISTING 9-19: **Creating a Static Field**

```
package com.allmycode.a09_19;

public class BagOfCheese {
  public String kind;
  public double weight;
  public int daysAged;
  public boolean isDomestic;

  public static int count = 0;

  public BagOfCheese() {
    count++;
  }
}
```

For each call to the `BagOfCheese` constructor, the constructor adds 1 to the value of `count`.

To refer to a class's static member, you preface the member's name with the name of the class, as shown in Listing 9-20.

LISTING 9-20: **Referring to a Static Field**

```
package com.allmycode.a09_20;

import android.support.v7.app.AppCompatActivity;
import android.os.Bundle;
import android.widget.TextView;

import com.allmycode.a09_19.BagOfCheese;

public class MainActivity extends AppCompatActivity {
  TextView textView;

  @Override
  protected void onCreate(Bundle savedInstanceState) {
    super.onCreate(savedInstanceState);
    setContentView(R.layout.activity_main);

    textView = (TextView) findViewById(R.id.textView);

    BagOfCheese bag1 = new BagOfCheese();
    BagOfCheese bag2 = new BagOfCheese();

    textView.setText(BagOfCheese.count + " bags");
  }
}
```

Fields aren't the only things that can be static. Methods can be static too. Consider the code in Listing 9-21.

LISTING 9-21: **A Static Field and a Static Method**

```
package com.allmycode.a09_21;

public class BagOfCheese {
  public String kind;
  public double weight;
  public int daysAged;
  public boolean isDomestic;
```

```
    private static int count = 0;

    public static int getCount() {
      return count;
    }

    public BagOfCheese() {
      count++;
    }
}
```

Listing 9-21 contains a static field and a static method. The static count field is private, so another class's code can't refer to BagOfCheese.count. But the method getCount is public. So, in place of BagOfCheese.count, another class can obtain the same information by calling BagOfCheese.getCount().

Android's official code style guidelines, posted at http://source.android.com/ source/code-style.html, tell you to start every nonpublic, nonstatic field name with a lowercase letter m. In an introductory Java book, I depart from these guidelines. But that's why, in a professionally written Android program, you'll see so many names start with the letter m.

To dot, or not

Consider the three ways to refer to a member (a field or a method):

>> **You can preface the member name with a name that refers to an object.**

For example, in Listing 9-11, I preface calls to toString with the names bag1 and bag2, each of which refers to an object:

```
textView.append(bag1.toString());
textView.append(bag2.toString());
```

When you do this, you're referring to something that belongs to each individual object. (You're referring to the object's nonstatic field, or calling the object's nonstatic method.)

>> **You can preface the member name with a name that refers to a class.**

For example, in Listing 9-20, I prefaced the field name count with the class name BagOfCheese.

When you do this, you're referring to something that belongs to the entire class. (You're referring to the class's static field, or calling the class's static method.)

>> **You can preface the member name with nothing.**

For example, in Listing 9-10, inside the `toString` method, I use the names `kind`, `weight`, `daysAged`, and `isDomestic` with no dots in front of them:

```java
public String toString() {
    return kind + ", " + weight + ", " + daysAged + ", " + isDomestic +
                                                      "\n";
}
```

A method can do this when it refers to its own object's fields, not when it refers to some other object's fields.

Java provides a loophole in which you break one of the three rules I just described. In Listing 9-20, you can replace `BagsOfCheese.count` with `bag1.count` or with `bag2.count`. That is, you can refer to a static member by prefacing it with the name of an object. This isn't a good a thing to do. It's just something that you're allowed to do.

A bad example

Don't do what I do in Listing 9-22.

LISTING 9-22: **Trouble in River City**

```java
// BAD CODE!!! GO TO YOUR ROOM, CODE.
package com.allmycode.a09_22;

public class BagOfCheese {
  public String kind;
  public double weight;
  public int daysAged;
  public boolean isDomestic;

  private int count = 0;

  public static int getCount() {
    return count;
  }

  public BagOfCheese() {
    count++;
  }
}
```

If you type the code in Listing 9-22 into Android Studio's editor and then hover the mouse over the `return count` statement, you see this ferocious-looking error message: `Non-static field 'count' cannot be referenced from a static context`. What gives? In my own code, I saw this error message dozens and dozens of times before I started feeling comfortable with the meaning of the word `static`.

If the `count` field isn't static, each instance of the `BagOfCheese` class has its own `count` field, and each `count` field belongs to an instance of the `BagOfCheese` class. But that's not true of the `getCount` method. In Listing 9-22, the `getCount` method is static. So the `getCount` method doesn't belong to any particular `BagOfCheese` instance. The `getCount` method belongs to the entire `BagOfCheese` class. See Figure 9-30.

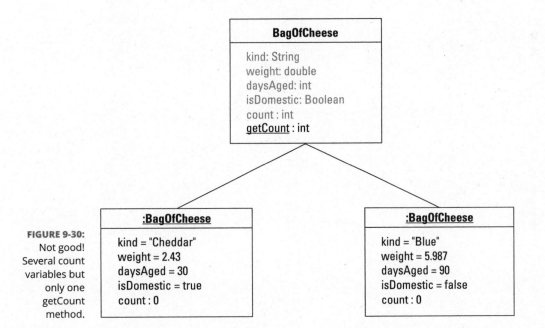

FIGURE 9-30:
Not good!
Several count
variables but
only one
getCount
method.

Inside of the `getCount` method, when Java sees the `return count` statement, Java doesn't know which instance's `count` to return. So Java refuses to compile your code. Android Studio displays an error message, and you're out of luck!

What's Next?

This chapter talks about individual classes. Most classes don't exist in isolation from other classes. Most classes belong to hierarchies of classes, subclasses, and sub-subclasses, so the next chapter covers the relationships among classes.

» Adding new life to old code

» Making changes without spending a fortune

Chapter **10**

Saving Time and Money: Reusing Existing Code

Wouldn't it be nice if every piece of software did just what you wanted it to do? In an ideal world, you could simply buy a program, make it work right away, plug it seamlessly into new situations, and update it easily whenever your needs changed. Unfortunately, software of this kind doesn't exist. (*Nothing* of this kind exists.) The truth is that no matter what you want to do, you can find software that does some of it, but not all of it.

This is one reason that object-oriented programming has been successful. For years, companies were buying prewritten code only to discover that the code didn't do what they wanted it to do. So the companies began messing with the code. Their programmers dug deep into the program files, changed variable names, moved subprograms around, reworked formulas, and generally made the code worse. The reality was that if a program didn't already do what you wanted (even if it did something ever so close to it), you could never improve the situation by mucking around inside the code. The best option was to chuck the whole program (expensive as that was) and start over. What a sad state of affairs!

Object-oriented programming has brought about a big change. An object-oriented program is, at its heart, designed to be modified. Using correctly written software, you can take advantage of features that are already built in, add new features of your own, and override features that don't suit your needs. The best aspect of this situation is that the changes you make are clean — no clawing and digging into other people's brittle program code. Instead, you make nice, orderly additions and modifications without touching the existing code's internal logic. It's the ideal solution.

The Last Word on Employees — Or Is It?

When you write an object-oriented program, you start by considering the data. You're writing about accounts. So what's an account? You're writing code to handle button clicks. So what's a button? You're writing a program to send payroll checks to employees. What's an employee?

In this chapter's first example, an employee is someone with a name and a job title — sure, employees have other characteristics, but for now I stick to the basics:

```
class Employee {
   String name;
   String jobTitle;
}
```

Of course, any company has different kinds of employees. For example, your company may have full-time and part-time employees. Each full-time employee has a yearly salary:

```
class FullTimeEmployee extends Employee {
   double salary;
}
```

In this example, the words extends Employee tell Java that the new class (the FullTimeEmployee class) has all the properties that any Employee has and, possibly, more. In other words, every FullTimeEmployee object is an Employee object (an employee of a certain kind, perhaps). Like any Employee, a FullTimeEmployee has a name and a jobTitle. But a FullTimeEmployee also has a salary. That's what the words extends Employee do for you.

A part-time employee has no fixed yearly salary. Instead, every part-time employee has an hourly pay rate and a certain number of hours worked in a week:

```
class PartTimeEmployee extends Employee {
   double hourlyPay;
   int hoursWorked;
}
```

So far, a PartTimeEmployee has four characteristics: name, jobTitle, hourlyPay, and number of hoursWorked.

Then you have to consider the big shots — the executives. Every executive is a full-time employee. But in addition to earning a salary, every executive receives a bonus (even if the company goes belly up and needs to be bailed out):

```
class Executive extends FullTimeEmployee {
    double bonus;
}
```

Java's extends keyword is cool because, by extending a class, you inherit all the complicated code that's already in the other class. The class you extend can be a class that you have (or another developer has) already written. One way or another, you're able to reuse existing code and to add ingredients to the existing code.

Here's another example: The creators of Android wrote the AppCompatActivity class, with its 460 lines of code. You get to use all those lines of code for free by simply typing extends AppCompatActivity:

```
public class MainActivity extends AppCompatActivity {
```

With the two words extends AppCompatActivity, your new MainActivity class can do all the things that a typical Android activity can do — start running, find items in the app's res directory, show a dialog box, respond to a low-memory condition, start another activity, return an answer to an activity, finish running, and much more.

Extending a class

So useful is Java's extends keyword that developers have several different names to describe this language feature:

» **Superclass/subclass:** The Employee class (see the earlier section "The Last Word on Employees — Or Is It?") is the *superclass* of the FullTimeEmployee class. The FullTimeEmployee class is a *subclass* of the Employee class.

» **Parent/child:** The Employee class is the *parent* of the FullTimeEmployee class. The FullTimeEmployee class is a *child* of the Employee class.

In fact, the Executive class extends the FullTimeEmployee class, which in turn extends the Employee class. So Executive is a *descendant* of Employee, and Employee is an *ancestor* of Executive. The Unified Modeling Language (UML) diagram in Figure 10-1 illustrates this point.

» **The "is a" relationship:** Every FullTimeEmployee object *is an* Employee object.

» **Inheritance:** The FullTimeEmployee class *inherits* the Employee class's members. (If any of the Employee class's members were declared to be private, the FullTimeEmployee class wouldn't inherit those members.)

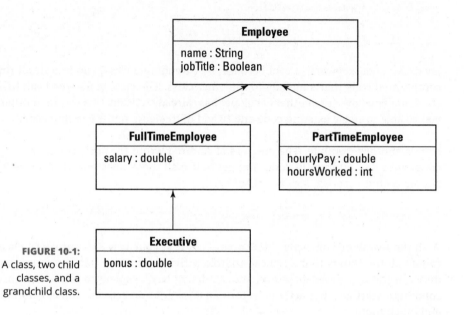

The Employee class has a name field, so the FullTimeEmployee class has a name field, and the Executive class has a name field. In other words, with the declarations of Employee, FullTimeEmployee, and Executive at the start of this section, the code in Listing 10-1 is legal.

All descendants of the Employee class have name fields, even though a name field is explicitly declared only in the Employee class itself.

LISTING 10-1: **Using the Employee Class and Its Subclasses**

```
Employee employee = new Employee();
employee.name = "Sam";

FullTimeEmployee ftEmployee = new FullTimeEmployee();
ftEmployee.name = "Jennie";

Executive executive = new Executive();
executive.name = "Harriet";
```

Almost every Java class extends another Java class. I write *almost* because one (and only one) class doesn't extend any other class. Java's built-in `Object` class doesn't extend anything. The `Object` class is at the top of Java's class hierarchy. Any class whose header has no `extends` clause automatically extends Java's `Object` class. So every other Java class is, directly or indirectly, a descendant of the `Object` class, as shown in Figure 10-2.

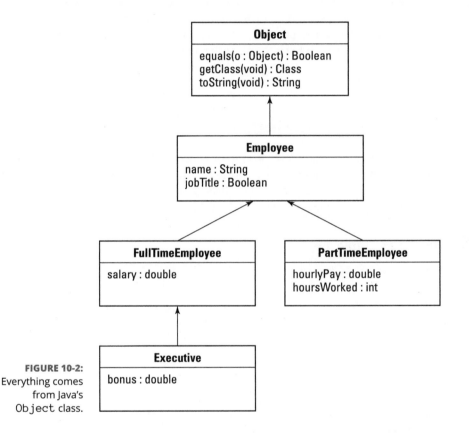

FIGURE 10-2:
Everything comes
from Java's
`Object` class.

The notion of extending a class is one pillar of object-oriented programming. In the 1970s, computer scientists were noticing that programmers tended to reinvent the wheel. If you needed code to balance an account, for example, you started writing code from scratch to balance an account. Never mind that other people had written their own account-balancing code. Integrating other peoples' code with yours, and adapting other peoples' code to your own needs, was a big headache. All things considered, it was easier to start from scratch.

Then, in the 1980s, object-oriented programming became popular. The notion of classes and subclasses provided a clean way to connect existing code (such as Android's `Activity` class code) with new code (such as your new `MainActivity` class code). By extending an existing class, you hook into the class's functionality, and you reuse features that have already been programmed.

REMEMBER

By reusing code, you avoid the work of reinventing the wheel. But you also make life easier for the end user. When you extend Android's `Activity` class, your new activity behaves like other peoples' activities because both your activity and the other peoples' activities inherit the same behavior from Android's `Activity` class. With so many apps behaving the same way, the user learns familiar patterns. It's a win-win situation.

Overriding methods

In this section, I expand on all the employee code snippets from the start of this chapter. From these snippets, I can present a fully baked program example. The example, as laid out in Listings 10-2 through 10-6, illustrates some important ideas about classes and subclasses.

LISTING 10-2: **What Is an Employee?**

```
package com.allyourcode.company;

public class Employee {
  public String name;
  public String jobTitle;

  public Employee() {
  }

  public Employee(String name, String jobTitle) {
    this.name = name;
    this.jobTitle = jobTitle;
  }

  public String getPayString() {
    return name + ", Pay not known\n";
  }
}
```

LISTING 10-3: **Full-Time Employees Have Salaries**

```java
package com.allyourcode.company;

import java.text.NumberFormat;
import java.util.Locale;
public class FullTimeEmployee extends Employee {
  public double salary;

  static NumberFormat currency = NumberFormat.getCurrencyInstance(Locale.US);

  public FullTimeEmployee() {
  }

  public FullTimeEmployee(String name, String jobTitle, double salary) {
    this.name = name;
    this.jobTitle = jobTitle;
    this.salary = salary;
  }

  public double pay() {
    return salary;
  }

  @Override
  public String getPayString() {
    return name + ", " + currency.format(pay()) + "\n";
  }
}
```

LISTING 10-4: **Executives Get Bonuses**

```java
package com.allyourcode.company;

public class Executive extends FullTimeEmployee {
  public double bonus;

  public Executive() {
  }

  public Executive(String name, String jobTitle, double salary, double bonus) {
    this.name = name;
    this.jobTitle = jobTitle;
```

(continued)

LISTING 10-4: *(continued)*

```java
    this.salary = salary;
    this.bonus = bonus;
  }

  @Override
  public double pay() {
    return salary + bonus;
  }
}
```

LISTING 10-5: Part-Time Employees Are Paid by the Hour

```java
package com.allyourcode.company;

import java.text.NumberFormat;
import java.util.Locale;

public class PartTimeEmployee extends Employee {
  public double hourlyPay;
  public int hoursWorked;

  static NumberFormat currency = NumberFormat.getCurrencyInstance(Locale.US);

  public PartTimeEmployee() {
  }

  public PartTimeEmployee(String name, String jobTitle,
                          double hourlyPay, int hoursWorked) {
    this.name = name;
    this.jobTitle = jobTitle;
    this.hourlyPay = hourlyPay;
    this.hoursWorked = hoursWorked;
  }

  public double pay() {
    return hourlyPay * hoursWorked;
  }

  @Override
  public String getPayString() {
    return name + ", " + currency.format(pay()) + "\n";
  }
}
```

LISTING 10-6: **Putting Your Employee Classes to the Test**

```
package com.allyourcode.a10_06;

import android.support.v7.app.AppCompatActivity;
import android.os.Bundle;
import android.widget.TextView;

import com.allyourcode.company.Employee;
import com.allyourcode.company.FullTimeEmployee;
import com.allyourcode.company.Executive;
import com.allyourcode.company.PartTimeEmployee;

public class MainActivity extends AppCompatActivity {
  TextView textView;

  @Override
  protected void onCreate(Bundle savedInstanceState) {
    super.onCreate(savedInstanceState);
    setContentView(R.layout.activity_main);

    textView = (TextView) findViewById(R.id.textView);

    Employee employee = new Employee("Barry", "Author");

    FullTimeEmployee ftEmployee =
        new FullTimeEmployee("Ed", "Manager", 10000.00);

    PartTimeEmployee ptEmployee =
        new PartTimeEmployee("Joe", "Intern", 8.00, 20);

    Executive executive =
        new Executive("Jane", "CEO", 20000.00, 5000.00);

    textView.setText("");

    textView.append(employee.getPayString());
    textView.append(ftEmployee.getPayString());
    textView.append(ptEmployee.getPayString());
    textView.append(executive.getPayString());
  }
}
```

Figure 10-3 shows a run of the code in Listings 10-2 through 10-6.

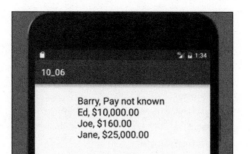

FIGURE 10-3:
Running the code
in Listings 10-2
through 10-6.

Figure 10-4 contains a UML diagram for the Employee class and its descendants.

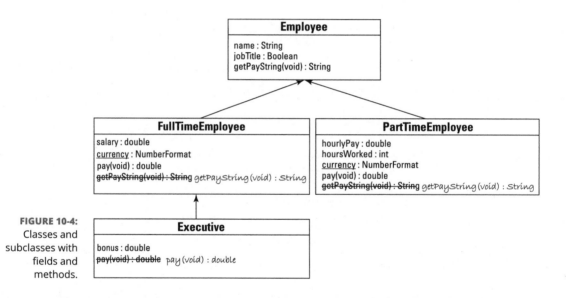

FIGURE 10-4:
Classes and
subclasses with
fields and
methods.

TECHNICAL
STUFF

In Figure 10-4, I use strikethrough text and simulated handwriting to represent overridden methods. These typographical tricks are my own inventions. Neither the strikethrough nor the simulated handwriting is part of the UML standard. In fact, the UML standard has all kinds of rules that I ignore in this book. My main purpose in showing you the rough UML diagrams is to help you visualize the hierarchies of classes and their subclasses.

Consider the role of the getPayString method in Figure 10-4 and in Listings 10-2 through 10-6. In the figure, getPayString appears in all except the Executive class; in the listings, I define getPayString in all except the Executive class.

The getPayString method appears for the first time in the Employee class (refer to Listing 10-2), where it serves as a placeholder for not knowing the employee's pay. The FullTimeEmployee class (refer to Listing 10-3) would inherit this vacuous getPayString class except that the FullTimeEmployee class declares its own version of getPayString. In the terminology from Chapter 4, the getPayString method in FullTimeEmployee *overrides* the getPayString method in Employee.

Listing 10-6 contains a call to a full-time employee's getPayString method:

```
FullTimeEmployee ftEmployee = ... Etc.
...
textView.append(ftEmployee.getPayString());
```

And in Figure 10-3, the call to ftEmployee. getPayString() gives you the FullTimeEmployee class's version of getPayString, not the Employee class's clueless version of getPayString. (If ftEmployee.getPayString() called the Employee class's version of getPayString, you'd see Ed, Pay not known in Figure 10-3.) Overriding a method declaration means taking precedence over that existing version of the method.

Of course, overriding a method isn't the same as obliterating a method. In Listing 10-6, the statements

```
Employee employee = ... Etc.
...
textView.append(employee.getPayString());
```

conjure up the Employee class's noncommittal version of showPay. It happens because an object declared with the Employee constructor has no salary field, no hourlyPay field, and no getPayString method other than the method declared in the Employee class. The Employee class, and any objects declared using the Employee constructor, could do their work even if the other classes (FullTime Employee, PartTimeEmployee, and so on) didn't exist.

REMEMBER

The only way to override a method is to declare a method with the same name and the same parameters inside a subclass. By *same parameters,* I mean the same number of parameters, each with the same type. For example, calculate(int count, double amount) overrides calculate(int x, double y) because both declarations have two parameters: The first parameter in each declaration is of type int, and the second parameter in each declaration is of type double. But calculate(int count, String amount) doesn't override calculate(int count, double amount). In one declaration, the second parameter has type double, and in the other declaration, the second parameter has type String. If you call calculate(42, 2.71828), you get the calculate(int x, double y) method, and if you call calculate(42, "Euler") you get the calculate(int count, String amount) method.

Listings 10-2 through 10-5 have other examples of overriding methods. For example, the Executive class in Listing 10-4 overrides its parent class's pay method, but not the parent class's getPayString method. Calculating an executive's pay is different from calculating an ordinary full-time employee's pay. But after you know the two peoples' pay amounts, showing an executive's pay is no different from showing an ordinary full-time employee's pay.

TECHNICAL STUFF

When I created this section's examples, I considered giving the Employee class a pay method (returning 0 on each call). This strategy would make it unnecessary for me to create identical getPayString methods for the FullTimeEmployee and PartTimeEmployee classes. For various reasons (none of them interesting), I decided against doing it that way.

Overriding works well in situations in which you want to tweak an existing class's features. Imagine having a news ticker that does everything you want except scroll sideways. (I'm staring at one on my computer right now! As one news item disappears toward the top, the next news item scrolls in from below. The program's options don't allow me to change this setting.) After studying the code's documentation, you can subclass the program's Ticker class and override the Ticker class's scroll method. In your new scroll method, the user has the option to move text upward, downward, sideways, or inside out (whatever that means).

Java's super keyword

You can inherit a lot from your parents. But one thing you can't inherit is their experiences of having been born. Yes, you can see pictures that your grandparents took. But that's not the same as having been there.

At this point, you may feel like quibbling. What would it mean to "inherit" your parents' birth experiences? Well, you can stop right there. I'm not trying to form a perfect metaphor. I'm only trying to introduce an important fact about Java programming — the fact that classes don't inherit constructors from their parent classes.

Look at the constructors in Listings 10-2 and 10-3.

>> The FullTimeEmployee class extends the Employee class.

>> Both classes have parameterless constructors.

>> Both classes have constructors that initialize all of their fields.

In fact, a FullTimeEmployee constructor initializes three fields. Only one of these fields — the salary field — is declared in the FullTimeEmployee class's code. The

FullTimeEmployee class inherits the other two fields — name and jobTitle — from the Employee class. This isn't a matter of FullTimeEmployee overriding its parent class's constructors. There are no constructors to override. Like any other subclass, the FullTimeEmployee class doesn't inherit its parent class's constructors.

Is there any way to avoid the loathsome redundancy of all the constructor declarations in Listings 10-2 to 10-5? There is. Java's super keyword can refer to a parent class's constructor:

```java
public FullTimeEmployee(String name, String jobTitle, double salary) {
  super(name, jobTitle);
  this.salary = salary;
}
```

In this code, the FullTimeEmployee constructor calls its parent class's constructor. The call to super has two parameters and, as luck would have it, the parent Employee class has a two-parameter constructor:

```java
public Employee(String name, String jobTitle) {
  this.name = name;
  this.jobTitle = jobTitle;
}
```

The super call sends two parameters to the parent class's constructor, and the parent class's constructor uses those two parameters to give name and jobTitle their initial values. Finally, the FullTimeEmployee class assigns a value to its own salary field. Everything works very nicely.

Java annotations

In Java, elements that start with an at-sign (@) are *annotations.* In Listings 10-3, 10-4, and 10-5, each @Override annotation reminds Java that the method immediately below the annotation has the same name and the same parameter types as a method in the parent class. The use of the @Override annotation is optional. If you remove all @Override lines from Listings 10-3, 10-4, and 10-5, the code works the same way.

Why use the @Override annotation? Imagine leaving off the annotation and mistakenly putting the following getPayString method (and no other getPayString method declaration) in Listing 10-3:

```java
public String getPayString(double salary) {
  return name + ", " + currency.format(salary) + "\n";
}
```

You might think that you've overridden the parent class's getPayString method, but you haven't! The Employee class's getPayString method has no parameters, and your new FullTimeEmployee class's getPayString method has a parameter. Android Studio looks at this stuff in the editor and says, "Okay, I guess the developer is inheriting the Employee class's parameterless getPayString method and declaring an additional version of getPayString. Both getPayString methods are available in the FullTimeEmployee class." (By the way, when Android Studio speaks, you can't see my lips moving.)

Everything goes smoothly until you run the code. The Java virtual machine sees the statement

```
textView.append(ftEmployee.getPayString());
```

in the main activity and calls the *parameterless* version of getPayString, which the FullTimeEmployee class inherits from its parent. That parent's method returns the useless Pay not known message. On the emulator screen, you see Ed, Pay not known for the full-time employee. That's not what you want.

The problem in this hypothetical example isn't so much that you commit a coding error — everybody makes mistakes like this one. (Yes, even I do. I make lots of them.) The problem is that, without an @Override annotation, you don't catch the error until you're running the program. That is, you don't see the error message as soon as you compose the code in the Android Studio editor. Waiting until runtime can be as painless as saying, "Aha! I know why this program didn't run correctly." But waiting until runtime can also be quite painful — as painful as saying, "My app was rated 1 on a scale of 5 because of this error that I didn't see until a user called my bad getPayString method."

Ideally, Android Studio is aware of your intention to override an existing method, and it can complain to you while you're staring at the editor. If you use the @Override annotation in conjunction with the bad getPayString method, the editor underlines @Override in red. When you hover the mouse over the word @Override, you see the message shown in Figure 10-5. That's good because you can fix the problem long before the problem shows up in a run of your code.

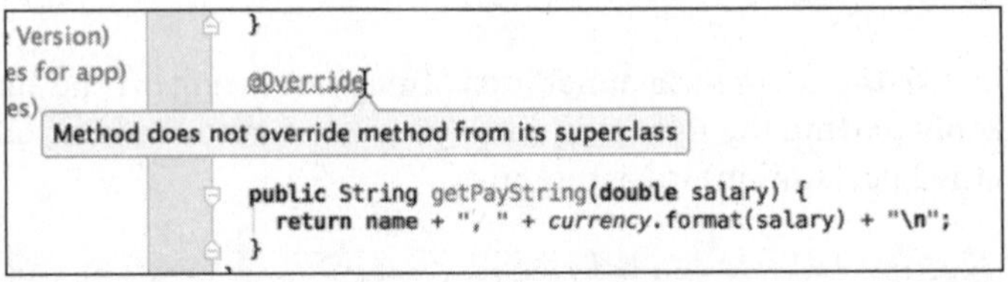

FIGURE 10-5:
The getPay
String method
doesn't override
the parent class's
getPayString
method.

In Chapter 9, Android Studio creates a `toString` method and puts another annotation — the `@NonNull` annotation — at the top of the method declaration. In Java, any reference type variable that doesn't point to anything has the value `null`. Consider the following cases:

» If you write `String greeting = "Hello"`, the `greeting` variable points to the characters H, e, l, l, o.

» If you write `String greeting = ""`, the `greeting` variable points to a string containing no characters. No, the string has no characters in it, but yes, it's still a string. If you execute

```
greeting.length()
```

you get the number 0.

» If you write `String greeting = null`, the `greeting` variable doesn't point to anything. In this case, if you execute

```
greeting.length()
```

your app crashes and you see a `NullPointerException` in Android Studio's Logcat pane.

In Chapter 9, the `@NonNull` annotation reminds Android Studio that the value returned by the new `toString` method must not be `null`. If Android Studio detects that the method returns `null`, you see a little yellow mark along the editor's rightmost edge. If you hover over that mark, you see a `'null' is returned by the method` warning.

More about Java's Modifiers

I start the conversation about Java's modifiers in Chapters 5 and 9. Chapter 5 describes the keyword `final` as it applies to variables, and Chapter 9 deals with the keywords `public` and `private`. In this section, I add a few more fun facts about Java modifiers.

The word `final` has many uses in Java programs. In addition to having final variables, you can have these elements:

» **Final class:** If you declare a class to be `final`, no one (not even you) can extend it.

>> **Final method:** If you declare a method to be `final`, no one (not even you) can override it.

Figures 10-6 and 10-7 put these rules into perspective. In Figure 10-6, I can't extend the `Stuff` class, because the `Stuff` class is `final`. And in Figure 10-7, I can't override the `Stuff` class's `increment` method because the `Stuff` class's `increment` method is `final`.

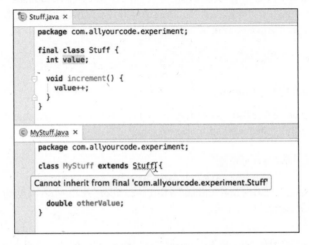

FIGURE 10-6:
Trying to extend a final class.

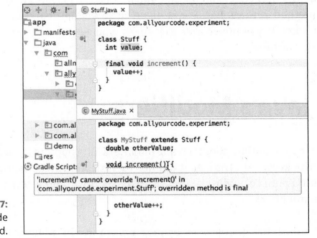

FIGURE 10-7:
Trying to override a final method.

You can apply Java's protected keyword to a class's members. This protected keyword has always seemed a bit strange to me. In common English usage, when my possessions are "protected," my possessions aren't as available as they'd normally be. But in Java, when you preface a field or a method with the protected keyword, you make that field or method a bit more available than it would be by default, as shown in Figure 10-8.

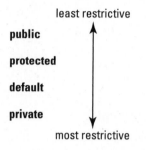

least restrictive

public

protected

default

private

most restrictive

FIGURE 10-8:
Access modes for
fields and
methods.

Here's what I say in Chapter 9 about members with default access:

> A default member of a class (a member whose declaration doesn't contain the words public, private, or protected) can be used by any code inside the same package as that class.

The same thing is true about a protected class member. But in addition, a protected member is inherited outside the class's package by any subclass of the protected member's class.

Huh? What does that last sentence mean? To make things concrete, Figure 10-9 shows you the carefree existence in which two classes are in the same package. With both Stuff and MyStuff in the same package, the MyStuff class inherits the Stuff class's default access value variable. The MyStuff class also inherits (and then overrides) the Stuff class's default access increment method.

If you move the Stuff class to a different package, MyStuff no longer inherits the Stuff class's default access value variable, as shown in Figure 10-10. In addition, the MyStuff class doesn't inherit the Stuff class's default access increment method.

But if, in the Stuff class, you turn value into a protected variable and you turn increment into a protected method, the MyStuff class again inherits its parent class's value variable and increment method, as shown in Figure 10-11.

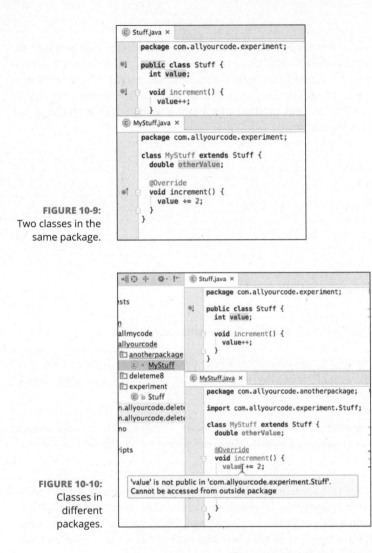

FIGURE 10-9:
Two classes in the same package.

FIGURE 10-10:
Classes in different packages.

Notice one more detail in Figure 10-11. I change the MyStuff class's increment method from default to public. I do this to avoid seeing an interesting little error message. You can't override a method with another method whose access is more restrictive than the original method. In other words, you can't override a public method with a private method. You can't even override a public method with a default method.

Java's default access is more restrictive than protected access. (Refer to Figure 10-8.) So you can't override a protected method with a default method. In Figure 10-11, I avoid the whole issue by making the MyStuff class's increment method be public. That way, I override the increment method with the least restrictive kind of access.

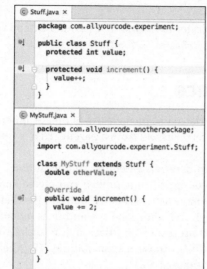

FIGURE 10-11:
Using the protected modifier.

Keeping Things Simple

Most programs operate entirely in the virtual realm. They have no bricks, nails, or girders. You can type a fairly complicated program in minutes. Even with no muscle and no heavy equipment, you can create a structure whose complexity rivals that of many complicated physical structures. You, the developer, have the power to build intricate, virtual bridges.

One goal of programming is to manage complexity. A good app isn't simply useful or visually appealing — a good app's code is nicely organized, easy to understand, and easy to modify.

Certain programming languages, like C++, support *multiple inheritance,* in which a class can have more than one parent class. For example, in C++ you can create a Book class, a TeachingMaterial class, and a Textbook class. You can make Textbook extend both Book and TeachingMaterial. This feature makes class hierarchies quite flexible, but it also makes those same hierarchies extremely complicated. You need tricky rules to decide how to inherit the move methods of both the computer's Mouse class and the rodent's Mouse class.

To avoid all this complexity, Java doesn't support multiple inheritance. In Java, each class has one (and only one) superclass. A class can have any number of subclasses. You can (and will) create many subclasses of Android's AppCompatActivity class. And other developers create their own subclasses of Android's AppCompatActivity class. But classes don't have multiple personalities. A Java class can have only one parent. The `Executive` class (refer to Listing 10-4) cannot extend both the `FullTimeEmployee` class and the `PartTimeEmployee` class.

Using an interface

The relationship between a class and its subclass is one of inheritance. In many real-life families, a child inherits assets from a parent. That's the way it works.

But consider the relationship between an editor and an author. The editor says, "By signing this contract, you agree to submit a completed manuscript by the fifteenth of August." Despite any excuses that the author gives before the deadline date, the relationship between the editor and the author is one of obligation. The author agrees to take on certain responsibilities; and, in order to continue being an author, the author must fulfill those responsibilities. (By the way, there's no subtext in this paragraph — none at all.)

Now consider Barry Burd. Who? Barry Burd — that guy who writes *Java Programming for Android Developers For Dummies,* 2nd Edition, and certain other *For Dummies* books (all from Wiley Publishing). He's a college professor, and he's also an author. You want to mirror this situation in a Java program, but Java doesn't support multiple inheritance. You can't make Barry extend both a `Professor` class and an `Author` class at the same time.

Fortunately for Barry, Java has interfaces. A class can extend only one parent class, but a class can implement many interfaces. A parent class is a bunch of stuff that a class inherits. On the other hand, as with the relationship between an editor and an author, an *interface* is a bunch of stuff that a class is obliged to provide.

Here's another example. Listings 10-2 through 10-5 describe what it means to be an employee of various kinds. Though a company might hire consultants, consultants who work for the company aren't employees. Consultants are normally self-employed. They show up temporarily to help companies solve problems and then leave the companies to work elsewhere. In the United States, differentiating between an employee and a consultant is important: So serious are the U.S. tax withholding laws that labeling a consultant an "employee" of any kind would subject the company to considerable legal risk.

To include consultants with employees in your code, you need a `Consultant` class that's separate from your existing `Employee` class hierarchy. On the other hand, consultants have a lot in common with a company's regular employees. For example, every consultant has a `getPayString` method. You want to represent this commonality in your code, so you create an interface. The interface obligates a class to give meaning to the method name `getPayString`, as shown in Listing 10-7.

LISTING 10-7:
Behold! An Interface!

```
package com.allyourcode.company;

public interface Payable {

  public String getPayString();
}
```

The element in Listing 10-7 isn't a class — it's a Java interface. Here's what the listing's code says:

> As an interface, my getPayString method has a header, but no body. In this interface, the getPayString method takes no arguments and returns a value of type String. A class that claims to implement me (the Payable interface) must provide (either directly or indirectly) a body for the getPayString method. That is, a class that claims to implement Payable must, in one way or another, implement the getPayString method.

> To find out about the difference between a method declaration's header and its body, see Chapter 4.

CROSS-
REFERENCE

Listings 10-8 and 10-9 implement the Payable interface and provide bodies for the getPayString method.

LISTING 10-8:
Implementing an Interface

```
package com.allyourcode.company;

import java.text.NumberFormat;
import java.util.Locale;

public class Consultant implements Payable {

  String name;
  double hourlyFee;
  int hoursWorked;

  static NumberFormat currency = NumberFormat.getCurrencyInstance(Locale.US);

  public Consultant() {
  }
```

(continued)

LISTING 10-8: *(continued)*

```java
public Consultant(String name, double hourlyFee, int hoursWorked) {
  this.name = name;
  this.hourlyFee = hourlyFee;
  this.hoursWorked = hoursWorked;
}

public double pay() {
  return hourlyFee * hoursWorked;
}

@Override
public String getPayString() {
  return name + ", " + currency.format(pay()) + "\n";
}
}
```

LISTING 10-9: **Another Class Implements the Interface**

```java
package com.allyourcode.company;

public class Employee implements Payable {
  String name;
  String jobTitle;
  int vacationDays;
  double taxWithheld;

  public Employee() {
  }

  public Employee(String name, String jobTitle) {
    this.name = name;
    this.jobTitle = jobTitle;
  }

  @Override
  public String getPayString() {
    return name + ", Pay not known\n";
  }
}
```

In Listings 10-8 and 10-9, both the Consultant and Employee classes implement the Payable interface — the interface that summarizes what it means to be paid by the company. With this in mind, consider the code in Listing 10-10.

LISTING 10-10: Using an Interface

```
package com.allyourcode.a10_10;

import android.support.v7.app.AppCompatActivity;
import android.os.Bundle;
import android.widget.TextView;

import com.allyourcode.company.Consultant;
import com.allyourcode.company.Employee;
import com.allyourcode.company.Payable;

public class MainActivity extends AppCompatActivity {
  TextView textView;

  @Override
  protected void onCreate(Bundle savedInstanceState) {
    super.onCreate(savedInstanceState);
    setContentView(R.layout.activity_main);

    textView = (TextView) findViewById(R.id.textView);

    Employee employee = new Employee("Barry", "Author");
    Consultant consultant = new Consultant("Willy", 100.00, 30);

    textView.setText("");

    displayPay(employee);
    displayPay(consultant);
  }

  void displayPay(Payable payable) {
    textView.append(payable.getPayString());
  }
}
```

A run of the code in Listing 10-10 is shown in Figure 10-12.

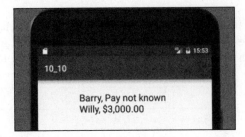

FIGURE 10-12:
Paying an
employee and a
consultant.

10_10

Barry, Pay not known
Willy, $3,000.00

In Listing 10-10, the displayPay method doesn't know anything about Employee classes or Consultant classes. All the displayPay method knows is that it wants its parameter to implement the Payable interface. As long as the object you pass to displayPay implements the Payable interface, the displayPay method's body can safely call the getPayString method.

Both the Employee and Consultant classes implement the Payable interface. So, in Listing 10-10, you can pass an Employee object to the displayPay method, and pass a Consultant object to the displayPay method. That flexibility — the ability to pass more than one kind of object to a method — illustrates the power of Java's interfaces.

In this section's example, two otherwise unrelated classes (Employee and Consultant) both implement the Payable interface. When I picture a Java interface, it's an element that cuts across levels of Java's class/subclass hierarchy, as shown in Figure 10-13.

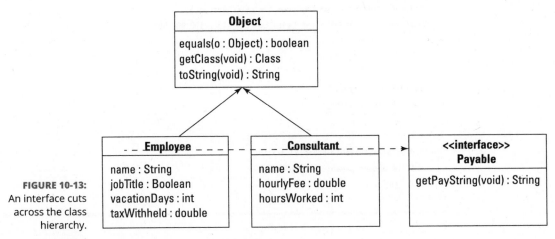

FIGURE 10-13:
An interface cuts
across the class
hierarchy.

TECHNICAL
STUFF

The dotted line in Figure 10-13 isn't part of standard UML. The folks who manage the standard have much better ways to represent interfaces than I use in this chapter's figures.

Some Observations about Android's Classes

When you start a new project, Android Studio offers to create an activity for your project. Android Studio offers you several different kinds of activities, such as a Basic Activity, an Empty Activity, a Login Activity, and so on. If you ask for an Empty Activity, you get the code shown in Listing 10-11.

LISTING 10-11: **Android Studio Creates a Main Activity**

```
package com.allyourcode.a10_11;

import android.support.v7.app.AppCompatActivity;
import android.os.Bundle;

public class MainActivity extends AppCompatActivity {

  @Override
  protected void onCreate(Bundle savedInstanceState) {
    super.onCreate(savedInstanceState);
    setContentView(R.layout.activity_main);
  }
}
```

The code declares a class named `MainActivity`. This name `MainActivity` isn't part of the Android API library. It's a name that you make up when you create a new Android project. (Actually, Android Studio makes up the name. You accept the name or change it to some other name when you follow the steps to create a new project.)

The `MainActivity` class in Listing 10-11 extends a class that belongs to Android's SDK library, namely, the `AppCompatActivity` class. In other words, the `MainActivity` object *is an* `AppCompatActivity` object. The `MainActivity` object has all the rights and responsibilities that any `AppCompatActivity` instance has. For example, the `MainActivity` has an `onCreate` method, which it overrides in Listing 10-11.

In fact, the `MainActivity` class inherits about 460 lines of code from Android's `AppCompatActivity` class, which inherits about 1,000 lines from Android's `FragmentActivity` class, which inherits about 6,700 lines from Android's `Activity` class. The inherited methods include ones such as `getCallingActivity`, `getCallingPackage`, `getParent`, `getTitle`, `getTitleColor`, `getWindow`, `onBackPressed`, `onKeyDown`, `onKeyLongPress`, `onLowMemory`, `onMenuItemSelected`, `setTitle`, `setTitleColor`, `startActivity`, `finish`, and many, many others. You inherit all this functionality with two simple words: `extends AppCompatActivity`.

REMEMBER

In the terminology of familial relationships, your `MainActivity` class is a descendant of Android's `Activity` class. Your `MainActivity` class is a kind of `Activity`.

Figure 10-14, taken directly from Android's online documentation, summarizes this information about the `AppCompatActivity` class.

TIP

For easy access to Android's API library documentation, bookmark `https://developer.android.com/reference/packages.html`.

In addition to being a subclass, the `AppCompatActivity` class implements a bunch of interfaces, including the `AppCompatCallback` interface, the `TaskStackBuilder` interface, and others. You don't have to remember any of this. If you ever need to know it, you can look it up on Android's documentation page. I write about the `MainActivity` class's genealogy to drive home the importance of classes and objects in Java programming.

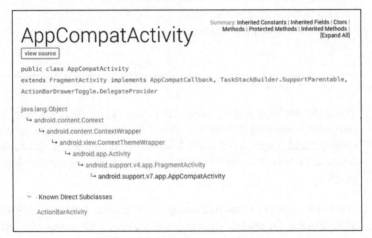

FIGURE 10-14:
An App
CompatActivity
family tree.

Java's super keyword, revisited

In an earlier section, the word `super` stands for the superclass's constructor. Listing 10-11, and many other listings, use the `super` keyword in a slightly different way. Yes, `super` always has something to do with a class's parent class. But, no, `super` doesn't always refer to the parent class's constructor.

In an onCreate method, the call super.onCreate(savedInstanceState) sends savedInstanceState to the parent class's onCreate method. In Listing 10-11, the parent class is the AppCompatActivity class. So Java calls the AppCompatActivity class's onCreate method.

The AppCompatActivity class's onCreate method contains its own call to super.onCreate(savedInstanceState). The AppCompatActivity class's parent is the FragmentActivity class. So Java passes savedInstanceState to the FragmentActivity class's onCreate method. And so on.

It's not until you get to the Activity class — your MainActivity class's great-grandparent — that the code makes direct use of the savedInstanceState variable. From this savedInstanceState information, the code puts the activity back the way it was before the system destroyed it.

CROSS-
REFERENCE

To find out why the poor activity may have been destroyed, see Chapter 4.

Casting, again

When you call findViewById, Java doesn't know what kind of view it will find. The findViewById method always returns a View instance, but lots of Android's classes extend the View class. For example, the classes Button, TextView, ImageView, CheckBox, Chronometer, and RatingBar all extend Android's View class. If you type the following code:

```
// DON'T DO THIS!!

TextView textView;

textView = findViewById(R.id.textView);
```

Java lets out a resounding, resentful roar: "How dare you assume that the object returned by a call to findViewById refers to an instance of the TextView class!" (Actually, Java quietly and mechanically displays an *Incompatible types* error message in Android Studio's editor. But I like to personify Java as though it's a stern taskmaster.)

In Chapter 6, *narrowing* means trying to assign a long value to an int value. A long value has 64 bits, and an int value has only 32 bits. So the attempt at narrowing fails. In this section, the bad findViewById call is another attempt to do narrowing — assigning the View value returned by a method call to a TextView variable. The TextView class is a subclass of the View class, so the assignment fails miserably.

But in so many of this book's examples, you prevent this failure. You appease the Java gods by adding a casting operator to the code. You tell Java to convert whatever pops out of the findViewById method call into a TextView object.

```
textView = (TextView) findViewById(R.id.textView1);
```

While you're typing the code, Java humors you and says, "Your casting operator shows me that you're aware of the difference between a TextView and any old View. I'll do my best to interpret the View object that I find at runtime as a TextView object." (Actually, while you're typing the code, Java says nothing. The fact that Java doesn't display any error messages when you use this casting trick is a good sign. Java's casting feature saves the day!)

REMEMBER

Casting prevents you from seeing an error message while you develop your code. In that way, casting is quite a useful feature of Java. But casting can't save you if your code contains runtime errors. When you type

```
textView = (TextView) findViewById(R.id.textView1);
```

you verify that the name textView represents a TextView widget. When the app runs, Java grabs the R.id.textView widget from the activity_main.xml file, and everything works just fine. But you may sometimes forget to check your R.java names against the components in the XML file. A call to findViewById surprisingly spits out a Button component when your casting tells Java to expect a TextView widget. When this happens, Java chokes on the casting operator and your app crashes during its run. Back to the drawing board!

CROSS-
REFERENCE

For a more complete discussion of casting, see Chapter 6.

4

Powering Android with Java Code

Chapter **11**
The Inside Story

I n common English usage, an *insider* is someone with information that's not available to most people. An insider gets special information because of her position within an organization.

American culture has many references to insiders. Author John Gunther became famous for writing *Inside Europe* and *Inside Africa* and other books in his *Inside* series. On TV crime shows, an inside job is a theft or a murder committed by someone who works in the victim's own company. So significant is the power of inside information that, in most countries, insider stock trading is illegal.

In the same way, a Java class can live inside another Java class. When this happens, the inner class has useful insider information. This chapter explains why.

A Button-Click Example

The last listing in Chapter 3 illustrates the industrial-strength way to make a button respond to a click. In Chapter 3, I treat the listing like a black box. I show you the listing, but I don't write much about it.

Now you're reading Chapter 11, and you know a lot about Java. You know about classes, about classes that extend other classes, and about interfaces. (Chapters 9 and 10 deal with these topics.) So in this chapter, I can introduce Java's inner classes, and I can build up to the code in that Chapter 3 listing.

I start with the code in Listings 11-1 and 11-2.

LISTING 11-1: **Your Main Activity**

```
package com.allmycode.a11_01;

import android.support.v7.app.AppCompatActivity;
import android.os.Bundle;
import android.widget.Button;
import android.widget.TextView;

public class MainActivity extends AppCompatActivity {
  Button button;
  TextView textView;

  @Override
  protected void onCreate(Bundle savedInstanceState) {
    super.onCreate(savedInstanceState);
    setContentView(R.layout.activity_main);

    button = (Button) findViewById(R.id.button);
    button.setOnClickListener(new MyOnClickListener(this));

    textView = (TextView) findViewById(R.id.textView);
  }

}
```

LISTING 11-2: **A Class Listens for Button Clicks**

```
package com.allmycode.a11_01;

import android.view.View;
import android.view.View.OnClickListener;

public class MyOnClickListener implements OnClickListener {
  MainActivity caller;

  public MyOnClickListener(MainActivity activity) {
    caller = activity;
  }
```

```
public void onClick(View view) {
    caller.textView.setText(R.string.you_clicked);
  }
}
```

A run of the code in Listings 11-1 and 11-2 is shown in Figures 11-1 and 11-2.

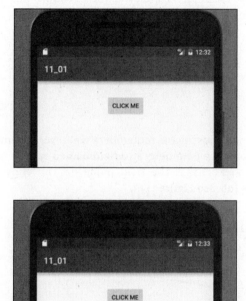

FIGURE 11-1:
Beginning a run
of the code in
Listings 11-1
and 11-2.

FIGURE 11-2:
What you see
after clicking the
button in
Listings 11-1
and 11-2.

**CROSS-
REFERENCE**

In Listing 11-2, the expression `R.string.you_clicked` stands for the string `"You clicked the button!"`. For details, see this chapter's later section "Android String resources (A slight detour)."

In Android, every button has a `setOnClickListener` method. When you call a button's `setOnClickListener` method, you tell Java that an object should respond when the user clicks the button. And what does *respond* mean? In the case of a button click, the responding object always runs its `onClick` method. So in Listing 11-1, the statement

```
button.setOnClickListener(new MyOnClickListener(this));
```

tells Java to run a particular object's `onClick` method when the user clicks the button.

In Listing 11-1, the responding object is a brand-new instance of the `MyOnClickListener` class. That's good, because I declare the `MyOnClickListener` class in Listing 11-2.

So far, so good. But, in Listing 11-1, what's that word `this` doing in the call to the `MyOnClickListener` constructor? To answer the question, take another peek at some code from Listing 11-2:

```
MainActivity caller;

public MyOnClickListener(MainActivity activity) {
   caller = activity;
}
```

The `MyOnClickListener` constructor remembers whatever parameter you pass to it. The constructor stores the parameter in a field named `caller`. So if you execute `new MyOnClickListener(this)`, the field name `caller` ends up referring to whatever `this` stands for. See Figure 11-3.

```
MainActivity caller;

public MyOnClickListener(MainActivity activity) {

   caller = activity;
}
```

The word `this` always stands for the object in which the word `this` appears. In Listing 11-1, the word `this` stands for the object that's described in Listing 11-1 — the `MainActivity` object. So in Listing 11-2, the field name `caller` ends up referring to the `MainActivity` described in Listing 11-1. That's interesting! Figure 11-4 illustrates the situation.

If `caller` refers to the stuff that's declared in Listing 11-1, `caller.textView` refers to the `textView` field in Listing 11-1. So, in Listing 11-2, the statement

```
caller.textView.setText(R.string.you_clicked);
```

tells Java to put the `R.string.you_clicked` string (the words `You clicked the button!`) into the activity's `textView` component. And that's how the words `You clicked the button!` get to appear on the screen shown in Figure 11-2. Figure 11-5 shows you what happens when Java runs the code.

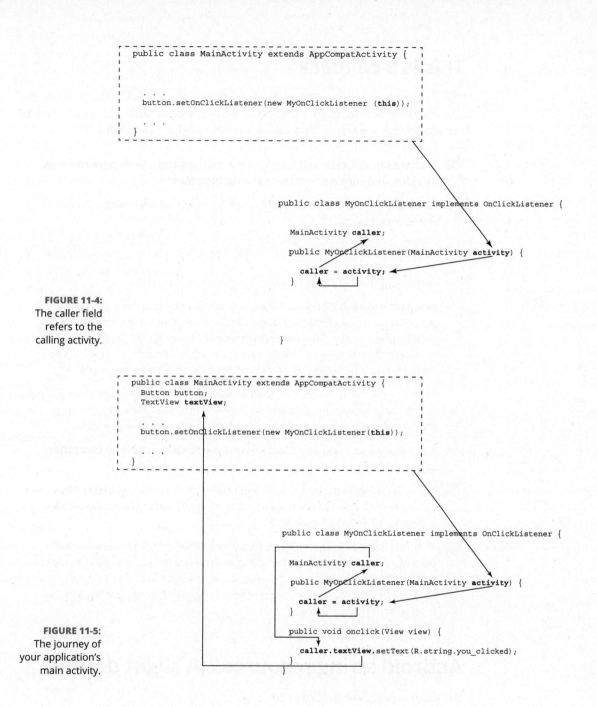

```
public class MainActivity extends AppCompatActivity {

    . . .
    button.setOnClickListener(new MyOnClickListener (this));

    . . .
}
```

```
public class MyOnClickListener implements OnClickListener {

    MainActivity caller;

    public MyOnClickListener(MainActivity activity) {

        caller = activity;
    }

}
```

FIGURE 11-4:
The caller field refers to the calling activity.

```
public class MainActivity extends AppCompatActivity {
    Button button;
    TextView textView;

    . . .
    button.setOnClickListener(new MyOnClickListener(this));

    . . .
}
```

```
public class MyOnClickListener implements OnClickListener {

    MainActivity caller;

    public MyOnClickListener(MainActivity activity) {

        caller = activity;
    }

    public void onclick(View view) {

        caller.textView.setText(R.string.you_clicked);
    }
}
```

FIGURE 11-5:
The journey of your application's main activity.

This is a callback

The pattern that I use in Listings 11-1 and 11-2 is known as a *callback*. When the user clicks the button, the `MyOnClickListener` object in Listing 11-2 calls back to the activity that created it. This callback is possible for two reasons:

>> **Android's built-in `setOnClickListener` method expects its parameter to implement Android's `OnClickListener` interface.**

I looked online for the first line of the `setOnClickListener` method's code. Here's what I found:

```
public void setOnClickListener(OnClickListener l)
```

Remember that `OnClickListener` is an interface, not a class.

When you call `setOnClickListener`, you pass an object to the method. The `setOnClickListener` method doesn't know much about that object's class. The method doesn't know whether you'll pass it one of your `MyOnClickListener` objects or a `BagOfCheese` object or a `WhateverElse` object. The `setOnClickListener` method wants the flexibility to accept any of those objects as its parameter.

All the `setOnClickListener` method knows is that it wants the object that you pass to it to implement Android's `OnClickListener` interface. That's why, in Listing 11-2, the `MyOnClickListener` class implements the `OnClickListener` interface.

>> **The `MyOnClickListener` object knows how to call back the activity that constructed it.**

Again, in Listing 11-1, the `MyOnClickListener` constructor call passes `this` to its new `MyOnClickListener` object. ("Call *me* back," says your activity's code in Listing 11-1.) Refer to Figure 11-5.

Then, in Listing 11-2, the `MyOnClickListener` constructor makes a mental note of who gets called back, by storing a reference to your activity in its own `caller` field. So, when push comes to shove, the code in Listing 11-2 calls back `caller.textView.setText`, which changes the words displayed in the original activity's `textView`.

Android string resources (A slight detour)

Here's an experiment for you to try:

1. **Start with this statement (or a statement much like this statement) in Android Studio's editor:**

```
textView.setText("You clicked the button!");
```

2. Click the mouse on the `"You clicked the button!"` string. When you do, you see a message about Android resources. (See Figure 11-6.)

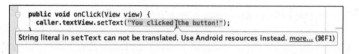

3. In response to the message, press Alt+Enter. When you do, you see a list of suggested actions. (See Figure 11-7.)

4. In the list of suggested actions, select the Extract String Resource action.

When you do, Android Studio displays an Extract Resource dialog box. (See Figure 11-8.)

5. **In the dialog box's name field, type you_clicked, or something like that.**

Type something with only letters, digits, and underscores — something that reminds you about the "You clicked the button!" string's text.

6. **In the Extract Resource dialog box, click OK.**

When you do all this, Android Studio replaces the "You clicked the button!" string with the expression R.string.you_clicked. (Refer to Listing 11-2.) This expression stands for the "You clicked the button!" string because Android Studio has also added a line to your project's app/res/values/strings.xml file:

```
<resources>
    <string name="app_name">11_01</string>
    <string name="you_clicked">You clicked the button!</string>
    <string name="click_me">CLICK ME</string>
</resources>
```

When you run the project, Android looks up the meaning of R.string.you_clicked the same way Android finds a TextView component when you write R.id.textView. Some details are in Chapter 3.

WARNING

Android Studio's editor doesn't always show you the text that's actually in your Java code. After you've followed the previous steps, you may still see

```
textView.setText("You clicked the button!");
```

in the editor. If you hover the mouse over the "You clicked the button!" string, you see a popup showing the text that's actually in your code — the R.string.you_clicked expression.

While you're looking at my little strings.xml file, notice the file's CLICK ME line. When I created the app belonging to Listings 11-1 and 11-2, I started by putting CLICK ME on the face of the button using the Designer tool's Properties pane. Then I changed the Designer tool to its Text mode, where I saw the following lines in the activity_main.xml file:

```
<Button
    android:text="CLICK ME"
```

I clicked my mouse on the code's "CLICK ME" value and followed steps similar to those for my "You clicked the button!" string. As a result, Android Studio changed the activity_main.xml file's lines to

```
<Button
    android:text="@string/click_me"
```

and added the CLICK ME line in the strings.xml file.

What's the purpose of all this R.string and @string stuff? Don't you have enough problems following your code's logic without having to look up the values of things like R.string.you_clicked? To discover an important advantage of string resources, try this experiment:

1. **Follow this section's steps to create an R.string.you_clicked resource.**

2. **Open your project's app/res/values/strings.xml file in Android Studio's editor.**

   At the top of the editor, you see a notification about something called the Translations editor.

3. **Click the translation notification's Open Editor link.**

   As a result, Android Studio's Translations Editor appears. (See Figure 11-9.)

Key	Default Value	Unt...
app_name	11_01	☐
click_me	CLICK ME	☐
you_clicked	You clicked the button!	☐

Key:
Default Value:
Translation:

FIGURE 11-9:
The Translations
editor.

4. **Near the top of the Translations Editor, click the Globe icon.**

   A list of language locales appears. (See Figure 11-10.)

   For the full scoop on language locales, visit www.iso.org/iso/country_codes.

ON THE
WEB

5. **Select a language locale from the list.**

   For this exercise, I select French (fr). As a result, the strings.xml branch in the Project tool window now has two subbranches. Both subbranches sport the label strings.xml, but the new subbranch's icon is a tiny picture of the flag of France. (See Figure 11-11.)

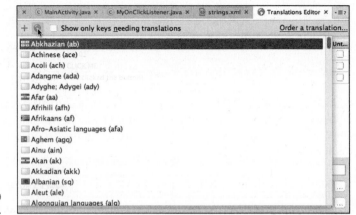

FIGURE 11-10
Select a language.

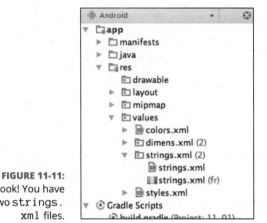

FIGURE 11-11:
Look! You have
two strings.
xml files.

In the Translations Editor, the term *you_clicked* is in red because you haven't yet translated *You clicked the button!* into French. The same is true for other terms that you haven't yet translated.

6. **Double-click the French (fr) column in the *you_clicked* row. In that column, type *Vous avez cliqué sur le bouton!* and then press Enter.**

Now, in the French version of the strings.xml file, you can find the following line:

```
<string name="you_clicked">Vous avez cliqué sur le bouton!</string>
```

(Sorry. The Translations Editor doesn't do any translating for you. The Translations Editor only adds code to your project when you type in the translations of words and phrases.)

7. **If you're ambitious, you can repeat these steps for the text on the face of the button.**

   With *R.string.click_me* referring to the English words *CLICK ME*, create the French translation *CLIQUEZ SUR-MOI*.

8. **Test your app.**

   As with most devices, the emulator has a setting for Language & Input. Change this setting to French (France), and suddenly your app looks like the display in Figure 11-12.

FIGURE 11-12:
C'est formidable!

REMEMBER

In most of this book's examples, I keep your life simple by putting Java `String` literals in calls to `setText`. I also put English language phrases in layout files by typing the phrases in Android Studio's Properties pane. It's all good for beginners, but professional Android developers favor this section's use of string resources. With string resources, you separate the words the user sees from the code, making it easy to provide translations. This is great because, when you upload an app to Google Play, the app is available to people in more than 137 countries.

Introducing Inner Classes

Does the diagram in Figure 11-5 seem unnecessarily complicated? Look at all those arrows! You might expect to see a few somersaults as the `caller` object bounces from place to place! The `MyOnClickListener` class (refer to Listing 11-2) devotes much of its code to obsessively keeping track of this `caller` object.

Another problem with Listings 11-1 and 11-2 is the way one class tinkers with the other class's value. In Listing 11-2, with the line

```
caller.textView.setText(R.string.you_clicked);
```

the `MyOnClickListener` class changes the text in the `MainActivity` class's `textView` variable. That's not good programming practice. It's like sneaking into someone's house and moving some furniture around. It may be okay, but it's always disconcerting.

Is there a better way to handle a simple button click?

There is. You can define a class inside another class. When you do, you're creating an *inner class*. It's a lot like any other class. But within an inner class's code, you can refer to the enclosing class's fields with none of the froufrou in Listing 11-2. That's why, at the beginning of this chapter, I sing the praises of insider knowledge.

One big class with its own inner class can replace both Listings 11-1 and 11-2. And the new inner class requires none of the exotic gyrations that you see in the old `MyOnClickListener` class. Listing 11-3 contains this wonderfully improved code.

LISTING 11-3:   **A Class within a Class**

```
package com.allmycode.a11_03;

import android.support.v7.app.AppCompatActivity;
import android.os.Bundle;
import android.view.View;
import android.view.View.OnClickListener;
import android.widget.Button;
import android.widget.TextView;

public class MainActivity extends AppCompatActivity {
  Button button;
  TextView textView;

  @Override
  protected void onCreate(Bundle savedInstanceState) {
    super.onCreate(savedInstanceState);
    setContentView(R.layout.activity_main);

    button = (Button) findViewById(R.id.button);
    button.setOnClickListener(new MyOnClickListener());

    textView = (TextView) findViewById(R.id.textView);
  }

  class MyOnClickListener implements OnClickListener {
```

```
    public void onClick(View view) {
        textView.setText(R.string.you_clicked);
    }
  }

}
```

When you run the code in Listing 11-3, you see the results shown earlier, in Figures 11-1 and 11-2.

Notice the relative simplicity of the new MyOnClickListener class in Listing 11-3. Going from the old MyOnClickListener class (refer to Listing 11-2) to the new MyOnClickListener inner class (refer to Listing 11-3), you reduce the number of files from two to one. But aside from the shrinkage, all the complexity of Figure 11-6 is absent from Listing 11-3. The use of this, caller, and textView in Listings 11-1 and 11-2 feels like a tangled rope. But in Listing 11-3, when you pull both ends of the rope, you find that the rope *isn't* knotted.

An inner class needs no fancy bookkeeping in order to keep track of its enclosing class's fields. Near the end of Listing 11-3, the line

```
textView.setText(R.string.you_clicked);
```

refers to the MainActivity class's textView field, which is exactly what you want. It's that straightforward.

REMEMBER

In this section, I show how a class can live inside of another class. An interface can live inside of a class, too. Look at two of the import declarations in Listing 11-3:

```
import android.view.View;
import android.view.View.OnClickListener;
```

Android's View class is in the android.view package. And Android's OnClickListener interface is an interface that's declared inside the View class.

No Publicity, Please!

Notice that the code in Listing 11-3 uses the MyOnClickListener class only once. (The only use is in a call to button.setOnClickListener.) So I ask: Do you really need a name for something that's used only once? No, you don't. (If there's only one cat in the house, you can name it "Cat.")

When you give a name to your disposable class, you have to type the name twice: once when you call the class's constructor:

```
button.setOnClickListener(new MyOnClickListener());
```

and a second time when you declare the class:

```
class MyOnClickListener implements OnClickListener {
```

To eliminate this redundancy, you can substitute the entire definition of the class in the place where you'd ordinarily call the constructor. When you do this, you have an *anonymous inner class*. Listing 11-4 shows you how it works.

LISTING 11-4: **A Class with No Name (Inside a Class with a Name)**

```
package com.allmycode.a11_04;

import android.support.v7.app.AppCompatActivity;
import android.os.Bundle;
import android.view.View;
import android.view.View.OnClickListener;
import android.widget.Button;
import android.widget.TextView;

public class MainActivity extends AppCompatActivity {
  Button button;
  TextView textView;

  @Override
  protected void onCreate(Bundle savedInstanceState) {
    super.onCreate(savedInstanceState);
    setContentView(R.layout.activity_main);

    button = (Button) findViewById(R.id.button);
    button.setOnClickListener(new OnClickListener() {
      public void onClick(View view) {
        textView.setText(R.string.you_clicked);
      }
    });

    textView = (TextView) findViewById(R.id.textView);
  }
}
```

A run of the code from Listing 11-4 is shown in Figures 11-1 and 11-2. In other words, the listing does exactly the same thing as its wordier counterparts in this chapter. The big difference is that, unlike this chapter's previous examples, the listing uses an anonymous inner class.

An anonymous inner class is a lot like an ordinary inner class. The big difference is that an anonymous inner class has no name. Nowhere in Listing 11-4 do you see a name like MyOnClickListener. Instead, you see what looks like an entire class declaration inside a call to button.setOnClickListener. It's as though the setOnClickListener call says, "The following listener class, which no one else refers to, responds to the button clicks."

Android Studio can turn the inner class code in Listing 11-3 into the anonymous class code in Listing 11-4. Here's how:

1. **View the code from Listing 11-3 in the Android Studio editor.**

2. **In the editor, click your mouse on either occurrence of the word MyOnClickListener.**

3. **On the Android Studio main menu, choose Refactor ➪ Inline.**

   The Inline to Anonymous Class dialog box appears, as shown in Figure 11-13.

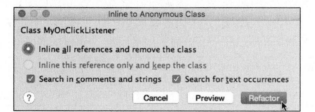

FIGURE 11-13: The Inline to Anonymous Class dialog box.

4. **In the dialog box, select the Inline All References and Remove the Class radio button.**

5. **Click OK.**

   As a result, Android Studio dismisses the dialog box and creates the code in Listing 11-4.

As far as I'm concerned, the most difficult aspect of using an anonymous inner class is keeping track of the code's parentheses, curly braces, and other non-alphabetic characters. Notice, for example, the string of closing punctuation characters — !");}}); — that straddles a few lines in Listing 11-4. The indentation in that listing helps a little bit when you try to read a big *mush* of anonymous inner class code, but it doesn't help a lot. Fortunately, there's a nice correspondence between the code in Listing 11-3 and the anonymized code in Listing 11-4. Figure 11-14 illustrates this correspondence.

I feel obliged to include a written explanation of the material in Figure 11-14. Here goes:

> To go from a named inner class to an anonymous inner class, you replace the named class's constructor call with the entire class declaration. In place of the class name, you put the name of the interface that the inner class implements (or, possibly, the name of the class that the inner class extends).

If you find my explanation helpful, I'm pleased. But if you don't find it helpful, I'm neither offended nor surprised. When I create a brand-new inner class, I find my gut feeling and Figure 11-14 to be more useful than Java's formal grammar rules.

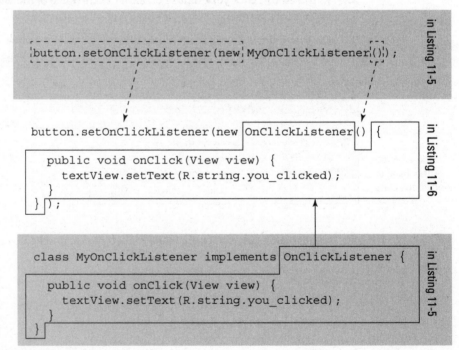

FIGURE 11-14: Turning ordinary inner class code into anonymous inner class code.

My humble advice: Start by writing code with no inner classes, such as the code in Listing 11-3. Later, when you become bored with ordinary Java classes, experiment by changing some of your ordinary classes into anonymous inner classes.

Lambda Expressions

If you open Listing 11-4 in Android Studio's editor and hover the mouse over the words `new OnClickListener`, you get an interesting surprise. (See Figure 11-15.) Android Studio tells you that you can replace the anonymous inner class with a lambda expression.

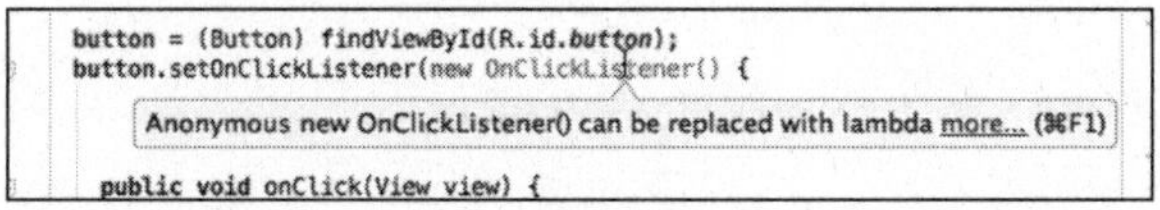

FIGURE 11-15:
You can create a lambda expression.

```
button = (Button) findViewById(R.id.button);
button.setOnClickListener(new OnClickListener() {

    Anonymous new OnClickListener() can be replaced with lambda more... (⌘F1)

    public void onClick(View view) {
```

Okay. What's a lambda expression? For starters, *lambda* is a letter in the Greek alphabet, and the term *lambda expression* comes from papers written in the 1930s by mathematician Alonzo Church.

In 2013, Oracle released Java 8, adding lambda expressions to the Java language. And in 2016, Google made Java 8 features available to Android developers.

I still haven't told you what a lambda expression is. A *lambda expression* is a concise way of declaring an interface that contains only one method. In Listing 11-4, the anonymous `OnClickListener` has only one method, namely, the `onClick` method. So you can replace this anonymous `OnClickListener` with a lambda expression.

If you respond to the message in Figure 11-15 by pressing Alt+Enter, Android Studio offers you a Replace with Lambda option. If you accept this option, Android Studio turns your code into the stuff shown in Listing 11-5.

LISTING 11-5: **Using a Lambda Expression**

```
package com.allmycode.a11_05;

import android.os.Bundle;
import android.support.v7.app.AppCompatActivity;
import android.widget.Button;
import android.widget.TextView;

public class MainActivity extends AppCompatActivity {
  Button button;
  TextView textView;
```

(continued)

LISTING 11-5:   *(continued)*

```
@Override
protected void onCreate(Bundle savedInstanceState) {
  super.onCreate(savedInstanceState);
  setContentView(R.layout.activity_main);

  button = (Button) findViewById(R.id.button);
  button.setOnClickListener(view -> textView.setText(R.string.you_clicked));

  textView = (TextView) findViewById(R.id.textView);
}

}
```

The code in Listing 11-5 does exactly the same thing as the code in Listings 11-1 to 11-6. The only difference is that Listing 11-5 uses a lambda expression. Figure 11-16 illustrates the transition from a class that implements a one-method interface to a lambda expression.

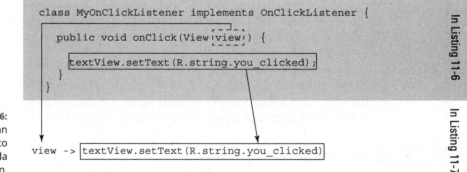

FIGURE 11-16: Turning an interface into a lambda expression.

In Figure 11-16, notice the lightweight role of the word view. When you declare an onClick method, you give the method a parameter of type View even if the statements inside the method don't use that parameter. In the same way, when you create a lambda expression for an onClick method, you preface the -> symbol with a parameter name, even if you don't use that parameter name to the left of the -> symbol.

TECHNICAL STUFF

In order to use lambda expressions, you must satisfy certain requirements. For example, you must compile your code with Java 8 or higher. Your Android Studio version must be 2.1 or higher. And your project's build.gradle file must include the following code:

```
android {
  ...
  defaultConfig {
    ...
    jackOptions {
      enabled true
    }
  }
  ...
}
```

TIP

A lambda expression may have more than one parameter to the left of the -> symbol. If it does, you must enclose all the parameters in parentheses and separate the parameters from one another with commas. For example, the expression

```
(price1, price2) -> price1 + price2
```

is a valid lambda expression.

If you're comfortable with lambda expressions, Listing 11-5 is much more readable than the earlier listings in this chapter. What started out as about ten lines of code in Listing 11-2 has become only part of a line in Listing 11-5.

Chapter **12**

Dealing with a Bunch of Things at a Time

All the world's a class,

And all the data, merely objects.

— JIMMY SHAKESPEARE, 11-YEAR-OLD COMPUTER GEEK

A *class* is a blueprint for things, and an *object* is a thing made from the blueprint. By *thing*, I mean a particular employee, a customer, an Android activity, or a more ethereal element, such as an `SQLiteOpenHelper`.

Android's `SQLiteOpenHelper` class assists developers in the creation of databases. An `SQLiteOpenHelper` doesn't look like anything in particular, certainly not like an employee or a bag of cheese. Nevertheless, `SQLiteOpenHelper` is a class.

This chapter covers another thing that you might not normally consider a class or an object — namely, a bunch of things. I use the word *bunch*, by the way, to avoid the formal terminology. (There's nothing wrong with the formal terminology, but I want to save it for this chapter's official grand opening, in the first section.)

Creating a Collection Class

A *collection class* is a class whose job is to store a bunch of objects at a time — a bunch of String objects, a bunch of BagOfCheese objects, a bunch of tweets, or whatever. You can create a collection class with the code in Listing 12-1.

LISTING 12-1: **Making an ArrayList**

```
package com.allmycode.a12_01;

import android.support.v7.app.AppCompatActivity;
import android.os.Bundle;
import android.widget.TextView;

import java.util.ArrayList;

public class MainActivity extends AppCompatActivity {
  TextView textView;

  @Override
  protected void onCreate(Bundle savedInstanceState) {
    super.onCreate(savedInstanceState);
    setContentView(R.layout.activity_main);

    textView = (TextView) findViewById(R.id.textView);

    ArrayList arrayList = new ArrayList();
    arrayList.add("Hello");
    arrayList.add(", ");
    arrayList.add("readers");
    arrayList.add("!");

    textView.setText("");

    for (int i = 0; i < 4; i++) {
      textView.append((String) arrayList.get(i));
    }
  }
}
```

When you run the code in Listing 12-1, you see the output shown in Figure 12-1.

FIGURE 12-1:
Running the code
in Listing 12-1.

The code in Listing 12-1 constructs a new ArrayList instance and makes the arrayList variable refer to that new instance. The ArrayList class is one of many kinds of collection classes.

REMEMBER

The statement ArrayList arrayList = new ArrayList() creates an empty list of things and makes the arrayList variable refer to that empty list. What does a list look like when it's empty? I don't know. I guess it looks like a blank sheet of paper. Anyway, the difference between having an empty list and having *no* list is important. Before executing ArrayList arrayList = new ArrayList(), you have no list. After executing ArrayList arrayList = new ArrayList(), you have a list that happens to be empty.

After calling arrayList.add, the list is no longer empty. The code in Listing 12-1 calls arrayList.add four times in order to put these four objects (all strings) into the list:

» "Hello"

» ", "

» "readers"

» "!"

Each object in the list has an *index* — a number from 0 to 3. You can think of an object's index as the object's position in the list. The string "Hello" has index 0, the string ", " has index 1, the string "readers" has index 2, and the string "!" has index 3.

REMEMBER

In a Java collection, the initial index is always 0, not 1.

An ArrayList instance's get method fetches the object for a particular index. So, in Listing 12-1, arrayList.get(0) is "Hello", arrayList.get(1) is ", ", and so on. To display all the strings in the list, the for statement in Listing 12-1 marches from index 0 to index 1, and then 2, and finally 3.

More casting

Notice the use of casting in Listing 12-1.

```
textView.append((String) arrayList.get(i));
```

When you create an ArrayList the way I did in Listing 12-1, Java assumes that the list contains things of type Object. In Java's class hierarchy, the Object class is the ancestor of all other classes. In fact, the parent class of Java's String class is the Object class.

When you call

```
arrayList.add("Hello");
```

Java says "That's nice. The developer has added a kind of Object to the arrayList." And Java is happy.

Notice what Java *doesn't* say. Java doesn't say "I'll remember that the developer added something of type String to the arrayList." In fact, Java forgets about this. By the time you get to the statement

```
textView.append((String) arrayList.get(i));
```

Java has forgotten all about the string "Hello". All Java knows is that you're trying to get an Object of some kind from the arrayList. So Java would get upset if you wrote

```
// With arrayList declared as in Listing 12-1, don't do this:
textView.append(arrayList.get(i));
```

The textView.append method wants its parameter to be a character sequence of some kind, and an Object that you obtain when you call the arrayList object's get method isn't necessarily a character sequence. That's why, in Listing 12-1, I have to cast the result of arrayList.get(i). This casting tells Java that, this time around, I expect the thing that it gets from the arrayList to be a String.

REMEMBER

Casting isn't a magic cure-all. The casting in Listing 12-1 is okay because all the objects in the arrayList have type String. But if, for some reason, the thing that Java obtains from (String) arrayList.get(i) isn't a String, the call to textView.append crashes and the person using your app gives you a bad rating on Google Play. You don't want that to happen.

Java generics

Starting with Java 5, the collection classes use generic types. You can recognize a generic type because of the angle brackets around its type name. For example, the following declaration uses String for a generic type:

```
ArrayList<String> arrayList = new ArrayList<>();
```

This improved declaration tells Java that the arrayList variable refers to a bunch of objects, each of which is an instance of String. When you substitute this new declaration in place of the nongeneric declaration from Listing 12-1, you don't need casting. Listing 12-2 has the code.

LISTING 12-2: **Using Java Generics**

```java
package com.allmycode.a12_02;

import android.support.v7.app.AppCompatActivity;
import android.os.Bundle;
import android.widget.TextView;

import java.util.ArrayList;

public class MainActivity extends AppCompatActivity {
  TextView textView;

  @Override
  protected void onCreate(Bundle savedInstanceState) {
    super.onCreate(savedInstanceState);
    setContentView(R.layout.activity_main);

    textView = (TextView) findViewById(R.id.textView);

    ArrayList<String> arrayList = new ArrayList<>();
    arrayList.add("Hello");
    arrayList.add(", ");
    arrayList.add("readers");
    arrayList.add("!");

    textView.setText("");
```

(continued)

LISTING 12-2: *(continued)*

```
    for (int i = 0; i < 4; i++) {
      textView.append(arrayList.get(i));
    }
  }
}
```

You can get away with using the nongeneric declaration in Listing 12-1. But creating a nongeneric collection has some disadvantages. When you don't use generics (as in Listing 12-1), you create a collection that might contain objects of any kind. In that case, Java can't take advantage of any special properties of the items in the collection. In Listing 12-1, you can't call `textView.append` without doing some casting. In some other code, nongeneric declarations may have other limitations.

REMEMBER

With its use of generics, the `ArrayList` declaration in Listing 12-2 has two pairs of angle brackets. The first pair contains the word `String` — the name of the class whose instances are being stuffed into the collection. The second pair of angle brackets is empty.

Here's another example using Java generics. Chapter 9 starts with a description of the `BagOfCheese` class. The declaration looks like this:

```
package com.allmycode.a09_01;

public class BagOfCheese {
  public String kind;
  public double weight;
  public int daysAged;
  public boolean isDomestic;
}
```

You can put a few `BagOfCheese` objects into a nongeneric collection:

```
ArrayList bags = new ArrayList();
```

But when your code gets items from the collection or makes use of the collection's items in any way, Java remembers only that the items in the collection are objects. Java doesn't remember that they're `BagOfCheese` objects. To display a bag's `kind` field, you can't write

```
// If arrayList isn't generic, don't do this:
textView.append(arrayList.get(i).kind);
```

In fact, you can't write arrayList.get(i).kind in any context, even if you're trying not to display what you got. Java doesn't remember that arrayList.get(i) is always a BagOfCheese instance. So Java refuses to reference the object's kind field.

Using casting, you can remind Java that the item you're getting from arrayList is a BagOfCheese instance:

```
textView.append(((BagOfCheese)arrayList.get(i)).kind);
```

But look at all the parentheses you need in order to make the casting work correctly. It's a mess.

If you tweak the code to make arrayList generic, Java knows that what you get from arrayList is always a BagOfCheese instance, and every BagOfCheese instance has a kind field:

```
ArrayList<BagOfCheese> bags = new ArrayList<>();
```

Then the statement textView.append(arrayList.get(i).kind) is okay.

You can use generics to create your own collection class. When you do, the generic type serves as a placeholder for an otherwise unknown type. Listing 12-3 contains a home-grown declaration of an OrderedPair class.

LISTING 12-3: **A Custom-Made Collection Class**

```
package com.allmycode.a12_04;

public class OrderedPair<T> {
  private T x;
  private T y;

  public T getX() {
    return x;
  }

  public void setX(T x) {
    this.x = x;
  }
  public T getY() {
    return y;
  }
```

(continued)

LISTING 12-3:   *(continued)*

```
public void setY(T y) {
  this.y = y;
 }
}
```

An OrderedPair object has two components: an x component and a y component. If you remember your high school math, you can probably plot ordered pairs of numbers on a two-dimensional grid. But who says that every ordered pair must contain numbers? The newly declared OrderedPair class stores objects of type T, and T can stand for any Java class or interface. In Listing 12-4, I show you how to create an ordered pair of BagOfCheese objects.

LISTING 12-4:   Using the Custom-Made Collection Class

```
package com.allmycode.a12_04;

import android.support.v7.app.AppCompatActivity;
import android.os.Bundle;
import android.widget.TextView;

import com.allmycode.a09_01.BagOfCheese;

public class MainActivity extends AppCompatActivity {
  TextView textView;

  @Override
  protected void onCreate(Bundle savedInstanceState) {
    super.onCreate(savedInstanceState);
    setContentView(R.layout.activity_main);

    textView = (TextView) findViewById(R.id.textView);

    OrderedPair<BagOfCheese> pair = new OrderedPair<>();

    BagOfCheese bag = new BagOfCheese();
    bag.kind = "Muenster";
    pair.setX(bag);

    bag = new BagOfCheese();
    bag.kind = "Brie";
    pair.setY(bag);
```

```
        textView.setText("");
        textView.append(pair.getX().kind);
        textView.append("\n");
        textView.append(pair.getY().kind);
    }
}
```

Java's wrapper classes

Chapters 5 and 9 describe primitive types and reference types:

>> **Each primitive type is baked into the language.**

Java has eight primitive types.

>> **Each reference type is a class or an interface.**

You can define your own reference type. So the number of reference types in Java is potentially endless.

The difference between primitive types and reference types is one of Java's most controversial features. Here's one of the primitive-versus-reference-type "gotchas:" You can't store a primitive value in an ArrayList. You can write

```
// THIS IS OKAY:
ArrayList<String> arrayList = new ArrayList<>();
```

because String is a reference type. But you can't write

```
// DON'T DO THIS:
ArrayList<int> arrayList = new ArrayList<>();
```

because int is a primitive type. Fortunately, each of Java's primitive types has a *wrapper* type, which is a reference type whose purpose is to contain another type's value. For example, an object of Java's Integer type contains a single int value. An object of Java's Double type contains a single double value. An object of Java's Character type contains a single char value. You can't create an ArrayList of int values, but you can create an ArrayList of Integer values:

```
// THIS IS OKAY:
ArrayList<Integer> arrayList = new ArrayList<>();
```

TIP

Every primitive type's name begins with a lowercase letter. Each of the corresponding wrapper types' names begins with an uppercase letter.

In addition to containing primitive values, wrapper classes provide useful methods for working with primitive values. For example, the `Integer` **wrapper class** contains `parseInt` and other useful methods for working with `int` values:

```
String string = "17";
int number = Integer.parseInt(string);
```

On the downside, working with wrapper types can be clumsy. For example, you can't use arithmetic operators with Java's numeric wrapper types. Here's the way I usually create two `Integer` values and add them together:

```
Integer myInteger = new Integer(3);
Integer myOtherInteger = new Integer(15);


Integer sum = myInteger.intValue() + myOtherInteger.intValue();
```

A call to `intValue` gets an ordinary primitive `int` from an `Integer`. I can use the plus sign to add these `int` values. Java lets me assign the resulting `int` value to the `Integer` variable `sum`.

Stepping Through a Collection

The program in Listing 12-1 uses a `for` loop with indexes to step through a collection. The code does what it's supposed to do, but it's a bit awkward. When you're piling objects into a collection, you shouldn't have to worry about which object is first in the collection, which is second, and which is third, for example.

Java has a few features that make it easier to step through a collection of objects. This section covers those features.

Using an iterator

If you have an `ArrayList` or some other kind of collection, you can make an *iterator* from that collection. Listing 12-5 shows you how an iterator works.

LISTING 12-5: **Iterating through a Collection**

```
package com.allmycode.a12_05;

import android.support.v7.app.AppCompatActivity;
import android.os.Bundle;
import android.widget.TextView;
```

```java
import java.util.ArrayList;
import java.util.Iterator;

public class MainActivity extends AppCompatActivity {
  TextView textView;

  @Override
  protected void onCreate(Bundle savedInstanceState) {
    super.onCreate(savedInstanceState);
    setContentView(R.layout.activity_main);

    textView = (TextView) findViewById(R.id.textView);

    ArrayList arrayList = new ArrayList();
    arrayList.add("Hello");
    arrayList.add(", ");
    arrayList.add("readers");
    arrayList.add("!");

    textView.setText("");

    Iterator<String> iterator = arrayList.iterator();

    while (iterator.hasNext()) {
      textView.append(iterator.next());
    }
  }
}
```

The output from running Listing 12-5 is shown earlier, in Figure 12-1.

When you have a collection (such as an ArrayList), you can create an iterator to go along with that collection. In Listing 12-5, you create an iterator to go along with the arrayList collection, by calling

```java
Iterator<String> iterator = arrayList.iterator();
```

After you've made this call, the variable iterator refers to something that can step through all values in the arrayList collection. Then, to step from one value to the next, you call iterator.next() repeatedly. And, to find out whether another iterator.next() call will yield results, you call iterator.hasNext(). The call to iterator.hasNext() returns a boolean value: true when there are more values in the collection and false when you've already stepped through all the values in the collection.

The enhanced for statement

An even nicer way to step through a collection is with Java's *enhanced* for *statement*. Listing 12-6 shows you how to use it.

LISTING 12-6: **Using the Enhanced** for **Statement**

```
package com.allmycode.a12_06;

import android.os.Bundle;
import android.support.v7.app.AppCompatActivity;
import android.widget.TextView;

import java.util.ArrayList;

public class MainActivity extends AppCompatActivity {
  TextView textView;

  @Override
  protected void onCreate(Bundle savedInstanceState) {
    super.onCreate(savedInstanceState);
    setContentView(R.layout.activity_main);

    textView = (TextView) findViewById(R.id.textView);

    ArrayList<String> arrayList = new ArrayList<>();
    arrayList.add("Hello");
    arrayList.add(", ");
    arrayList.add("readers");
    arrayList.add("!");

    textView.setText("");

    for (String string : arrayList) {
      textView.append(string);
    }
  }
}
```

An enhanced for statement doesn't have a counter. Instead, the statement has the format shown in Figure 12-2.

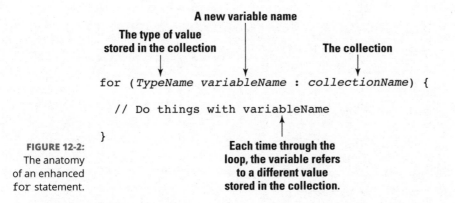

A new variable name

The type of value stored in the collection

The collection

```
for (TypeName variableName : collectionName) {

    // Do things with variableName

}
```

Each time through the loop, the variable refers to a different value stored in the collection.

FIGURE 12-2:
The anatomy of an enhanced for statement.

The enhanced for statement in Listing 12-6 achieves the same effect as the iterator in Listing 12-5 and the ordinary for statement in Listing 12-1. That is, the enhanced for statement steps through the values stored in the arrayList collection.

The enhanced for statement was introduced in Java 5.0. It's "enhanced" because, for stepping through a collection, it's easier to use than a pre-Java 5.0 for statement.

A cautionary tale

In an enhanced for statement, the variable that repeatedly stands for different values in the collection never refers directly to any of those values. Instead, this variable always contains a copy of the value in the collection. So, if you assign a value to that variable, you don't change any values inside the collection.

Here's a quiz. (Don't be scared. The quiz isn't graded.) What do you see when you run the following code?

```java
package com.allmycode.badcode;

import android.os.Bundle;
import android.support.v7.app.AppCompatActivity;
import android.widget.TextView;

import java.util.ArrayList;

public class MainActivity extends AppCompatActivity {
    TextView textView;
```

```
@Override
protected void onCreate(Bundle savedInstanceState) {
    super.onCreate(savedInstanceState);
    setContentView(R.layout.activity_main);

    textView = (TextView) findViewById(R.id.textView);

    ArrayList<String> arrayList = new ArrayList<>();
    arrayList.add("Hello");
    arrayList.add(", ");
    arrayList.add("readers");
    arrayList.add("!");

    textView.setText("");

    // THIS IS PRETTY BAD CODE
    for (String string : arrayList) {
        string = "Oops!";
        textView.append(string);
    }

    textView.append("\n");

    for (String string : arrayList) {
        textView.append(string);
    }
}
}
```

A run is shown in Figure 12-3.

FIGURE 12-3:
Running this
section's bad
code.

In the first `for` statement, the variable `string` is reassigned to refer to the word "Oops!" each time through the loop. Calls to `textView.append` display that word "Oops!" four times. But these reassignments to the string variable have no effect on the values in the arrayList. The arrayList still contains the values "Hello", ", ", "readers", and "!".

So, when Java executes the second for loop, that loop displays the words Hello, readers!.

Functional programming techniques

With Java 8 comes yet another way to step through a collection. Check the code in Listing 12-7.

LISTING 12-7: **Using a Stream**

```
package com.allmycode.a12_07;

import android.os.Bundle;
import android.support.v7.app.AppCompatActivity;
import android.widget.TextView;

import java.util.ArrayList;

public class MainActivity extends AppCompatActivity {
  TextView textView;

  @Override
  protected void onCreate(Bundle savedInstanceState) {
    super.onCreate(savedInstanceState);
    setContentView(R.layout.activity_main);

    textView = (TextView) findViewById(R.id.textView);

    ArrayList<String> arrayList = new ArrayList<>();
    arrayList.add("Hello");
    arrayList.add(", ");
    arrayList.add("readers");
    arrayList.add("!");

    textView.setText("");

    arrayList.stream().forEach(string -> textView.append(string));
  }
}
```

A *stream* is a little bit like a person working in a bucket brigade. A stream takes things in, makes few changes to the things if necessary, and then sends things out the other end. A stream modifies what it receives and then passes the modified goods on to the next stream in the line.

In Listing 12-7, the expression `arrayList.stream()` represents a stream. It's a stream that sends out the things in the `arrayList`. Those things end up in the lap of the `forEach` method call. And the `forEach` method call does something with each of those things.

What does the `forEach` method call do with each thing that it receives? To each thing, the `forEach` method call applies the lambda expression `string ->` `textView.append(string)`.

CROSS-REFERENCE

Lambda expressions pop up in the conversation in Chapter 11.

The lambda expression `string -> textView.append(string)` takes whatever it receives, calls that thing by the parameter name `string`, and then applies the `textView.append` method to `string`. In other words, the lambda expression displays (in the activity's `textView` component) whatever you give it.

Java's streams are an example of the *functional programming* style. With functional programming, you avoid *do this, then do that* solutions to problems. Instead, you call methods, which hand their results to other methods, which in turn may hand their results to other methods, and so on. You chain method calls one after another until the result that you want pops out in the end.

WARNING

Streams work only on devices running Android SDK 24 or higher. If you intend to use Java streams in a project, then, when you create the project, set the Minimum SDK to 24. If you've already created a project with Minimum SDK less than 24, open the project's `Gradle Scripts/build.grade (Module: app)` file. In that file, look for a number after the word `minSdkVersion`. Change that number to 24.

Java's Many Collection Classes

The `ArrayList` class that I use in many of this chapter's examples is only the tip of the Java collections iceberg. The Java library contains many collections classes, each with its own advantages. Table 12-1 contains an abbreviated list.

TABLE 12-1	Some Collection Classes
Class Name	Characteristic
ArrayList	A resizable array.
LinkedList	A list of values, each having a field that points to the next one in the list.
Stack	A structure (which grows from bottom to top) that's optimized for access to the topmost value. You can easily add a value to the top or remove it from the top.
Queue	A structure (which grows at one end) that's optimized for adding values to one end (the rear) and removing values from the other end (the front).
PriorityQueue	A structure, like a queue, that lets certain (higher-priority) values move toward the front.
HashSet	A collection containing no duplicate values.
HashMap	A collection of key/value pairs.

Each collection class has its own set of methods (in addition to the methods that it inherits from AbstractCollection, the ancestor of all collection classes).

ON THE
WEB

To find out which collection classes best meet your needs, visit the Android API documentation pages at http://developer.android.com/reference.

Arrays

In the "Stepping Through a Collection" section, earlier in this chapter, I cast aspersions on the use of an index in Listing 12-1. "You shouldn't have to worry about which object is first in the collection, which is second, and which is third," I write. Well, that's my story and I'm sticking to it, except in the case of an array. An array is a particular kind of collection that's optimized for indexing. That is, you can easily and efficiently find the 100th value stored in an array, the 1,000th value stored in an array, or the 1,000,000th value stored in an array.

The array is a venerable, tried-and-true feature of many programming languages, including newer languages such as Java and older languages such as FORTRAN. In fact, the array's history goes back so far that most languages (including Java) have special notation for dealing with arrays. Listing 12-8 illustrates the notation for arrays in a simple Java program.

LISTING 12-8: **Creating and Using an Array**

```
package com.allmycode.a12_08;

import android.support.v7.app.AppCompatActivity;
import android.os.Bundle;
import android.widget.TextView;

public class MainActivity extends AppCompatActivity {
  TextView textView;

  @Override
  protected void onCreate(Bundle savedInstanceState) {
    super.onCreate(savedInstanceState);
    setContentView(R.layout.activity_main);

    textView = (TextView) findViewById(R.id.textView);

    String[] myArray = new String[4];
    myArray[0] = "Hello";
    myArray[1] = ", ";
    myArray[2] = "readers";
    myArray[3] = "!";

    textView.setText("");

    for(int i = 0; i < 4; i++) {
      textView.append(myArray[i]);
    }

    textView.append("\n");

    for (String string : myArray) {
      textView.append(string);
    }
  }
}
```

Figure 12-4 shows the output of a run of the code in Listing 12-8. Both the ordinary for loop and the enhanced for loop display the same output.

FIGURE 12-4:
Running the code
in Listing 12-8.

In Listing 12-8, the ordinary `for` loop uses indexes, with each index marked by square brackets. As it is with all Java collections, the initial value's index is 0, not 1. Notice also the number 4 in the array's declaration — it indicates that "you can store 4 values in the array." The number *4 doesn't* indicate that "you can assign a value to `myArray[4]`." In fact, if you add a statement such as `myArray[4] = "Oops!"` to the code in Listing 12-8, you get a nasty error message (`Array IndexOutOfBoundsException`) when you run the program.

REMEMBER

The statement `String[] myArray = new String[4]` creates an empty array and makes the `myArray` variable refer to that empty array. The array can potentially store as many as four values. But, initially, that variable refers to an array that contains no values. It's not until Java executes the first assignment statement (`myArray[0] = "Hello"`) that the array contains any values.

You can easily and efficiently find the 100th value stored in an array (`myArray[100]`) or the 1,000,000th value stored in an array (`myArray[1000000]`). Not bad for a day's work. So, what's the downside of using an array? The biggest disadvantage of an array is that each array has a fixed limit on the number of values it can hold. When you create the array in Listing 12-8, Java reserves space for as many as four `String` values. If, later in the program, you decide that you want to store a fifth element in the array, you need some clumsy, inefficient code to make yourself a larger array. You can also overestimate the size you need for an array, as shown in this example:

```
String[] myArray = new String[20000000];
```

When you overestimate, you probably waste a lot of memory space.

Another unpleasant feature of an array is the difficulty you can have in inserting new values. Imagine having a wooden box for each year in your collection of *Emperor Constantine Comics*. The series dates back to the year 307 A.D., when Constantine became head of the Roman Empire. You have only 1,700 boxes because you're missing about six years (mostly from the years 1150 to 1155). The boxes aren't numbered, but they're stacked one next to another in chronological order in a line that's 200 meters long. (The line is as long as the 55th floor of a skyscraper is tall.)

At a garage sale in Istanbul, you find a rare edition of *Emperor Constantine Comics* from March 1152. After rejoicing over your first comic from the year 1152, you realize that you have to insert a new box into the pile between the years 1151 and 1153, which involves moving the year 2016 box about ten centimeters to the right, and then moving the 2015 box in place of the 2016 box, and then moving the 2014 box in place of the 2015 box. And so on. Life for the avid *Emperor Constantine Comics* collector is about to become tiresome! Inserting a value into the middle of a large array is equally annoying.

String resource arrays

In Chapter 11, I introduce Android's string resource feature. You put a string of characters into an `app/res/values/strings.xml` file. Then, in your Java code, you refer to that string with an `R.string.`*something_or_other* expression.

You can do the same kind of thing with an entire array of strings. First, you put a `string-array` element in your `strings.xml` file:

```
<resources>
    <string name="app_name">12_08</string>
    <string-array name="greeting_words">
        <item>Hello</item>
        <item>, </item>
        <item>readers</item>
        <item>!</item>
    </string-array>
</resources>
```

Then, in Listing 12-8, you can replace

```
String[] myArray = new String[4];
myArray[0] = "Hello";
myArray[1] = ", ";
myArray[2] = "readers";
myArray[3] = "!";
```

with the following code:

```
Resources res = getResources();
String[] myArray = res.getStringArray(R.array.greeting_words);
```

Java's varargs

In an app of some kind, you need a method that displays a bunch of words as a full sentence. How do you create such a method? You can pass a bunch of words to the sentence. In the method's body, you display each word, followed by a blank space, as shown here:

```
for (String word : words) {
  System.out.print(word);
  System.out.print(" ");
}
```

To pass words to the method, you create an array of `String` values:

```
String[] stringsE = { "Goodbye,", "kids." };
displayAsSentence(stringsE);
```

Notice the use of the curly braces in the initialization of `stringsE`. In Java, you can initialize any array by writing the array's values, separating the values from one another by commas, and surrounding the entire bunch of values with curly braces. When you do this, you create an *array initializer*.

Listing 12-9 contains an entire program to combine words into sentences.

LISTING 12-9: **A Program without Varargs**

```
package com.allmycode.a12_09;

import android.support.v7.app.AppCompatActivity;
import android.os.Bundle;
import android.widget.TextView;

public class MainActivity extends AppCompatActivity {
  TextView textView;

  @Override
  protected void onCreate(Bundle savedInstanceState) {
    super.onCreate(savedInstanceState);
    setContentView(R.layout.activity_main);

    textView = (TextView) findViewById(R.id.textView);

    String[] stringsA = { "Hello,", "I", "must", "be", "going." };
    String[] stringsB = { "     ", "-Groucho" };
```

(continued)

LISTING 12-9: *(continued)*

```java
        String[] stringsC = { "Say", "Goodnight,", "Gracie." };
        String[] stringsD = { "     ", "-Nathan Birnbaum" };
        String[] stringsE = { "Goodbye,", "kids." };
        String[] stringsF = { "     ", "-Clarabell" };

        textView.setText("");

        displayAsSentence(stringsA);
        displayAsSentence(stringsB);
        displayAsSentence(stringsC);
        displayAsSentence(stringsD);
        displayAsSentence(stringsE);
        displayAsSentence(stringsF);
    }

    void displayAsSentence(String[] words) {
        for (String word : words) {
            textView.append(word);
            textView.append(" ");
        }
        textView.append("\n");
    }
}
```

When you run the code in Listing 12-9, you see the output shown in Figure 12-5.

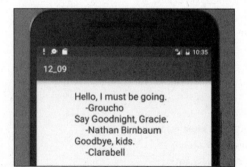

FIGURE 12-5:
Running the code
in Listing 12-9.

The code in Listing 12-9 is awkward because you have to declare six different arrays of String values. You can't combine the variable declarations and the method call. A statement such as

```java
displayAsSentence("Say", "Goodnight,", "Gracie.");
```

is illegal because the call's parameter list has three values, and because the `displayAsSentence` method (in Listing 12-9) has only one parameter (one array). You can try fixing the problem by declaring `displayAsSentence` with three parameters:

```
void displayAsSentence(String word0, String word1, String word2) {
```

But then you're in trouble when you want to pass five words to the method.

To escape from this mess, Java 5.0 introduces varargs. A parameter list with *varargs* has a type name followed by three dots. The dots represent any number of parameters, all of the same type. Listing 12-10 shows you how it works.

LISTING 12-10: **A Program with *Varargs***

```
package com.allmycode.a12_10;

import android.support.v7.app.AppCompatActivity;
import android.os.Bundle;
import android.widget.TextView;

public class MainActivity extends AppCompatActivity {
  TextView textView;

  @Override
  protected void onCreate(Bundle savedInstanceState) {
    super.onCreate(savedInstanceState);
    setContentView(R.layout.activity_main);

    textView = (TextView) findViewById(R.id.textView);

    textView.setText("");

    displayAsSentence("Hello,", "I", "must", "be", "going.");
    displayAsSentence("    ", "-Groucho");
    displayAsSentence("Say", "Goodnight,", "Gracie.");
    displayAsSentence("    ", "-Nathan Birnbaum");
    displayAsSentence("Goodbye,", "kids.");
    displayAsSentence("    ", "-Clarabell");
  }

  void displayAsSentence(String... words) {
    for (String word : words) {
```

(continued)

LISTING 12-10: *(continued)*

```
        textView.append(word);
        textView.append(" ");
      }
      textView.append("\n");
    }
}
```

In Listing 12-10, the parameter list (String... words) stands for any number of String values — one String value, one hundred String values, or even no String values. So, in Listing 12-10, I can call the displayAsSentence method with two parameters ("Goodbye,", "kids."), with three parameters ("Say", "Good night,", "Gracie."), and with five parameters ("Hello,", "I", "must", "be", "going.").

In the body of the displayAsSentence method, I treat the collection of parameters as an array. I can step through the parameters with an enhanced for statement, or I can refer to each parameter with an array index. For example, in Listing 12-10, during the first call to the displayAsSentence method, the expression words[0] stands for "Hello". During the second call to the displayAsSentence method, the expression words[2] stands for "Goodnight". And so on.

Using Collections in an Android App

If you look at the Palette in Android Studio's Designer tool, you can find the *Spinner* component. You can drag a Spinner component from the Palette onto one of your app's preview screens. A Spinner component is a drop-down list — a bunch of alternatives for the user to choose from. (See Figures 12-6, 12-7, and 12-8.) That "bunch" of alternatives is a collection of some sort. In this section, I use an array to implement the collection.

FIGURE 12-6:
A TextView
component and a
spinner.

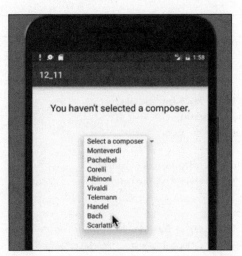

FIGURE 12-7:
The user expands
the spinner's
choices.

FIGURE 12-8:
The user has
selected Bach.

Listing 12-11 has the code.

LISTING 12-11: **Creating a Spinner**

```
package com.allmycode.a12_11;

import android.os.Bundle;
import android.support.v7.app.AppCompatActivity;
import android.view.View;
import android.widget.AdapterView;
import android.widget.AdapterView.OnItemSelectedListener;
import android.widget.ArrayAdapter;
import android.widget.Spinner;
import android.widget.TextView;

public class MainActivity extends AppCompatActivity {
```

(continued)

LISTING 12-11: *(continued)*

```
TextView textView;

@Override
protected void onCreate(Bundle savedInstanceState) {
  super.onCreate(savedInstanceState);
  setContentView(R.layout.activity_main);

  Spinner spinner = (Spinner) findViewById(R.id.spinner);
  textView = (TextView) findViewById(R.id.textView);
  String[] choices =
      {"Select a composer",
          "Monteverdi", "Pachelbel", "Corelli", "Albinoni",
          "Vivaldi", "Telemann", "Handel","Bach", "Scarlatti"};

  ArrayAdapter<String> adapter =
    new ArrayAdapter<>(this, android.R.layout.simple_spinner_item, choices);

  spinner.setAdapter(adapter);
  spinner.setOnItemSelectedListener(new MyItemSelectedListener());
}

class MyItemSelectedListener implements OnItemSelectedListener {

  @Override
  public void onItemSelected(AdapterView<?> adapterView, View view,
                             int position, long id) {

    if (position == 0) {
      textView.setText("You haven't selected a composer.");
    } else {
      textView.setText(adapterView.getItemAtPosition(position).toString());
    }
  }

  @Override
  public void onNothingSelected(AdapterView<?> adapterView) {
    // Do nothing
  }
}
}
```

To make a spinner do its job, you create a listener and an adapter.

The listener

A spinner's listener is much like a button's listener. It's a piece of code that listens for user actions and responds when an appropriate action occurs. (See Chapter 11.)

In Listing 12-11, I create a listener (an instance of my own MyItemSelectedListener class). I tell Android to notify the listener when the user selects one of the spinner's items:

```
spinner.setOnItemSelectedListener(new MyItemSelectedListener());
```

The MyItemSelectedListener class's onItemSelected method must tell Android what to do in response to the user's selection.

The adapter

You may guess that you add an item to a spinner with a call like this:

```
// Don't do this:
spinner.addRow("Monteverdi");
```

But that's not the way it works. When an Android developer thinks about a spinner, the developer thinks about two different concepts:

>> **A spinner has data.**

In Figure 12-7, the spinner's data consists of the values "Select a composer", "Monteverdi", "Pachelbel", and so on.

>> **A spinner has a "look."**

This section's spinner has a simple look. In Figure 12-6, the spinner has text on the left side and a tiny downward arrow on the right side. In Figure 12-7, each of the spinner's items has text on the left side.

A spinner's incarnation on the screen (the "look") is an object in and of itself. It's an instance of Android's AdapterView class. A similar-sounding thing, an instance of the SpinnerAdapter class, connects a spinner's data with a spinner's "look." See Figure 12-9.

The data

```
String[] choices =
    {"Select a composer",
        "Monteverdi", "Pachelbel", "Corelli", "Albinoni",
        "Vivaldi", "Telemann", "Handel","Bach", "Scarlatti"};
```

The spinner adapter

The adapter view

FIGURE 12-9:
How a spinner
works.

There are several kinds of spinner adapter, including the `ArrayAdapter` and `CursorAdapter` classes:

>> An `ArrayAdapter` gets data from a collection, such as an array or an `ArrayList`.

>> A `CursorAdapter` gets data from a database query.

In Listing 12-11, I use an `ArrayAdapter`. The `ArrayAdapter` constructor has three parameters:

>> **The first parameter is a context.**

I use `this` for the context. As in Chapter 9, the word `this` represents whatever object contains the current line of code. In Listing 12-11, `this` refers to the `MainActivity`.

>> **The second parameter is a layout.**

In Listing 12-11, the name `android.R.layout.simple_spinner_item` refers to a standard layout for one of the items in Figure 12-7.

>> **The third parameter is the source of the data.**

In Listing 12-11, I provide `choices`, which I declare to be an array of `String` values.

In Listing 12-11, notice the `onItemSelected` method's `position` parameter. When the user selects the topmost item in the spinner's list (the Select a Composer item in Figure 12-7), Android gives that `position` parameter the value 0. When the user selects the next-to-topmost item (the Monteverdi item in Figure 12-7), Android gives that `position` parameter the value 1. And so on.

In the `onItemSelected` method's body, the code checks to make sure that `position` isn't 0. If `position` isn't 0, the code plugs that `position` value into the `adapterView.getItemAtPosition` method to get the string on whatever item the user clicked. The code displays that string (`Monteverdi`, `Pachelbel`, or whichever) in a `textView` component.

Chapter **13**

An Android Social Media App

A reader from Vancouver (in British Columbia, Canada) writes:

> "Hello, Barry. I just thought I would ask that you include the area that seems to get attention from app developers: programs connecting with social sites. I look forward to reading the new book! Best regards, David."

Well, David, you've inspired me to create a Twitter app. This chapter's example does two things: Post a new tweet and get a twitter user's timeline. The app can perform many more Twitter tasks — for example, search for tweets, look for users, view trends, check friends and followers, gather suggestions, and do lots of other things that Twitter users want done. For simplicity, though, I have the app perform only two tasks: tweet and display a timeline.

I can summarize the essence of this chapter's Twitter code in two short statements. To post a tweet, the app executes

```
twitter.updateStatus("This is my tweet.");
```

And, to display a user's timeline, the app executes

```
List<twitter4j.Status> statuses = twitter.getUserTimeline("allmycode");
```

Of course, these two statements only serve as a summary, and a summary is never the same as the material it summarizes. Imagine standing on the street in Times Square and shouting this statement: "Twitter dot update status: 'This is my tweet.'" Nothing good happens because you're issuing the correct command in the wrong context. In the same way, the context surrounding a call to `twitter.updateStatus` in an app matters an awful lot.

This chapter covers all the context surrounding your calls to `twitter.updateStatus` and `twitter.getUserTimeline`. In the process, you can read about Java's exceptions — a vital feature that's available to all Java programmers.

The Twitter App's Files

You can download this chapter's code from my website (`http://allmycode.com/Java4Android`) by following the instructions in Chapter 2. As is true for any Android app, this chapter's Android Studio project contains hundreds of files. In this chapter, I concentrate on the project's `MainActivity.java` file. But a few other files require some attention.

The Twitter4J API jar file

Android has no built-in support for communicating with Twitter. Yes, the raw materials are contained in Android's libraries, but to deal with all of Twitter's requirements, someone has to paste together those raw materials in a useful way. Fortunately, several developers have done all the pasting and made their libraries available for use by others. The library that I use in this chapter is Twitter4J. Its website is `http://twitter4j.org`.

A `.jar` file is a compressed archive file containing a useful bunch of Java classes. For this chapter's example to work, your project must include a `.jar` file containing the Twitter4J libraries. If you've successfully imported this book's code into Android Studio, the `13_01` project contains the necessary `.jar` file.

TIP

You can view the contents of a `.jar` file by using WinZip or StuffIt Expander or the operating system's built-in unzipping utility. To do so, you may or may not have to change the filename from *whatever*`.jar` to *whatever*`.zip`.

If you're creating this chapter's example on your own, or if you're having trouble with the project's existing .jar files, you can add Twitter4J libraries to your project. The following instructions worked for me in mid-2016.

WARNING

Google changes these steps once in a while. So if these steps don't work for you, send me an email — the address is Java4Android@allmycode.com.

1. Visit http://twitter4j.org.

2. Find the link to download the latest stable version of Twitter4J.

To run this chapter's example, I use Twitter4J version 4.0.4. If you download a later version, it'll probably work. But I make no promises about the backward compatibility, forward compatibility, or sideward compatibility of the various Twitter4J versions. If my example doesn't run properly for you, you can search the Twitter4J site for a download link to version 4.0.4.

3. Click the link to download the Twitter4J software.

The file that I downloaded is twitter4j-4.0.4.zip.

4. Look for a twitter4j-core.jar file inside the downloaded .zip file.

In the .zip file that I downloaded, I found a file named twitter4j-core-4.0.4.jar.

5. Extract the twitter4j-core.jar file to this project's app/libs directory.

Use your operating system's File Explorer or Finder to do the extracting and copying.

6. On Android Studio's main menu, choose File ⇨ Project Structure.

The Project Structure dialog box appears.

7. In the panel on the left side of the dialog box, select App.

8. In the main body of the dialog box, select the Dependencies tab.

A list of dependencies appears. Look for a plus sign that's associated with the list of dependencies.

9. Click the plus sign.

A context menu appears.

10. On the context menu, select File Dependency.

Android Studio displays the Select Path dialog box.

11. In the Select Path dialog box, navigate to the directory containing your twitter4j-core.jar file.

REMEMBER

What I refer to as your `twitter4j-core.jar` file is probably named `twitter4j-core-4.0.4.jar` or similar.

12. Select the `twitter4j-core.jar` file and click OK.

Doing so adds your `twitter4j-core.jar` file to the Dependencies tab's list.

13. Click OK to dismiss the Project Structure dialog box.

Your project can now use the Twitter4J library's code.

The manifest file

Every Android app has an `AndroidManifest.xml` file. Listing 13-1 contains the `AndroidManifest.xml` file for this chapter's Twitter app.

LISTING 13-1: **The AndroidManifest.xml File**

```xml
<?xml version="1.0" encoding="utf-8"?>
<manifest xmlns:android="http://schemas.android.com/apk/res/android"
        package="com.allmycode.a13_01">

    <uses-permission android:name="android.permission.INTERNET"/>

    <application
        android:allowBackup="true"
        android:icon="@mipmap/ic_launcher"
        android:label="@string/app_name"
        android:supportsRtl="true"
        android:theme="@style/AppTheme">
        <activity
            android:name=".MainActivity"
            android:windowSoftInputMode="adjustPan">
            <intent-filter>
                <action android:name="android.intent.action.MAIN"/>
                <category android:name="android.intent.category.LAUNCHER"/>
            </intent-filter>
        </activity>
    </application>

</manifest>
```

When you create a new Android application project, Android Studio writes most of the code in Listing 13-1 automatically. For this chapter's project, I have to add two additional snippets of code:

>> **The** `windowSoftInputMode` **attribute tells Android what to do when the user activates the onscreen keyboard.**

The `adjustPan` value tells Android how to adjust the screen's components when the keyboard appears. (Take my word for it: The app looks ugly without this `adjustPan` value.)

>> **The** `uses-permission` **element warns Android that my app requires Internet connectivity.**

If you forget to add this `uses-permission` element (as I often do), the app doesn't obey any of your Twitter commands. And when your app fails to contact the Twitter servers, Android often displays only cryptic, unhelpful error messages.

REMEMBER

The error messages from an unsuccessful run of this chapter's Android app range from extremely helpful to extremely unhelpful. One way or another, it never hurts to read these messages. You can find most of the messages on Android Studio's Logcat pane.

CROSS-REFERENCE

For more information about `AndroidManifest.xml` files, see Chapter 4.

The main activity's layout file

Chapter 3 introduces the use of a layout file to describe the look of an activity on the screen. The layout file for this chapter's example has no extraordinary qualities. I include it in Listing 13-2 for completeness. As usual, you can import this chapter's code from my website (`http://allmycode.com/Java4Android`). But if you're living large and creating the app on your own from scratch, you can copy the contents of Listing 13-2 to the project's `res/layout/activity_main.xml` file. Alternatively, you can use Android Studio's toolset to drag and drop, point and click, or type and tap your way to the graphical layout shown in Figure 13-1.

LISTING 13-2: **The Layout File**

```
<RelativeLayout xmlns:android="http://schemas.android.com/apk/res/android"
            xmlns:tools="http://schemas.android.com/tools"
            android:layout_width="match_parent"
            android:layout_height="match_parent"
            android:paddingBottom="@dimen/activity_vertical_margin"
            android:paddingLeft="@dimen/activity_horizontal_margin"
            android:paddingRight="@dimen/activity_horizontal_margin"
            android:paddingTop="@dimen/activity_vertical_margin"
            tools:context=".MainActivity" >
```

(continued)

LISTING 13-2:   *(continued)*

```
<TextView
    android:id="@+id/textView2"
    android:layout_width="wrap_content"
    android:layout_height="wrap_content"
    android:layout_alignBaseline="@+id/editTextUsername"
    android:layout_alignBottom="@+id/editTextUsername"
    android:layout_alignLeft="@+id/editTextTweet"
    android:text="@string/at_sign"
    android:textAppearance="?android:attr/textAppearanceLarge"/>

<EditText
    android:id="@+id/editTextUsername"
    android:layout_width="wrap_content"
    android:layout_height="wrap_content"
    android:layout_above="@+id/timelineButton"
    android:layout_toRightOf="@+id/textView2"
    android:ems="10"
    android:hint="@string/type_username_here"/>

<TextView
    android:id="@+id/textViewTimeline"
    android:layout_width="wrap_content"
    android:layout_height="wrap_content"
    android:layout_alignLeft="@+id/timelineButton"
    android:layout_below="@+id/timelineButton"
    android:maxLines="100"
    android:scrollbars="vertical"
    android:text="@string/timeline_here"/>

<Button
    android:id="@+id/timelineButton"
    android:layout_width="wrap_content"
    android:layout_height="wrap_content"
    android:layout_alignLeft="@+id/textView2"
    android:layout_centerVertical="true"
    android:onClick="onTimelineButtonClick"
    android:text="@string/timeline"/>

<Button
    android:id="@+id/tweetButton"
    android:layout_width="wrap_content"
    android:layout_height="wrap_content"
    android:layout_above="@+id/editTextUsername"
```

```
        android:layout_alignLeft="@+id/editTextTweet"
        android:layout_marginBottom="43dp"
        android:onClick="onTweetButtonClick"
        android:text="@string/tweet"/>

    <EditText
        android:id="@+id/editTextTweet"
        android:layout_width="wrap_content"
        android:layout_height="wrap_content"
        android:layout_above="@+id/tweetButton"
        android:layout_alignParentLeft="true"
        android:layout_marginLeft="14dp"
        android:ems="10"
        android:hint="@string/type_your_tweet_here"/>

    <TextView
        android:id="@+id/textViewCountChars"
        android:layout_width="wrap_content"
        android:layout_height="wrap_content"
        android:layout_alignBaseline="@+id/tweetButton"
        android:layout_alignBottom="@+id/tweetButton"
        android:layout_toRightOf="@+id/timelineButton"
        android:text="@string/zero"/>

</RelativeLayout>
```

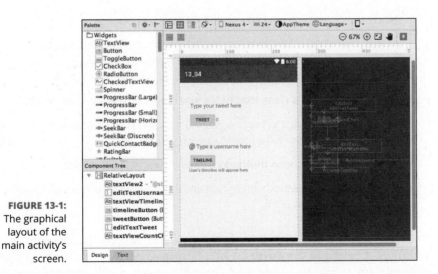

FIGURE 13-1:
The graphical layout of the main activity's screen.

How to Talk to the Twitter Server

Listing 13-3 contains a snippet of code from the main activity in this chapter's example.

LISTING 13-3: **Some Fake Java Code (Yes, It's Fake!)**

```
Twitter twitter;

// ... and later in the code ...

ConfigurationBuilder builder = new ConfigurationBuilder();
builder
    .setOAuthConsumerKey("00000000000000000000000000")
    .setOAuthConsumerSecret("1111111111111111111111111111111111111111111111111")
    .setOAuthAccessToken("222222222-333333333333333333333333333333333333333333")
    .setOAuthAccessTokenSecret("4444444444444444444444444444444444444444444444");

TwitterFactory factory = new TwitterFactory(builder.build());
twitter = factory.getInstance();
```

The code in Listing 13-3 creates an instance of the `Twitter` class.

Here's some information regarding the Twitter4J API:

>> **A `Twitter` object is a gateway to the Twitter servers.**

   A call to one of the methods belonging to a `Twitter` object can post a brand-new tweet, get another Twitter user's timeline, make favorites, add friendships, create blocks, search for users, and do other cool things.

>> **`TwitterFactory` is a class that helps you create a new `Twitter` object.**

   As the name suggests, `TwitterFactory` is a factory class. In Java, a *factory* class is a class that can call a constructor on your behalf.

>> **Calling the `getInstance` method creates a new `Twitter` object.**

   The `getInstance` method's body contains the actual constructor call. That's how factory methods work.

REMEMBER

The `ConfigurationBuilder`, `TwitterFactory`, and `Twitter` classes that I use in Listing 13-3 belong to the Twitter4J API. If, instead of using Twitter4J, you use a different API to communicate with Twitter servers, you'll use different class names. What's more, those classes probably won't match up, one for one, with the Twitter4J classes.

Using OAuth

When you run this chapter's example, the code has to talk to Twitter on your behalf. And normally, to talk to Twitter, you supply a username and password. But should you be sharing your Twitter password with any app that comes your way? Probably not. Your password is similar to the key to your house. You don't want to give copies of your house key to strangers, and you don't want an Android app to remember your Twitter password.

So how can your app post a tweet without having your Twitter password? One answer is *OAuth*, a standardized way to have apps log on to host computers.

The big, ugly strings in Listing 13-3 are OAuth strings. You get strings like this from the Twitter website. If you copy the gobbledygook correctly, your app acquires revocable permission to act on behalf of the Twitter user. And the app never gets hold of the user's password.

Now, here come the disclaimers:

>> **A discussion of how OAuth works, and why it's safer than using ordinary Twitter passwords, is far beyond the scope of this book.**

I don't pretend to explain OAuth and its mysteries in this chapter.

>> **True app security requires more than what you see in Listing 13-3.**

The goal of this chapter is to show how an app can talk to a social media site. In this chapter's code, I use OAuth and Twitter4J commands to achieve that goal as quickly as I can, without necessarily showing you the "right" way to do it. For more comprehensive coverage of OAuth, visit `https://oauth. net/`: the official website for OAuth developers.

>> **The long strings of characters in Listing 13-3 don't work.**

I'm not prepared to share my own OAuth strings with the general public, so to create Listing 13-3, I took the general outline of my real `ConfigurationBuilder` code and then pressed my nose against the keyboard to replace the characters in the OAuth strings.

To run this chapter's app, you must create your own set of OAuth keys and copy them into your Java code. The later section "Getting OAuth keys and tokens" outlines the steps.

Making a ConfigurationBuilder

In Listing 13-3, the chaining of `set` method calls, one after another, is called the *builder pattern*.

Here's the basic idea. A configuration builder has lots of properties, and you can imagine several different ways of setting those properties. For example, you could have one enormous constructor:

```
// This is not correct Twitter4J code:
ConfigurationBuilder builder = new ConfigurationBuilder(
                    "0000000000000000000", "1111111111111111111",
                    "2222222-33333333333333333", "4444444444444444444");
```

This approach is cumbersome because you must remember which string belongs in which position. In fact, it gets worse. A configuration builder has 46 different properties, and you may want to set more than four of these properties. However, a constructor with 46 parameters would be truly awful.

Another possibility is to create a blank-slate configuration builder and then set each of its properties with separate method calls.

```
// This is not correct Twitter4J code:
ConfigurationBuilder builder = new ConfigurationBuilder();
builder.setOAuthConsumerKey("0000000000000000000");
builder.setOAuthConsumerSecret("1111111111111111111");
builder.setOAuthAccessToken("2222222-33333333333333333");
builder.setOAuthAccessTokenSecret("4444444444444444444");
```

This is less awkward than having a giant constructor, but there's a better way. In the Twitter4J API, the ConfigurationBuilder class has 46 set methods. Each method applies to an existing ConfigurationBuilder instance. And each method returns, as its result, a new ConfigurationBuilder instance. So, in Listing 13-3, the statement

```
ConfigurationBuilder builder = new ConfigurationBuilder();
```

creates a blank-slate configuration builder. The next piece of code

```
builder
    .setOAuthConsumerKey("0000000000000000000000000")
```

applies to the blank-slate instance. But the value of this piece of code is a ConfigurationBuilder instance with a particular OAuth consumer key. To this enhanced instance you apply

```
.setOAuthConsumerSecret("111111111111111111111111111111111111111111111111")
```

The combined code's value is an even better ConfigurationBuilder instance — one with a particular OAuth consumer key and an OAuth consumer secret.

And so on. Each application of a `set` method takes an existing instance and yields an instance with more and better properties.

Notice how readable Listing 13-3 is compared to the incorrect code snippets in this section. This elegant way of adding properties to an object is the builder pattern.

After adding enough properties to a configuration builder, you call the builder's own `build` method to create a factory. Then you can use the factory to create an instance of the `Twitter` class:

```
TwitterFactory factory = new TwitterFactory(builder.build());
twitter = factory.getInstance();
```

Getting OAuth keys and tokens

For your Android app to communicate with Twitter servers, you need your own OAuth keys and tokens. To get them, follow this section's steps.

WARNING

The following instructions apply to the Twitter web pages for developers at the time of this book's publication. Twitter might change the design of its website at any time without notice. (At any rate, it won't notify me!)

1. **Sign in to your Twitter user account (or register for an account if you don't already have one).**

2. **Visit** `https://dev.twitter.com/apps/new`.

    If the stars are aligned harmoniously, you should see Twitter's Create an Application page.

3. **On the Create an Application page, fill in all required fields along with the (misleadingly optional) Callback URL field.**

    When I visit the page, I see the Name field, the Description field, the Website field, and the Callback URL field. All but the Callback URL field are listed as being required.

    Typing your app's name in the Name field is a no-brainer. But what do you use for the other fields? After all, you aren't creating an industrial-strength Android app. You're creating only a test app — an app to help you see how to use Twitter4J.

    The good news is that you can type almost anything in the Description field. The same is true for the Website and Callback URL fields, as long as you type things that look like real URLs.

I've never tried typing a `twitter.com` URL in either the Website or Callback URL fields, but I suspect that typing a `twitter.com` URL doesn't work.

To communicate with Twitter via an Android app, you need a callback URL. In other words, for this chapter's example, the callback URL isn't optional. Neither the Website field nor the Callback URL field has to point to a real web page. But you must fill in those two fields.

The Callback URL field isn't marked as being required. Nevertheless, you must type a URL in the Callback URL field.

4. **After agreeing to the terms, and doing the other stuff to prove that you're a good person, click the Create Your Twitter Application button.**

   Doing so brings you to a page where you manage your new application. The page has four tabs, labeled Details, Settings, Keys and Access Tokens, and Permissions.

5. **Near the top of the page, select the Permissions tab.**

6. **On the Permissions page, look for a choice of access types. Change your app's access from Read and Write (the default) to Read, Write and Access Direct Messages.**

   For this toy application, you select Read, Write and Access Direct Messages — the most permissive access model that's available. This option prevents your app from hitting brick walls because of access problems.

When you develop a real-life application, you do the opposite of what I suggest in this step. For a real-live app, you select the least permissive option that suits your application's requirements.

First change your app's access level, and then create the app's access token (as explained in Step 9). Don't create the access token before changing the access level. If you try to change the access level after you've created the access token, your app won't work. What's worse, Twitter's app setup page doesn't warn you about the problem. Believe me — I've wasted hours of my life on this Twitter quirk.

7. **Click the button that offers to update your application's settings.**

   Doing so changes your app's access level to Read, Write and Access Direct Messages.

8. **Near the top of the page, select the Keys and Access Tokens tab.**

   You can find a few buttons on that page.

9. **Click the button that offers to create your access token.**

   After doing so, your app's Keys and Access Tokens tab displays your app's access token and the access token secret, in addition to your app's access level, consumer key, and consumer secret.

10. Copy the four codes (Consumer Key, Consumer Secret, Access Token, and Access Token Secret) from your app's Details tab to the appropriate lines in your `MainActivity` **class's code. (See Listing 13-3.)**

Whew! You're done putting OAuth keys and tokens in your Java code.

TECHNICAL STUFF

In the OAuth world, an app whose code communicates with Twitter's servers is a *consumer.* To identify itself as a trustworthy consumer, an app must send passwords to Twitter's servers. In OAuth terminology, these passwords are called the *consumer key* and the *consumer secret.*

The Application's Main Activity

What's a *Java Programming for Android Developers For Dummies,* 2nd Edition, without some Java code? Listing 13-4 contains the Twitter app's Java code.

LISTING 13-4: **The *MainActivity.java* File**

```
package com.allmycode.a13_04;

import android.os.AsyncTask;
import android.os.Bundle;
import android.support.v7.app.AppCompatActivity;
import android.text.Editable;
import android.text.TextWatcher;
import android.text.method.ScrollingMovementMethod;
import android.view.View;
import android.widget.EditText;
import android.widget.TextView;

import java.util.List;

import twitter4j.Twitter;
import twitter4j.TwitterException;
import twitter4j.TwitterFactory;
import twitter4j.conf.ConfigurationBuilder;

public class MainActivity extends AppCompatActivity {
    TextView textViewCountChars, textViewTimeline;
    EditText editTextTweet, editTextUsername;
    Twitter twitter;
```

(continued)

LISTING 13-4: *(continued)*

```java
@Override
protected void onCreate(Bundle savedInstanceState) {
  super.onCreate(savedInstanceState);
  setContentView(R.layout.activity_main);
  editTextTweet = (EditText) findViewById(R.id.editTextTweet);
  editTextTweet.addTextChangedListener(new MyTextWatcher());
  textViewCountChars = (TextView) findViewById(R.id.textViewCountChars);
  editTextUsername = (EditText) findViewById(R.id.editTextUsername);
  textViewTimeline = (TextView) findViewById(R.id.textViewTimeline);
  textViewTimeline.setMovementMethod(new ScrollingMovementMethod());
  ConfigurationBuilder builder = new ConfigurationBuilder();
  builder
      .setOAuthConsumerKey("00000000000000000000000000")
      .setOAuthConsumerSecret("11111111111111111111111111111111111111111111")
      .setOAuthAccessToken("222222222-3333333333333333333333333333333333")
      .setOAuthAccessTokenSecret("4444444444444444444444444444444444444444");
  TwitterFactory factory = new TwitterFactory(builder.build());
  twitter = factory.getInstance();
}


// Button click listeners

public void onTweetButtonClick(View view) {
  new MyAsyncTaskTweet().execute(editTextTweet.getText().toString());
}


public void onTimelineButtonClick(View view) {
  new MyAsyncTaskTimeline().execute(editTextUsername.getText().toString());
}


// Count characters in the Tweet field

class MyTextWatcher implements TextWatcher {
  @Override
  public void afterTextChanged(Editable s) {
    textViewCountChars.setText("" + editTextTweet.getText().length());
  }

  @Override
  public void beforeTextChanged
      (CharSequence s, int start, int count, int after) {
  }
```

```
    @Override
    public void onTextChanged
        (CharSequence s, int start, int before, int count) {
    }
}


// The AsyncTask classes

public class MyAsyncTaskTweet extends AsyncTask<String, Void, String> {
  @Override
  protected String doInBackground(String... tweet) {
    String result = "";
    try {
      twitter.updateStatus(tweet[0]);
      result = getResources().getString(R.string.success);
    } catch (TwitterException twitterException) {
      result = getResources().getString(R.string.twitter_failure);
    } catch (Exception e) {
      result = getResources().getString(R.string.general_failure);
    }
    return result;
  }


  @Override
  protected void onPostExecute(String result) {
    editTextTweet.setHint(result);
    editTextTweet.setText("");
  }
}

public class MyAsyncTaskTimeline extends AsyncTask<String, Void, String> {
  @Override
  protected String doInBackground(String... username) {
    String result = new String("");
    List<twitter4j.Status> statuses = null;
    try {
      statuses = twitter.getUserTimeline(username[0]);
    } catch (TwitterException twitterException) {
      result = getResources().getString(R.string.twitter_failure);
    } catch (Exception e) {
      result = getResources().getString(R.string.general_failure);
    }
    for (twitter4j.Status status : statuses) {
      result += status.getText();
```

(continued)

LISTING 13-4:   *(continued)*

```
        result += "\n";
      }
      return result;
    }


    @Override
    protected void onPostExecute(String result) {
      editTextUsername.setText("");
      textViewTimeline.setText(result);
    }
  }
}
```

WARNING

Twitter's network protocols require that the device that runs this chapter's app is set to the correct time. I don't know how correct the "correct time" has to be, but I've had lots of trouble running the app on emulators. Either my emulator is set to get the time automatically from the network (and it gets the time incorrectly) or I set the time manually and the *seconds* part of the time isn't close enough. One way or another, the error message that comes back from Twitter (usually specifying a null authentication challenge) isn't helpful. So I avoid emulators whenever I test this code. Rather than run an emulator, I set my phone to get the network time automatically. Then I run this chapter's app on that phone. If you have trouble running this section's app, try running the app on a real phone.

When you run the app, you see two areas. One area contains a Tweet button; the other area contains a Timeline button, as shown in Figure 13-2.

FIGURE 13-2:
The main activity, in its pristine state.

360   PART 4 Powering Android with Java Code

In Figure 13-2, the words *Type your tweet here* and *Type a username here* are light gray. This happens because I use `android:hint` attributes with the `EditText` components in Listing 13-2. A *hint* is a bunch of characters that appear only when a text field is otherwise empty. When the user clicks inside the text field, or types any text inside the text field, the hint disappears.

Type a tweet into the text field on top, and then press the Tweet button, as shown in Figure 13-3. If your attempt to tweet is successful, the message `Success!` replaces the tweet in the text field, as shown in Figure 13-4. If, for one reason or another, your tweet can't be posted, the message `Call to Twitter failed` replaces the tweet in the text field, as shown in Figure 13-5.

FIGURE 13-3:
The user types a tweet.

FIGURE 13-4:
The app indicates a successful tweet.

Next, type a username in the lower text field, and then click Timeline. If all goes well, a list of the user's most recent tweets appears below the Timeline button, as shown in Figure 13-6. You can scroll the list to see more of the user's tweets.

FIGURE 13-5:
The app brings
bad tidings
to the user.

FIGURE 13-6:
The @fordum-
mies timeline.

The onCreate method

The onCreate method in Listing 13-4 calls findViewById to locate some of the components declared in Listing 13-2.

CROSS-
REFERENCE

For insight into the workings of Android's findViewById method, see Chapter 3.

The onCreate method also creates a MyTextWatcher instance to listen for changes in the field where the user types a tweet. Android notifies the MyTextWatcher instance whenever the user types a character in (or deletes a character from) the app's editTextTweet field. The MyTextWatcher class's afterTextChanged method counts the number of characters in the editTextTweet field. The method displays the count in the tiny textViewCountChars field.

The count includes the characters in Twitter handles even though Twitter no longer counts such things toward the 140-character limit. Also, the app doesn't do anything special if a user types more than 140 characters into the editTextTweet field. In a real-life app, I'd add code to deal with these issues. But when I create sample apps, I like to keep the code as uncluttered as possible.

TECHNICAL STUFF

Android actually notifies the `MyTextWatcher` instance three times for each text change in the `editTextTweet` field: once before changing the text, once during the change of the text, and once after changing the text. In Listing 13-4, I don't make `MyTextWatcher` execute any statements before or during the changing of the text. In `MyTextWatcher`, the only method whose body contains statements is the `after TextChanged` method. Even so, in order to implement Android's `TextWatcher` interface, the `MyTextWatcher` class must provide bodies for the `before TextChanged` and the `onTextChanged` methods.

Finally, in the `onCreate` method, the call to `setMovementMethod(new Scrolling MovementMethod())` permits scrolling on the list of items in a user's timeline.

The button listener methods

Listing 13-2 describes two buttons, each with its own `onClick` method. I declare the two methods in Listing 13-4: the `onTweetButtonClick` method and the `onTimelineButtonClick` method. Each of the methods has a single statement in its body — a call to execute a newly constructed `AsyncTask` of some kind. Believe me, this is where the fun begins!

The trouble with threads

Imagine that you're talking to a poorly designed robot. The robot executes only one set of instructions at a time. You give this robot the following set of instructions:

```
1. Visit allmycode.com/Java4Android.
2. Download the code listings.
3. Uncompress the downloaded file.
```

You have a slow Internet connection, so the robot takes a long time to download the code listings. (The robot stares vacantly into the air during the download.) In the middle of the download, you have a craving for a glass of orange juice. So you say the following:

```
1. Go to the refrigerator.
2. Pour a glass of orange juice.
3. Bring the glass to me.
```

The robot continues to stare vacantly because the robot executes only one set of instructions at a time. You wave your hands in front of the robot's glassy eyes, but nothing happens. You robot seems to be paralyzed during the long, laborious download.

Life would be better if the robot could perform two *threads* of execution at once. With two threads of execution, the robot would share its time between two different sets of instructions:

```
1. Visit allmycode.com/Java4Android.
2. Download the code listings.         1. Go to the refrigerator.
3. Uncompress the downloaded file.     2. Pour a glass of orange juice.
                                       3. Bring the glass to me.
```

How would the robot manage to perform two threads of execution at the same time? It doesn't matter how. In one possible scenario, the robot has two brains and each brain works on one of the threads. In another scenario, the robot's single brain jumps back and forth from one thread to the other, devoting a bit of time to one thread, and then some time to the other thread, and then some time to the first thread again, and so on.

Creating more than one thread means executing more than one piece of code at the same time. For the Java developer, things become very complicated very quickly. Juggling several simultaneous pieces of code is like juggling several raw eggs: One way or another, you're sure to end up with egg on your face.

To help fix all this, the creators of Android developed a multi-threading framework. Within this framework, you bundle all your delicately timed code into a carefully defined box. This box contains all the ready-made structure for managing threads in a well-behaved way. Rather than worry about where to put your Internet request and display the result in a timely fashion, you simply plug certain statements into certain places in the box and let the box's ready-made structure take care of all the routine threading details.

This marvelous box belongs to Android's AsyncTask classes. To understand these classes, you need a bit of terminology explained:

>> **Thread:** A bunch of statements to be executed in the order prescribed by the code

>> **Multi-threaded code:** A bunch of statements in more than one thread

Java executes each thread's statements in the prescribed order. But if your program contains two threads, Java might not execute all the statements in one thread before executing all the statements in the other thread. Instead, Java might intermingle execution of the statements in the two threads. For example, I ran the following code several times:

```
new OneThread().start();
new AnotherThread().start();

class OneThread extends Thread {
  public void run() {
    for (int i = 0; i < 2000; i++) {
      output(i);
    }
  }
}

class AnotherThread extends Thread {
  public void run() {
    for (int i = 2000; i < 4000; i++) {
      output(i);
    }
  }
}
```

(I didn't really use a method named *output*. Instead, I used an elaborate bunch of statements that aren't worth worrying about here.)

The first time I ran the code, the output looked like this:

```
0 1 2 ... 189 2000 2001 ... 2144 190 191 ...
```

The second time, the output looked like this:

```
2000 2001 ... 2650 0 1 2 ...
```

The third time, the output looked like this:

```
0 1 2 ... 48 2000 49 50 ... 58 2001 59 60 2002 ...
```

The output 0 always comes before the output 1 because the statements to output 0 and 1 are in the same thread. But you can't predict whether Java will display 0 or 2000 first, because the statements to output 0 and 2000 are in two different threads.

TECHNICAL STUFF

>> **The UI thread:** The thread that displays components on the screen

In an Android program, your main activity runs primarily in the UI thread.

The *UI* in *UI thread* stands for user interface. Another name for the UI thread is the *main thread*. The use of this terminology predates the notion of a main activity in Android.

>> **A background thread:** Any thread other than the UI thread

In an Android program, when you create an AsyncTask class, some of that class's code runs in a background thread.

In addition to all the terminology, you should know about two rules concerning threads:

>> **Any time-consuming code should be in a background thread — not in the UI thread.**

This chapter's example reaches out on the Internet and posts a tweet or grabs a Twitter user's timeline. Either of these chores might take a noticeable amount of time. As a result, all the app's components may come to a standstill while the app waits for a response from the Internet. The entire user interface is temporarily frozen. The app looks like my poorly designed, paralyzed robot. You don't want that to happen.

>> **Any code that modifies a property of the screen must be in the UI thread.**

If, in a background thread, you have code that modifies text on the screen, you're either gumming up the UI thread or creating code that doesn't compile. Either way, you don't want to do it.

Understanding Android's AsyncTask

A class that extends Android's AsyncTask looks like the outline in Listing 13-5.

LISTING 13-5: **The Outline of an *AsyncTask* Class**

```
public class MyAsyncTaskName extends AsyncTask<Type1, Type2, Type3> {

  @Override
  protected void onPreExecute () {
    // Execute statements in the UI thread before starting background thread.
    // For example, display an empty progress bar.
  }
```

```
@Override
protected Type3 doInBackground(Type1... param1) {
  // Execute statements in the background thread.
  // For example, get info from Twitter.

  return resultValueOfType3;
}


@Override
protected void onProgressUpdate(Type2... param) {
  // Update a progress bar (or some other kind of progress indicator) during
  // execution of the background thread.
}


@Override
protected void onPostExecute(Type3 resultValueOfType3) {
  // Execute statements in the UI thread after finishing the statements in the
  // background thread. For example, display info from Twitter in the
  // activity's components.
  }
}
```

When you create an AsyncTask class, Android executes each method in its appropriate thread. In the doInBackground method (refer to Listing 13-5), you put code that's too time-consuming for the UI thread. So Android executes the doInBackground method in the background thread. (Big surprise!) In Listing 13-5's other three methods (onPreExecute, onProgressUpdate, and onPostExecute), you put code that updates the components on the device's screen. Android executes these methods in the UI thread, as shown in Figure 13-7.

Android also makes your life easier by coordinating the execution of an AsyncTask class's methods. For example, onPostExecute doesn't change the value of a screen component until after the execution of doInBackground. (See Figure 13-7.) In this chapter's Twitter app, the onPostExecute method doesn't update the screen until after the doInBackground method has fetched a user's timeline from Twitter. The user doesn't see a timeline until the timeline is ready to be seen.

You'd think that with all this coordination of method calls, you lose any benefit from having more than one thread. But that's not the case. Because the doInBackground method runs outside the UI thread, your activity can respond to the user's clicks and drags while the doInBackground method waits for a response from the Twitter servers. It's all good.

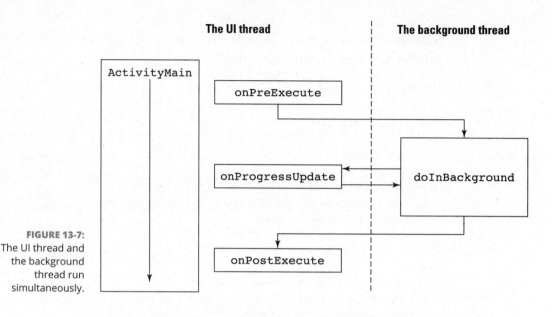

The UI thread　　　　　　　　　　**The background thread**

ActivityMain

onPreExecute

onProgressUpdate ← doInBackground

onPostExecute

FIGURE 13-7:
The UI thread and
the background
thread run
simultaneously.

My Twitter app's AsyncTask classes

Listing 13-5 contains four methods. But in Listing 13-4, I override only two of the methods: doInBackground and onPostExecute. The MyAsyncTaskTweet and MyAsyncTaskTimeline classes in Listing 13-4 inherit the other two methods from their superclass.

Notice (in Listings 13-4 and 13-5) the use of generic type names in an AsyncTask class. An AsyncTask is versatile enough to deal with all types of values. In Listing 13-4, the first generic parameter of MyAsyncTaskTweet has type String because a tweet is a string of as many as 140 characters. But someone else's AsyncTask might accept an image or a music file as its input.

When you create an AsyncTask class, you "fill in the blanks" by putting the following three type names inside the angle brackets:

» **The first type name (*Type1* in Listing 13-5) stands for a value (or values) that you pass to the** doInBackground **method.**

   The doInBackground method, with its varargs parameter, uses these values to decide what has to be done.

» **The second type name (*Type2* in Listing 13-5) stands for a value (or values) that mark the background thread's progress in completing its work.**

TECHNICAL
STUFF

This chapter's example has no progress bar, nor a progress indicator of any kind. So in Listing 13-4, the second type name is Void.

In Java, the Void class is a wrapper class for the void value. Put that in your black hole of nothingness!

» **The third type name (*Type3* in Listing 13-5) stands for a value that the doInBackground method returns and that the onPostExecute method takes as a parameter.**

In the doInBackground method of Listing 13-4, this third type name is String. It's String because the doInBackground method returns the word "Success!" or the words "Call to Twitter failed", and the onPostExecute method displays these words in the screen's editTextTweet field.

Figure 13-8 summarizes the way generic type names influence the methods' types in Listing 13-4, and Figure 13-9 summarizes how values move from one place to another in the MyAsyncTaskTweet class of Listing 13-4.

```
new MyAsyncTaskTweet().execute(editTextTweet.getText().toString());


public class MyAsyncTaskTweet extends AsyncTask<String, Void, String> {
  @Override
  protected String doInBackground(String... tweet) {
    String result = "";

    try {
      twitter.updateStatus(tweet[0]);
      result = getResources().getString(R.string.success);
    } catch (TwitterException twitterException) {
      result = getResources().getString(R.string.twitter_failure);
    } catch (Exception e) {
      result = getResources().getString(R.string.general_failure);
    }
    return result;
  }

  @Override
  protected void onPostExecute(String result) {
    editTextTweet.setHint(result);
    editTextTweet.setText("");
  }
}
```

FIGURE 13-8:
The use of types in an AsyncTask class.

An AsyncTask can be fairly complicated. But when you compare Android's AsyncTask to the do-it-yourself threading alternatives, the AsyncTask idea isn't bad at all. In fact, when you get a little practice and create a few of your own AsyncTask classes, you get used to thinking that way. The whole business starts to feel quite natural.

```
new MyAsyncTaskTweet().execute(editTextTweet.getText().toString());


public class MyAsyncTaskTweet extends AsyncTask<String, Void, String> {
  @Override
  protected String doInBackground(String... tweet) {
    String result = "";

    try {
      twitter.updateStatus(tweet[0]);
      result = getResources().getString(R.string.success);
    } catch (TwitterException twitterException) {
      result = getResources().getString(R.string.twitter_failure);
    } catch (Exception e) {
      result = getResources().getString(R.string.general_failure);
    }
    return result;
  }

  @Override
  protected void onPostExecute(String result) {
    editTextTweet.setHint(result);
    editTextTweet.setText("");
  }
}
```

FIGURE 13-9:
The flow of
values in an
AsyncTask
class.

WARNING

Despite my glowing remarks in this chapter, Android's AsyncTask isn't a cure-all for your multitasking problems. An AsyncTask doesn't always give you the kind of control you need over your code. And, if your activity gets destroyed in the middle of an AsyncTask execution, you may have some trouble. But when you first write code that makes network requests, AsyncTask is a good place to start.

Cutting to the chase, at last

At the beginning of this chapter, I promise that a statement like

```
twitter.updateStatus("This is my tweet.");
```

lies at the heart of the code to post a tweet. You can see this by looking at the code in Listing 13-4. Here's a summary:

```
Twitter twitter;

...


ConfigurationBuilder builder = new ConfigurationBuilder();
builder
    .setOAuthConsumerKey // ... Etc.
```

```
TwitterFactory factory = new TwitterFactory(builder.build());
twitter = factory.getInstance();

...

twitter.updateStatus(tweet[0]);
```

In the Twitter4J API,

>> A `ConfigurationBuilder` **helps you create a** `TwitterFactory`**.**

>> **The** `TwitterFactory` **class helps you create a new** `Twitter` **object.**

A call to the factory's `getInstance` method calls a `Twitter` constructor on your behalf. This creates a new `Twitter` object for you to use.

>> **A** `Twitter` **object is a gateway to the Twitter servers.**

>> **A call to the** `Twitter` **object's** `updateStatus` **method posts a brand-new tweet.**

In Listing 13-4, the parameter to the `updateStatus` method is an array element. That's because, in the `doInBackground` method's header, `tweet` is a varargs parameter. You can pass as many values to `doInBackground` as you want. In the body of the method, you treat `tweet` as though it's an ordinary array. The first tweet value is `tweet[0]`. If there were a second `tweet` value, it would be `tweet[1]`. And so on.

CROSS-
REFERENCE

For the lowdown on varargs parameters, see Chapter 12.

In Listing 13-4, the code to fetch a user's timeline looks something like this:

```
List<twitter4j.Status> statuses = null;

...

statuses = twitter.getUserTimeline(username[0]);
```

A fellow named Yusuke Yamamoto developed Twitter4J (or at least, Yusuke Yamamoto was the Twitter4J project leader), and at some point Mr. Yamamoto decided that the `getUserTimeline` method returns a collection of `twitter4J.Status` objects. (Each `twitter4J.Status` instance contains one tweet.) To honor the contract set by calling the `getUserTimeline` method, the code in Listing 13-4 declares `statuses` to be a collection of `twitter4J.Status` objects.

A few lines later in the code, an enhanced `for` statement steps through the collection of `statuses` values and appends each value's text to a big result string. The loop adds `"\n"` (Java's go-to-the-next-line character) after each tweet for good measure. In the `onPostExecute` method, the code displays the big result string in the screen's `textViewTimeline` field.

TECHNICAL STUFF

In Listing 13-4, in the second `doInBackground` method, I use the fully qualified name `twitter4j.Status`. I do this to distinguish the `twitter4J.Status` class from Android's own `AsyncTask.Status` class (an inner class of the `AsyncTask` class).

CROSS-REFERENCE

For insight into Java's inner classes, refer to Chapter 11.

Java's Exceptions

Have I ever had something go wrong during the run of a program? (*Hint:* The answer is yes.) Have you ever tried to visit a website and been unable to pull up the page? (Indubitably, the answer is yes.) Is it possible that Java statements can fail when they try to access the Twitter server? (Absolutely!)

In Java, most of the things that go wrong during the execution of a program are *exceptions*. When something goes wrong, your code *throws* an exception. If your code provides a way to respond to an exception, your code *catches* the exception.

Like everything else in Java, an exception is an object. Every exception is an instance of Java's `Exception` class. When your code tries to divide by zero (which is always a "no-no"), your code throws an instance of the `ArithmeticException` class. When your code can't read from a stored file, your code throws an instance of the `IOException` class. When your code can't access a database, your code throws an instance of the `SQLException` class. And when your Twitter4J code gets a bad response from the Twitter servers, your code throws an instance of the `TwitterException` class.

The classes `ArithmeticException`, `IOException`, `SQLException`, `TwitterException`, and many, many others are subclasses of Java's `Exception` class. Each of the classes `Exception`, `ArithmeticException`, `IOException`, and `SQLException` is part of Java's standard API library. The class `TwitterException` is declared separately in the Twitter4J API.

Java has two kinds of exceptions: unchecked exceptions and checked exceptions. The easiest way to tell one kind of exception from the other is to watch Android Studio's response when you type and run your code:

>> When you execute a statement that can throw an *unchecked* exception, you don't have to add additional code.

For example, an `ArithmeticException` is an unchecked exception. You can write and run the following (awful) Java code:

```
// Don't do this:
int i = 3 / 0;
```

When you try to run this code, the program crashes. In Android Studio's Logcat pane, you see a message like the one shown in Figure 13-10.

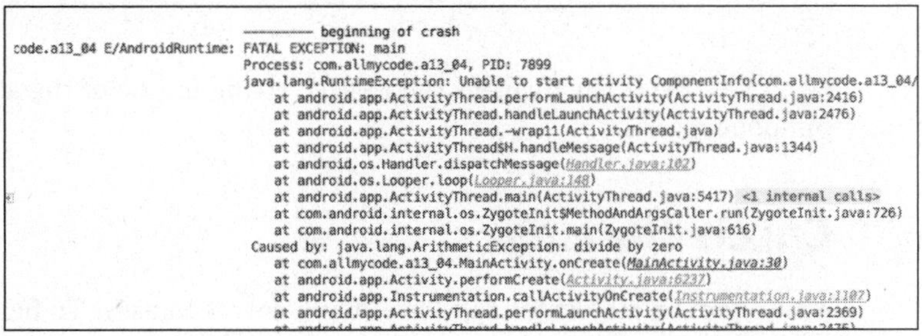

```
------- beginning of crash
code.a13_04 E/AndroidRuntime: FATAL EXCEPTION: main
                Process: com.allmycode.a13_04, PID: 7899
                java.lang.RuntimeException: Unable to start activity ComponentInfo{com.allmycode.a13_04/
                    at android.app.ActivityThread.performLaunchActivity(ActivityThread.java:2416)
                    at android.app.ActivityThread.handleLaunchActivity(ActivityThread.java:2476)
                    at android.app.ActivityThread.-wrap11(ActivityThread.java)
                    at android.app.ActivityThread$H.handleMessage(ActivityThread.java:1344)
                    at android.os.Handler.dispatchMessage(Handler.java:102)
                    at android.os.Looper.loop(Looper.java:148)
                    at android.app.ActivityThread.main(ActivityThread.java:5417) <1 internal calls>
                    at com.android.internal.os.ZygoteInit$MethodAndArgsCaller.run(ZygoteInit.java:726)
                    at com.android.internal.os.ZygoteInit.main(ZygoteInit.java:616)
                Caused by: java.lang.ArithmeticException: divide by zero
                    at com.allmycode.a13_04.MainActivity.onCreate(MainActivity.java:30)
                    at android.app.Activity.performCreate(Activity.java:6237)
                    at android.app.Instrumentation.callActivityOnCreate(Instrumentation.java:1107)
                    at android.app.ActivityThread.performLaunchActivity(ActivityThread.java:2369)
                    at android.app.ActivityThread.handleLaunchActivity(ActivityThread.java:2416)
```

FIGURE 13-10:
Shame on you!
You divided
by zero.

» **When you execute a statement that can throw a *checked* exception, you must add code.**

A `TwitterException` is an example of a checked exception, and a call to `getUserTimeline` can throw a `TwitterException`. To find out what happens when you call `getUserTimeline` without adding code, see a portion of Android Studio's editor in Figure 13-11.

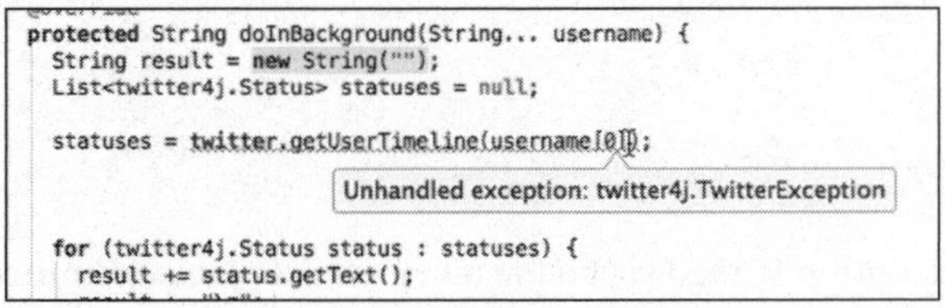

```
@Override
protected String doInBackground(String... username) {
  String result = new String("");
  List<twitter4j.Status> statuses = null;

  statuses = twitter.getUserTimeline(username[0]);
                          ┌─────────────────────────────────────────────┐
                          │ Unhandled exception: twitter4j.TwitterException │
                          └─────────────────────────────────────────────┘
  for (twitter4j.Status status : statuses) {
    result += status.getText();
```

FIGURE 13-11:
Java insists that
you add code to
acknowledge an
exception.

In Figure 13-11, the error message indicates that by calling the `getUserTimeline` method, you run the risk of throwing a `TwitterException`. The word *Unhandled* means that `TwitterException` is one of Java's checked exceptions and that you haven't provided any code to address the possibility of the exception's being thrown. That is, if the app can't communicate with the Twitter servers, and Java throws a `TwitterException`, your code has no "Plan B."

In Listing 13-4, I add Java's try / catch **statement to my** getUserTimeline **call.** Here's the translation of the try / catch **statement:**

```
try to execute the following statement(s): {
    statuses = twitter.getUserTimeline(username[0]);


} If you throw a TwitterException while you're trying, {
    set the result to whatever string R.string.twitter_failure represents.
} If you throw some other kind of exception while you're trying, {
    set the result to whatever string R.string.general_failure represents.
}
```

Eventually, my code displays the result **string in one of the activity's** TextView **components.**

Catch clauses

A try / catch **statement can have many** catch **clauses. To help illustrate** catch **clauses, I've added a few new lines to one of the** try / catch **statements in Listing 13-4:**

```
try {
    count = numberOfTweets / averagePerDay;
    statuses = twitter.getUserTimeline(username[0]);
} catch (TwitterException twitterException) {
    result = getResources().getString(R.string.twitter_failure);
} catch (ArithmeticException a) {
    result = getResources().getString(R.string.divide_by_zero);
} catch (Exception e) {
    result = getResources().getString(R.string.general_failure);
}

result += "\n";
```

When an exception is thrown inside a try clause, Java examines the accompanying list of catch clauses. Every catch clause has a parameter list, and every parameter list contains a type of exception.

Java starts at whatever catch clause appears immediately after the try clause and works its way down the program's text. For each catch clause, Java asks: Is the exception that was just thrown an instance of the class in this clause's parameter list?

>> **If it isn't,** Java skips the catch clause and moves on to the next catch clause in line.

>> **If it is,** Java executes the catch clause and then skips past all other catch clauses that come with this try clause.

Java goes on and executes whatever statements come after the whole try / catch statement.

Look at this section's code snippet. Java starts executing the numberOfTweets / averagePerDay calculation. If averagePerDay is zero, the calculation fails and the code throws an ArithmeticException. As a result, Java skips past the statuses = twitter... statement. If there were any other statements between the failed calculation and the word catch, Java would skip those statements too.

Java goes directly to the catch clauses, starting with the topmost catch clause. The topmost catch clause is for TwitterException instances, but dividing by zero doesn't throw a TwitterException. So Java marches onward to the next catch clause.

The next catch clause is for ArithmeticException instances. Yes, dividing by zero threw an ArithmeticException. So Java executes the statement inside that catch clause. Java sets result to the string that R.string.divide_by_zero represents.

Then Java jumps out of the try / catch statement. Java executes the statement immediately after the try / catch statement, adding the end-of-line character ("\n") to the result string. Then Java executes any other statements after the result += "\n" statement.

TIP

In the sample code with three catch clauses, I end the chain of catch clauses with an Exception e clause. Java's Exception class is an ancestor of Twitter Exception and ArithmeticException and all the other exception classes. No matter what kind of exception your code throws inside a try clause, that exception matches the Exception e catch clause. You can always rely on an Exception e clause as a last resort for handling a problem.

A finally clause

In addition to tacking on catch clauses, you can also tack a finally clause on to your try / catch statement. Java's finally keyword says, in effect, "Execute the finally clause's statements whether the code threw an exception or not." For example, in the following code snippet, Java always adds "\n" to the result variable, whether or not the call to getUserTimeline throws an exception:

```
try {
  statuses = twitter.getUserTimeline(username[0]);
} catch (TwitterException e) {
  result = getResources().getString(R.string.twitter_failure);
} finally {
  result += "\n";
}
```

Passing the buck

Here's a handy response to use whenever something goes wrong: "Don't blame me — tell my supervisor to deal with the problem." (I should have added the Tip icon to this paragraph!) When dealing with an exception, a Java method can do the same thing and say, "Don't expect me to have a try / catch statement — pass the exception on to the method that called me."

Here's how it works: In the MyAsyncTaskTimeline class of Listing 13-4, move the code that creates a result to a method of its own. (See Listing 13-6.)

LISTING 13-6: **Nipping an Exception in the Bud**

```
public class MyAsyncTaskTimeline extends AsyncTask<String, Void, String> {

  @Override
  protected String doInBackground(String... username) {
    String result = new String("");
    result = getResult(username);
    return result;
  }

  String getResult(String... username) {
    String result = new String("");
    List<twitter4j.Status> statuses = null;
    try {
      statuses = twitter.getUserTimeline(username[0]);
    } catch (TwitterException twitterException) {
      result = getResources().getString(R.string.twitter_failure);
    }
    for (twitter4j.Status status : statuses) {
      result += status.getText();
      result += "\n";
    }
    return result;
  }
```

```
@Override
protected void onPostExecute(String result) {
  editTextUsername.setText("");
  textViewTimeline.setText(result);
  }
}
```

In Listing 13-6, the getResult method says "Try to get a user's timeline. If you get a bad response from the Twitter server, handle it by displaying the R.string. twitter_failure message." To keep things simple, I have only one catch clause in Listing 13-6.

You can get rid of the try / catch statement in the getResult method, as long as the next method upstream acknowledges the exception's existence. To see what I mean, look at Listing 13-7.

LISTING 13-7:   **Make the Calling Method Handle the Exception**

```
public class MyAsyncTaskTimeline extends AsyncTask<String, Void, String> {

  @Override
  protected String doInBackground(String... username) {
    String result = new String("");
    try {
      result = getResult(username);
    } catch (TwitterException twitterException) {
      result = getResources().getString(R.string.twitter_failure);
    }
    return result;
  }

  String getResult(String... username) throws TwitterException {
    String result = new String("");
    List<twitter4j.Status> statuses = null;

    statuses = twitter.getUserTimeline(username[0]);

    for (twitter4j.Status status : statuses) {
      result += status.getText();
      result += "\n";
    }
    return result;
  }
```

(continued)

LISTING 13-7: *(continued)*

```
@Override
protected void onPostExecute(String result) {
  editTextUsername.setText("");
  textViewTimeline.setText(result);
}
}
```

In Listing 13-7, the getResult method's header contains a throws clause. With this throws clause, the getResult method says "If I experience a Twitter Exception, I won't deal with the exception in my own try / catch statement. Instead, I'll pass the exception on to whichever method called me." Because the doInBackground method calls getResult, Java insists that the doInBackground method contain code to acknowledge the possibility of a TwitterException. To fulfill this responsibility, the doInBackground method surrounds the getResult call with a try / catch statement.

In this example, the buck must stop with my doInBackground method. My doInBackground method's header can't have a throws TwitterException clause. Instead, the doInBackground method must contain a catch clause for the TwitterException. My code's doInBackground method overrides Android's own doInBackground method, and Android's doInBackground method doesn't throw a TwitterException. Here's the general rule: Imagine some exception that I'll call XYZException. If a method's header doesn't say throws XYZException, you can't override that method with a header that says throws XYZException.

Of course, the buck doesn't always have to stop after the first throws clause. You could say, "Don't blame me — tell my supervisor to deal with the problem." And then your supervisor could say, "Don't blame me — tell *my* supervisor to deal with the problem." (Where my wife works, things like this happen all the time.) Listing 13-8 has an admittedly contrived example.

LISTING 13-8: **Keep Passing the Hot Potato**

```
public class MyAsyncTaskTimeline extends AsyncTask<String, Void, String> {

  @Override
  protected String doInBackground(String... username) {
    String result = new String("");
    try {
      result = getResult(username);
    } catch (TwitterException twitterException) {
```

```
        result = getResources().getString(R.string.twitter_failure);
    }
    return result;
}

String getResult(String... username) throws TwitterException {
    String result = new String("");
    List<twitter4j.Status> statuses = null;

    statuses = getStatuses(username);

    for (twitter4j.Status status : statuses) {
        result += status.getText();
        result += "\n";
    }
    return result;
}

List<twitter4j.Status> getStatuses(String[] username)
                                            throws TwitterException {
    List<twitter4j.Status> statuses;
    statuses = twitter.getUserTimeline(username[0]);
    return statuses;
}

@Override
protected void onPostExecute(String result) {
    editTextUsername.setText("");
    textViewTimeline.setText(result);
}
}
```

If you get a bad response from the Twitter server, the getStatuses method passes the exception to the getResult method, which in turn passes the exception to the doInBackground method. The doInBackground method takes the ultimate responsibility by surrounding the getResult call in a try / catch statement.

Chapter **14**

Hungry Burds: A Simple Android Game

What started as a simple pun involving the author's last name has turned into Chapter 14 — the most self-indulgent writing in the history of technical publishing.

The scene takes place in south Philadelphia in the early part of the 20th century. My father (then a child) sees his father (my grandfather) handling an envelope. The envelope has just arrived from the old country. My grandmother grabs the envelope out of my grandfather's hands. The look on her face is one of superiority. "I open the letters around here," she says with her eyes.

While my grandmother opens the letter, my father glances at the envelope. The last name on the envelope is written in Cyrillic characters, so my father can't read it. But he notices a short last name in the envelope's address. Whatever the characters are, they're more likely to be a short name like Burd than a longer name like Burdinsky or Burdstakovich.

The Russian word for *bird* is *ptitsa*, so there's no etymological connection between my last name and our avian friends. But as I grew up, I would often hear kids yell, "Burd is the word" or "Hey, Burdman" from across the street. Today, my one-person Burd Brain Consulting firm takes in a small amount of change every year.

Introducing the Hungry Burds Game

When the game begins, the screen is blank. Then, for a random amount of time (averaging one second), a Burd fades into view, as shown in Figure 14-1.

If the user does nothing, the Burd disappears after fading into full view. But if the user touches the Burd before it disappears, the Burd gets a cheeseburger and remains onscreen, as shown in Figure 14-2.

After ten Burds have faded in (and the unfed ones have disappeared), the screen displays a Game Over pop-up message. (See Figure 14-3.)

Two icons serve as menu items at the top of the screen. If the user selects the Info icon, a pop-up message shows the number of fed Burds in the current run of the game. The message also shows the high score for all runs of the game. (See Figure 14-4.) If the user selects the Rewind icon, the game begins again.

FIGURE 14-3:
The game ends.

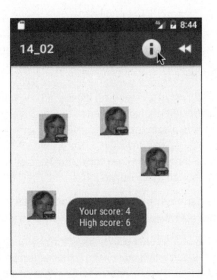

FIGURE 14-4:
The score sheet.

The Hungry Burds Java code is about 150 lines long. (Compare this with one of the Android game developer's books that I bought. In that book, the simplest example has 2,300 lines of Java code.) To keep the Hungry Burds code from consuming dozens of pages, I've omitted some features that you might see in a more realistically engineered game:

>> **The Hungry Burds game doesn't access data over a network.**

The game's high-score display doesn't tell you how well you scored compared with your friends or with other players around the world. The high-score display applies to only one device — the one you're using to play the game.

>> **The game restarts whenever you change the device's orientation.**

If you tilt the device from Portrait mode to Landscape mode, or from Landscape mode to Portrait mode, Android calls the main activity's lifecycle methods. Android calls the activity's `onPause`, `onStop`, and `onDestroy` methods. Then it reconstitutes the activity by calling the activity's `onCreate`, `onStart`, and `onResume` methods. As a result, whatever progress you've made in the game disappears and the game starts itself over again from scratch.

CROSS-
REFERENCE

For an introduction to an activity's lifecycle methods, see Chapter 4.

>> **The screen measurements that control the game are crude.**

Creating a visual app that involves drawing, custom images, or motion of any kind involves some math. You need math to make measurements, estimate distances, detect collisions, and complete other tasks. To do the math, you produce numbers by making Android API calls, and you use the results of your calculations in Android API library calls.

To help me cut to the chase, my Hungry Burds game does only a minimal amount of math, and it makes only the API calls I believe to be absolutely necessary. As a result, some items on the screen don't always look their best.

>> **The game has no settings.**

The number of Burds displayed, the minimum length of time for each Burd's display, and the maximum additional time of each Burd's display are all hardcoded in the game's Java file. In the code, these constants are `NUMBER_OF_BURDS`, `MINIMUM_DURATION`, and `MAXIMUM_ADDITIONAL_DURATION`. As a developer, you can change the values in the code and reinstall the game. But the ordinary player can't change these numbers.

>> **The game may not be challenging with the default `NUMBER_OF_BURDS`, `MINIMUM_DURATION`, and `MAXIMUM_ADDITIONAL_DURATION` values.**

I admit it: On this front, I'm at a distinct disadvantage. I'm a lousy game player. I remember competing in video games against my kids when they were young. I lost every time. At first it was embarrassing; in the end it was ridiculous. I could never avoid being shot, eaten, or otherwise squashed by my young opponents' avatars.

I don't presume to know what values of `NUMBER_OF_BURDS`, `MINIMUM_DURATION`, and `MAXIMUM_ADDITIONAL_DURATION` are right for you. And if no values are right for you (and the game isn't fun to play no matter which values you have), don't despair. I've created Hungry Burds as a teaching tool, not as a replacement for Pokémon GO.

If changing the `AVERAGE_SHOW_TIME` and `MINIMUM_SHOW_TIME` doesn't make Hungry Burds feel like a real game, try running the game on a real-life device.

TIP

The Main Activity

I start with an outline of the main activity's code. The outline is in Listing 14-1. (If outlines don't work for you and you want to see the code in its entirety, refer to Listing 14-2, a little later in this chapter.)

LISTING 14-1: **An Outline of the App's Java Code**

```
package com.allmycode.a14_02;

public class MainActivity extends AppConpatActivity
    implements OnClickListener, AnimationListener {

  // Declare fields

  /* Activity lifecycle methods */

  @Override
  public void onCreate(Bundle savedInstanceState) {
    super.onCreate(savedInstanceState);
    setContentView(R.layout.activity_main);

    // Find the layout

    // Get the size of the device's screen
  }

  @Override
  public void onResume() {
    startPlaying();
  }

  /* Game play methods */
  void startPlaying() {
    // Set this run's score (countClicked) to zero
    // Remove any images from the previous game

    showABurd();
  }

  void showABurd() {
    // Add a Burd in some random place
    // At first, the Burd is invisible
```

(continued)

LISTING 14-1: *(continued)*

```
// Create an AlphaAnimation to make the Burd
//      fade in (from invisible to fully visible)

burd.startAnimation(animation);
}


/* OnClickListener method */

public void onClick(View view) {
  countClicked++;

  // Change the image to a Burd with a cheeseburger
}


/* AnimationListener methods */

public void onAnimationEnd(Animation animation) {
  if (++countShown < NUMBER_OF_BURDS) {
    showABurd(); // Again!
  } else {
    // Display the "Game Over" message
  }
}


/* Menu methods */

public boolean onCreateOptionsMenu(Menu menu) {
  // Make the menu
}

public boolean onOptionsItemSelected(MenuItem item) {
  // Show the scores or start a new game
}

private void showScores() {
  // Get high score from SharedPreferences
  // If this score is greater than the high score, update SharedPreferences
  // Display high score and this run's score
}
}
```

The heart of the Hungry Burds code is the code's game loop. Here's a sneak preview of the full Hungry Burds app's code:

```
@Override
public void onResume() {
  super.onResume();
  startPlaying();
}


void startPlaying() {
  countClicked = countShown = 0;
  layout.removeAllViews();
  showABurd();
}


void showABurd() {
  // Add a Burd in some random place.
  // At first, the Burd is invisible ...

  burd.setVisibility(View.INVISIBLE);

  // ... but the animation will make the Burd visible.

  AlphaAnimation animation = new AlphaAnimation(0.0F, 1.0F);
  animation.setDuration(duration);
  animation.setAnimationListener(this);
  burd.startAnimation(animation);
}


public void onAnimationEnd(Animation animation) {
  if (++countShown < NUMBER_OF_BURDS) {
    showABurd(); // Again!
  } else {
    // Display the "Game Over" message
  }
}
```

When Android executes the onResume method, the code calls the startPlaying method, which in turn calls the showABurd method. The showABurd method does what its name suggests, by animating an image from alpha level 0 to alpha level 1. (Alpha level 0 is fully transparent; alpha level 1 is fully opaque.)

When the animation ends, the onAnimationEnd method checks the number of Burds that have already been displayed. If the number is less than ten, the onAnimationEnd method calls showABurd again, and the game loop continues.

By default, a Burd returns to being invisible when the animation ends. But the main activity implements OnClickListener, and when the user touches a Burd, the class's onClick method makes the Burd permanently visible, as shown in the following snippet:

```
public void onClick(View view) {
    countClicked++;
    ((ImageView) view).setImageResource(R.drawable.burd_burger);
    view.setVisibility(View.VISIBLE);
}
```

TECHNICAL
STUFF

In an activity's onCreate method, you put code that runs when the activity comes into existence. In contrast, in the onResume method, you put code that runs when the user begins interacting with the activity. The user isn't aware of the difference because the app starts running so quickly. But for you, the developer, the distinction between an app's coming into existence and starting to interact is important. In Listings 14-1 and 14-2, the onCreate method contains code to restore any previous state, set the activity's layout, and measure the screen size. The onResume method is different. With the onResume method, the user is about to touch the device's screen. So In Listings 14-1 and 14-2, the onResume method displays something for the user to touch: the first of several hungry Burds.

TECHNICAL
STUFF

When you override Android's onResume method, the first statement in the method body must be super.onResume(). A similar rule holds for Android's onCreate method, and for all of Android's activity lifecycle methods.

The code, all the code, and nothing but the code

Following the basic outline of the game's code in the earlier section "The Main Activity," Listing 14-2 contains the entire text of the game's MainActivity.java file.

LISTING 14-2: **The App's Java Code**

```
package com.allmycode.a14_02;

import android.content.SharedPreferences;
import android.graphics.Point;
```

```java
import android.os.Bundle;
import android.support.v7.app.AppCompatActivity;
import android.view.Display;
import android.view.Menu;
import android.view.MenuItem;
import android.view.View;
import android.view.View.OnClickListener;
import android.view.animation.AlphaAnimation;
import android.view.animation.Animation;
import android.view.animation.Animation.AnimationListener;
import android.widget.ImageView;
import android.widget.RelativeLayout;
import android.widget.RelativeLayout.LayoutParams;
import android.widget.Toast;

import java.util.Random;

public class MainActivity extends AppCompatActivity
    implements OnClickListener, AnimationListener {

  final int NUMBER_OF_BURDS = 10;
  final int MINIMUM_DURATION = 500;
  final int MAXIMUM_ADDITIONAL_DURATION = 1000;
  int countShown = 0, countClicked = 0;
  Random random = new Random();

  RelativeLayout layout;
  int displayWidth, displayHeight;

  /* Activity lifecycle methods */

  @Override
  public void onCreate(Bundle savedInstanceState) {
    super.onCreate(savedInstanceState);
    setContentView(R.layout.activity_main);

    layout = (RelativeLayout) findViewById(R.id.relativeLayout);

    Display display = getWindowManager().getDefaultDisplay();
    Point size = new Point();
    display.getSize(size);
    displayWidth = size.x;
    displayHeight = size.y;
  }
```

(continued)

LISTING 14-2: *(continued)*

```java
@Override
public void onResume() {
  super.onResume();
  startPlaying();
}

/* Game play methods */

void startPlaying() {
  countClicked = countShown = 0;
  layout.removeAllViews();
  showABurd();
}

void showABurd() {

  long duration =
      MINIMUM_DURATION + random.nextInt(MAXIMUM_ADDITIONAL_DURATION);

  LayoutParams params = new LayoutParams
      (LayoutParams.WRAP_CONTENT, LayoutParams.WRAP_CONTENT);

  params.leftMargin = random.nextInt(displayWidth) * 3 / 4;
  params.topMargin = random.nextInt(displayHeight) * 5 / 8;

  ImageView burd = new ImageView(this);
  burd.setImageResource(R.drawable.burd);
  burd.setLayoutParams(params);
  burd.setOnClickListener(this);
  burd.setVisibility(View.INVISIBLE);

  layout.addView(burd);

  AlphaAnimation animation = new AlphaAnimation(0.0F, 1.0F);
  animation.setDuration(duration);
  animation.setAnimationListener(this);
  burd.startAnimation(animation);
}

/* OnClickListener method */

public void onClick(View view) {
  countClicked++;
  ((ImageView) view).setImageResource(R.drawable.burd_burger);
```

```java
    view.setVisibility(View.VISIBLE);
  }


  /* AnimationListener methods */

  public void onAnimationEnd(Animation animation) {
    if (++countShown < NUMBER_OF_BURDS) {
      showABurd();
    } else {
      Toast.makeText(this, "Game Over", Toast.LENGTH_LONG).show();
    }
  }


  public void onAnimationRepeat(Animation arg0) {
  }


  public void onAnimationStart(Animation arg0) {
  }

  /* Menu methods */

  @Override
  public boolean onCreateOptionsMenu(Menu menu) {
    getMenuInflater().inflate(R.menu.menu_main, menu);
    return true;
  }


  @Override
  public boolean onOptionsItemSelected(MenuItem item) {
    switch (item.getItemId()) {
      case R.id.show_scores:
        showScores();
        return true;
      case R.id.play_again:
        startPlaying();
        return true;
    }
    return super.onOptionsItemSelected(item);
  }

  private void showScores() {
    SharedPreferences prefs = getPreferences(MODE_PRIVATE);
    int highScore = prefs.getInt("highScore", 0);
```

(continued)

LISTING 14-2:   *(continued)*

```
if (countClicked > highScore) {
  highScore = countClicked;
  SharedPreferences.Editor editor = prefs.edit();
  editor.putInt("highScore", highScore);
  editor.commit();
}

Toast.makeText(this, "Your score: " + countClicked +
    "\nHigh score: " + highScore, Toast.LENGTH_LONG).show();
}
}
```

Measuring the display

You want to randomly choose places on the device's screen to display Burd images. To do this, it may help to know the size of the device's screen. How complicated can that be? You can measure the screen size with a ruler, and you can determine a device's resolution by reading the specs in the user manual.

Of course, Android programs don't have opposable thumbs, so they can't use plastic rulers. And a layout's characteristics can change, depending on several runtime factors, including the device's orientation (portrait or landscape) and the amount of screen space reserved for Android's notification bar and buttons. If you don't play your cards right, you can easily call methods that prematurely report a display's width and height as zero values.

Fortunately, the `android.view.Display` class's `getSize` method gives you useful answers without too much coding. So, here and there in Listing 14-2, you find the following code:

```java
public class MainActivity extends AppCompatActivity {

  int displayWidth, displayHeight;

  public void onCreate(Bundle savedInstanceState) {

    Display display = getWindowManager().getDefaultDisplay();
    Point size = new Point();
    display.getSize(size);
    displayWidth = size.x;
    displayHeight = size.y;
  }
```

```
void showABurd() {

    LayoutParams params = new LayoutParams
        (LayoutParams.WRAP_CONTENT, LayoutParams.WRAP_CONTENT);

    params.leftMargin = random.nextInt(displayWidth) * 3 / 4;
    params.topMargin = random.nextInt(displayHeight) * 5 / 8;

}
```

An instance of Android's Point class is basically an object with two components: an x component and a y component. In the Hungry Burds code, a call to getWindowManager().getDefaultDisplay() retrieves the device's display. The resulting display's getSize method takes an instance of the Point class and fills its x and y fields. The x field's value is the display's width, and the y field's value is the display's height, as shown in Figure 14-5.

A LayoutParams object stores information about the way a component should appear as part of an activity's layout. (Each kind of layout has its own Layout Params inner class, and the code in Listing 14-2 imports the RelativeLayout. LayoutParams inner class.) A LayoutParams instance has a life of its own, apart from any component whose appearance the instance describes. In Listing 14-2, I construct a new LayoutParams instance before applying the instance to any particular component. Later in the code, I call

```
burd.setLayoutParams(params);
```

to apply the new LayoutParams instance to one of the Burds.

Constructing a new LayoutParams instance with a double dose of LayoutParams. WRAP_CONTENT (one LayoutParams.WRAP_CONTENT for width and one LayoutParams. WRAP_CONTENT for height) indicates that a component should shrink-wrap itself around whatever content is drawn inside it. Because the code eventually applies this LayoutParams instance to a Burd, the Burd will be only wide enough and only tall enough to contain a picture of yours truly from the project's res/drawable directory.

TECHNICAL STUFF

The alternative to WRAP_CONTENT is MATCH_PARENT. With two MATCH_PARENT parameters in the LayoutParams constructor, a Burd's width and height would expand to fill the activity's entire relative layout. In this example, that layout would fill most of the device's screen.

A LayoutParams instance's leftMargin field stores the number of pixels between the left edge of the display and the left edge of the component. Similarly, a Layout Params instance's topMargin field stores the number of pixels between the top edge of the display and the top edge of the component. (See Figure 14-5.)

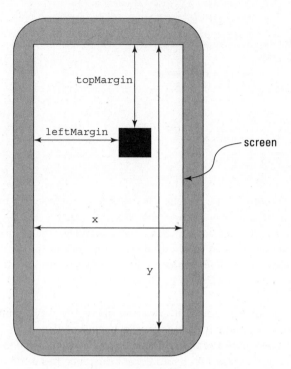

FIGURE 14-5:
Measuring
distances on the
screen.

In Listing 14-2, I generate values randomly to position a new Burd. A Burd's left edge (`params.leftMargin`) is no farther than ¾ths of the way across the screen, and the Burd's top edge (`params.topMargin`) is no lower than ⅝ths of the way down the screen. If you don't multiply the screen's width by ¾ (or some such fraction), an entire Burd can be positioned beyond the right edge of the screen. The user sees nothing while the Burd comes and goes. The same kind of thing can happen if you don't multiply the screen's height by ⅝.

TECHNICAL
STUFF

The fractions ¾ and ⅝, which I use to determine each component's position, are crude guesstimates of a portrait screen's requirements. A more refined app would carefully measure the available turf and calculate the optimally sized region for positioning new Burds.

In Listing 14-2, I also generate numbers randomly to decide how many milliseconds each Burd takes to fade into full view. The `MAXIMUM_ADDITIONAL_DURATION` is 1000, so the expression `random.nextInt(MAXIMUM_ADDITIONAL_DURATION)` stands for a value from 0 to 999. By adding `MINIMUM_DURATION` (refer to Listing 14-2), I make `duration` be a number between 500 and 1499. So a Burd takes between 500 and 1499 milliseconds to fade into view.

CROSS-
REFERENCE

I introduce the `java.util.Random` class in Chapter 8.

Constructing a Burd

Android's `ImageView` class represents objects that contain images. Normally, you put an image file (a `.png` file, a `.jpg` file, or a `.gif` file) in your project's `res/drawable` directory, and a call to the `ImageView` object's `setImageResource` method associates the `ImageView` object with the image file. In Listing 14-2, the following lines fulfill this role:

```
ImageView burd = new ImageView(this);
burd.setImageResource(R.drawable.burd);
```

Because of the `R.drawable.burd` parameter, Android looks in the project's *app*/res/drawable directory for a file named `burd.png`, `burd.jpg`, or `burd.gif`.

You can find `burd.png` in the stuff that you download from this book's website (`www.allmycode.com/Java4Android`).

The statement

```
burd.setVisibility(View.INVISIBLE);
```

makes the Burd be completely transparent. The next statement

```
layout.addView(burd);
```

normally makes a component appear on the user's screen. But with the `View.INVISIBLE` property, the Burd doesn't show up. It's not until I start the code's fade-in animation that the user begins seeing a Burd on the screen.

When the user clicks on a Burd, Android calls the `onClick` method in Listing 14-2. The `onClick` method's `view` parameter represents the `ImageView` object that the user clicked. In the body of the `onClick` method, the statement

```
((ImageView) view).setImageResource(R.drawable.burd_burger);
```

assures Java that `view` is indeed an `ImageView` instance and changes the picture on the face of that instance from a hungry author to a well-fed author. (In the *app*/res/drawable directory, Android grabs a file named `burd_burger.png`, `burd_burger.jpg`, or `burd_burger.gif`.) The `onClick` method also sets the `ImageView` instance's visibility to `View.VISIBLE`. That way, when this Burd's animation ends, the happy Burd remains visible on the user's screen.

DISPLAYING THINGS ON THE DEVICE'S SCREEN

When you create an Android activity, you fill most of the activity's screen with something called a view group. A *view group* holds components such as `Button` components, `EditText` components, `TextView` components, `ImageView` components, and other such things. To make a particular component appear on an activity's screen, you add that component to the activity's view group.

The Android API has several kinds of view groups, including these:

- `LinearLayout`: Arranges components in a line across the screen, or in a column down the screen.

- `GridLayout`: Arranges components in a rectangular grid (that is, in the cells of a table whose borders are invisible).

- `RelativeLayout`: Arranges components by describing their positions relative to one another. For example, you can place `button2` to the right of `button1` or make the top of `button2` be 50 pixels below the bottom of `button1`.

- `ConstraintLayout`: Has more features than `RelativeLayout` for describing components' relative positions. For example, you can center a component in a layout by constraining the component to the top, bottom, left, and right of the layout. You can move the component from the center by assigning a bias constraint.

To add a component to a view group, you have two alternatives:

- **In a file such as** `activity_main.xml`, **you can use XML code to describe the component.**

  I do that in most of this book's examples without making a big fuss about it.

- **In a file such as** `MainActivity.java`, **you can use Java code to describe the component.**

  I do that in Listing 14-2 because each component (each Burd) appears at a different time during the app's run.

With Android Studio's Designer tool, you drag components onto a preview screen. When you do, Android Studio composes the `activity_main.xml` file for you. You see the `activity_main.xml` file's code when you switch to the Designer tool's Text tab.

The layout file (`activity_main.xml`) for this chapter's app is quite short:

```
<?xml version="1.0" encoding="utf-8"?>

<RelativeLayout xmlns:android= "http://schemas.android.com/apk/res/
    android"
                xmlns:tools="http://schemas.android.com/tools"
                android:id="@+id/relativeLayout"
                android:layout_width="match_parent"
                android:layout_height="match_parent"
                tools:context=".MainActivity">
</RelativeLayout>
```

The file tells Android that most of the screen is taken up with a `RelativeLayout`, and that the RelativeLayout's id is `relativeLayout`. You can create this file (or a file very much like this file) on the Designer tool's Design tab. To do so, follow these steps:

1. **Remove any `TextView` components or other components from inside the preview screens.**

2. **At the top of the component tree, look for the word *RelativeLayout*.**

    If you see the word *RelativeLayout*, go to Step 3.

    If you see some other word (such as *ConstraintLayout* or *LinearLayout*), drag a RelativeLayout item from the Palette to one of the preview screens. Then select the new RelativeLayout in the component tree and look at the Properties pane. In the Properties pane, make sure that both the `layout_width` and `layout_height` properties have the value `match_parent`.

3. **If you haven't already done so, select the RelativeLayout in the component tree.**

4. **In the Properties pane's ID field, type `relativeLayout`.**

    Android Studio may have already filled this field with the name `activity_main`. But I find this name confusing because, with this name, the app has two things — one named `R.layout.activity_main` and another named `R.id.activity_main` — and they're not quite the same thing. In Listing 14-2, I refer to `R.id.relative Layout`. And in the Designer tool, I set the ID accordingly.

In Listing 14-2, the statement

```
layout = (RelativeLayout) findViewById(R.id.relativeLayout);
```

(continued)

(continued)

makes the variable `layout` refer to the activity's one and only view group. Later in Listing 14-2, the statement

```
layout.addView(burd)
```

adds a Burd to the activity's view group, setting the stage for displaying the Burd on the screen. Elsewhere in Listing 14-2, the statement

```
layout.removeAllViews();
```

removes all Burds from the activity's view group in preparation for the start of the Hungry Burds game.

Android animation

Android has two types of animation:

>> **View animation:** A system that comes in two different flavors:

- *Tweening:* You tell Android how an object should look initially and how the object should look eventually. You also tell Android how to change from the initial appearance to the eventual appearance. (Is the change gradual or sudden? If the object moves, does it move in a straight line or in a curve of some sort? Will it bounce a bit when it reaches the end of its path?)

   With tweening, Android considers all your requirements and figures out exactly how the object looks *between* the start and the finish of the object's animation.

- *Frame-by-frame animation:* You provide several snapshots of the object along its path. Android displays these snapshots in rapid succession, one after another, giving the appearance of movement or of another change in the object's appearance.

   Movie cartoons are the classic example of frame-by-frame animation, even though, in modern moviemaking, graphics specialists use tweening to create sequences of frames.

>> **Property animation:** A system in which you can modify any property of an object over a period of time.

   With property animation, you can change anything about any kind of object, whether the object appears on the device's screen or not. For example, you can increase an `earth` object's average temperature from 15° Celsius to 18° Celsius over a period of ten minutes. Rather than display the `earth` object, you can watch the way average temperature affects water levels and plant life, for example.

Unlike view animation, the use of property animation changes the value stored in an object's field. For example, you can use property animation to change a component from being invisible to being visible. When the property animation finishes, the component remains visible.

The Hungry Burds code uses view animation, which includes these specialized animation classes:

>> AlphaAnimation: Fades into view or fades out of view

>> RotateAnimation: Turns around

>> ScaleAnimation: Changes size

>> TranslateAnimation: Moves from one place to another

In particular, the Hungry Burds code uses AlphaAnimation. In the statement

```
AlphaAnimation animation = new AlphaAnimation(0.0F, 1.0F);
```

the alpha level of 0.0 indicates complete transparence, and the alpha level of 1.0 indicates complete opaqueness. (The AlphaAnimation constructor expects its parameters to be float values, so I plug the float values 0.0F and 1.0F into the constructor call.)

The call

```
animation.setAnimationListener(this);
```

tells Java that the code to respond to the animation's progress is in this main activity class. Indeed, the class header at the top of Listing 14-2 informs Java that the HungryBurds class implements the AnimationListener interface. And to make good on the implementation promise, Listing 14-2 contains bodies for the methods onAnimationEnd, onAnimationRepeat, and onAnimationStart. (Nothing happens in the onAnimationRepeat and onAnimationStart methods. That's okay.)

The onAnimationEnd method does what I describe earlier in this chapter: The method checks the number of Burds that have already been displayed. If the number is less than ten, the onAnimationEnd method calls showABurd again and the game loop continues.

REMEMBER

An object's `visibility` property doesn't change when a view animation makes the object fade in or fade out. In this chapter's example, a Burd starts off with `View.INVISIBLE`. A fade-in animation makes the Burd appear slowly on the screen. But when the animation finishes, the Burd's `visibility` field still contains the original `View.INVISIBLE` value. Normally, when the animation ends, the Burd simply disappears. It's only when the user touches a hungry Burd that the code's `onClick` method calls `view.setVisibility(View.VISIBLE)`, making the Burd image remain on the screen.

Creating menus

A strip at the top of the screen shown earlier, in Figure 14-1, is the activity's *action bar* (also known as the *app bar*). The right side of the action bar displays *action buttons*. The Hungry Burds game has two action buttons: an Info button and a Rewind button.

Defining the XML file

To describe your activity's action bar, you create an XML file in your project's *app/res/menu* directory. Listing 14-3 contains the XML file for the Hungry Burds game.

LISTING 14-3: **Description of a Menu**

```xml
<menu xmlns:android="http://schemas.android.com/apk/res/android"
    xmlns:app="http://schemas.android.com/apk/res-auto"
    xmlns:tools="http://schemas.android.com/tools"
    tools:context="com.allmycode.a14_02.MainActivity">

    <item
        android:id="@+id/show_scores"
        android:icon="@drawable/ic_dialog_info"
        android:title="@string/scores"
        app:showAsAction="ifRoom|withText"
        />

    <item
        android:id="@+id/play_again"
        android:icon="@drawable/ic_media_rew"
        android:title="@string/again"
        app:showAsAction="ifRoom|withText"
        />
</menu>
```

In Listing 14-3, each `item` element describes an action button. Each `item` element has four attributes:

>> **The `android:id` attribute gives the action button a name.**

You refer to this name in the main activity's Java code.

>> **The `android:icon` attribute points to a file containing an image.**

The file lives in your project's *app*/`res`/`drawable` directory. If there's room, Android displays this image on the action bar. (Refer to Figure 14-1.)

If there's no room, the action appears only when the user selects the action bar's Overflow icon. (See Figures 14-6 and 14-7.)

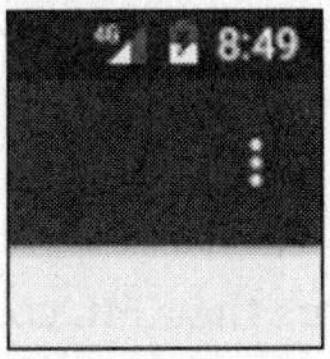

FIGURE 14-6:
This phone's
Overflow icon has
three dots
aligned vertically.

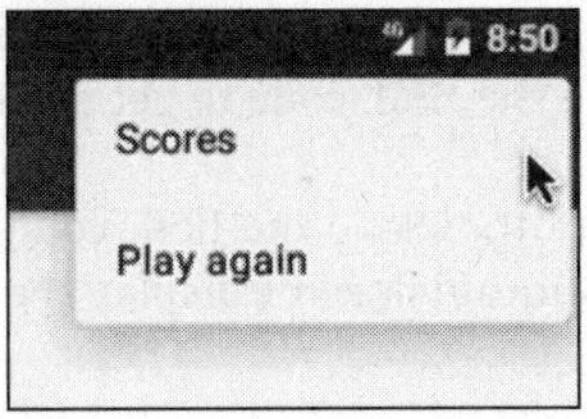

FIGURE 14-7:
Expanding the
Overflow icon.

>> **The `android:title` attribute points to some helpful text.**

That text may or may not appear along with the icon, depending on the size of the screen and the next attribute's options.

In Listing 14-3, the attribute `android:showAsAction="ifRoom|withText"` tells Android two things:

>> `ifRoom`: **Show this icon on the action bar if there's room for it.**

If there isn't enough room, reveal this icon when the user presses the Overflow icon.

>> `withText`: **Show this item's title on the action bar if there's room for it.**

Figure 14-8 shows each icon along with the icon's title.

FIGURE 14-8:
There's room for
the icons' titles.

REMEMBER

Use Java's bitwise or operator (|) to separate the word ifRoom from the word withText.

Listing 14-3 is very nice, but the XML file in Listing 14-3 isn't enough to put items on your app's action bar. For that, you need to inflate the XML file. That's why I put the following method in Listing 14-2:

```
@Override
public boolean onCreateOptionsMenu(Menu menu) {
    getMenuInflater().inflate(R.menu.menu_main, menu);
    return true;
}
```

When you *inflate* an XML document, Android turns the XML code into something resembling Java code (a Java object, perhaps).

In the preceding code, you get a MenuInflater that's capable of inflating menus from XML resources. Then you inflate the XML code to get a real, live Java object.

REMEMBER

When you implement the onCreateOptionsMenu method, you must return either true or false. If you return false, Android doesn't display the menu. How rude!

Handling user actions

In the menu's XML file (refer to Listing 14-3), you describe how the menu items look. And in the onOptionsItemSelected method (refer to Listing 14-2), you describe what happens when the user clicks any of those menu items.

Take a gander at the onOptionsItemSelected method in Listing 14-2. When the user clicks an item, the code calls the item's getItemId method. Depending on the getItemId method's return value, the code calls either the showScores method or the startPlaying method.

The onOptionsItemSelected method returns a boolean value. A true return value tells Android that you've finished handling the user's selection. If you return false, Android passes the selection event to whatever other code might be waiting for it.

402   PART 4 Powering Android with Java Code

Shared preferences

When a user selects the Scores menu item (the Info icon), the app displays the score for the current game and the high score for all games. (Refer to Figure 14-3.) The high score display applies to only one device — the device that's running the current game. To remember the high score from one run to another, I use Android's Shared Preferences feature.

TECHNICAL STUFF

Android provides several ways to store information from one run of an app to the next. In addition to using shared preferences, you can store information in the device's SQLite database. (Every Android device has SQLite database software.) You can also store information in an ordinary Linux file or on a network host of some kind.

Here's how you wield a set of shared preferences:

>> **To create shared preferences, you call the activity's** getShared Preferences **method.**

In fact, the getSharedPreferences method belongs to Android's Context class, and the Activity class is a subclass of the Context class.

In Listing 14-2, I call getSharedPreferences in the activity's showScores method. The call's parameter, MODE_PRIVATE, tells Android that no other app can read from or write to this app's shared preferences. (I know — there's nothing "shared" about something that no other app can use. But that's the way Android's terminology works.)

Aside from MODE_PRIVATE, the alternatives are described in this list:

● MODE_WORLD_READABLE: Other apps can read from these preferences.

● MODE_WORLD_WRITEABLE: Other apps can write to these preferences.

● MODE_MULTI_PROCESS: Other apps can write to these preferences even while an app is in the middle of a read operation. Weird things can happen with this much concurrency. If you use MODE_MULTI_PROCESS, watch out!

You can combine modes with Java's bitwise *or* operator (|). A call such as

```
getSharedPreferences(MODE_WORLD_READABLE | MODE_WORLD_WRITEABLE);
```

makes your preferences both readable and writable for all other processes.

>> **To start adding values to a set of shared preferences, you use an instance of the** SharedPreferences.Editor **class.**

In Listing 14-2, I make a new editor object. Then I use the editor to add ("highScore", highScore) to the shared preferences. Taken together, ("highScore", highScore) is a *key/value pair*. The *value* (whatever number my `highscore` variable holds) is the actual information. The *key* (the string `"highScore"`) identifies that particular piece of information. (Every value has to have a key. Otherwise, if you've stored several different values in your app's shared preferences, you have no way to retrieve any particular value.)

In Listing 14-2, I call `putInt` to store an `int` value in shared preferences. Android's `Editor` class (an inner class of the `SharedPreferences` class) has methods such as `putInt`, `putFloat`, `putString`, and `putStringSet`.

>> **To finish adding values to a set of shared preferences, you call the editor's `commit` method.**

In the `showScores` method in Listing 14-2, the statement `editor.commit()` does the job.

>> **To read values from an existing set of shared preferences, you call `getBoolean`, `getInt`, `getFloat`, or one of the other get methods belonging to the `SharedPreferences` class.**

In the `showScores` method in Listing 14-2, the call to `getInt` takes two parameters. The first parameter (the string `"highscore"`) is the key that identifies a particular piece of information. The second parameter (the `int` value 0) is a default value. So when you call `prefs.getInt("highScore", 0)`, the following applies:

- If `prefs` has no pair with key `"highscore"`, the method call returns 0.

- If `prefs` has a previously stored `"highscore"` value, the method returns that value.

Informing the user

Near the bottom of Figure 14-3, a capsule-shaped pop-up contains the words *Game Over*. Figure 14-4 has a similar pop-up. These pop-ups illustrate the use of Android's `Toast` class. A *toast* is an unobtrusive little view that displays some useful information for a brief period. A `Toast` view pops up on the screen the way a hot piece of bread pops up from a toaster. (Rumor has it that the Android class name `Toast` comes from this goofy analogy.)

The `Toast` class has two extremely useful methods: `makeText` and `show`.

>> **The static `Toast.makeText` method creates an instance of the `Toast` class.**

The `makeText` method has three parameters:

- The first parameter is a context (the word `this` in the `makeText` calls in Listing 14-2).

- The second parameter is either a resource (such as R.string.scores) or a String expression (such as "Game Over").

  If you call makeText with a String expression, the user sees the String when Android displays the toast. If you call makeText with a resource, Android looks for the resource in your project's *app*/res/values/strings.xml file. In Listing 14-2, the code calls makeText twice with a String expression in each call.

  If you use an int value (42, for example) for the second parameter of the makeText method, Android doesn't display the characters *42* in the Toast view. Instead, Android looks for a resource whose value in R.java is 42. Your R.java file probably doesn't contain the number 42. So, instead of a Toast view, you get a ResourceNotFound exception. Your app crashes, and you groan in dismay.

- The makeText method's third parameter is either Toast.LENGTH_LONG or Toast.LENGTH_SHORT. With LENGTH_LONG, the Toast view appears for 3.5 seconds. With LENGTH_SHORT, the Toast view appears for 2 seconds.

» **The show method tells Android to display the Toast view.**

In Listing 14-2, notice that I call both makeText and show in one Java statement. If you forget to call the show method, the Toast view doesn't appear. You stare in disbelief wondering why you don't see the Toast view. ("Who stole my toast?" you ask.) When you finally figure out that you forgot to call the show method, you feel foolish. (At least that's the way I felt when I forgot earlier today.)

To display the Toast view for more than 3.5 seconds, put the Toast statement inside a loop. For example, to display the word *Hello* for ten seconds, use the following code:

```
for (int i = 0; i < 5; i++) {
    Toast.makeText(this, "Hello", Toast.LENGTH_SHORT).show();
}
```

It's Been Fun

This chapter has been fun, and this book has been fun! I love writing about Android and Java. And I love hearing from readers. Remember that you can send email to me at java4android@allmycode.com, and you can reach me on Twitter (@allmycode) and on Facebook (/allmycode).

Occasionally, I hear from a reader who says something like this: "If I read your whole book, will I know everything I have to know about Java?" The answer is always "No, no, no!" (That's not only one "no." It's "no" times three.) No matter what topic you study, there's always more to learn. So keep reading, keep practicing, keep learning, and, by all means, keep in touch.

5

The Part of Tens

IN THIS CHAPTER

» **Checking your capitalization and value comparisons**

» **Watching out for fall-through**

» **Putting methods, listeners, and constructors where they belong**

» **Using static and nonstatic references**

» **Avoiding other heinous errors**

Chapter **15**

Ten Ways to Avoid Mistakes

"The only people who never make mistakes are the people who never do anything at all." One of my college professors said that. I don't remember the professor's name, so I can't give him proper credit. I guess that's my mistake.

Putting Capital Letters Where They Belong

Java is a case-sensitive language, so you really have to mind your *p*s and *q*s — along with every other letter of the alphabet. Here are some concepts to keep in mind as you create Java programs:

» Java's keywords are all completely lowercase. For instance, in a Java i f statement, the word *if* can't be *If* or *IF*.

» When you use names from Android's Application Programming Interface (API), the case of the names has to match what appears in the API.

>> The names you make up yourself must be capitalized the same way through-out the entire program. If you declare a myAccount variable, you can't refer to it as MyAccount, myaccount, or Myaccount. If you capitalize the variable name two different ways, Java thinks you're referring to two completely different variables.

For more info on Java's case-sensitivity, see Chapter 4.

Breaking Out of a switch Statement

If you don't break out of a switch statement, you get fall-through. For instance, if the value of roll is 7, the following code prints all three words — win, continue, and lose:

```
switch (roll) {
case 7:
  textView.setText("win");
case 10:
  textView.setText("continue");
case 12:
  textView.setText("lose");
}
```

For the full story, see Chapter 8.

Comparing Values with a Double Equal Sign

When you compare two values, you use a double equal sign. The line

```
if (inputNumber == randomNumber)
```

is correct, but the line

```
if (inputNumber = randomNumber)
```

is not correct. For a full report, see Chapter 5.

Adding Listeners to Handle Events

You want to know when the user clicks a widget, when an animation ends, or when something else happens, so you create listeners:

```
public class MainActivity extends Activity
    implements OnClickListener, AnimationListener {
...
public void onClick(View view) {
    ...
}
public void onAnimationEnd(Animation animation) {
    ...
}
```

When you create listeners, you must remember to set the listeners:

```
ImageView widget = new ImageView(this);
widget.setOnClickListener(this);
...
AlphaAnimation animation = new AlphaAnimation(0.0F, 1.0F);
animation.setAnimationListener(this);
...
```

If you forget the call to setOnClickListener, nothing happens when you click the widget. Clicking the widget harder a second time doesn't help.

For the rundown on listeners, see Chapter 11.

Defining the Required Constructors

When you define a constructor with parameters, as in

```
public Temperature(double number)
```

Java no longer creates a default parameterless constructor for you. In other words, you can no longer call

```
Temperature roomTemp = new Temperature();
```

unless you explicitly define your own parameterless Temperature constructor. For all the gory details on constructors, see Chapter 9.

Fixing Nonstatic References

If you try to compile the following code, you get an error message:

```
class WillNotWork {
  String greeting = "Hello";

  static void show() {
      textView.setText(greeting);
  }
}
```

You get an error message because the show method is static, but greeting isn't static. For the complete guide to finding and fixing this problem, see Chapter 9.

Staying within Bounds in an Array

When you declare an array with ten components, the components have indexes 0 through 9. In other words, if you declare

```
int guests[] = new int[10];
```

you can refer to the guests array's components by writing guests[0], guests[1], and so on, all the way up to guests[9]. You can't write guests[10], because the guests array has no component with index 10.

For the latest gossip on arrays, see Chapter 12.

Anticipating Null Pointers

A NullPointerException comes about when you call a method on an expression that has no "legitimate" value. Here's an example:

```
public class MainActivity extends AppCompatActivity {
  TextView textView;
```

```
@Override
protected void onCreate(Bundle savedInstanceState) {
  super.onCreate(savedInstanceState);
  setContentView(R.layout.activity_main);

  // You forget the findViewById line.
}


public void onButtonClick(View view) {
    textView.setText("Hello");
}
}
```

In Java, a reference type variable that doesn't point to anything has the value null. So in this example, the textView variable's value is null.

You can't call the setText method on the null value. For that matter, you can't call any method on the null value. When Java tries to execute textView.setText("Hello"), the app crashes. The user sees an *Application has stopped* message. If you're testing the app using Android Studio, you see NullPointerException in the Logcat pane.

To avoid this kind of calamity, think twice about any method call in your code. If the expression before the dot can possibly be null, add exception-handling code to your program:

```
public void onButtonClick(View view) {
  try {
    textView.setText("Hello");
  } catch(NullPointerException e) {
    Toast.makeText(this, "The app has recovered from an error.",
                                    Toast.LENGTH_LONG).show();

  }
}
```

For the story on handling exceptions, see Chapter 13.

Using Permissions

Some apps require explicit permissions. For example, the app in Chapter 13 talks to Twitter's servers over the Internet. This doesn't work unless you add a `<uses-permission>` element to the app's `AndroidManifest.xml` file:

```
<uses-permission android:name= "android.permission.INTERNET"/>
```

If you forget to add the `<uses-permission>` element to your `AndroidManifest.xml` file, the app can't communicate with Twitter's servers. The app fails without displaying a useful error message. Too bad!

The Activity Not Found

If you create a second activity for your app, you must add a new `<activity>` element in the app's `AndroidManifest.xml` file. The element can be as simple as

```
<activity android:name=".MySecondActivity"/>
```

but, in most cases, the element is a bit more complicated.

If you don't add this `<activity>` element, Android can't find the `MySecondActivity` class, even though the `MySecondAcitivity.java` file is in the app's project directory. Your app crashes with an `ActivityNotFoundException`.

And that makes all the difference.

Chapter **16**

Ten Websites for Developers

This chapter lists ten useful and fun websites. Each one has resources to help you use Java more effectively. And as far as I know, none of these sites uses adware or pop-ups or other grotesque programs.

This Book's Websites

For all matters related to the technical content of this book, visit www.allmycode.com/Java4Android.

For business issues (for example, "How can I purchase 100 copies of *Java Programming for Android Developers For Dummies,* 2nd Edition?"), simply go to www.dummies.com and type Java programming for Android developers in the Search box. If a list of titles is returned, click on the second edition of this book.

The Horse's Mouth

Oracle's official website for Java is www.oracle.com/technetwork/java.

Programmers and developers interested in sharing Java technology can go to www.java.net.

For everything an Android developer needs to know, visit http://developer.android.com.

Finding News and Reviews

For the latest info about Android, visit Android Authority at www.androidauthority.com.

For articles by the tech experts, visit The Server Side at www.theserverside.com, InfoQ at www.infoq.com, and TechCrunch at http://techcrunch.com.

For discussions by everyone (including many very smart people), visit JavaRanch at www.javaranch.com.

Check it out!

Index

Symbols and Numerics

J

.jar files, 346–348

Java. *See also specific topics*

about, 15–17, 99–101, 129–130, 187

accessing fields and methods, 253–257

annotations, 279–281

assignment operators, 146–147

assignments, 134–136

bytecode instructions, 21–22

case-sensitivity in, 84, 101

code listings, 131

collection classes, 332–333

decision-making, 187–199

from development to execution with, 20–26

editing program files, 46

exceptions, 372–379

expressions, 136

extending classes, 124

`false`, 148–149

form of `if` statements in, 189–191

generic types, 321–325

information in, 130–142

initializations, 134–136

literals, 136

logical operators, 150–155

method calls, 111–114

method declarations, 111–114

methods, 105–116

modifiers, 251–255, 281–285

names of classes, 103–104

overriding methods, 124–125

parentheses, 155–156

plus sign in, 144–145

primitive types, 140–142

repeating instructions, 199–214

setting up, 33–35

source code, 20

statements, 106–108, 118

static, 260–263

super keyword, 278–279

`true`, 147–148

type names, 133–134

types, 142–156

using getters and setters, 257–260

varargs, 337–340

variable names, 133

website, 416

what the code does, 88–93

wrapper classes, 325–326

Java 2 Standard Edition 1.2, 16

Java Development Kit (JDK), 16, 28

Java Mobile Edition (Java ME), 16

Java Programming For Android Developers For Dummies, 2nd Edition (Burd), 286

Java types

about, 109

method parameters and, 173–174

rules, 163–168

strings, 157–163

Java virtual machine (JVM), 25

javadoc comments, 121

JavaRanch (website), 416

JDK (Java Development Kit), 16, 28

JVM (Java virtual machine), 25

K

kernel, 19

keys, OAuth, 355–357

keywords

about, 99, 102–103

super, 278–279, 292–293

L

lambda expressions, 313–315

launching

Android Studio, 42–43

Android Studio IDE, 38–39

apps, 61–63

Control Panel screen, 35

IDE, 57

sample programs, 40–42

SDK Manager, 49

IDE, 57
sample programs, 40–42
SDK Manager, 49
operating system, 19
operators
addition (+), 142–143
arithmetic, 142–143
assignment, 146–147
bitwise, 402
cast, 167
compound assignment, 147
division (/), 142–143
logical, 150–155
multiplication (*), 142–143
remainder upon division (%), 142–143
subtraction (–), 142–143
Oracle (website), 34, 416
OrderedPair class, 324
overloading, 110, 237
overriding methods, 124–125, 272–278

P

package declaration, 103, 118
Packages view (Android Studio), 45
paragraph class, 251–253
parameter passing, 179
parameter types code listing, 171–172
parameters
constructors with, 235–239
method, 108–109
number of, 109–111
parent class, 269
parentheses (()), 118, 155–156
PartTimeEmployee class, 278–279, 280–281, 286
pass-by reference, 250
pass-by value, 177–186, 250
passing primitive types, 247–251
permissions, using, 414
physical devices
about, 50
mimicking, 51
testing apps on, 65–67

platform number, 13
Point class, 393
portability, 25
postdecrementing, 143
postincrementing, 143
precedence rules, 155
predecrementing, 143
preferences, shared, 403–404
preincrementing, 143
priming loops, 206
primitive types
about, 140–142, 247, 325
going to from strings, 159–160
going to strings from, 158–159
pass-by value and, 177–186
passing, 247–251
printer driver, 242
PriorityQueue class, 333
private member, of classes, 254
programming, object-oriented (OOP)
about, 217–219, 267–268
Android classes, 291–294
calling constructors, 230–231
classes, 219–232
constructors with parameters, 235–239
creating objects, 223–227
default constructor, 239–240
examples, 268–269
extending classes, 269–272
Java annotations, 279–281
Java modifiers, 281–285
Java super keyword, 278–279
members of classes, 245
methods, 232–251
objects, 219–232
overriding methods, 272–278
passing primitive types, 247–251
reference types, 246–247
responsibility of objects, 242–245
reusing names, 227–230
simplicity, 285–290

Java, 109, 142–156, 157–163, 163–168, 173–174
logical, 142
long, 141, 165–166, 167, 247
methods and, 170–177
passing primitive, 247–251
primitive, 140–142, 158–160, 177–186, 247–251, 325
reference, 140, 246–247, 325
return, 171–172, 174–175
short, 141, 247
String, 140, 144, 157–163, 198, 202–203, 247
variable, 131
of variables, 131
wrapper, 158, 199

U

UI thread, 366
UML (Unified Modeling Language), 223
underscore character (_), 133
Unicode, 137
Unified Modeling Language (UML), 223
unzipping, 32
updates, 214
updateStatus method, 371
UseAccount class, 255, 257
UseAccountFromOutside class, 255–256, 257
user actions, handling, 402
user input, getting, 160–163
users, informing, 404–405
uses–permission element, 349
UseSprite class, 257
UseSpriteFromOutside class, 257

V

values, comparing, 410
varargs (Java), 337–340
variable names, 133, 136
variable types, 131

versions
  of Android, 13–15
  installing of Android, 49–50
  removing existing, 36
view animation, 398
view group, 396
view.getId( ), 193–195
virtual devices, creating, 50–54
virtual machine, 24–26
visibility property, 400
Visual Studio Emulator for Android (website), 65

W

Warning icon, 6
websites
  Android, 416
  Android API documentation page, 333
  Android Authority, 416
  Android SDK, 37
  Android Studio, 37
  book, 29, 112, 415
  built-in API classes, 122
  Burd, Barry (author), 7
  Cheat Sheet, 7
  code style guidelines, 263
  Dedexer program, 22
  for developers, 415–416
  Dummies, 7
  emulators, 64–65
  Hello World app, 55
  Java, 33, 416
  JavaRanch, 416
  language locales, 305
  news and reviews, 416
  Oracle, 34, 416
  precedence rules, 155
  sample programs, 32
  The Server Side, 416

About the Author

Barry Burd received a master of science degree in computer science at Rutgers University and a PhD in mathematics at the University of Illinois. As a teaching assistant in Champaign-Urbana, Illinois, he was elected five times to the university-wide List of Teachers Ranked As Excellent By Their Students.

Since 1980, Dr. Burd has been a professor in the Department of Mathematics and Computer Science at Drew University in Madison, New Jersey. He has lectured at conferences in the United States, Europe, Australia, and Asia. He hosts podcasts and videos about software and other technology topics. He is the author of many articles and books, including *Java For Dummies*, *Beginning Programming with Java For Dummies*, and *Android Application Development All-in-One For Dummies*, all from Wiley.

Dr. Burd lives in Madison, New Jersey, with his wife of n years, where $n > 35$. In his spare time, he enjoys being a workaholic.

Dedication

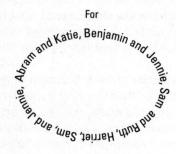

For

Abram and Katie, Benjamin and Jennie, Sam and Ruth, Harriet, Sam, and Jennie

Acknowledgments

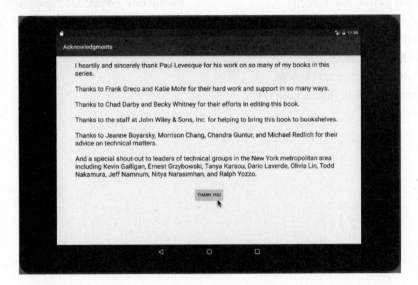

Publisher's Acknowledgments

Acquisitions Editor: Katie Mohr

Senior Project Editor: Paul Levesque

Copy Editor: Becky Whitney

Technical Editor: Chad Darby

Editorial Assistant: Serena Novosel

Sr. Editorial Assistant: Cherie Case

Production Editor: Siddique Shaik

Cover Image: photovibes/Shutterstock

Apple & Mac

iPad For Dummies,
6th Edition
978-1-118-72306-7

iPhone For Dummies,
7th Edition
978-1-118-69083-3

Macs All-in-One
For Dummies, 4th Edition
978-1-118-82210-4

OS X Mavericks
For Dummies
978-1-118-69188-5

Blogging & Social Media

Facebook For Dummies,
5th Edition
978-1-118-63312-0

Social Media Engagement
For Dummies
978-1-118-53019-1

WordPress For Dummies,
6th Edition
978-1-118-79161-5

Business

Stock Investing
For Dummies, 4th Edition
978-1-118-37678-2

Investing For Dummies,
6th Edition
978-0-470-90545-6

Personal Finance
For Dummies, 7th Edition
978-1-118-11785-9

QuickBooks 2014
For Dummies
978-1-118-72005-9

Small Business Marketing
Kit For Dummies,
3rd Edition
978-1-118-31183-7

Careers

Job Interviews
For Dummies, 4th Edition
978-1-118-11290-8

Job Searching with Social
Media For Dummies,
2nd Edition
978-1-118-67856-5

Personal Branding
For Dummies
978-1-118-11792-7

Resumes For Dummies,
6th Edition
978-0-470-87361-8

Starting an Etsy Business
For Dummies, 2nd Edition
978-1-118-59024-9

Diet & Nutrition

Belly Fat Diet For Dummies
978-1-118-34585-6

Mediterranean Diet
For Dummies
978-1-118-71525-3

Nutrition For Dummies,
5th Edition
978-0-470-93231-5

Digital Photography

Digital SLR Photography
All-in-One For Dummies,
2nd Edition
978-1-118-59082-9

Digital SLR Video &
Filmmaking For Dummies
978-1-118-36598-4

Photoshop Elements 12
For Dummies
978-1-118-72714-0

Gardening

Herb Gardening
For Dummies, 2nd Edition
978-0-470-61778-6

Gardening with Free-Range
Chickens For Dummies
978-1-118-54754-0

Health

Boosting Your Immunity
For Dummies
978-1-118-40200-9

Diabetes For Dummies,
4th Edition
978-1-118-29447-5

Living Paleo For Dummies
978-1-118-29405-5

Big Data

Big Data For Dummies
978-1-118-50422-2

Data Visualization
For Dummies
978-1-118-50289-1

Hadoop For Dummies
978-1-118-60755-8

Language &
Foreign Language

500 Spanish Verbs
For Dummies
978-1-118-02382-2

English Grammar
For Dummies, 2nd Edition
978-0-470-54664-2

French All-in-One
For Dummies
978-1-118-22815-9

German Essentials
For Dummies
978-1-118-18422-6

Italian For Dummies,
2nd Edition
978-1-118-00465-4

Available in print and e-book formats.

Available wherever books are sold. **For more information or to order direct visit www.dummies.com**

Math & Science

Algebra I For Dummies,
2nd Edition
978-0-470-55964-2

Anatomy and Physiology
For Dummies, 2nd Edition
978-0-470-92326-9

Astronomy For Dummies,
3rd Edition
978-1-118-37697-3

Biology For Dummies,
2nd Edition
978-0-470-59875-7

Chemistry For Dummies,
2nd Edition
978-1-118-00730-3

1001 Algebra II Practice
Problems For Dummies
978-1-118-44662-1

Microsoft Office

Excel 2013 For Dummies
978-1-118-51012-4

Office 2013 All-in-One
For Dummies
978-1-118-51636-2

PowerPoint 2013
For Dummies
978-1-118-50253-2

Word 2013 For Dummies
978-1-118-49123-2

Music

Blues Harmonica
For Dummies
978-1-118-25269-7

Guitar For Dummies,
3rd Edition
978-1-118-11554-1

iPod & iTunes
For Dummies, 10th Edition
978-1-118-50864-0

Programming

Beginning Programming
with C For Dummies
978-1-118-73763-7

Excel VBA Programming
For Dummies, 3rd Edition
978-1-118-49037-2

Java For Dummies,
6th Edition
978-1-118-40780-6

Religion & Inspiration

The Bible For Dummies
978-0-7645-5296-0

Buddhism For Dummies,
2nd Edition
978-1-118-02379-2

Catholicism For Dummies,
2nd Edition
978-1-118-07778-8

Self-Help & Relationships

Beating Sugar Addiction
For Dummies
978-1-118-54645-1

Meditation For Dummies,
3rd Edition
978-1-118-29144-3

Seniors

Laptops For Seniors
For Dummies, 3rd Edition
978-1-118-71105-7

Computers For Seniors
For Dummies, 3rd Edition
978-1-118-11553-4

iPad For Seniors
For Dummies, 6th Edition
978-1-118-72826-0

Social Security
For Dummies
978-1-118-20573-0

Smartphones & Tablets

Android Phones
For Dummies, 2nd Edition
978-1-118-72030-1

Nexus Tablets
For Dummies
978-1-118-77243-0

Samsung Galaxy S 4
For Dummies
978-1-118-64222-1

Samsung Galaxy Tabs
For Dummies
978-1-118-77294-2

Test Prep

ACT For Dummies,
5th Edition
978-1-118-01259-8

ASVAB For Dummies,
3rd Edition
978-0-470-63760-9

GRE For Dummies,
7th Edition
978-0-470-88921-3

Officer Candidate Tests
For Dummies
978-0-470-59876-4

Physician's Assistant Exam
For Dummies
978-1-118-11556-5

Series 7 Exam For Dummies
978-0-470-09932-2

Windows 8

Windows 8.1 All-in-One
For Dummies
978-1-118-82087-2

Windows 8.1 For Dummies
978-1-118-82121-3

Windows 8.1 For Dummies,
Book + DVD Bundle
978-1-118-82107-7

Available in print and e-book formats.

DEC -- 2016

Available wherever books are sold. **For more information or to order direct visit www.dummies.com**